THE ANCIENT LANGUAG E
AND A

This book, derived from the acclaimed *Cambridge Encyclopedia of the World's Ancient Languages*, describes the ancient languages of Syria-Palestine and Arabia, for the convenience of students and specialists working in that area. Each chapter of the work focuses on an individual language or, in some instances, a set of closely related varieties of a language. Providing a full descriptive presentation, each of these chapters examines the writing system(s), phonology, morphology, syntax, and lexicon of that language, and places the language within its proper linguistic and historical context. The volume brings together an international array of scholars, each a leading specialist in ancient language study. While designed primarily for scholars and students of linguistics, this work will prove invaluable to all whose studies take them into the realm of ancient language.

Roger D. Woodard is the Andrew Van Vranken Raymond Professor of the Classics at the University of Buffalo. His chief research interests lie generally within the areas of Greek and Roman myth and religion, Indo-European culture and linguistics, the origin and development of writing among the Greeks, and the interaction between Greece and the ancient Near East. His other books include *The Cambridge Companion to Greek Mythology* (2007), *Indo-European Sacred Space* (2006), *The Cambridge Encyclopedia of the World's Ancient Languages* (2004); *Ovid's Fasti* (with A. J. Boyle, 2000); *Greek Writing from Knossos to Homer: A Linguistic Interpretation of the Origins of the Greek Alphabet* (1997), and *On Interpreting Morphological Change* (1990). He has also published numerous articles and served as President of the Society for the Study of Greek and Latin Language and Linguistics from 1992 to 2001.

The Ancient Languages of Syria-Palestine and Arabia

Edited by

ROGER D. WOODARD

CAMBRIDGE
UNIVERSITY PRESS

CAMBRIDGE UNIVERSITY PRESS
Cambridge, New York, Melbourne, Madrid, Cape Town, Singapore, São Paulo, Delhi

Cambridge University Press
The Edinburgh Building, Cambridge CB2 8RU, UK

Published in the United States of America by Cambridge University Press, New York

www.cambridge.org
Information on this title: www.cambridge.org/9780521684989

Previously published in 2004 as chapters 9–16 of Woodard,
Roger D., *The Cambridge Encyclopedia of the World's Ancient Languages*
© Cambridge University Press 2004

First published 2008

Printed in the United Kingdom at the University Press, Cambridge

A catalogue record for this publication is available from the British Library

ISBN 978-0-521-68498-9 paperback

Contents

	List of figures		*page* vi
	List of tables		vii
	List of maps		viii
	List of contributors		ix
	Notes on numbering and cross-referencing		x
	List of abbreviations		xi
	Preface	ROGER D. WOODARD	xv
	Preface to the first edition	ROGER D. WOODARD	xix
1	Language in ancient Syria-Palestine and Arabia: an introduction	ROGER D. WOODARD	1
2	Ugaritic	DENNIS PARDEE	5
3	Hebrew	P. KYLE MCCARTER, JR.	36
4	Phoenician and Punic	JO ANN HACKETT	82
5	Canaanite dialects	DENNIS PARDEE	103
6	Aramaic	STUART CREASON	108
7	Ancient South Arabian	NORBERT NEBES and PETER STEIN	145
8	Ancient North Arabian	M. C. A. MACDONALD	179
	Appendix 1. Afro-Asiatic	JOHN HUEHNERGARD	225
	Appendix 2. Full tables of contents from The Cambridge Encyclopedia of the World's Ancient Languages, *and from the other volumes in the paperback series*		247
	Index of general subjects		252
	Index of grammar and linguistics		255
	Index of languages		258
	Index of named linguistic laws and principles		262

Figures

3.1 The seven full vowels of Tiberian Hebrew *page* 43

4.1 Vowel phonemes of Standard Phoenician 87

7.1 The great inscription of Karib'il Watar (*c.* 685 BC) R3945: section of lines 11–20 148

8.1 Pre-Islamic Arabia 180

8.2 Examples of the Ancient North Arabian scripts 182

8.3 Letter-forms in the Ancient North Arabian scripts 187

Tables

2.1	The Ugaritic cuneiform consonantal script	*page* 8
2.2	The Ugaritic noun: absolute state	13
2.3	The Ugaritic verb: G-stem	23
3.1	The Hebrew alphabet	39
3.2	The Tiberian representation of the principal Hebrew vowels	40
3.3	The consonantal phonemes of Hebrew	42
3.4	The vowel classes of Hebrew verbs	68
4.1	The Phoenician consonantal script	85
4.2	The consonantal phonemes of Standard Phoenician	86
4.3	The enclitic personal pronouns of Standard Phoenician	92
6.1	Aramaic consonantal scripts	110
6.2	Aramaic vowel diacritics	111
6.3	Old Aramaic consonantal phonemes	113
7.1	The Ancient South Arabian consonantal script	147
7.2	The consonantal phonemes of Ancient South Arabian	149
8.1	The consonantal phonemes of Ancient North Arabian	188
8.2	The cardinal numerals in Dadanitic	213
A.1	The consonantal phonemes of Common Semitic	229
A.2	Proto-Semitic personal pronouns	237

Map

Contributors

STUART CREASON	University of Chicago
JO ANN HACKETT	Harvard University
JOHN HUEHNERGARD	Harvard University
M. C. A. MACDONALD	University of Oxford
P. KYLE MCCARTER, JR.	The Johns Hopkins University
NORBERT NEBES	Friedrich-Schiller-Universität Jena
DENNIS PARDEE	University of Chicago
PETER STEIN	Friedrich-Schiller-Universität Jena
ROGER D. WOODARD	University of Buffalo (The State University of New York)

Notes on numbering and cross-referencing

This volume is one of five paperbacks derived from *The Cambridge Encyclopedia of the World's Ancient Languages* (*WAL*), with the content now organized by region for the convenience of students and specialists wishing to focus on a given area of the ancient world.

Cross-references to material within this volume use its own internal chapter numbers. Any cross-references to other chapters of the original *WAL* refer to the chapter numbers in that work, and are prefixed by *WAL*. The contents list of *WAL* is reproduced at the back of this volume, as are the contents of the respective volumes of the paperback series derived from it.

Abbreviations

Any abbreviation that deviates from the form given below is noted within the text of the individual chapter or within a chapter-specific list.

Linguistic terms

abl.	ablative
abs.	absolutive
acc.	accusative
act.	active
adj.	adjective
adv.	adverb (adverbial)
all.	allative
anim.	animate
aor.	aorist
art.	article
asp.	aspirated
aux.	auxiliary (verb)
caus.	causative
cl.	clause
coll.	collective
com.	common
comp.	comparative
comt.	comitative
conj.	conjunction
conjv.	conjunctive
conn.	connective
cons.	consonant
constr.	construct (state)
cont.	continuant
cop.	copula
dat.	dative
def. art.	definite article
dem.	demonstrative
det.	determinate
detv.	determinative
dial.	dialect
dir.	directive
dir. obj.	direct object
disj.	disjunctive
du.	dual
dur.	durative
emph.-pcl.	emphatic particle
encl.	enclitic
eq.	equative
erg.	ergative
ext.	extended
fem.	feminine
final-pcl.	final-particle
fut.	future
gdve.	gerundive
gen.	genitive
ger.	gerund
impf.	imperfect
impftv.	imperfective
impv.	imperative
inan.	inanimate
inc.	inclusive
indef. art.	indefinite article
indet.	indeterminate
indic.	indicative
inf.	infinitive
instr.	instrumental
interr.	interrogative
intr.	intransitive
iter.	iterative
juss.	jussive
loc.	locative
mediopass.	mediopassive
mid.	middle

N.	noun
neg.	negative
neut.	neuter
nom.	nominative
NP	noun phrase
num.	number
obj.	object
obl.	oblique
opt.	optative
part.	participle
pass.	passive
pcl.	particle
per.	person
perf.	perfect
perfv.	perfective
perfvz.	perfectivizer
pert.	pertinentive
pl.	plural
pluperf.	pluperfect
poss. suff.	possessive suffix
postp.	postposition
PP	prepositional phrase
prec.	precative
preC.	preconsonantal
pref.	prefix
prep.	preposition
pres.	present
pret.	preterite
preV.	prevocalic
pro.	pronoun
prosp.	prospective
quot.	quotative particle
refl.	reflexive
rel. pro.	relative (pronoun)
rel./connec.	relative/connective
sg.	singular
soc.	sociative case
SOV	Subject–Object–Verb (word order)
spec.	specifier
splv.	superlative
stat.	stative
subj.	subject
subjunc.	subjunctive
subord.	subordinate/subordinator/ subordination marker
subord.-pcl.	subordinating particle
suff.	suffix
s.v.	*sub voce*
top.	topicalizer
tr.	transitive
V.	verb
var.	variant
vent.	ventive
voc.	vocative
vow.	vowel
VP	verbal phrase

Languages

Akk.	Akkadian
Ar.	Arabic
Ass.	Assyrian
Av.	Avestan
Bab.	Babylonian
Cis. Gaul.	Cisalpine Gaulish
Eg.	Egyptian (Old, Late, Earlier)
Eng.	English
Etr.	Etruscan
Gk.	Greek
Gmc.	Germanic
Go.	Gothic
Hisp.-Celt.	Hispano-Celtic
Hitt.	Hittite
IE	Indo-European
Lat.	Latin
Lep.	Lepontic
Luv.	Luvian
Lyc.	Lycian
MA	Middle Assyrian
MB	Middle Babylonian
NA	Neo-Assyrian
NB	Neo-Babylonian
OA	Old Assyrian
O. Akk.	Old Akkadian
O. Av.	Old Avestan
OB	Old Babylonian
OHG	Old High German
OP	Old Persian
PG	Proto-Greek
PGmc.	Proto-Germanic
PIE	Proto-Indo-European
PIIr.	Proto-Indo-Iranian
PIr.	Proto-Iranian
PMS	Proto-Mije-Sokean
PS	Proto-Semitic
PSo.	Proto-Sokean
SB	Standard Babylonian

Skt.	Sanskrit
Sum.	Sumerian
Y. Av.	Young Avestan

Other

abbr.	abbreviation
dict.	dictionary
intro.	introduction
lit.	literally
NA	not applicable
NS	new series
trad.	traditional
translit.	transliteration

Preface

Preliminary remarks

What makes a language ancient? The term conjures up images, often romantic, of archeologists feverishly copying hieroglyphs by torchlight in a freshly discovered burial chamber; of philologists dangling over a precipice in some remote corner of the earth, taking impressions of an inscription carved in a cliff-face; of a solitary scholar working far into the night, puzzling out some ancient secret, long forgotten by humankind, from a brittle-leafed manuscript or patina-encrusted tablet. The allure is undeniable, and the literary and film worlds have made full use of it.

An ancient language is indeed a thing of wonder – but so is every other language, all remarkable systems of conveying thoughts and ideas across time and space. And ancient languages, as far back as the very earliest attested, operate just like those to which the linguist has more immediate access, all with the same familiar elements – phonological, morphological, syntactic – and no perceptible vestiges of Neanderthal oddities. If there was a time when human language was characterized by features and strategies fundamentally unlike those we presently know, it was a time prior to the development of any attested or reconstructed language of antiquity. Perhaps, then, what makes an ancient language different is our awareness that it has outlived those for whom it was an intimate element of the psyche, not so unlike those rays of light now reaching our eyes that were emitted by their long-extinguished source when dinosaurs still roamed across the earth (or earlier) – both phantasms of energy flying to our senses from distant sources, long gone out.

That being said, and rightly enough, we must return to the question of what counts as an ancient language. As *ancient* the editor chose the upward delimitation of the fifth century AD. This *terminus ante quem* is one which is admittedly "traditional"; the fifth is the century of the fall of the western Roman Empire (AD 476), a benchmark which has been commonly (though certainly not unanimously) identified as marking the end of the historical period of *antiquity*. Any such chronological demarcation is of necessity arbitrary – far too arbitrary – as linguists accustomed to making such diachronic distinctions as *Old English, Middle English, Modern English* or *Old Hittite, Middle Hittite, Neo-Hittite* are keenly aware. Linguistic divisions of this sort are commonly based upon significant political events and clearly perceptible cultural shifts rather than upon language phenomena (though they are surely not without linguistic import as every historical linguist knows). The choice of the boundary in the present concern – the ancient-language boundary – is, likewise (as has already been confessed), not mandated by linguistic features and characteristics of the languages concerned.

However, this arbitrary choice, establishing a *terminus ante quem* of the fifth century, is somewhat buttressed by quite pragmatic linguistic considerations (themselves consequent to the whim of historical accident), namely the co-occurrence of a watershed in language documentation. Several early languages first make a significant appearance in the historical record in the fourth/fifth century: thus, Gothic (fourth century; see *WAL* Ch. 36), Ge'ez (fourth/fifth century; see *WAL* Ch. 14, §1.3.1), Classical Armenian (fifth century; see *WAL* Ch. 38), Early Old Georgian (fifth century; see *WAL* Ch. 40). What newly comes into clear light in the sixth century is a bit more meager – Tocharian and perhaps the very earliest Old Kannada and Old Telegu from the end of the century. Moreover, the dating of these languages to the sixth century cannot be made precisely (not to suggest this is an especially unusual state of affairs) and it is equally possible that the earliest attestation of all three should be dated to the seventh century. Beginning with the seventh century the pace of language attestation begins to accelerate, with languages documented such as Old English, Old Khmer, and Classical Arabic (though a few earlier inscriptions preserving a "transitional" form of Arabic are known; see Ch. 8, § 1.1.1). The ensuing centuries bring an avalanche of medieval European languages and their Asian contemporaries into view. Aside from the matter of a culturally dependent analytic scheme of historical periodization, there are thus considerations of language history that motivate the upper boundary of the fifth century.

On the other hand, identifying a *terminus post quem* for the inclusion of a language in the present volume was a completely straightforward and noncontroversial procedure. The low boundary is determined by the appearance of writing in human society, a graphic means for recording human speech. A system of writing appears to have been first developed by the Sumerians of southern Mesopotamia in the late fourth millennium BC (see *WAL* Ch. 2, §§1.2; 2). Not much later (beginning in about 3100 BC), a people of ancient Iran began to record their still undeciphered language of Proto-Elamite on clay tablets (see *WAL* Ch. 3, §2.1). From roughly the same period, the Egyptian hieroglyphic writing system emerges in the historical record (see *WAL* Ch. 7, §2). Hence, Sumerian and Egyptian are the earliest attested, understood languages and, *ipso facto*, the earliest languages treated in this volume.

It is conjectured that humans have been speaking and understanding language for at least 100,000 years. If in the great gulf of time which separates the advent of language and the appearance of Sumerian, Proto-Elamite, and Egyptian societies, there were any people giving written expression to their spoken language, all evidence of such records and the language or languages they record has fallen victim to the decay of time. Or the evidence has at least eluded the archeologists.

Format and conventions

Each chapter, with only the occasional exception, adheres to a common format. The chapter begins with an overview of the history (including prehistory) of the language, at least up to the latest stage of the language treated in the chapter, and of those peoples who spoke the language (§1, HISTORICAL AND CULTURAL CONTEXTS). Then follows a discussion of the development and use of the script(s) in which the language is recorded (§2, WRITING SYSTEMS); note that the complex Mesopotamian cuneiform script, which is utilized for several languages of the ancient Near East – Sumerian (*WAL* Ch. 2), Elamite (*WAL* Ch. 3), Hurrian (*WAL* Ch. 4), Urartian (*WAL* Ch. 5), Akkadian and Eblaite (*WAL* Ch. 8), Hittite (*WAL* Ch. 18), Luvian (*WAL* Ch. 19) – and which provides the inspiration and graphic raw materials for others – Ugaritic (*WAL* Ch. 9) and Old Persian (*WAL* Ch. 28) – is treated in most detail in *WAL* Chapter 8, §2. The next section presents a discussion of phonological elements of the language (§3, PHONOLOGY), identifying consonant and vowel phonemes, and treating matters such as allophonic and morphophonemic variation, syllable structure and phonotaxis, segmental length, accent (pitch and stress), and synchronic and diachronic phonological processes. Following next is discussion of morphological phenomena (§4, MORPHOLOGY), focusing on topics such as word structure, nominal and pronominal categories and systems, the categories and systems of finite verbs and other verbal elements (for explanation of the system of classifying Semitic verb stems – G stem, etc. – see Appendix 1, §3.3.5.2), compounds, diachronic morphology, and the system of numerals. Treatment of syntactic matters then follows (§5, SYNTAX), presenting discussion of word order and coordinate and subordinate clause structure, and phenomena such as agreement, cliticism and various other syntactic processes, both synchronic and diachronic. The description of the grammar closes with a consideration of the lexical component (§6, LEXICON); and the chapter comes to an end with a list of references cited in the chapter and of other pertinent works (BIBLIOGRAPHY).

To a great extent, the linguistic presentations in the ensuing chapters have remained faithful to the grammatical conventions of the various language disciplines. From discipline to discipline, the most obvious variation lies in the methods of transcribing sounds. Thus, for example, the symbols *ś*, *ṣ*, and *ṭ* in the traditional orthography of Indic language scholarship represent, respectively, a voiceless palatal (palato-alveolar) fricative, a voiceless retroflex fricative, and a voiceless retroflex stop. In Semitic studies, however, the same symbols are used to denote very different phonetic realities: *ś* represents a voiceless lateral fricative while *ṣ* and *ṭ* transcribe two of the so-called emphatic consonants – the latter a voiceless stop produced with a secondary articulation (velarization, pharyngealization, or glottalization), the former either a voiceless fricative or affricate, also with a secondary articulation. Such conventional symbols are employed herein, but for any given language, the reader can readily determine phonetic values of these symbols by consulting the discussion of consonant and vowel sounds in the relevant phonology section.

Broad phonetic transcription is accomplished by means of a slightly modified form of the International Phonetic Alphabet (IPA). Most notably, the IPA symbols for the palato-alveolar fricatives and affricates, voiceless [ʃ] and [tʃ] and voiced [ʒ] and [dʒ], have been replaced by the more familiar [š], [č], [ž], and [ǰ] respectively. Similarly, [y] is used for the palatal glide rather than [j]. Long vowels are marked by either a macron or a colon.

In the phonology sections, phonemic transcription, in keeping with standard phonological practice, is placed within slashes (e.g., /p/) and phonetic transcription within square brackets (e.g., [p]; note that square brackets are also used to fill out the meaning of a gloss and are employed as an element of the transcription and transliteration conventions for certain languages, such as Elamite [*WAL* Ch. 3] and Pahlavi [*WAL* Ch. 30]). The general treatment adopted in phonological discussions has been to present transcriptions as phonetic rather than phonemic, except in those instances in which explicit reference is made to the phonemic level. Outside of the phonological sections, transcriptions are usually presented using the conventional orthography of the pertinent language discipline. When potential for confusion would seem to exist, transcriptions are enclosed within angled brackets (e.g., <p>) to make clear to the reader that what is being specified is the *spelling* of a word and not its *pronunciation*.

Further acknowledgments

The enthusiastic reception of the first edition of this work – and the broad interest in the ancient languages of humankind that it demonstrates – has been and remains immensely gratifying to both editor and contributors. The editor would like to take this opportunity, on behalf of all the contributors, to express his deepest appreciation to all who have had a hand in the success of the first edition. We wish too to acknowledge our debt of gratitude to Cambridge University Press and to Dr. Kate Brett for continued support of this project and for making possible the publication of this new multivolume edition and the increased accessibility to the work that it will inevitably provide. Thanks also go to the many kind readers who have provided positive and helpful feedback since the publication of the first edition, and to the editors of *CHOICE* for bestowing upon the work the designation of Outstanding Academic Title of 2006.

Roger D. Woodard
Vernal Equinox 2007

Preface to the first edition

In the following pages, the reader will discover what is, in effect, a linguistic description of all known ancient languages. Never before in the history of language study has such a collection appeared within the covers of a single work. This volume brings to student and to scholar convenient, systematic presentations of grammars which, in the best of cases, were heretofore accessible only by consulting multiple sources, and which in all too many instances could only be retrieved from scattered, out-of-the-way, disparate treatments. For some languages, the only existing comprehensive grammatical description is to be found herein.

This work has come to fruition through the efforts and encouragement of many, to all of whom the editor wishes to express his heartfelt gratitude. To attempt to list all – colleagues, students, friends – would, however, certainly result in the unintentional and unhappy neglect of some, and so only a much more modest attempt at acknowledgments will be made. Among those to whom special thanks are due are first and foremost the contributors to this volume, scholars who have devoted their lives to the study of the languages of ancient humanity, without whose expertise and dedication this work would still be only a *desideratum*. Very special thanks also go to Dr. Kate Brett of Cambridge University Press for her professionalism, her wise and expert guidance, and her unending patience, also to her predecessor, Judith Ayling, for permitting me to persuade her of the project's importance. I cannot neglect mentioning my former colleague, Professor Bernard Comrie, now of the Max Planck Institute, for his unflagging friendship and support. Kudos to those who masterfully translated the chapters that were written in languages other than English: Karine Megardoomian for Phrygian, Dr. Margaret Whatmough for Etruscan, Professor John Huehnergard for Ancient South Arabian. Last of all, but not least of all, I wish to thank Katherine and Paul – my inspiration, my joy.

Roger D. Woodard
Christmas Eve 2002

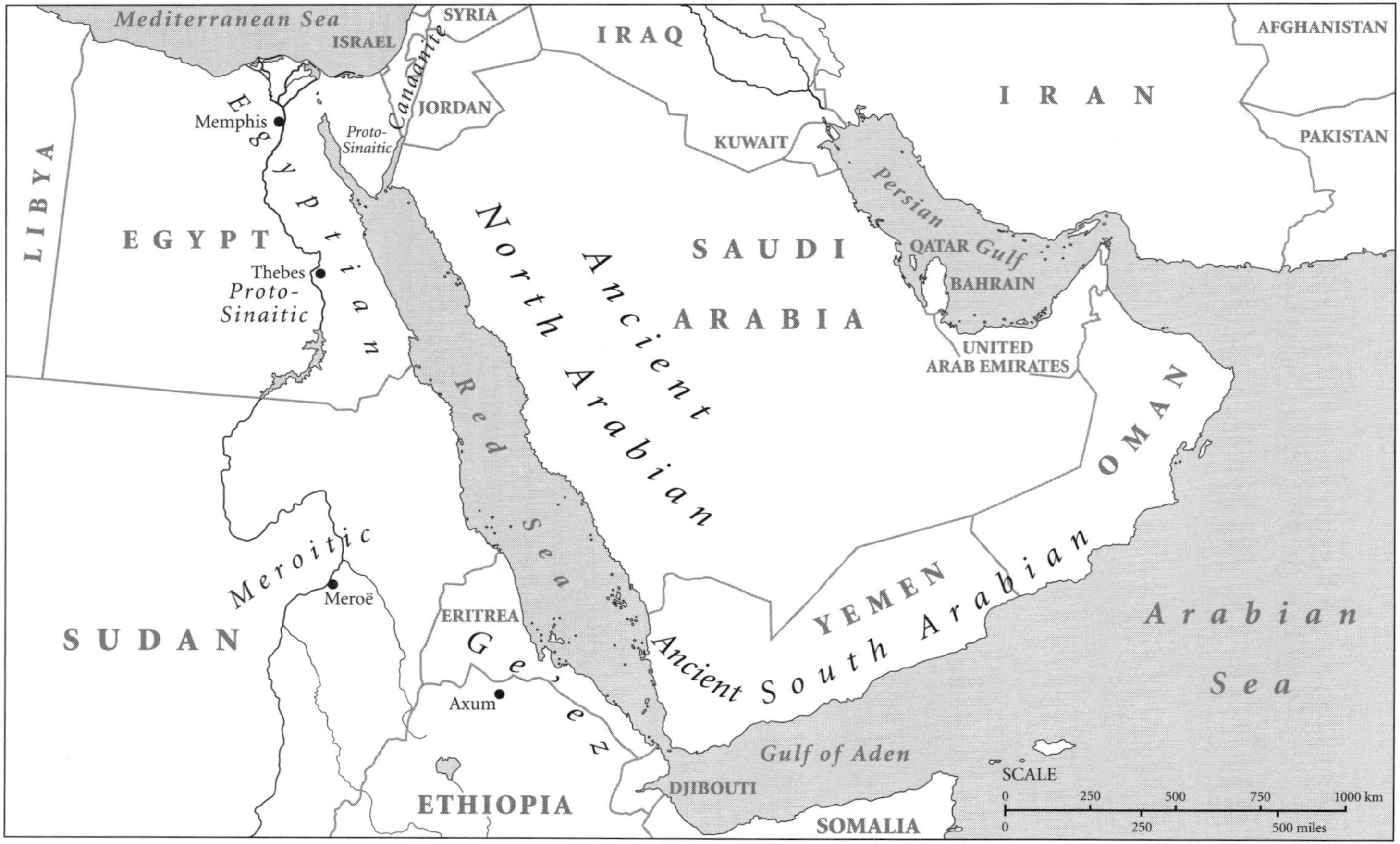

Map 1. The ancient languages of Northeastern Africa and Arabia

CHAPTER 1

Language in Ancient Syria-Palestine and Arabia: an introduction

ROGER D. WOODARD

Pedra
It seems no work of man's creative hand,
By labor wrought as wavering fancy plann'd,
But from the rock as by magic grown,
Eternal, silent, beautiful, alone!
Not virgin-white like the old Doric shrine
Where erst Athena held her rites divine;
Not saintly-grey, like many a minster fane,
That crowns the hill, and consecrates the plain;
But rosy-red as if the blush of dawn
That first beheld them were not yet withdrawn;
The hues of youth upon a brow of woe,
Which man deemed old two thousand years ago.
Match me such marvel save in Eastern clime,
A rose-red city half as old as Time.
John William Burgon

Often rehearsed, sometimes parodied, there remains something hauntingly arresting about John William Burgon's sonnet in praise of Petra, Jordon's "rose-red city," lying at the threshold of the Arabian Peninsula, on the southeastern fringe of ancient Syria-Palestine (the term is used herein to denote the region encompassing the modern political states of Jordon, Israel, Lebanon, and Syria; on the notion of "Syria-Palestine," a geographic construct popularized by W. F. Albright, see Dever 1997). Now home to a Bedouin community, Petra was once the thriving capital city of the ancient Nabataeans, whose kingdom flourished in the late centuries BC and the early centuries AD. Arid Petra's prosperity flowed not only from the desert caravans that passed through the city, located at the nexus of intersecting trade routes, but from its abundant water supply, captured by an elaborate system of Nabataean-engineered ducts, dams, and cisterns. Strabo, the first-century (BC and AD) Greek geographer, knew of just such a Petra: "The chief city of the Nabataeans is called Petra, for it lies in a place that is otherwise smooth and flat, but guarded by encircling rock [Greek πέτρα (*pétra*)]. It is steep and sheer on the outside, but on the inside it possesses no short supply of streaming water, both for the fetching and for irrigating gardens" (*Geography* 16.4.21).

A bit further along, Strabo, in commenting on the Arabian harbor town that he calls *Leuke Kome* (Λευκὴ Κώμη 'White Village'), asserts that "to and from this place camel-caravaners journey safely and easily, going into Petra and out of Petra, with so many people and camels that they are not at all different from an army" (*Geography* 16.4.24).

These prosperous Nabataeans left behind abundant language evidence, and much of it, but by no means all of it, comes from Petra itself. Linguistic life among the Nabataeans, as throughout most of the ancient Near East, was complex. Some of the nomadic peoples living in the vicinity of Petra were speakers of the Ancient North Arabian language of Hismaic (see Ch. 8, §1.1.2). Ancient South Arabian (see Ch. 7) must have been commonly heard in Petra on the lips of traders traveling with the frankincense-, myrrh-, and nard-laden camel caravans coming north from South Arabia – as were undoubtedly other tongues from even more distant locales. The principal inscriptional language of the Nabataeans themselves was Aramaic, the lingua franca of the time and place. The Nabateans were, however, an Arab people and speakers of Old Arabic (see Ch. 8, §1.1.1): Old Arabic names and forms surface in Nabataean Aramaic inscriptions, and the earliest text written in Old Arabic *language* is written with the Nabataean Aramaic *script*. This Nabatean script is in fact the historical source of the present-day Arabic writing system.

The frenetic complexity of living Petra's linguistic milieu lies placid beneath the stone city's Nabataean Aramaic inscriptional remains. This language, Aramaic, shares at least two traits in common with the other languages that comprise this volume. First, Aramaic and the other languages concerned are members of a single language family – the Semitic family. Second, each of these languages is written using a consonantal script – a writing system in which each symbol represents a single consonant and in which (to generalize slightly) vowels are not explicitly represented.

With regard to the first trait (Semitic family membership), the language profile of Syria-Palestine and the Arabian Peninsula differs somewhat from that of the neighboring regions of Mesopotamia and Northeast Africa (treated in the companion volume, *The Ancient Languages of Mesopotamia, Egypt, and Aksum*) where both Semitic and non-Semitic languages were indigenous in antiquity, and many (though not all) of the non-Semitic languages are well attested and well understood (though, we should note, the Egyptian language is Afro-Asiatic and, hence, ultimately related to Semitic; see Appendix 1 at the end of this volume). Syria-Palestine and Arabia, in contrast, are places where only Semitic languages are attested in antiquity, with the possible exception of what has been called Byblic.

Byblic is a language attested by only a small number of inscriptions. In the course of his excavations at the site of the ancient city of Byblos (Biblical Gebal) on the coast of the modern state of Lebanon, the French archeologist Maurice Dunand unearthed inscriptions, on bronze and stone, executed in a previously unknown script. Many of the symbols are of a hieroglyphic nature, some apparently descended from or inspired by characters of the Egyptian hieroglyphic script; the Byblian script thus bears the tag *Pseudo-Hieroglyphic*, or, less commonly, *Proto-Byblic*. The script, judging by the number of identified symbols (114 by Dunand's analysis), is likely syllabic. As early as 1946 (a year after Dunand's publication of the inscriptions), the decipherment of Byblian Pseudo-Hieroglyphic was announced by a distinguished French philologist, Edouard Dhorme, who read the language of the script as Phoenician. Dhorme's proposed decipherment and others which have followed (see Daniels 1996:29–30 for discussion of subsequent attempts) have not been received with confidence and the script and its language still reside in the undeciphered file.

While Syria-Palestine and Arabia might thus be viewed as places of relative linguistic homogeneity (vis-à-vis Mesopotamia and Northeast Africa), within the domain of the Semitic family itself they prove to be linguistically quite heterogeneous regions. The Semitic family is divided fundamentally into an East Semitic and a West Semitic branch; on at least the West Semitic side, further subdivisions can be identified. Each of the several constituent groups of the Semitic family is represented within the geographic space that is Syria-Palestine and the Arabian Peninsula, with the possible exception of the subgroup to which Ge'ez (Ethiopic) belongs, depending upon how one subcategorizes that aspect of the family (see below). Eblaite, a language of second-millennium BC northern Syria is East Semitic (and is treated together with the Mesopotamian East Semitic Akkadian languages in *WAL* Chapter 8, owing to its close relationship to those languages). Aramaic (Ch. 6) and the Canaanite languages of Phoenician (Ch. 4), Ugaritic (Ch. 2), and Hebrew (Ch. 3), along with lesser-known Canaanite languages (dubbed "Canaanite dialects"), such as Moabite, Ammonite, and Edomite (Ch. 5), are West – specifically Northwest – Semitic languages; all were spoken in Syria-Palestine. The early languages of Arabia are Ancient South Arabian (Ch. 7) and Ancient North Arabian (Ch. 8); their geographic distribution within Arabia is self-evident. Ancient North Arabian is now commonly bracketed with the Northwest Semitic languages to form a Central Semitic group within West Semitic. Some Semitists would include Ancient South Arabian in this same Central cluster; others would identify a separate South Semitic group, within West Semitic, in which South Arabian and Ge'ez – languages separated by the Red Sea – share membership (on Ge'ez, see *WAL* Ch. 14).

In his *De inventoribus rerum* (*On the Invention of Things*), the Italian Renaissance scholar Polydore Vergil examines the question of *Quis primus literas invenerit?* ("Who first invented letters?"), exploring what the Greek and Roman authors had to say on the subject. Invoking the Greek historian Diodorus Siculus, Vergil tells his readers (translation here and below is that of Copenhaver 2002):

> Diodorus . . . seems to attribute the invention of letters (about their inventor I note great disagreement among the relevant authors) to the Egyptians, writing thus: The Egyptians claim that they discovered letters, the motions of the stars, geometry, and most of the arts. Some maintain that a man named Menon invented them in Egypt. But one must not fail to mention that instead of letters they used pictures of animals which in fact represented mental notions. (1.6.2)

A bit further along, Vergil rehearses the views of Eusebius, the third-/fourth-century bishop of Caesarea, who himself cites the Jewish historian Eupolemus:

> Eusebius believes that Eupolemus actually relates the true origin of letters when he affirms that Moses (who lived long before Cadmus, according to the same Eusebius in his *Chronicle* and in book 10 of the *Preparation for the Gospel*) first taught letters to the Jews, that the Phoenicians got them from the Jews and finally that the Greeks got them from the Phoenicians. (1.6.6)

While the Egyptians may or may not have invented writing (see the Introduction to *The Ancient Languages of Mesopotamia, Egypt, and Aksum*), the consonantal writing systems used to record the ancient Semitic languages of Syria-Palestine and Arabia – the second shared trait noted above – almost certainly have their common origin in the land of the Pharaohs, where their inception was crucially dependent on the Egyptian script (pictorial, as Diodorus claims, though representing sounds, not mere "mental notions"; see *WAL* Ch. 7, §2.1). The ancestor of these various Syro-Palestinian and Arabian writing systems is the so-called Proto-Sinaitic script, likely devised within Egypt by a Semitic people living there during the early second millennium BC (see Darnell *et al.* 2005:90–91; Hamilton 2006). The earliest-known examples of the script come from Wadi el-Hol in Upper Egypt and date to *c.* 1850 BC (see Darnell *et al.* 2005:86–90). Slightly less ancient examples (*c.* 1700 BC) come from Serabit al-Khadem in the Sinai Peninsula – preserved in inscriptions produced by Semitic workers in the turquoise mines of the region. Fundamentally, this script was devised by assigning to pictorial symbols of the Egyptian writing system the value of the consonant that begins the Semitic name for the object symbolized (the so-called "acrophonic principle"; see Ch. 4, §2). On the basis of existing evidence, the creation of the Proto-Sinaitic consonantal script may perhaps be dated to *c.* 2000 BC.

We should mention that very recent work has revealed an earlier use – perhaps *c.* 2400 BC, or earlier still – of Egyptian *symbols* used with Egyptian (rather than Semitic) *phonetic values* to spell Semitic words. These Semitic-language inscriptions, recording spells used for protection against snakes, were found in the pyramid of the Pharaoh Unas in the Egyptian city of Ṣaqqārah; they would appear to preserve a third-millennium BC form of Northwest Semitic (see Steiner 2007).

A form of the Proto-Sinaitic script is attested in Syria-Palestine as well; its occurrences in the latter region, dating to *c.* the seventeenth century BC and later, are given the name Proto-Canaanite. An offshoot of the Proto-Canaanite script – perhaps quite an early one – gave rise to the Arabian writing systems, both South (see Ch. 7, §2) and North Arabian (see Ch. 8, §2); the South Arabian consonantal script evolved further into the Ethiopic syllabary of Ge'ez (see *WAL* Ch. 14, §2). By the fourteenth century BC, the Proto-Canaanite script had also spawned the writing system that is best attested from the remains of the city of Ugarit on the Syrian coast – unique among Canaanite scripts both in the cuneiform-shape of its symbols and in the addition of three syllabic characters to the script's repertory of consonantal letters (see Ch. 2, §2).

Elsewhere in Syria-Palestine the Proto-Canaanite script continued to evolve, with its curvilinear, pictorial propensities dissolving into more conventionalized linear forms beginning in about the eleventh century BC, and being used to record the Canaanite language of Phoenician (see Ch. 4, §§1–2). It is this Linear Phoenician script that would be acquired for writing Aramaic (*c.* eleventh century BC; see Ch. 6, §2.1) and then Hebrew (*c.* tenth century BC; see Ch. 3, §§1–2) – and not the other way around as Eupolemus, per Eusebius, imagined.

And what of Eusebius' Cadmus, long preceded by Moses? Cadmus is the Phoenician prince of Greek tradition who sailed west through the Mediterranean in search of his abducted sister Europa. The Linear Phoenician consonantal script is the source not only of the Aramaic and Hebrew writing systems, but of the Greek alphabet as well, and Cadmus is one of several figures to whom the Greeks gave the credit for introducing writing to Greece. But that story must await another volume.

Bibliography

Burgon, J. 1936. "Pedra." In H. Felleman (ed.), *The Best Loved Poems of the American People*, p. 80. Garden City, NY: Garden City Books.

Copenhaver, B. (trans.). 2002. *Polydore Vergil: On Discovery*. Cambridge, MA: Harvard University Press.

Daniels, P. 1996. "The first civilizations." In Daniels and Bright 1996, pp. 21–32.

Daniels, P. and W. Bright (eds.). 1996. *The World's Writing Systems*. Oxford: Oxford University Press.

Darnell, J. *et al.* 2005. "Two early alphabetic inscriptions from the Wadi El-Hôl: new evidence for the origin of the alphabet from the Western Desert of Egypt." *The Annual of the American Schools of Oriental Research* 59:63–124.

Dever, W. 1997. "Syria-Palestine." In Meyers 1997, vol. 5, p. 147.

Dhorme, E. 1946. "Déchiffrement des inscriptions pseudo-hiéroglyphiques de Byblos." *Syria* 25:1–35.

Dunand, M. 1945. *Byblia grammata: Documents et recherches sur le développement de l'écriture en Phénicie*. Beirut: Ministry of Education of Lebanon.

Hamilton, G. 2006. *The Origins of the West Semitic Alphabet in Egyptian Scripts*. Washington: Catholic Biblical Association.

Meyers, E. (ed.). 1997. *The Oxford Encyclopedia of Archaeology in the Near East* (5 vols.). Oxford: Oxford University Press.

Steiner, R. 2007. "Proto-Canaanite Spells in the Pyramid Texts: A First Look at the History of Hebrew in the Third Millennium BCE." Academy of the Hebrew Language. http://hebrew-academy.huji.ac.il/new.html.

CHAPTER 2

Ugaritic

DENNIS PARDEE

1. HISTORICAL AND CULTURAL CONTEXTS

Ugaritic is the only well-attested example known today of the West Semitic languages spoken in the Levantine area in the second millennium BC. The position of Ugaritic among the Semitic languages has been a matter of dispute, in part because of a confusion of categories, namely between literary and linguistic criteria. Literarily, the poetic texts show strong formal (poetic parallelism), lexical, and thematic affinities with Biblical Hebrew poetry. Linguistically, however, Ugaritic is considerably more archaic than any of the well-attested Northwest Semitic languages, and probably descends directly from a Levantine "Amorite" dialect. All indications are that it is not more directly related to East Semitic (Akkadian) than to West Semitic. Within the latter branch, it shares certain important isoglosses with Northwest Semitic as opposed to Arabic (e.g., roots I*w* → I*y*) and with Canaanite as opposed to Aramaic (e.g., /ḍ/ → /ṣ/). The isoglosses shared with Arabic (e.g., consonantal inventory) represent for the most part features commonly inherited from Proto-Semitic.

Ugaritic is a one-period language, attested only for the last part of the Late Bronze Age, approximately 1300–1190 BC. This is because the writing system in which known Ugaritic texts are inscribed was not invented (at least according to present data) until the early thirteenth century, whereas the city of Ugarit – virtually the only site where Ugaritic texts have been discovered – was destroyed early in the twelfth century. In recent years it has become clearer that the greatest number of texts date from the last few decades of the site and there is, therefore, no basis on which to define a "late" Ugaritic over against the main body of texts (contra Tropper 1993b), for the main body of texts *is* late Ugaritic. The only clear strata of the language are the poetic dialect in which most mythological texts are written and the prose dialect used for everyday communication and administration.

Virtually all Ugaritic texts have been discovered at the site of the ancient city of Ugarit, modern Ras Shamra, excavated by the French more or less continuously since 1929 (Yon 1997). The site had been inhabited since the Neolithic period (Contenson 1992), but texts are presently attested only for the Late Bronze Age; the Middle Bronze levels, where finds of Akkadian texts are to be expected, have hardly been penetrated. In recent years, Ugaritic texts have been discovered at neighboring Ras Ibn Hani, a suburb of Ugarit (Bordreuil *et al.* 1987). From rare mentions of Ugarit in texts from other sites (Mari, el-Amarna), it is clear that the inhabitants of the city were of so-called Amorite stock, for they bear Amorite names and maintained cultural relations with the other Amorite kingdoms of the eighteenth century BC.

The area under the control of Ugarit was limited on the north and east by important natural boundaries (the Jebel al-Aqraᶜ on the north and the Jebel Ansariyeh on the east), with occasional control of areas bordering these boundaries (e.g., southern portions of the state of Mukish to the north). The southern boundary was at the southern extremity of the Gebleh Plain, and also varied (e.g., at times including the kingdom of Siyannu). The average territory may have been approximately 2,000 sq. km. (Saadé 1979:33).

There are approximately 50 mythological texts in poetry and some 1,500 texts in prose (including decipherable fragments). The primary types of prose texts are (i) religious (ritual, pantheon, votive); (ii) ominological (astral, malformed births, extispicy); (iii) medical (hippiatric); (iv) epistolary; (v) administrative (contracts, lists of many sorts); and (vi) didactic (abecedaries, exercises).

The prose texts originated largely from the palace administration of the city of Ugarit. The administration was headed by a king, often in vassal position to a king of a larger political entity, particularly the Hittite king in the period documented. Many of the letters emanate directly from the royal family; many of the ritual texts specifically mention the king; most of the administrative texts deal with one aspect or another of royal control of the resources of the kingdom (real estate, taxes, management of royal goods, working of royal raw materials, etc.). The hundred-plus epistolary documents, in particular, reveal the Ugaritic that was in everyday use in the city.

Because they provide a mythical and literary background to the Hebrew Bible, the poetic texts have made Ugarit famous. They are, however, comparatively few in number and the poetic dialect presents many difficulties of interpretation. Several of the tablets bearing the major mythological texts are signed by a scribe named Ilimilku who some now suspect may have lived near the end of the kingdom of Ugarit, rather than nearly a century earlier, the generally accepted view (Pardee 1997:241 note 3). The poems that he and other scribes wrote down had in all likelihood been passed down by oral tradition for centuries.

The nature of the corpus and of the writing system places limits on our ability to describe the language. The number of texts is relatively small and virtually all are damaged to some degree, leaving few long stretches of text for analysis. This is especially true of the prose texts, which were usually written on tablets smaller than those bearing the major mythological texts. There are no prose narrative texts as yet from which to derive a narrative prose syntax. The poetic texts are largely narrative rather than lyrical, but are of little use, because of their archaic form, for projecting a prose syntax. The upshot is that phonology is described largely in terms of graphemes; morphology is to a significant degree reconstructed; reasonably comprehensive descriptions of morphosyntax and of poetic syntax are possible; the prose discourse syntax particular to letters is reasonably well known, while narrative prose syntax is known primarily from narrative sections of letters.

The Ugaritic language was only one of at least eight languages (and/or writing systems) in use at Ugarit. The one other Semitic language attested is Akkadian, the international lingua franca of the time, in which approximately 2,000 texts are written in syllabic cuneiform, primarily epistolary, legal, and administrative. A number of texts have also been found in Sumerian, Hittite (written in standard syllabic cuneiform and in hieroglyphic), Egyptian, Hurrian (written in Ugaritic consonantal cuneiform and in standard syllabic cuneiform), and Cypro-Minoan (not fully deciphered).

2. WRITING SYSTEMS

2.1 The consonant alphabets

The Ugaritic writing system is unique in that it adapts the cuneiform principle (wedges inscribed in clay) to represent graphemes of a consonantal type for the purpose of writing a

West Semitic language. The Semitic consonantal writing system had been devised some two to four centuries before the earliest attested Ugaritic texts, and there is no particular reason to believe that it was not in use at Ugarit before the invention of the Ugaritic cuneiform characters. Indeed, it is not unlikely that the cuneiform system is a representation in clay of a linear alphabet (i.e., one written with ink), though presently available data do not allow a precise description of the origin of the cuneiform alphabet of Ugarit.

At present, three consonantal systems are attested at Ugarit: (i) the *long alphabet*, well attested by abecedaries; (ii) the *short alphabet*, very rarely attested and of uncertain composition (no abecedary has yet been discovered representing this script); (iii) a South Semitic type alphabet, presently attested at Ugarit by a single abecedary (RS 88.2215), showing South Arabian character order (i.e., *h*, *l*, *ḥ*, *m* . . .), very similar to an abecedary discovered in 1933 at Beth-Shemesh in Palestine but only recently deciphered (bibliography in Bordreuil-Pardee 1995b; 2001, text 32).

The long alphabet was clearly intended for writing Ugaritic, for virtually all texts, whether in prose, in poetry, or of a didactic nature, are written in it. The short alphabet shows merging of phonemes (and thus graphemes) on the Phoenician model (e.g., /š/ and /ṯ/ written *ṯ*), and the few texts in consonantal cuneiform discovered beyond the borders of Ugarit appear to be written in variants of the alphabet script (Dietrich and Loretz 1988; cf. Bordreuil 1981). It seems, therefore, to be an adaptation of the long alphabet to a Phoenician-type consonantal repertory. The language of at least one text written in this system has been identified as Phoenician (Greenstein 1976; Bordreuil 1979). Though the abecedary in South Arabian order consists of the same number of signs as the basic consonantal repertory of the long alphabet, it shows several variant sign forms and was not, therefore, a simple reorganization of the Ugaritic script along South Arabian lines. Because only abecedaries are attested in this version of the script, one can only speculate as to the language that it was used to convey.

Several examples of the (long) consonantal alphabet written out partially or in full (i.e., abecedaries) provide our oldest witnesses to the concept of a repertory of consonants existing in a fixed order. The Ugaritic abecedary consists of twenty-seven symbols denoting the consonants of the language, plus an additional three characters appended to the end. The Ugaritic symbols follow the order customary for the later Northwest Semitic alphabets, which, however, contain only twenty-two signs:

Semitic abecedaries

Northwest Semitic

ʾ	b	g		d	h	w	z	ḥ	ṭ	y	k		l	m		n		s	ʿ	p	ṣ	q	r	š		t

Ugaritic

ả	b	g	ḫ	d	h	w	z	ḥ	ṭ	y	k	š	l	m	ḏ	n	ẓ	s	ʿ	p	ṣ	q	r	ṯ	ġ	t
ỉ	ủ	s̀																								

The five extra signs of Ugaritic (*ḫ*, *š*, *ḏ*, *ẓ*, *ġ*) are dispersed at apparent random within the order, seemingly suggesting the invention of the Northwest Semitic alphabet for a language, such as Ugaritic, which had a larger consonantal inventory than those of the well-known first-millennium languages.

The origin of the three additional signs (*ỉ*, *ủ*, *s̀*) appended to the end of the abecedary is in dispute. The patent similarity of *form* between the Ugaritic symbol transliterated *s̀*, and the *s*-character of the later Northwest Semitic script makes a common origin likely, but the reason for the addition of this sign to the Ugaritic alphabet is unclear (compare Segert

Table 2.1 The Ugaritic cuneiform consonantal script

Character	Transcription	Character	Transcription
𐎀	ả	𐎏	ḏ
𐎁	b	𐎐	n
𐎂	g	𐎑	ẓ
𐎃	ḫ	𐎒	s
𐎄	d	𐎓	ʿ
𐎅	h	𐎔	p
𐎆	w	𐎕	ṣ
𐎇	z	𐎖	q
𐎈	ḥ	𐎗	r
𐎉	ṭ	𐎘	ṯ
𐎊	y	𐎙	ġ
𐎋	k	𐎚	t
𐎌	š	𐎛	ỉ
𐎍	l	𐎜	ủ
𐎎	m	𐎝	s̉

1983:201–218; Dietrich and Loretz 1988). In *function*, *s̉* is like Ugaritic *s*, but only in certain words – other *s*-words are never written with *s̉*.

2.2 The syllabic characters

The typification of the Ugaritic script as "consonantal" requires some qualification. The initial character *ả* and the two "supplemental" characters *ỉ* and *ủ* function as *syllabic* symbols, having the CV value of glottal stop plus the vowel *a*, *i*, or *u*. The reason for the presence of these syllabic *alif* (the name of the Northwest Semitic character for the glottal stop) signs is uncertain (perhaps they were added for the purpose of writing a language such as Akkadian, which permits syllables to begin with vowels; Akkadian texts written with the Ugaritic script have been found, but they are rare). To represent a syllable-final glottal stop, *ỉ* is used. The situation presents difficulties, however, for a syllable-final glottal stop seems sometimes to quiesce, sometimes to be followed by a very brief vowel (compare "secondary opening" in Biblical Hebrew). See Verreet 1983:223–258; another hypothesis is proposed by Tropper 1990b.

3. PHONOLOGY

3.1 Consonants

The Ugaritic consonantal system is typically described in terms of *graphemes* rather than in phonetic terms. By comparison with the later West Semitic languages, and in comparison with other contemporary languages (Akkadian, Egyptian, Hurrian), however, the phonetic system can be approximated (see Tropper 1994a; Gordon 1997):

Ugaritic obstruents

	Bilabial	*Inter-dental*	*Dental*	*Palato-alveolar*	*Velar*	*Pharyngeal*	*Glottal*
Stops							
Voiceless	p		t		k		ʾ (/ʔ/)
Voiced	b		d		g		
Emphatic			ṭ (/t'/)		q (/k'/)		
Fricatives							
Voiceless		ṯ (/θ/)	s	š	ḫ (/x/)	ḥ (/ħ/)	h
Voiced		ḏ (/ð/)	z		ǵ (/γ/)	ʿ(/ʕ/)	
Emphatic		ẓ (/ð'/)	ṣ (/s'/)				

The fricative transcribed *ś* may be lateral fricative /ɬ/ instead.

In addition, the following sonorants occur:

	Bilabial	*Dental*	*Palatal*
Nasals	m	n	
Liquids		r, l	
Glides	w		y

In comparison with Arabic, Ugaritic had one fewer consonantal phoneme, there being no sign for **ḍ*, which had shifted to *ṣ*. The Ugaritic writing system made no distinction between *š* and *ś*. Indeed, there being no evidence from graphic confusions within Ugaritic for the survival of **ś* (unlike Hebrew), it appears likely that it had merged with /š/ (Blau 1977:106; Tropper 1994a:29–30).

The graphic system does not correspond precisely to the phonetic one. The symbol *ẓ* is used for etymological *ẓ̄* (/ð'/), but certain words containing etymological *ẓ̄* are regularly written with symbol *ǵ* (e.g., *nǵr* "guard" from the root *NẒR*), probably expressing a phonetic shift, itself reflective of a dual articulation of ẓ (dental and laryngeal; cf. Aramaic /ð'/ ≈ < q > → /ʕ/; Segert 1988). The use of the symbol *ẓ* for /t'/ is not nearly as widespread as has been claimed (see Freilich and Pardee 1984), appearing only in *CTA* 24 and probably in *RIH* 78/14 (Bordreuil and Caquot 1980:352–353; Tropper 1994b; Pardee 2000:859–71).

Etymological /ð/ poses particular problems: it is sometimes written with the character *ḏ*, but usually with *d*. Apparent confusion of /ð/ and /z/ characterizes certain roots: for example, *nḏr*/*nzr* "vow" (both in Ugaritic); *ḏmr*/*zmr* "sing"; *ḏrʿ*/*zrʿ* "seed/arm." Though there is, therefore, certainly evidence for disparities between the graphic and phonetic systems, the situation was probably not as confused as some have thought. Examination of the confusions claimed by Tropper 1994a reveals that the interpretations of the texts, and hence of the phoneto-semantic identifications, are sometimes either dubious or faulty: for example, *šỉr* and *ṯỉr* are not the same word (Tropper 1994a:38) –the first is "flesh, meat," while the second denotes a kinship status; the two terms only become homophonous in Hebrew with the coalescence of /š/ and /θ/.

3.2 Vowels

Because the Ugaritic writing system does not include vowel characters, Ugaritic vocalic phonology represents an uneasy truce between description and reconstruction. It has this feature in common with all of the pre-Christian era Northwest Semitic languages; however, those attested in the first millennium BC either make use of *matres lectionis* ("mothers of reading," consonant characters used to signal the presence of a vowel) and have later vocalization systems on the basis of which some retrojection can be done (Aramaic, Hebrew), or else have later congeners in which *matres lectionis* are used (late Phoenician, Punic, Neo-Punic). The reconstruction of the Ugaritic vocalic system must rely, therefore, on two types of internal sources: (i) the "extra" *alif* signs in the Ugaritic script (see §2.2); and (ii) Ugaritic words in syllabically written texts. The latter appear in three distinct forms: (i) the so-called polyglot vocabularies (Ugaritic words written in ancient "dictionary" entries); (ii) Ugaritic words in Akkadian texts; and (iii) proper names. For the first two types, see Nougayrol 1968: texts 130–142 and indices pp. 351–352, and Huehnergard 1987; the third type is more difficult to use for reliable results because of the presence of archaic elements in Ugaritic names and of non-Ugaritic names. If one wishes to reconstruct a form or a word where these internal sources are silent, one must rely on comparative Semitic considerations.

The Ugaritic vocalic system is assumed to have consisted of the same six phonemes reconstructed for Proto-Semitic, /a/, /i/, /u/, /ā/, /ī/, /ū/, to which two secondary long vowels were added by monophthongization, /ê/ < */ay/ and /ô/ < */aw/. There is no evidence for secondary lengthening of the short vowels (e.g., /a/ → *qameṣ* in Biblical Hebrew), nor for any shifts of the long vowels (e.g., the "Canaanite shift" /ā/ → /ō/). Apparent anomalous uses of the *alif* signs may indicate the presence of glide vowels following certain of the laryngeal and pharyngeal consonants (Verreet 1983), though these data are susceptible to other interpretations (Tropper 1990b).

4. MORPHOLOGY

4.1 Word formation and word classes

Like the other Semitic languages, Ugaritic morphology is of the inflecting (or fusional) type. The traditional view according to which a Semitic word consists of a consonantal *root* + *internal vowel(s)* + *additional morphemes* still has merit today. Though there are clearly nominal roots, which include a vocalic element (e.g., *kalb-* "dog"), and verbal roots in which vocalic variation is the rule and which serve as the basis for nominal derivation (see below), both types of roots generate derivatives. Morphology thus consists of an abstract entity known as a *root*, which exists in concrete form as a set of consonants, usually two or three, which in a nominal root may include a vowel, and which is modified by internal vowel change (*ablaut*), by suffixation, and/or by prefixation. Thus, a Ugaritic dictionary, organized by root (according to the tradition of Semitic-language dictionaries), will begin with the simplest form attested, either a verb or a noun, and will proceed from this simple form through the attested verbal forms (if any such exist), then through entries characterized by suffixation, then through those characterized by prefixation and/or by further suffixation: for example, *MLK* "to rule," *mlk* "king," *mlkt* "queen," **mmlkt* "kingdom."

Though it is not a useless thing to analyze an old West Semitic text according to the grammatical categories commonly used for the modern languages of scholarship, a descriptive analysis of these languages gives three primary categories of words: *nouns* (see §4.2), *verbs* (see §4.4), and *particles* (see §4.6). There is, nonetheless, a significant degree of overlap within these categories (e.g., verbal nouns and particles derived from nouns) and there are clearly definable subcategories (e.g., adjectives and adverbs). The three-division description is nevertheless important, for the elements belonging to overlapping categories and to subcategories are clearly definable according to one or other of the primary categories (e.g., verbal nouns will have nominal morphology along with certain syntactic and lexical features of verbs; adjectives will have nominal morphology not verbal morphology; verbal adjectives will have nominal morphology along with certain syntactic and lexical features of verbs, etc.).

Nouns and adjectives are marked for gender, number, and case, but not for definiteness and only partially for state. These grammatical categories are expressed by affixation. Internal vowel variation and prefixation function primarily in nouns to mark lexical categories rather than grammatical ones.

Verbs are marked for aspect/tense, for person, for voice, and for mood. There are (i) two aspects – perfective and imperfective, the first marked only by suffixation, the second by prefixation and suffixation; (ii) three voices – active, middle, and passive, marked by internal vowel change and by prefixed consonantal morphemes; and (iii) five moods, all marked by suffixation to the imperfective verb. The position of the person markers indicates aspect/tense; in other words, person is expressed by suffixation in the perfective, by prefixation in the imperfective.

Particles are characterized by the absence of the morphological markers of nouns and verbs. This is completely true, however, of only the most basic particles, for many are secondarily derived from nouns or pronouns and may thus include markers characteristic of the nominal system.

The following presentation of the morphological categories will follow this three-way division, with an attempt to delineate clearly the overlapping categories and the subcategories. In the ensuing discussions and tables Ø is used to indicate forms that are expected to exist but that are not attested in the texts presently extant, while *-ø* is used for forms without a consonantal indicator of a morpheme otherwise indicated consonantally in the paradigm or for a form ending with hypothetical *zero* vowel.

4.2 Nominal morphology

4.2.1 Nominal formation

Nominal forms may consist of the following:

1. *ROOT + internal vowel(s)*: for example, *MaLK-* "king"; *DaKaR-* "male."
2. *Nominal prefix + ROOT + internal vowel(s)*: for example, *maL'aK-* "messenger."
3. *ROOT + internal vowel(s) + nominal suffix*: for example, *Ra'aB ān-* "famine."
4. *Combinations of 2 and 3*: for example, *'aL'iYān-* "mighty."

There are also a certain number of reduplicated (e.g., *qdqd* "top of head," *ysmsm* "beauteous") and quadriconsonantal (e.g., *'rgz* "walnut"?) nominal forms.

The most common nominal prefixes are *m-* (concrete entities), *t-* (abstract entities); much rarer are *'-* and *y-* (both for concrete entities).

The most common nominal suffixes are *-n* (*-ān-*, more rarely *-an-*) and *-t* (perhaps, as in the later Northwest Semitic languages, *-īt-* and *-ūt-* for abstracts).

The data are inconsistent on the matter of whether nouns of the *qatl*/*qitl*/*qutl* types had monosyllabic or bisyllabic stems in the plural (as in Hebrew: *melek* < *malk*, *məlākīm* < *malak-*). Either the bisyllabic plural base was in the process of development from an originally monosyllabic one (Sivan 1992), or else the plural stem was already bisyllabic in Proto-Ugaritic and the second vowel was inconsistently elided in Ugaritic (Huehnergard 1987:304–307).

4.2.2 Case

Case-markers are suffixed and consist of a combination of vocalic and consonantal elements. A *triptotic* case system – nominative, genitive, accusative – is used in the singular, a *diptotic* one – nominative, oblique – in the dual and plural. This system is consistent with case systems known from fully vocalized languages and is demonstrated internally by the reasonably consistent use of the appropriate *alif* sign (see §2.2) in writing nouns of which ʾ ([ˀ]) is the final consonant: for example, sg.masc.nom. *ksủ* = [kussaˀu]; sg.masc.gen. *ksỉ* = [kussaˀi]; sg.masc.acc. *ksả* = [kussaˀa]; pl.masc.nom. *rpủm* = [rapaˀūma]; pl.masc.obl. *rpỉm* = [rapaˀīma].

There is no separate case for the expression of the vocative. There are two lexical vocative markers, *l* and *y* (cf. Arabic *ya*), but a noun may be vocative without the use of a lexical marker. There is some evidence that the oblique case was used in the plural (Singer 1948) and one datum (*ksỉ* "O throne") for the genitive in the singular, perhaps by analogy with the case that normally follows the preposition *l* (Bordreuil and Pardee 1991:158).

The accusative case is used both for the object(s) of transitive verbs and for various adverbial notions.

There are some nouns, particularly those bearing a nominal suffix containing a long vowel (e.g., *-ān*, *-īt*) that have a diptotic singular system: *-u* nominative, *-a* oblique (Liverani 1963; Huehnergard 1987:299.)

4.2.3 Gender

Gender is marked by suffixed morphemes: the singular masculine by *-ø*; singular feminine by *-t* (= [-(a)t-]); plural masculine by lengthening of case-vowel (lengthened genitive singular = plural oblique); plural feminine by *-t* (= [-āt-]). The dual morpheme was probably attached to the singular stem, masculine or feminine.

Several nouns that take feminine agreement do not bear the *-t-* morpheme (e.g., *ủm* "mother"); while the plural morphemes do not correspond in every case to the sex/gender of the entity devoted (e.g., *grnt*, pl. of *grn* "threshing-floor," probably masculine as in Hebrew).

4.2.4 Number

Singular, dual, and plural are productive number categories, marked by variations in the case-vowel, with affixation of *-m* to the dual and plural (for the problem of the quality of the vowel after this *-m* on the dual, see Huehnergard 1987:298, who posits that it was originally *i* on the dual, *a* on the plural).

4.2.5 Definiteness

There is no quasi-lexical marker of definiteness in Ugaritic (cf. *h-* in Hebrew), though the unusually frequent use of *hn* in one text may be a precursor of such a development (Liverani 1964:181–182; Pardee, 1984a:218, n. 23).

4.2.6 State

A fifth grammatical category, morphosyntactic in nature, is useful in describing the ancient Semitic languages; this is the category of state. There are two primary states, absolute and construct; a third, the pronominal state, is useful in describing some of the later Northwest Semitic languages where vowel reduction is prevalent, and will be referred to briefly here.

Table 2.2 The Ugaritic noun: absolute state

	Singular		Dual	Plural
Masculine				
Nominative	malku	*Nominative*	malkāmi *or* malkāma	malakūma *or* malkūma
Genitive	malki	*Oblique*	malkêmi *or* malkêma	malakīma *or* malkīma
Accusative	malka			
Feminine				
Nominative	malkatu	*Nominative*	malkatāmi *or* malkatāma	malakātu *or* malkātu
Genitive	malkati	*Oblique*	malkatêmi *or* malkatêma	malakāti *or* malkāti
Accusative	malkata			

Absolute describes a noun in unbound form, *construct* a noun bound to a following one in the genitive relationship, and *pronominal* a noun bound to a following pronoun also in the genitive relationship.

An example of typical masculine and feminine nouns in the absolute state, indicating the markers of case, gender, and number, is presented in Table 2.2. Note that in the dual and plural numbers, variant forms occur. The vowel /ê/ is from earlier */ay/ (see §3.2).

4.2.6.1 *Construct state*

In Ugaritic, the case-vowel is preserved in the first word(s) of genitive phrases (in traditional grammar the head noun is called the *nomen regens*, the second noun the *nomen rectum*). Thus, in the singular, the genitive relationship is marked only by the genitive case-vowel on the second element of the phrase. This feature is shared with, for example, classical Arabic, whereas in other Semitic languages the first word also shows some form of modification (e.g., Akkadian *šarru* becomes *šar* in construct, Hebrew *dāḇār* becomes *dəḇar*; for another view of the Ugaritic data, see Zevit 1983; refutation by Huehnergard 1987:300–301). In the dual and the plural the *-m* of the *nomen regens* is usually dropped in construct.

Singular	malku qarîti	"The/A king (NOM.) of the/a city"
Dual	malkā qarîti	"[The] two kings (NOM.) of the/a city"
Plural	mal(a)kū qarîti	"[The] kings (NOM.) of the/a city"

4.2.6.2 *Pronominal state*

The case-vowel is also preserved in the pronominal state, again in contrast with Akkadian where the case-vowel drops; here Hebrew shows remnants of a system similar to the Ugaritic one (*dəbārᵊkā* for *dabar + V + ka*).

Singular	malkuhu	"his king" (NOM.)
Dual	malkāhu	"his two kings" (NOM.)
Plural	mal(a)kūhu	"his kings" (NOM.)

4.2.7 Adjectives

Adjectival morphology is identical to that of nouns. An adjective used independently ("substantivally," according to the traditional grammatical term), not as a modifier of a noun, functions itself as a noun. When an adjective modifies a noun, it agrees in gender, number, and case with the noun. It is by this morphosyntactic feature that adjectives are most clearly differentiated from nouns, for a noun used to modify another noun does not vary in gender (e.g., the phrase "the woman is a man" in Ugaritic would be *ảt̲t mt hy* (lit. "[The] woman, a man [is] she"), where *ảt̲t* retains its feminine marker and *mt* its masculine marker). Attributive adjectives normally follow the noun they modify; predicate adjectives either precede or follow the noun.

The primary adjectival suffix is the so-called gentilic or *nisbe* ending consisting of *vowel + -y (= [-yy-]) + case-vowel.* The quality of the first vowel is uncertain. The only apparently explicit indication shows [u], *qnủym* "people who work with royal purple dye or with lapis lazuli" (*CAT* 2.73:17 [line 39 in Pardee 1983–1984]).

Comparative and superlative adjectival markers do not exist and such notions must thus be expressed lexically (e.g., by forms of the root *M'D* "much") or syntactically (e.g., *nʿmt šnt ỉl*, "the best years of El" [*CAT* 1.108:27], a substantified adjective in construct with a noun, lit. "the good ones of the years of El").

A nominal genitive formation is often used in place of an adjectival one, e.g., *ảt̲t ṣdqh* (= [ʔaθθatu ṣidqihu]) "the wife of his legitimacy" = "his legitimate wife" (*CTA* 14:12 [Gordon 1965:113, §13.22]).

4.2.8 Numerals

In Ugaritic, numerals belong to nominal categories: cardinal numbers are nouns, ordinals adjectives. Numbers in texts may be either fully written out or expressed by number signs, using the same system as is used in Akkadian texts (a single vertical wedge = "1," a single oblique wedge = "10," etc.).

The Ugaritic repertory of numerals is largely similar to the standard West Semitic inventory:

	Cardinals	*Ordinals* (where different)
1	ảḥd/ảḥt and ʿšty	?
2	t̲n/t̲t	
3	t̲lt̲/t̲lt̲t	
4	ảrbʿ/ảrbʿt	rbʿ
5	ḫmš/ḫmšt	
6	t̲t/t̲t̲t	t̲dt̲
7	šbʿ/šbʿt	
8	t̲mn(y)/t̲mnt	
9	tšʿ/tšʿt	
10	ʿšr/ʿšrt	
11	ʿšty ʿšr/ʿšrh	
12	t̲n ʿšr/ʿšrh *etc.*	
20	ʿšrm *etc.*	
100	mỉt (sing.)/mảt (pl.)	
1,000	ảlp	
10,000	rbt	

With the exception of words containing an *alif* sign, the vocalism of numerals can be reconstructed only from comparative data.

The primary distinctive feature of the Ugaritic numerals is in their morphosyntax: as opposed to the other ancient Semitic languages, where the numerals 3 through 10 observe *chiastic concord* (i.e., incongruent gender agreement, feminine-looking numbers with masculine nouns and vice versa), the distribution of numbers marked with -φ versus -*(a)t* shows less regularity.

Other features of numerals deserving special comment:

1. The formant *ʿšty* is used for for the number "one," as in Akkadian, not just in the number "eleven" as in Hebrew.
2. The only attested forms of the absolute case of the number 2 are *ṯn* and *ṯt* (*ṯnm* is adverbial, "twice," in *CTA* 18 IV 22, 33; 19 II 78; *CAT* 1.104:18, 20). This form constitutes an isogloss with Akkadian (*šine*) against the other West Semitic languages (e.g., Hebrew *šnayim*). See Pardee 2000:195.
3. The alternate form with *-h* of the 10-word found in the cardinals of the teens is not used only to modify feminine nouns as in Hebrew. Moreover, the presence of *h* in the Ugaritic spelling shows that the origin of the element was consonantal, though its form (i.e., the vowel[s] with which the consonant is associated) and its function are uncertain.
4. The ordinals may have a long vowel between the second and third radicals, though its quality is unknown; hence the difference between 6 and 6th: respectively *ṯiṯṯu* (< **ṯidṯu*) versus *ṯadīṯu*, or the like. The ordinals are certainly not formed with the *nisbe* suffix (as in Hebrew), for that morpheme appears in Ugaritic as *-y* (see §4.2.7).

Fractions are very poorly known: *ḫṣt* appears in prose in the meaning "half" of a given quantity (*CTA* 34:10) while *nṣp* apparently means "half" of a (sheqel-)weight in administrative texts.

In a mythological text (*CTA* 14 I 16–20) one finds a series of D-stem passive feminine participles of denominative verbs formed from numbers, designating a series of women: *mṯlṯt, mʿrbt, mḫmšt, mṯdṯt, mšbʿt* "the third one . . . the seventh one." From context these forms refer back to *mtrḫt* (line 13) "the married one," namely "the third woman (taken in marriage)," "the fourth . . . ," etc. These words are thus neither fractions nor multiplicatives, as has often been claimed.

In the number phrase, the noun denoting the counted entity may be either in the same case as the number (i.e., the numeral and the noun are in apposition) or in the genitive case (Blau 1972:78–79).

In poetry, several cases are found of the ordinal number preceding the noun it modifies, in apparent contradiction to the rule that attributive adjectives follow the noun they modify (Gordon 1965:48–49, §7.44; Blau 1972:79). It is likely that such constructions were genitival; in other words, the adjective was in construct with the noun, rather than appositional, as is the case when the attributive adjective follows the noun it modifies, though the semantic nuance of the genitival construction is unknown. One encounters, for example, *b šbʿ ymm* (*CTA* 17 I 16), probably [bi šabīʕi yamīma] "on the seventh of days.") Rarer is a prepositional formulation: *hn šb*[ʿ] *b ymm* (*CTA* 17 V 3–4), probably [hanna šabīʕa bi yamīma], literally "Behold on the seventh among days."

The preposition *l* is often used to join the unit to the ten in compound numbers, as in *ṯn l ʿšrm* "twenty-two" (Pardee 1976:302).

4.3 Pronouns

In their function as replacing nouns, pronouns share features with nouns, though they are not as consistently marked for case, gender, number, and state as are nouns and adjectives.

4.3.1 Personal pronouns

Ugaritic possesses both independent and clitic personal pronouns.

4.3.1.1 Independent personal pronouns

The primary function of independent personal pronouns is to express the grammatical concept of person on the noun side of the grammar (person is expressed grammatically in verbs, but not in nouns); this function entails the marking for gender. Case is also marked, apparently diptotically, though the oblique forms are rarely attested. Nominative case forms are as follows:

	Singular	*Dual*	*Plural*
1st com.	ảnk/ản	Ø	Ø
2nd masc.	ảt	ảtm	ảtm
2nd fem.	ảt	Ø	Ø
3rd masc.	hw	hm	hm
3rd fem.	hy	Ø	Ø

In the oblique case, separate forms are attested for only the following:

	Singular	*Dual*	*Plural*
3rd masc.	hwt	hmt	hmt
3rd fem.	hyt	Ø	Ø

These forms function both as accusatives (i.e., direct object of a transitive verb: *kbd hyt* "honor her"; *kbd hwt* "honor him" (*CTA* 3 III 7, VI 20)) and as genitives (*ṯbr dỉy hwt* "he broke the pinions of him"; *ṯbr dỉy hyt* "he broke the pinions of her" (*CTA* 19 III 122, 144))'.

The first- and the second-person forms consist, as in most of the Semitic languages, of a deictic element *ản* followed by the pronominal element proper. The vocalization of these forms can then be approximated as follows:

	Singular	*Dual*	*Plural*
1st com.	[ˀanāku] (<[ˀan + āku])		
2nd masc.	[ˀatta] (<[ˀan + ta])	[ˀattumā] (<[ˀan + tumā])	[ˀattumu] (<[ˀan + tumu])
2nd fem.	[ˀatti] (<[ˀan + ti])		

The optional first-person singular form *ản* already shows the dropping of the consonantal element *-k-*, though its vocalization is unknown ([ˀanā], as in Aramaic, or [ˀanī], by analogy with other first-person pronominal forms, as in Hebrew?).

The third-person singular forms consist of an augmented form of the primitive pronoun: [hu] > [huwa], [hi] > [hiya].

4.3.1.2 Clitic personal pronouns

Proclitic and enclitic pronouns, clearly related historically to the independent forms just cited, are also attested. Historically speaking, finite verbal forms (see §4.4.2) are made up of a pronominal element providing the notion of person, plus the verbal element. These pronominal elements were *suffixed* in the *perfective*, essentially *prefixed* in the *imperfective*:

	PERFECTIVE			IMPERFECTIVE		
	Singular	Dual	Plural	Singular	Dual	Plural
1st com.	-t	-ny	-n	ʾ	n-	n-
2nd masc.	-t	-tm	-tm	t-	t-	t-
2nd fem.	-t	Ø	-tn	t-	t-	t-
3rd masc.	-ϕ ([-a])	-ϕ ([-ā])	-ϕ ([-ū])	y-	y-/t-	y-/t-
3rd fem.	-t	-t	-ϕ ([-ā])	y-	t-	t-

As it is absent in the other Semitic languages while being attested in Egyptian, the first common dual *-ny* (also attested as a genitive enclitic) appears to be an archaic retention in Ugaritic. Other dual forms indicated were apparently differentiated from identically written plural forms (or singular in the case of the 3rd fem. perf.) by vocalic pattern.

Enclitic personal pronouns are also attached to nouns, with a genitive function, and to verbs, with a primarily accusative function (occasionally dative). Here the second person is marked by *-k-* rather than by *-t-*:

	Singular	*Dual*	*Plural*
1st com.	-y/-ϕ/-n	-ny	-n
2nd masc.	-k	-km	-km
2nd fem.	-k	Ø	-kn
3rd masc.	-h	-hm	-hm
3rd fem.	-h	-hm	-hn

The forms indicated for the first person are distributed according to function: *-y/-ϕ* is genitive (i.e., attached to nouns); *-n* accusative (i.e., attached to transitive verbs). The former set is distributed according to the case of the singular noun to which the genitive suffix is attached (nom. = *-ϕ*; gen./acc. = *-y*); the *-ϕ* form is assumed to have arisen through syncope (*[-uya] → long vowel, usually identified as [-ī]). This distribution differs from early Phoenician, where the suffix on nominative/accusative nouns is identical (i.e., orthographic *-ϕ*), *-y* only appearing in the genitive. As with the independent and prefixed pronominal elements, most of the dual forms were apparently differentiated from identically written plural forms by vocalic pattern.

Accusative enclitic pronouns on imperfect verbs show a great deal of variation because of assimilation to *-n* verbal forms and apparent reanalysis. For example, singular third masculine can appear as *-h* (= [-hu]); as *-n* (= [-annu] < [-an] + [hu]); as *-nh* (= [-annahu] < [anna] + [hu]); as *-nn* (= [-annannu]; apparently from [-anna] + [nnu], through reanalysis of [nnu] as a pronominal suffix); and finally even *-nnn* (apparently = [-annannannu], through double reanalysis). See Pardee 1984b:244–245, n. 14.

4.3.2 Relative pronouns

The relative pronoun is composed of *$\underline{d}$ ([ð]) + vowel, nearly always written with *d*, marked for gender and number, though the forms are not used consistently. This particle is directly related to the *$\underline{d}$ū $\underline{d}$ā $\underline{d}$ī* series in Arabic and to the *ze^h/zōʾt* series in Hebrew (used sporadically as a relative pronoun there), and its basic function is therefore deictic, as is shown in Ugaritic by the enclitic use of *-d* in demonstrative pronouns and adjectives (see §4.3.3) and in adverbials. The gender and number categories indicated here represent agreement between the relative pronoun and its antecedent:

d (sg. masc.) *dt* (pl. masc. and fem.; not used consistently,
interchangeable with *dt*)
dt (sg. fem., also interchangeable with *dt*)

4.3.3 Demonstrative pronouns

The primary demonstrative pronouns and adjectives are compounds consisting of the deictic particle *hn* (probably essentially the same particle as the Hebrew definite article and as the deictic particle *hēn/hinnē^h^* in that language), to which explicating elements are joined: either the relative pronoun *d* (cf. Arabic *ʾillāḏī*) in the case of the proximal demonstrative; or *k*, of uncertain origin, in the distal. The forms are identical to those of the demonstrative adjectives, and the two categories are defined, therefore, by their syntactic characteristics:

Proximal hnd ~ hndt
Distal hnk ~ hnkt

The forms with and without *-t* are not distributed consistently according to gender, and the *-t* may thus be the enclitic particle and not the feminine morpheme *-t*.

Though the usage is rare and to date attested only in the oblique case, the third-person independent pronouns could also be used as demonstrative adjectives, apparently, as in Hebrew, with a distal connotation: for example, *mlk hwt* "that king" (*CAT* 1.103:43); *ḥwt hyt* "that land" (*CAT* 45′, 55′, 56′; for the reading of line 45′, see Pardee 1986:119, 124).

4.3.4 Other pronouns

The other pronominal elements do not show the primary morphological characteristics of nouns and thus overlap with the category of particles. They are included here in order to provide a complete picture of pronouns.

4.3.4.1 Interrogative pronouns

The attested interrogative pronouns are *my* "who?" and *mh* "what?" Comparing *mh*, of which the *-h* is consonantal, with Biblical Hebrew *mah* leads to the conclusions that (i) the gemination following the Hebrew pronoun represents assimilation of the *-h*; and (ii) the presence of the <h> in the orthography is therefore historical writing (this solution appears more likely than positing a Proto-Hebrew form *man* and identifying the orthographic <h> as a secondary *mater lectionis*).

4.3.4.2 Indefinite pronouns

The indefinite pronouns and adjectives are *mn*/*mnk* and *mnm*. As presently attested, *mn* and *mnk* denote human entities ("whoever"), *mnm* inanimate ones ("whatever"). The basic particle was plausibly [mVn] with the distinction between human and nonhuman referents expressed by ablaut (e.g., [min-] for humans, [man-] for nonhumans); *-k* and *-m* are expanding elements of uncertain semantic content. Because "enclitic" *-m* may be attached to any part of speech, it would not be surprising to encounter the form *mnm* applied to humans; it would have been distinguished from the nonhuman reference by its characteristic vowel.

4.4 Verbal morphology

The verbal system represents an archaic form of West Semitic, one with an N-stem; a D-stem (characterized by the doubling of the middle radical); a causative stem in Š; *t*-stems built off the G-, D-, and Š-stems; as well as some less well-attested stems. For discussion of the conventional classification of Semitic verb-stems, see Appendix 1, §3.3.5.2.

As in the other Semitic languages, the basic verbal form can itself express various sorts of action. The primary opposition is *transitive* versus *intransitive.* Of the latter sort, there are two primary types: verbs of *motion* and *stative* verbs. Verbs of motion are themselves of two primary types: verbs that express only motion and those that express either the motion or the state achieved (e.g., *qm* "arise" or "be standing"). Stative verbs also can denote either the state itself or the attainment thereof (e.g., *qrb* "be near" or "become near," i.e., "approach"). These distinctions are reflected in the verbal system: only transitive verbs can be passivized and tend to take double accusatives in the causative, single accusatives in the D-stem. Stative verbs are factitivized in the D-stem, cannot be passivized in the G-stem, and have a stative participial form rather than the active one. Verbs of motion cannot be passivized in the G-stem, appear rarely in the D-stem, and are transitivized in the Š-stem, where they take the single accusative construction. There are of course, a certain number of verbs that either cross-categorize or defy classification.

4.4.1 Verb-stems

The attested verbal stems are as follows:

1. *G-stem*: base stem, or simple stem; active and passive voices.
2. *Gt-stem*: *-t-* infixed after first radical of G-stem; middle/reflexive in function.
3. *D-stem*: doubled middle radical; factitive in function; active and passive voices.
4. *tD-stem*: *t-* prefixed to D-stem (see Huehnergard 1986); middle/reflexive in function.
5. *N-stem*: preformative *n-*; middle/passive in function.
6. *Š-stem*: preformative *š-*; causative in function; active and passive voices.
7. *Št-stem*: *-t-* infixed after *š-* of causative stem; middle/reflexive in function; the few forms attested indicate that the form may no longer have been productive.
8. *L-stem*: lengthened vowel after first radical and reduplicated second or third radical; intensive or factitive in function.
9. *R-stem*: reduplication of both radicals of biconsonantal root, of second and third radicals of triconsonantal root; factitive in function.
10. *tR-* or *Rt-stem*: *t* prefixed to first root consonant or infixed after first root consonant of R-stem; factitive-reflexive in function.

The following examples are given with vocalization in order to illustrate the phonetic distinctions between the forms (see below). Many details of the vocalizations are, however, still uncertain. Here, an asterisk before a G-stem form indicates that the verb is only attested in Ugaritic in the following derived stem (and does not indicate that the form is reconstructed).

1. *LḤM* "to eat (something)" (G-stem transitive, *laḥama*); *LḤM* "to provide (someone) with food" (D-stem, *liḥḥama*); *ŠLḤM* "to cause (someone) to eat (something)" (Š-stem, *šalḥima*).
2. *RḤṢ* "to wash" (G-stem transitive, *raḥaṣa*); *(ʾI)RTḤ Ṣ* "to wash oneself" (Gt-stem, *ʾirtaḥaṣa*)

3. *NTK* "to pour out" (G-stem transitive, *nataka*); *NTK* "to pour forth" (N-stem, *nattaka* < *nantaka*).
4. **BKR* "to be the first born" (G-stem stative, *bakura*); *BKR* "to promote (someone) to the status of first born" (D-stem, *bikkara*).
5. **KMS* "to squat" (G-stem intransitive, *kamasa*); *TKMS* "to collapse" (tD-stem, *takammasa*).
6. ʿRB "to enter" (G-stem verb of movement, *ʿaraba*); *ŠʿRB* "to cause (someone) to enter" (Š-stem, *šaʿriba*).
7. *RḤQ* "to be far off or to move far off" (G-stem stative, *raḥuqa*); *ŠRḤQ* "to cause to be far off" (Š-stem, *šarḥiqa*).
8. *QL* "to fall" (G-stem intransitive, *qāla*?); *ŠQL* "to cause (something) to fall" (Š-stem, *šaqīla*); *(ʾI)ŠTQL* "to cause oneself to fall" → "to arrive" (Št-stem, *ʾīštaqīla*).
9. *RM* "to be or become high" (G-stem stative, *rāma*); *RMM* "to raise" (L-stem, *rāmama*).
10. **KR(R)* "to turn" (G-stem verb of movement, *karra*); *KRKR* "to turn, twist, snap" (said of what one does with the fingers) (R-stem *karkara*); cf. the adjectival form *YSMSM* "beautiful" < *YSM* (G-stem stative *yasuma* "to be beautiful").
11. **YPY* "to be beautiful" (G-stem stative, *yapiya*); *TTPP* "she makes herself beautiful" (only form attested of Rt- or tR-stem, *titêpêpî* < **titaypaypiyu* or *tîtapêpî* < **tiytapaypiyu*).

4.4.2 Verb conjugations (aspect/tense)

There are two verbal conjugations marked for person, gender, and number: one is characterized by STEM + PRONOMINAL ELEMENT and expresses acts viewed as complete (*perfective*, often called the "perfect" though the term is technically incorrect), the other is characterized by PRONOMINAL ELEMENT + STEM (+ AFFIX) and expresses acts not viewed as complete (*imperfective*, often called the "imperfect"). The pronominal elements (see §4.3.1.2) were joined to the verbal elements in an archaic stage of the language. This description of the form and function of the two verbal conjunctions is accurate for the prose texts. In poetry the distribution of the two forms just described has thus far defied complete description. Usage seems to reflect an older stage of the language, when the zero-ending imperfect form (see §4.4.6, **4**) functioned as a preterite, like Akkadian *iprus*. In the West Semitic verbal system, the permansive came to function as perfective, the "subjunctive" (*iprusu*) as an imperfective, and the preterite as a jussive (and, particularly in Biblical Hebrew, as a frozen preterite after *wa-*).

In spite of the problems of description and categorization of the verbal system in the poetic texts, many scholars, e.g., Tropper 1995, have preferred to classify the Ugaritic verbal system on the basis of poetic usage, rather than on that of the prose texts (similar attempts, of course, have been made in the classification of Biblical Hebrew). It appears legitimate to see in the poetic texts remnants of a previous stage of the language (plausibly closer to East Semitic), remnants that seem not to be used consistently because they are no longer representative of the spoken language, while the prose texts reflect spoken Ugaritic in the thirteenth–twelfth centuries BC. Only in these prose texts is a reasonably consistent system visible (cf. Mallon 1982).

The Ugaritic verbal system is here classified as *aspectual*, rather than *tensed*, primarily because of its similarity to the prose system of Biblical Hebrew (Pardee 1993a, 1993b, 1995). While tense is a real-world phenomenon (past–present–future), aspectual systems include a greater degree of subjectivity; in other words, the speaker may express a situation as complete or incomplete according to several criteria. Because of the nature of tense, aspectual systems cannot ignore temporal considerations; accordingly, a language may not be identified as a tensed language simply because it reflects real-world temporal considerations. On the other hand, a language may be classed as aspectual if it ignores real-world temporality, as in the use of the imperfect in Biblical Hebrew prose to express past-tense iteratives (e.g., *yišmaʿ* "he used to hear").

The perfective may have been characterized by internal ablaut for active (*katab-*) versus stative (*katib-*, *katub-*), but all internal evidence is for the *katib-* type (writings of the middle radical with : *l'ik*=[laʔika] "he sent"; *š'il*=[šaʔila] "he asked"). Syllabic writings attest some *katab-* forms (Huehnergard 1987:319–320).

The imperfective was characterized by internal ablaut, perhaps for active (*yaktub-*) versus stative (*yiktab-*, *yaktib-*). There are few data for these differentiations, but those that do exist tend to agree with the data from the later West Semitic languages, making the conclusions plausible. In addition, the imperfective is also marked, by affixation to the stem, for mood (see §4.4.4). The *Barth–Ginsberg Law* of *a*-dissimilation (*yaktab* → *yiktab*) was operative in Ugaritic.

No certain evidence exists for a present-future form corresponding to Akkadian *iparras* (Fenton 1970).

4.4.3 Voice

Active verbs are of two primary types, transitive and intransitive (e.g., *halaka* "he went"; *maḫaṣa ʾêba* "he smote the enemy"). The concept of transitivity is not a useless one in Semitics, for not only do certain verbs take complements that correspond to what in other languages would be direct objects, but distinctively marked passive forms, used almost exclusively for verbs that in other languages would be qualified as transitive, are common. Though lack of vocalization in Ugaritic makes identification difficult, it is likely that all transitive forms (i.e., G-stem transitive verbs, D-stem, and Š-stem) had passive forms that were differentiated from the active by ablaut (for a contrary view on the G-passive finite forms, see Verreet 1986:324–330; brief refutation in Tropper 1993a:478–479). In addition, the N-stem, basically an intransitivizing and deagentifying stem, can be used as a passive (such a usage of the *t*-stems, which became common in Hebrew, is not clear in Ugaritic.) Passives are attested for finite forms (e.g., *tšt išt* "fire is placed" [*CTA* 4 VI 22]) as well as for participles. There is as yet no evidence for ablaut-passive imperatives, though there was almost certainly an N-stem imperative (*RS* 34.126:13 *ibky* and *ibid.* 18 *išḫn*, the first of which appears to function as a passive "be bewept" [Bordreuil and Pardee 1991:157–159]). On the basis of comparative data, one would not expect a passive infinitive necessarily to have existed.

Between the two extremes marked by the clearly transitive and passive forms, there is a whole middle range of forms denoting reflexivity, reciprocity, advantage or disadvantage to actor and so forth. These notions are clearest in the *t*-stems (Gt, tD, and Št). The primary function of the N-stem in Ugaritic, as in several of the Semitic languages, was for the expression of patient-oriented acts and it is thus used for both the passive and the middle.

4.4.4 Mood

Verbal mood was in Ugaritic, as in the other West Semitic languages, marked by variations to the imperfective stem.

4.4.4.1 Imperative

The imperative in Ugaritic does not have the preformative element characteristic of the imperfective, but the fact that its stem-vowel is identical to that of the imperfective leaves no doubt as to the historical linkage of the imperative to the imperfective. Its form is thus ROOT + stem-vowel (+ additional PRONOMINAL ELEMENT). The question of an additional vowel between the first two radicals is unresolved: imperfective *yaktub-*; imperative *kVtub-* or *ktub-*. In the case of *kVtub-*, the quality of the first vowel is unknown. Is it always identical to the stem-vowel or sometimes different? To the basic imperative element may be added the *-a(n)(na)* elements; see §4.4.4.2. The imperative existed only in the second person and only for positive commands (negative commands are expressed by *ảl* + jussive).

4.4.4.2 *Other moods*

All other moods are marked by affixation to the full imperfective stem (the stem *YKTB*/*yaktub-* will be used below for STEM):

Nonimperatival moods of Ugaritic

Jussive	YKTB + ϕ	yaktub
Indicative	YKTB + u	yaktubu
Volitive	YKTB + a	yaktuba
Energic 1	YKTB + (a)n	yaktubVn
Energic 2	YKTB + anna	yaktubanna

The morphosemantic values of these moods are largely derived from comparison with other Semitic languages, for the forms are not used consistently in the poetic texts and the prose texts have not yet furnished sufficient material to establish usage with certainty. Because of the absence of vowel indicators, the usage of one mood or another can be determined only when the root ends in *alif* or *yod*: the form of *alif* will indicate the quality of the following vowel, while the presence or absence of *yod* may indicate the presence or absence of a following vowel (*yabniyu* = <ybny>; **yabniy* → *yabni* = <ybn>). These III-weak roots (see §4.4.6) thus provide us with the primary internal data on the aspectual and modal systems in Ugaritic, but inconsistency of usage, particularly in the case of III-*y* roots, also creates a significant degree of uncertainty.

The *-a* form does not function primarily as a marker of syntactic dependency (Verreet 1988), but as a *volitive* (Tropper 1991; 1993a:473–474; Pardee 1993b), and its traditional classification – namely "subjunctive" – borrowed from Arabic, is thus not appropriate (this is to be understood not as a claim that the *-a* form cannot appear in subordinate clauses, but as a denial that such is its principal function).

The two *energic* forms are only distinguishable when followed by a suffix (see §4.3.1.2) and their semantic import is uncertain. The distribution of these suffixed forms clearly indicates the existence of two energic forms, *-an* and *-anna* (as in Arabic). Whether there also existed a similar form built on the "indicative" (*-u+n(a)*), as apparently in old Canaanite (Rainey 1996, II:234–244), has not been determined.

Mood distinction in forms containing a suffixed pronominal subject element (e.g., pl. 3rd masc. *yaktub* + *ū*) is variable in the later languages and impossible to determine in Ugaritic (except where the distinction was marked by consonantal *-n* – there the problem is the precise function of the *-n*).

4.4.5 Strong verb paradigm

The G-stem of the Ugaritic strong verb is illustrated in Table 2.3 (particularly doubtful reconstructions are indicated with one or more question marks); KTB is the root meaning to "to write." More extensive paradigms, with proposed vocalizations, can be found in Segert 1984.

Table 2.3 The Ugaritic verb: G-stem

	Perfective	Imperfective	Jussive	Imperative
Singular				
1st com.	katabtu	ʾaktubu	ʾaktub	
2nd masc.	katabta	taktubu	taktub	kutub(a)
2nd fem.	katabti	taktubīna	taktubī	kutubī
3rd masc.	kataba	yaktubu	yaktub	
3rd fem.	katabat	taktubu	taktub	
Dual				
1st com.	katabnayā (?)	naktubā (?)	naktubā?	
2nd masc.	katabtumā	taktubā(ni)	taktubā	kutubā
2nd fem.	Ø	Ø	Ø	Ø
3rd masc.	katabā (?)	yaktubā(ni)	yaktubā	
		taktubā(ni)	taktubā	
3rd fem.	katabtā (?)	taktubā(ni)	taktubā	
Plural				
1st com.	katabnū	naktubu	naktub	
2nd masc.	katabtum(u)	taktubū(na)	taktubū	kutubū
2nd fem.	katabtin(n)a	taktubna (?)	taktubna (??)	kutubā (?)
3rd masc.	katabū	yaktubūna	yaktubū	
		taktubūna	taktubū	
3rd fem.	katabā	taktub(ā)na (?)	taktubā (??)	

The third-person dual and plural imperfectives often have preformative *t*-, rather than *y*- (Verreet 1988). The presence of different forms in similar texts appears to show that *t*-preformative cannot in and of itself mark a distinction either of gender (masc. vs. fem.) or of number (dual vs. pl.): for example, *t ʿrbn g̱trm* "the *g̱trm* will enter" (*CTA* 33:9); *yrdn g̱trm* "the *g̱trm* will descend" (*CAT* 1.112:18); cf. *tʿln i̇lm* "the gods will ascend" (*CAT* 1.112:8).

Second-person feminine dual forms are not attested, but the graphic identity of third-person masculine and feminine pronominal forms indicates that a distinction would, in any case, have been vocalic and thus indeterminable in the consonantal orthography.

The N-stem imperative had *i* in the preformative syllable: for example, *i̇šḫn* ([ˀiššaxin-] < *[ˀinšaxin-]) "be hot!" (*RS* 34.126:18, cf. *i̇bky* "be bewept!" in line 13; Bordreuil and Pardee 1991:157–158). The same holds for the Gt perfective: thus, *i̇tdb*, generally taken as a scribal error for *i̇tbd* ([ˀîtabada] < *[ˀiˀtabada]) "it has perished" (*CTA* 14 I 8).

The Gt and tD were apparently characterized by different stem-vowels in the imperfective, *i* versus *a*: *yštˀil* (Gt) versus *yštˀal* (tD) "ask, importune" (Huehnergard 1986).

It is highly unlikely that there existed an H-causative (Hebrew *Hiphil*) or a ʾ-causative (*Aphel*) alongside the Š-causative (Merrill 1974; Tropper 1990a).

4.4.6 Weak verbs

In Ugaritic, a *weak verb* is in essence one that contains an *alif*; one that at a proto-stage contained *y or *w in any of the root positions; or one which contains a geminate (i.e., $C_1C_2C_2$). Some peculiarities of the weak verb roots of Ugaritic are outlined below. Roman numerals are used to designate the position of the weak consonant in the root (1st, 2nd, 3rd).

1. Some I-*alif* roots show vagaries in orthography that indicate some form of mutation of the *alif* (quiescence, "secondary opening"?): for example, *yỉḫd* versus *yủḫd*, both meaning "he seizes" (see Verreet 1983; Tropper 1990b).
2. I-*y*/*w* roots have all (with very rare exceptions) become I-*y* in the perfective. Most imperfectives show a bisyllabic stem, with *a* in the prefix syllable: thus, *ảrd* ([ˀarid-]) "I descend"; *YD*ʿ "to know" has *i* in the prefix syllable, *ỉd*ʿ ([ˀidaʕ-] "I know," probably reflecting an *a* stem-vowel, because of the final guttural, and the Barth–Ginsberg Law (see §4.4.2).
3. *Hollow roots* have no consonantal element in the slot occupied by consonant II in triconsonantal roots. Most attested imperfectives have preformative vowel *a*: *ảbn* ([ˀabīn-]) "I understand." The root *B*ˀ "to enter" is written with *ủ*, apparently representing [u]:*ủbủ* ([ˀubūˀu]) "I enter" (indicative), ủbả ([ˀubūˀa]) "that I might enter" (-*a* volitive). See Pardee 1988:221.
4. III-*y*/*w* roots have shifted almost entirely to III-*y*; exceptions are attested for *ảšlw* "I relax" (*CTA* 14 III 149) and *ảtwt* "you have come" (*CTA* 4 IV 32). The zero-ending imperfective (jussive, historical "preterite") has apparently monophthongized (**yabniy* → *yabni*) but, as noted above, usage is not consistent in the poetic texts, and use of historical writing (i.e., [yabni] = <ybn/ybny>) may be at the origin of some forms. See Verreet 1988 (and Sivan 1982 for III-weak nominal forms).

4.4.7 Nonfinite verbals

There are two productive forms, the infinitive and the participle, which are associated with the verb but not marked for aspect or person. These forms belong by their morphology to the noun side of the grammar, by their syntax to both the noun and the verb (i.e., complementation can be either accusatival or genitival).

4.4.7.1 Infinitives

There was one abstract verbal noun (infinitive). The pattern in the G-stem does not seem to have been fixed (Huehnergard 1987:320), though it is likely that *katāb-* was the most common for strong roots; compare *bšảl* ([bi šaˀāli], the preposition *b* + infinitive). The infinitive in the derived stems was formed by ablaut: no *m*-preformative infinitives are attested. The nominal character of the infinitive will, of course, have appeared also in its case morphology and morphosyntax.

Though there is a syntactic usage corresponding to the so-called *infinitive absolute* construction, there does not seem to have been in Ugaritic a productive separate form so used in contradistinction to the verbal noun. One will note that it is the *katāb-* form that became the infinitive absolute in Biblical Hebrew, whereas this form functions frequently as a verbal noun in Ugaritic. Where discernible (i.e., in III-ˀ roots), the infinitive in "absolute" usage ends in *u*, homophonous with the nominative, though its origin may be different: *hm ǵmủ ǵmỉt* ([himma ɣamāˀu ɣamiˀti]) "If you are indeed thirsty" (*CTA* 4 IV 34 [Gordon 1965:79, 121, §§9.27; 13.57]).

4.4.7.2 Participles

Each verbal stem has at least one corresponding verbal adjective (participle). If the stem is transitive, there will be a participle for each voice, the active and the passive. In addition, it is likely that the G-stem had two *stative verbal adjectives*, for a total of four: thus, active *kātib-*; stative *katib-* and *katub-*; passive *katūb-*.

All the derived stems except the N-stem form the participle with a prefixed *m*-. The D-stem had *u* in the preformative of the participle (cf. *mu-na-aḫ-ḫi-mu*, the syllabic writing of the personal name *mnḥm* "the one who brings comfort").

The morphology of the verbal adjectives, is like that of the other adjectives and the nominal case system could in most instances specify a participle where ambiguity was potential. For example, *raḥuqu*, with final -*u*, could only be a stative participle, while *raḥuqa* could be either verbal or adjectival, but only the latter if the word could be construed as in the accusative case.

Several nouns, nonparticipial in form, are built from the Š-stem: for example, *šʿtqt* "she who causes to pass on"; *šmrr* "that which causes bitterness" (i.e., "venom").

4.5 Adverbs

Adverbials may be expressed by adverbial lexemes or by adverbialization of a noun, that is, by prefixing a preposition, by suffixation of an adverbial morpheme (see §4.6.2), or by using a particular form of the noun. Adverbial lexemes are either etymological nouns of which the derivation is clear (e.g., *ʿt* "now," *ʿln* (*ʿl*+-*n*) "above") or particles (e.g., *ṯm*, "there"). The accusative case was the primary case used for adverbialization of nouns: for example, *qdqd* "on the head," *ym* "for a day," *šmm* "to the heavens."

4.6 Particles

4.6.1 Deictic particles

The standard presentative particle is *hn* (conventional translation "behold"). The basic element is *h*-, for alongside *hn* one finds *hl*, *hln*, *hlny* (on expanding particles see §4.6.5). It is likely that this particle *hn* is at the origin of the Phoenician/Hebrew definite article (*ha* + gemination), while variant forms thereof appear in other West Semitic languages (e.g., Arabic *ʾil*- and the Aramaic postpositive article, if from *hʾ* or the like).

In epistolary usage, the functions of *hn*- and *hl*- are distinct in that only the latter is used in a clearly local sense of "here" (*RS* 15.174:7; RS 29.093:11) whereas both function deictically, "behold." This analysis of previously known texts is reinforced by the following recent examples in which *hl*- appears immediately before *hn*-: *RS* 92.2005:9 *hln hn ʿmn* ("Here, behold with me"); RS 94.2497:5 *hlny hnn b bt mlk* ("Here, behold in the house of the king").

Rhetorical "now" is expressed by a form of this deictic particle with affixed -*t* (see §4.6.2).

The deictic element -*d*- (< /-ð/) was quite productive, functioning independently as a relative pronoun (see §4.3.2) and enclitically as part of the demonstrative pronoun and adjective (see §4.3.3), and as an adverbial (see §4.6.2).

4.6.2 Adverbial particles

As noted in §4.5, adverbials may be expressed by adverbial lexemes or by adverbialization of a noun (i.e., by prefixing a preposition, by use of the accusative case, or by suffixation of an adverbial morpheme).

The following are examples of adverbial particles: *hn*, *hnn*, *hnny* "here"; *hl*, *hlh*, *hlny* "here," *ṯm*, *ṯmn*, *ṯmny* "there"; *ht* rhetorical "now" (probably *hn* + -*t*), and *ảp* "also."

Interrogative adverbs are *ỉy* and *ản* "where?"; *ỉk*(*y*) "how?"; *lm* (probably *l* "to/for" + *m* "what?") "why?" The particle *ỉk* is often used as a rough equivalent of *lm*: for example, *ỉk mǵy gpn wủgr* "how is it that *gpn-w-ủgr* have come?" (not: "how have *gpn-w-ủgr* come?") (*CTA* 3 III 33). The interrogative particles normally come at the head of the sentence. Judging from passages difficult to understand if taken as declarative, it is likely that interrogation could also be indicated by voice inflection. There is no interrogative particle in Ugaritic such as Hebrew *hă-* which marks a following phrase as a question.

Negative adverbs are *l* (primarily indicative) and *ỉl* (primarily volitive). The particle *ỉn* is used, as in Hebrew, primarily to negate nominal phrases; *bl* is rare, attested primarily in poetry and with nouns.

The primary asseveratives and negatives were written the same but probably had different vocalizations: *l*= [lā] "not" and [la] "indeed" (Huehnergard 1983:583–584); *ỉl*= [ˀal] "must not" and [ˀallu] (?) "must."

Prepositional adverbialization is extremely common: for example, *l* (preposition) + *ˁlm* (noun) = "for a long time."

The two most common adverbial suffixes attached to nouns are *-m* and *-h*. The first cannot be defined precisely, for it appears on virtually all parts of speech. One common occurrence is on adverbial nouns, perhaps only augmenting the adverbial accusative. The second corresponds to the locative/directive *he* in Biblical Hebrew and is used both locally and temporally: thus, *šmmh* "to the heavens," *ˁlmh* "for a long time." Note that, in contrast to Hebrew where the *hê* is written without *mappīq*, the Ugaritic *-h* is consonantal.

4.6.3 Conjunctions

The most common coordinating conjunction is *w-*, capable of linking phrases at all levels (word, clause, sentence, paragraph). The conjunction *p* (cf. Arabic *fa*) occurs more rarely, usually with a notion of cause-and-effect linkage; *ỉp* "also" (and expanded forms) functions most commonly at the paragraph level, and is in all probability a form of *p* produced by prefixing [ˀ]. The conjunction *ủ* functions both independently and correlatively (*ủ* ... *ủ* "either ... or") and probably covers two lexemes: (i) [ˀū] "and"; (ii) [ˀô] (< *[au]) "either/or."

The most common subordinating conjunction is *k* "because, when, if" (comparable to Hebrew *kī*), expanded with *-y* and with *-m* (same meaning), and rarely with *-d* (the same particle as the relative pronoun), with no appreciable change of meaning. Both *ỉm* and *hm* are attested as conditional conjunctions meaning "if."

4.6.4 Prepositions

Ugaritic overlaps significantly with the other West Semitic languages in its prepositional system. Some of these are primitive particles (e.g., *b* "in," *k* "like," *l* "at"); others are derived from clearly identifiable verbal or nominal roots (e.g., *ˁl* "upon," *tḥt* "under," *ỉḫr* "after"); still others are combinations of the two processes (e.g., *l* + *pn* "in front of," *b* + *yd*, "in the hand/control of," *b* + *tk* "in the midst of"). One also finds similarities in nuances and translation values (e.g., *b* = "in, within, through, by the intermediary of, by the price of," etc.). The status of compound prepositions (i.e., those formed of two primary prepositions) is as yet uncertain: the only example attested to date is *l* + *b*, apparently meaning something like "within," though the identity of the first element is uncertain (Rainey 1973:56; Freilich 1986:119–130).

The primary peculiarity of Ugaritic is the absence of a prepositional lexeme expressing the ablatival notion "from, away from." This absence is compensated by a complex system of verb + preposition combinations, where the translation value of the preposition can be determined only by usage and by context (Pardee 1975, 1976, with a discussion of prepositional semantic ambiguity). The prepositional system as a whole appears to function primarily to denote position rather than direction, a stative notion rather than a motional one. Directionality and motion were supplied primarily by the verb. What this means in practice is that virtually any preposition may appear in expressions of the ablative and the modern reader must depend on elements other than the preposition itself to reach a proper interpretation of a passage. The following passage is instructive, for it includes a preposition with "opposite meanings" in the expression of a "from ... to" situation, but along standard Ugaritic lines – that is, by means of different verb + preposition combinations (*yrd l* "descend from," *yṯb l* "sit upon"): *yrd l ks ỉyṯb l hdm w l hdm yṯb l ảrṣ* "he descends from the throne, he sits upon the footstool, and [he descends] from the footstool, he sits upon the earth" (*CTA* 5 VI 12–14).

There are also certain functional differences between Ugaritic and the other Semitic languages: for example, the increased use of *ʿm* "with" to denote the end-point of a trajectory; *l* used to form compound numbers. Moreover, different lexemes occur: for example, *ẓr* "back," yielding "on top of".

The substantive following a preposition is, as nearly as can be determined, always in the genitive case (as in Akkadian, Arabic, etc.). This is shown for Ugaritic by nominal phrases spelled with a final *alif* character: for example, *l ksỉ* [lê kussaʔi] "to the chair/throne"; *b nšỉ* [bi našāʔi] "in his lifting, when he lifts."

The case system still being in force, no prepositional particle has developed in Ugaritic to mark the direct object of a transitive verb, such as, for example, Phoenician *ʾyt*, Hebrew *ʾōt-* and *ʾet/ʾēt*).

4.6.5 Enclitic particles

Ugaritic makes use of a baroque array of enclitic particles (Aartun 1974, 1978), the disentanglement of which is made all the more difficult by the absence of vocalized texts. These particles can be joined to all parts of speech and are capable of accretion one to another (e.g., *h+n+n+y*). Particles that apparently have little more than an "emphatic" function may develop a paradigmatic function alongside particles of more precisely definable origin: for example, *hnd* "this" = *h* (deictic particle) + *n* (particle) + *d* (relative pronoun), alongside *hnk* "that" = *h* (deictic particle) + *n* (particle) + *k* (particle). The principal enclitic particles are these:

1. *-d* – relative pronoun that can function as a compounding element with nouns (e.g., *šbʿd*, "sevenfold") and with other particles (e.g., *hnd* "this"), and is expandable (e.g., *šbʿịd*, also "sevenfold").
2. *-h* = adverbial (see §4.6.2).
3. *-y* = enclitic particle, particularly as expander to another particle (e.g., *hn+n+y*).
4. *-k* = enclitic particle, particularly in *hnk* "that."
5. *-m* = enclitic particle used on all parts of speech (see §4.6.2 for use with adverbials).
6. *-n* = enclitic particle used on all parts of speech. One particularly striking usage is the "*n* of apodosis" (Hoftijzer 1982); in certain omen texts characterized by a repetitive protasis–apodosis structure, the first word in the apodosis, if a singular noun in the absolute state, has enclitic *-n* (Pardee 1986:126, 129; Tropper 1994b:466–469).
7. *-t* = enclitic particle, particularly as expander to another particle (e.g., *ht* < *hn+t* with assimilation; *hn+d+t*).

4.7 Compounds

Compound verbs are virtually unknown in old West Semitic, and compound nouns are rare (the primary case cited for Ugaritic is *bl mt* "not death" used in parallel with *ḥym* "life" in

CTA 17 VI 27). Complex prepositional phrases, made up of a preposition and a common noun, are certainly well attested (see §4.6.4, and the list and discussion in Pardee 1976:306–310), but it is in most cases dubious that the complex phrase had evolved as a lexical entity of which the compositional elements were no longer perceived.

4.8 Derivational processes

Because Ugaritic is a poorly attested one-period language, it is hardly possible to describe synchronic derivational processes. Viewing the language comparatively, however, it appears clear that the known state of the language reflects a number of such processes, for one can spot certain morphemes of which the function is best described as derivational.

Within categories, the generating of new particles by particle accretion is perhaps the clearest derivational process (better so termed perhaps than as compounding), though the semantics of the process are unclear in most cases.

Across categories, the nominal system, particularly the *m*- and *t*- prefixes and the -*n* suffix noted in §4.2.1, and certain ablaut forms (e.g., *qattāl* to express a *nomen professionalis*), usually reflect a deverbal notion rather than an inner-nominal process. The suffixing of particles to nominal elements, to the extent that these particles were not perceived by native speakers as lexical items, also represents a form of derivation.

Across subcategories, the case of the *nisbe* ending, by which nouns are transformed into adjectives (see §4.2.7), is the clearest case of a derivational morpheme.

5. SYNTAX

The relative dearth of prose texts mentioned in the introduction makes it difficult to ascertain a normative prose syntax, while the lack of vocalized texts makes some aspects of morphosyntax difficult to ascertain precisely.

5.1 Word order

On the phrase level, there are two primary nominal phrases: the genitival and the adjectival.

The *genitival phrase* is the common Semitic construct state: X of Y (see §4.2.6.1). The first element is in the case required by context, the second in the genitive. It can denote the various relationships well known elsewhere (subjective genitive, objective genitive, genitive of identification, genitive of material, etc.). No lexical or pronominal element may intervene between the members of a construct chain, only enclitic particles.

The *adjectival phrase* is of two types, (i) the phrase-level or attributive, in which the adjective follows the noun and agrees in gender, number, and case; and (ii) the sentence-level or predicative, in which the adjective may either precede or follow the noun and agrees in gender, number, and case. An attributive adjective modifying any member of a construct chain must come at the end of the chain (e.g., *ḥbr kṯr ṭbm* "the companions of Kothar, the good ones" [*CAT* 1.108:5]). Apparent attributive adjectives preceding the noun they modify are most frequently substantives in construct with the noun (*nʿmt šnt il* "the excellent ones of the years of El" = "the most excellent years of El" (*CAT* 1.108:27)).

In nominal sentences, word order is essentially free with fronting used for topicalization. Thus *hw mlk* will denote "he, not someone else, is king" (an "identifying" sentence), *mlk hw* "he is king, he is not something else" (a "classifying" sentence).

In the simplest verb phrase, consisting of verb + pronoun, the subject pronoun is part of the verbal form itself, suffixed in the perfective, prefixed in the imperfective. The primary variation occurs through addition of an independent pronoun for "emphasis," creating a formal *casus pendens* (e.g., *ảtm bštm w ản šnt* "as for you, you may tarry but as for me, I'm off" (*CTA* 3 IV 77)). The independent pronoun may precede or follow the verbal unit. The simple verb phrase is by definition a sentence: SUBJECT + PREDICATE (imperfective) or PREDICATE + SUBJECT (perfective).

In verbal sentences one finds fronting for topicalization as in, for example, the following (*RS* 34.124:25–28 [Bordreuil and Pardee 1991:148]):

ybnn	hlk	ʿm	mlk	ảmr	wybl	hw	mỉt	ḫrṣ
Yabninu	went	to	king of	Amurru	and he took	he	one hundred of	gold

SUBJECT : VERB :: VERB : SUBJECT

"Yabninu (not someone else) went to the king of Amurru, and he took, did he, one hundred [pieces of] gold"

According to one study, there is a strong tendency in poetry to place the object phrase close to the verb, either before it or after it (Wilson 1982:26).

The verb is usually fronted in subordinate clauses where the subject is known (*CAT* 2.16: 6–8):

ủmy	tdʿ	ky	ʿrbt	l	pn	špš
My mother	must know	that	I entered	to	face of	Sun

"May my mother know that I have entered before the 'Sun' "

The *subject–verb(–object–modifier)* order is regular in the first clause of apodoses in texts of the omen and hippiatric genres (the basis structure of sentences in both genres is protasis–apodosis). This order cannot be demonstrated to be the result of influence from another language (Pardee 1986:128–129), and probably reflects, therefore, systematized topicalization (Tropper 1994b:469–471), though the general absence of *w-* of apodosis (see §5.3.2) and the presence of *-n* of apodosis (see §4.6.5) in these texts must be included in an explanation of the phenomenon.

On the basis of present evidence, therefore, it is impossible to say that Ugaritic is a primarily VSO language, though, as in Biblical Hebrew, this is certainly the case in subordinate clauses.

5.2 Coordinate clauses

Coordination is indicated most commonly by *w-*, by *p-* when effect is denoted (for coordinating conjunctions see §4.6.3). Asyndesis is fairly frequent at the sentence (and paragraph) level, common at the phrase level.

5.3 Subordinate clauses

The principal types of subordinate clauses are (i) relative, (ii) conditional, and (iii) a variety of temporal/circumstantial, causal, resultative, and completative (object) clauses most commonly introduced by *k* ([kī]) when lexically marked (the conjunction is written both *k* and *ky* [Pardee 1984a:214–215]). The whole concept of "subordinate" clause is rendered murky by the frequent use of the so-called *w* (or more rarely *p*) of apodosis (see §5.3.2) – that is, heading the main clause with *w* or *p* when it follows the "subordinate" clause. The details have not been worked out for Ugaritic, and the state of the corpus renders a comprehensive view difficult; points of similarity with Biblical Hebrew indicate that the overall situation in Ugaritic may not have been dissimilar (cf. Gross 1987).

5.3.1 Relative clauses

Explicit relative clauses are marked by a preceding *d*/*dt*. Relative adverbials are usually marked: for example, *ảdrm d b grn* "the leaders who are at the threshing floor" (*CTA* 17 V 7). Unmarked relative verbal clauses are difficult to spot because the notion of person is marked in the verb, and SUBJECT is by definition included in both verbs. An example upon which there is general agreement is *yd mḫṣt ảqht ġzr tmḫṣ ảlpm ỉb* "The hand [that] struck Hero Aqhat will strike the enemy by thousands" (*CTA* 19 IV 220–221).

The relative pronoun functions at both the phrase level – *il d pỉd* "god of mercy" (*CTA* 4 II 10 and frequent) – and at the sentence level – subject (A), object (B), adverbial (C) below:

A.	ỉl . . .	d	yšr			
	god- . . .	who	he sings			
	"the god . . . who sings" (*CAT* 1.108:2–3);					
B.	skn	d	š‘lyt	ṯryl		
	sacred stone	that	she caused to ascend	Ṯarriyelli		
	"Sacred stone which Ṯarriyelli offered" (*CAT* 6.13:1–2)					
C.	mt	hrnmy	d	ỉn	bn	lh
	Man	Harnamite	who	there is not	son	to him
	"the Harnamite man to whom there is no son" = "who has no son" (*CTA* 17 I 19)					

Note the relative genitive construction.

ḥry . . .	d	k	n‘m	‘nt	n‘mh
'Ḥurraya . . .	who	like	beauty of	Anat	her beauty'
"whose beauty is like Anat's" (*CTA* 14 VI 289–292)					

The relative pronoun may either have an explicit antecedent, as in the examples just cited, or be used "absolutely": for example, *p d ỉn b bty ttn* "For what is not in my house shall you give" (*CTA* 14 III 142).

The conjunction *k*(*y*) does not function as a relative particle (see §5.3.3).

5.3.2 Conditional clauses

Conditions may be marked by *hm* or (less frequently) *ỉm* and tend to precede the main clause. Conditional clauses may be unmarked. A lexical distinction between real and irreal conditions is as yet unknown. The main clause following the conditional clause may or may not be preceded by the so-called *w* or *p* of apodosis (for [A] below see Bordreuil and Caquot 1980:359–360; Pardee 1984a:222; and for [B], see Bordreuil and Pardee 1991:147):

A.	hm	ymt	w	ỉlḥmn	ảnk					
	If	he dies	and	I indeed fight	I					
	"If he should die, I will go on fighting on my own" (*RIH* 78/12:19–22)									
B.	ỉm	ht	l	b	mṣqt	yṯbt	qrt	p	mn	lỉkt
	If	behold	to	in	distress	she/it is sitting	city	and	what	I sent

ảnk	lḥt	bt	mlk	ảmr
I	tablet	of daughter of	king of	Amurru

"So if the city is remaining undecided, then for what reason did I send a letter regarding the daughter of the king of Amurru?" (*RS* 34.124:20–24).

5.3.3 Other subordinate clauses

Temporal/circumstantial phrases may be expressed as a true clause, that is, as conjunction + finite verb (*k tdbr* "when you speak"), or as a prepositional phrase consisting of preposition + infinitive (*b šảl* "in [his] asking" = "when he asks").

Causal and resultative clauses are not nearly so frequent as in Biblical Hebrew. Causal clauses, particularly, are often difficult to distinguish from temporal/circumstantial clauses. A reasonably clear example of each, respectively, follows:

A.

tšmḫ . . .	ảṯrt	. . . k	mt	ảlỉyn	bʿl
She rejoices . . .	Athirat	. . . that	is dead/has died	most mighty	Baal

"May Aṯirat rejoice because Mighty Baal is dead" (*CTA* 6 I 39–42)

B.

mn (!)	krt	k	ybky
What	Kirta	that	he weeps

"Who/what is Kirta that he should weep?" (*CTA* 14 I 38–39)

The principal marker of completative (object) clauses is *k*(*y*):

ủmy	tdʿ	ky	ʿrbt	l	pn	špš
My mother	must know	that	I entered	to	face of	Sun

"May my mother know that I have entered before the 'Sun' "

A particularly common word order in letters is a construction in which a *casus pendens* is followed by a subordinate clause marked by *k*(*y*), with the main clause coming only after these two clauses

lḥt	šlm	k	lỉkt	ủmy	ht	ʿmny
Tablet of	well being	that CONJ.	she sent	my mother	behold	with me

kll	šlm
everything	is well

"As for the letter of greeting, as for the fact that my mother sent [it], behold with me everything is fine" (*CAT* 2.34:5–7)

For this interpretation of the structure, see Pardee 1977:7–8.

5.4 Agreement

Personal pronouns agree in (i) person, gender, and number with an appositional verbal form (*ảnk ảḥwy* "I give life" [*CTA* 17 VI 32]); and (ii) gender, number, and case with an appositional or predicate noun (*ảt ủmy* "you, my mother" [*CAT* 2.30:20–21]; *ảt ảḫ* "you are my brother" [*CTA* 18 I 24]) and with predicate adjectives (*dbḥn ndbḥ hw* "the sacrifice [-*n* of apodosis], sacrificed is it") (where *ndbḥ* is an N-stem participle; *CTA* 40:9 and parallels). The relative pronoun agrees in gender and number with its antecedent; whether the case of the relative pronoun itself is decided by the case of the antecedent or by the function of the relative pronoun in its clause cannot be determined (cf. Arabic, where case agreement is decided in the relative clause).

Adjectives agree in gender, number, and case with the modified noun. Demonstrative pronouns agree in gender and number with the antecedent (case unknown), while demonstrative adjectives agree in gender, number, and case with the modified noun.

Interrogatives and indefinite pronouns do not show agreement.

6. LEXICON

Ugaritic fits the common Semitic and common West Semitic pattern in kinship terms (*ảb* "father," *ủm* "mother," etc.), tree names (*ảrz* "cedar," etc.), geographical terms (*nhr* "river," etc.), with some notable peculiarities: for example, *ḥwt* ([ħuwwat-]) "land (geographical–political entity)," alongside *ảrṣ* "earth, ground" and *bld* "homeland."

When deciphering a Ugaritic text, one finds points of lexical contact with all of the Semitic languages. Because of the small number of texts, the image of the Ugaritic scholar deciphering a text on the basis of various Semitic dictionaries is not totally false, though with the increase in number of reasonably well-understood texts, inner-Ugaritic lexicography is becoming more practicable. The apparent heterogeneity of the Ugaritic lexicon may be explained in two ways: (i) the archaic nature of the language (cognates with other Semitic languages will thus be largely with retentions in those languages); (ii) the relatively poor corpus of texts in the languages with which Ugaritic appears most closely related linguistically (thus, if Hebrew and Phoenician were attested more extensively, there would be fewer exclusive isoglosses between Arabic and Ugaritic).

The principal motion verbs are useful language/dialect isoglosses (e.g., for all the similarities between Hebrew and Aramaic, the systems of motion verbs are quite different in the two languages). Here Ugaritic falls directly in the Hebrew/Phoenician group: *hlk* "go," *yrd* "descend," *ʿly* "ascend," *bʾ* "enter" (alongside *ʿrb*), *yṣʾ* "exit," *ṯb* "return." Some verbs of movement that can also denote the state attained are: *qm* "arise," *škb* "lie down," *ʿmd* "stand," *rkb* "mount." Primary motion verbs peculiar to Ugaritic are *tbʿ* "go away," *mǵy* "go to, arrive at" (apparently < *MẒY*), and *yštql* "he arrives," used only in poetry and in the imperfective.

Expressions of existence resemble most closely the later Northwest Semitic pattern: there are positive and negative quasi-verbs, *ỉṯ* and *ỉn*, respectively, corresponding, for example, to Hebrew *yēš* and *ʾayin*/ *ʾē*^{y}*n*, as well as the verb *kn* (*nʿmn ykn* "there will be prosperity" [*RIH* 78/14:3, Bordreuil and Caquot 1980:352–353]), which corresponds to the regular verb "to be" in Phoenician (and Arabic) and to the more strongly marked verb "to be stable" in Hebrew.

In spite of the cosmopolitan nature of the city of Ugarit, there are relatively few readily identifiable loanwords: *ḥṯṯ* "silver" is an apparent example from Hittite, *kḥṯ* "chair, throne" an example from Hurrian.

References and abbreviations

Aartun, K. 1974. *Die Partikeln des Ugaritischen*, part 1. Alter Orient und Altes Testament 21/1. Kevelaer: Butzon and Bercker; Neukirchen-Vluyn: Neukirchener Verlag.

———. 1978. *Die Partikeln des Ugaritischen*, part 2. Alter Orient und Altes Testament 21/2. Kevelaer: Butzon and Bercker; Neukirchen-Vluyn: Neukirchener Verlag.

Blau, J. 1972. "Marginalia Semitica." *Israel Oriental Studies* 2:57–82.

———. 1977. "'Weak' phonetic change and the Hebrew *śîn*." *Hebrew Annual Review* 1:67–119.

Bordreuil, P. 1979. "L'inscription phénicienne de Sarafand en cunéiformes alphabétiques." *Ugarit-Forschungen* 11:63–68.

Bordreuil, P., A. Bounni, N. Saliby, E. Lagarce, and J. Lagarge. 1987. "Les fouilles de Ras Ibn Hani (Syrie) en 1984 et 1986." *Académie des Inscriptions et Belles-Lettres, Comptes Rendus*, pp. 274–301.

Bordreuil, P., and A. Caquot. 1980. "Les textes en cunéiformes alphabétiques découverts en 1978 à Ibn Hani." *Syria* 57:343–373.

Bordreuil, P., and D. Pardee. 1991. *Une bibliothèque au sud de la ville (Quartier "Sud-Centre"). Les textes de la 34e campagne (1973), deuxième partie: les textes en cunéiformes alphabétiques.* Ras Shamra-Ougarit VII. Paris: Editions Recherche sur les Civilisations.

______. 1995a. "L'épigraphie ougaritique: 1973–1993." In M. Yon, M. Sznycer, and P. Bordreuil (eds.), *Le pays d' Ougarit autour de 1200 av. J-C*, pp. 27–32. Ras Shamra-Ougarit XI. Paris: Editions Recherche sur les Civilisations.

______. 1995b. "Un abécédaire du type sud-sémitique découvert en 1988 dans les fouilles archéologiques françaises de Ras Shamra-Ougarit." *Académie des Inscriptions et Belles-Lettres, Comptes Rendus*, pp. 855–860.

______. 2001. "Textes alphabétiques enougaritique." In M. Yon, D. Arnaud (ed.), *Études Ougaritiques. I. Travaux 1985–1995.* Ras Sharma-Ougarit XIV. Paris: Editions Recherche sur les Civilisations.

CAT 1995 = Dietrich, M., O. Loretz, and J. Sanmartín. *The Cuneiform Alphabetic Texts from Ugarit, Ras Ibn Hani and Other Places* (KTU: 2nd enlarged edition). Abhandlungen zur Literatur Alt-Syrien-Palästinas und Mesopotamiens 8. Münster: UGARIT-Verlag.

Contenson, H. de. 1992. *Préhistoire de Ras Shamra: Les sondages stratigraphiques de 1955 à 1976.* Ras Shamra-Ougarit VIII/1–2. Paris: Editions Recherche sur les Civilisations.

CTA 1963 = Herdner, A. *Corpus des tablettes en cunéiformes alphabétiques découvertes à Ras Shamra-Ugarit de 1929 à 1939.* Mission de Ras Shamra 10. Bibliothèque Archéologique et Historique 79. Paris: Imprimerie Nationale; Paul Geuthner.

Cunchillos, J.-L. 1993. *Banco de Datos Filológicos Semíticos Noroccidentales. Primera Parte: Datos Ugaríticos. I. Textos Ugaríticos.* Madrid: Instituto de Filología.

______. 1995. *Banco de Datos Filológicos Semíticos Noroccidentales. Primera Parte: Datos Ugaríticos. II/1–3. Concordancia de Palabras Ugaríticos en Morfología Desplegada.* Madrid: Instituto de Filología.

Dietrich, M., and O. Loretz. 1988. *Die Keilalphabete. Die phönizisch-Kanaanäische und altarabischen Alphabete in Ugarit.* Abhandlungen zur Literatur Alt-Syrien-Palästinas 1. Münster: UGARIT-Verlag.

Fenton, T. 1970. "The absence of a verbal formation **yaqattal* from Ugaritic and Northwest Semitic." *Journal of Semitic Studies* 15:31–41.

Freilich, D. 1986. "Is there an Ugaritic deity *Bbt*?" *Journal of Semitic Studies* 31:119–130.

Freilich, D., and D. Pardee. 1984. "{ẓ} and {ṭ} in Ugaritic: a re-examination of the sign-forms." *Syria* 61:25–36.

Gordon, C. 1965. *Ugaritic Textbook: Grammar, Texts in Transliteration, Cuneiform Selections, Glossary, Indices.* Analecta Orientalia 38. Rome: Pontifical Biblical Institute.

______. 1997. "Ugaritic phonology." In A. S. Kaye (ed.), *Phonologies of Asia and Africa*, pp. 49–54. Winona Lake, IN: Eisenbrauns.

Greenstein, E. 1976. "A Phoenician inscription in Ugaritic script?" *Journal of the Ancient Near Eastern Society of Columbia University* 8:49–57.

Gross, W. 1987. *Die Pendenskonstruktion im Biblischen Hebräisch. Arbeiten zu Text und Sprache im Alten Testament 22.* St. Ottilien: EOS Verlag.

Hoftijzer, J. 1982. "Quodlibet Ugariticum." In G. van Driel, Th. J. H. Krispijn, M. Stohl, *et al.* (eds.), *Zikir Šumim. Assyriological Studies Presented to F. R. Kraus on the Occasion of his Seventieth Birthday*, pp. 121–127. Nederlands Instituut voor het Nabije Oosten Studia Francisci Scholten Memoriae Dicata 5. Leiden: Brill.

Huehnergard, J. 1983. "Asseverative **la* and hypothetical **lu/law* in Semitic." *Journal of the American Oriental Society* 103:569–593.

______. 1986. "A Dt stem in Ugaritic?" *Ugarit-Forschungen* 17:402.

______. 1987. *Ugaritic Vocabulary in Syllabic Transcription.* Harvard Semitic Studies, 32. Atlanta: Scholars Press.

Liverani, M. 1963. "Antecedenti del diptotismo arabo nei testi accadici di Ugarit." *Rivista degli Studi Orientali* 38:131–160.

———. 1964. "Elementi innovativi nell'ugaritico non letterario." *Atti della Accademia Nazionale dei Lincei, Rendiconti della Classe di Scienze morali, storiche e filologiche*, vol. VIII, fascicle 19, pp. 173–191.
Mallon, E. 1982. *The Ugaritic Verb in the Letters and Administrative Documents*. Ph.D. dissertation, The Catholic University of America. Ann Arbor, MI: University Microfilms.
Merrill, E. 1974. "The Aphel causative: does it exist in Ugaritic?" *Journal of Northwest Semitic Languages* 3:40–49.
Nougayrol, J. 1968. "Textes suméro-accadiens des archives et bibliothèques privées d'Ugarit." In J.-C. Courtois (ed.), *Ugaritica V. Nouveaux textes accadiens, hourrites et ugaritiques des archives et bibliothèques privées d'Ugarit, commentaires des textes historiques (première partie)*, pp. 1–446. Bibliothèque Archéologique et Historique 80. Mission de Ras Shamra 16. Paris: Imprimerie Nationale.
Pardee, D. 1975. "The preposition in Ugaritic." *Ugarit-Forschungen* 7:329–378.
———. 1976. "The preposition in Ugaritic." *Ugarit-Forschungen* 8:215–322, 483–493.
———. 1977. "A new Ugaritic letter." *Bibliotheca Orientalis* 34:3–20.
———. 1983–1984. "The Letter of Puduḫepa: the text." *Archiv für Orientforschung* 29–30:321–329.
———. 1984a. "Further studies in Ugaritic epistolography." *Archiv für Orientforschung* 31:213–230.
———. 1984b. "Three Ugaritic tablet joins." *Journal of Near Eastern Studies* 43:239–245.
———. 1986. "The Ugaritic *šumma izbu* text." *Archiv für Orientforschung* 33:117–147.
———. 1988. *Les textes para-mythologiques de la 24ᵉ campagne (1961)*. Ras Shamra-Ougarit IV. Paris: Editions Recherche sur les Civilisations.
———. 1993a. Review of *The Syntax of the Verb in Classical Hebrew Prose*, by Alviero Niccacci, 1990. *Journal of Near Eastern Studies* 52:313–314.
———. 1993b. Review of *Modi ugaritici: Eine morpho-syntaktische Abhandlung über das Modalsystem in Ugaritische*, by E. Verreet, 1988. *Journal of Near Eastern Studies* 52:314–317.
———. 1995. Review of *Studies in Verbal Aspect and Narrative Technique in Biblical Hebrew Prose*, by Mats Eskhult, 1990. *Journal of Near Eastern Studies* 54:64–66.
———. 1997. *The Baʿlu Myth: The Context of Scripture*. In W. Hallo and K. Younger (eds.), *The Context of Scripture. Vol. I: Canonical Compositions from the Biblical World*, pp. 241–274. Leiden: Brill.
———. 2000. *Les textes rituels*. Ras Shamra Ougarit. Paris: Editions Recherche sur les Civilisations.
Rainey, A. 1973. "Gleanings from Ugarit." *Israel Oriental Studies* 3:34–62.
———. 1996. *Canaanite in the Amarna Tablets. A Linguistic Analysis of the Mixed Dialect Used by Scribes from Canaan* (4 vols.). Handbuch der Orientalistik 25. Leiden: Brill.
RIH = text discovered at Ras Ibn Hani.
RS = text discovered at Ras Shamra.
Saadé, G. 1979. *Ougarit: Métropole cananéenne*. Beirut: Imprimerie Catholique.
Segert, S. 1983. "The last sign of the Ugaritic alphabet." *Ugarit-Forschungen* 15:201–218.
———. 1984. *A Basic Grammar of the Ugaritic Language*. Berkeley: University of California Press.
———. 1988. "The Ugaritic voiced postvelar in correspondence to the emphatic interdental." *Ugarit-Forschungen* 20:287–300.
Singer, A. 1948. "The vocative in Ugaritic." *Journal of Cuneiform Studies* 2:1–10.
Sivan, D. 1982. "Final triphthongs and final *yu/a/i* – *wu/a/i* dipththongs in Ugaritic nominal forms." *Ugarit-Forschungen* 14:209–218.
———. 1992. "Notes on the use of the form *qatal* as the plural base for the form *qatl* in Ugaritic." *Israel Oriental Studies* 12:235–238.
Tropper, J. 1990a. *Der ugaritische Kausativstamm und die Kausativbildungen des semitischen. Eine morphologisch-semantische Untersuchung zum Š-Stamm und zu den umstrittenen nichtsibilantischen Kausativstämmen des Ugaritischen*. Abhandlungen zur Literatur Alt-Syrien-Palästinas 2. Münster: UGARIT-Verlag.
———. 1990b. "Silbenschliešendes Aleph im Ugaritischen – Ein neuer Versuch." *Ugarit-Forschungen* 22:359–369.
———. 1991. "Finale Sätze und *yqtla*-Modus im Ugaritischen." *Ugarit-Forschungen* 23:341–352.
———. 1993a. "Auf dem Weg zu einer ugaritischen Grammatik." In M. Dietrich and O. Loretz (eds.), *Mesopotamica–Ugaritica–Biblica. Festschrift für Kurt Bergerhof zur Vollendung seines 70.*

Lebensjahres am 7. Mai 1992, pp. 471–480. Alter Orient und Altes Testament 232. Kevelaer: Butzon and Bercker; Neukirchen-Vluyn: Neukirchener Verlag.

______. 1993b. "Morphologische Besonderheiten des Spätugaritischen." *Ugarit-Forschungen* 25:389–394.

______. 1994a. "Das ugaritische Konsonanteninventar." *Journal of Northwest Semitic Languages* 20(2):17–59.

______. 1994b. "Zur Grammatik der ugaritischen Omina." *Ugarit-Forschungen* 24:457–472.

______. 1995. "Das altkanaanäische und ugaritische Verbalsystem." In M. Dietrich, and O. Loretz (eds.), *Ugarit. Ein ostmediterranes Kulturzentrum im Alten Orient. Ergebnisse und Perspektiven der Forschung. Band I: Ugarit und seine altorientalische Umwelt*, pp. 159–170. Abhandlungen zur Literatur Alt-Syrien-Palästinas, 7. Münster: UGARIT-Verlag.

Verreet, E. 1983. "Das silbenschliessende Aleph im Ugaritischen." *Ugarit-Forschungen* 15:223–258.

______. 1986. "Beobachtungen zum ugaritischen Verbalsystem II," I17:319–344.

______. 1988. *Modi Ugaritici. Eine Morpho-syntaktische Abhandlung über das Modalsystem im Ugaritischen.* Orientalia Lovaniensia Analect, 27. Leiden: Peeters.

Wilson, G. 1982. "Ugaritic word order and sentence structure in KRT." *Journal of Semitic Studies* 27:17–32.

Yon, Marguerite. 1997. *La cité d'Ougarit sur le tell de Ras Shamra. Guides Archéologiques de l'Institut Français d'Archéologie du Proche-Orient, No. 2.* Paris: Editions Recherche sur les Civilisations.

Zevit, Z. 1983. "The question of case endings on Ugaritic nouns in *status constructus*." *Journal of Semitic Studies* 28:225–232.

Nota bene: A monumental grammar of Ugaritic appeared too late to be used in preparing this overview. It must be considered essential for the future study of Ugaritic.

Tropper, J. 2000. *Ugaritische Grammatik.* Alter Orient und Altes Testament 273. Münster: Ugarit-Verlag.

CHAPTER 3

Hebrew

P. KYLE McCARTER, JR.

1. HISTORICAL AND CULTURAL CONTEXTS

1.1 The position of Hebrew within the Semitic languages

Hebrew, the language of ancient Israel and Judah and their descendant Jewish communities, is a Northwest Semitic language. Northwest Semitic and Arabic constitute Central Semitic, which is a subgroup of West Semitic, one of the two primary divisions of the Semitic branch of the larger Afro-Asiatic family (Appendix 1, §§1–2). Within Northwest Semitic, Hebrew is classified as Canaanite as distinct from Aramaic. Other members of the Canaanite subgroup include the dialect of the city-state of Ugarit (cf. Ch. 2, §1) in the Late Bronze Age (*c.* 1550–1200 BC), and the languages of Israel's immediate neighbors in the Iron Age (*c.* 1200–586 BC), namely, Phoenician (Ch. 4) and the Transjordanian languages of Ammonite, Moabite, and Edomite (Ch. 5).

1.2 Stages in the development of Ancient Hebrew

Although linguistic features found in the limited surviving evidence for the Canaanite dialects of the Late Bronze Age anticipate some of the distinctive characteristics of Iron Age Hebrew, it is unlikely that Hebrew emerged as a discrete language before the end of the Late Bronze Age and the beginning of the Iron Age. Prosodic and linguistic studies suggest that the earliest poetry preserved in the Hebrew Bible may have been composed before the end of the second millennium BC, and this poetry represents the first identifiable phase of the language, which is called *Archaic* or *Archaic Biblical Hebrew* (before *c.* 1000 BC).

No extant inscription that can be identified specifically as Hebrew antedates the tenth century BC, and Hebrew inscriptions in significant numbers do not begin to appear before the early eighth century BC. Nevertheless, the Hebrew of the Iron Age inscriptions that do survive, especially those from Judah, is essentially the same as the Hebrew found in the biblical Primary History (Genesis–2 Kings) and the original portions of the books of the pre-exilic prophets. This form of Hebrew constitutes the classical phase of the language, which is known as *Classical* or *Biblical Hebrew* (BH) and corresponds to the speech of the kingdom of Judah from its formation to the Babylonian Exile (*c.* tenth–sixth centuries BC). The Hebrew of post-exilic Judah, which is represented by inscriptions of the Persian and Hellenistic periods and especially by the later biblical literature (*c.* sixth–second centuries BC), is called *Late Classical* or *Late Biblical Hebrew* (LBH). The Samaritan Pentateuch, which seems to have been independent of Jewish tradition by the late second century BC, is also an important witness to the Hebrew of this period.

The Hebrew of the early post-biblical period is represented by the Hebrew of the Dead Sea Scrolls and especially that of the Mishnah and other rabbinical literature. As noted below (§1.3), the literary documents from Qumran exhibit substantial continuity with Late Biblical Hebrew, while the few nonliterary documents stand much closer linguistically to Rabbinic Hebrew. From the viewpoint of the development of the language, there is a distinction between the Hebrew of the early rabbinical works – the Mishnah, the Tosefta and certain other, primarily halakhic compositions (*c.* first–third centuries AD) – and that of the later rabbinical works – the Jerusalem and Babylonian Talmuds and certain other, primarily haggadic compositions (fourth century AD and later). Viewed as a whole, this phase in the development of the language is called *Middle* or *Rabbinic Hebrew* (RH). Another important witness to Hebrew in late antiquity is the Hexapla, the six-column critical edition of the Old Testament compiled by the Church father Origen of Caesarea; in his second column (Secunda), Origen produced a Greek transliteration of the Hebrew text that reflects the pronunciation of the first half of the third century AD.

In this chapter, primary attention is given to the classical phase of Hebrew (BH), but important divergent or innovative features of the other ancient phases of Hebrew (LBH and RH) are noted. The subsequent phases of the language – *Medieval Hebrew* and *Modern* or *Israeli Hebrew* – fall outside the scope of the discussion.

1.3 The speech communities of Ancient Hebrew

In a general sense, the emergence of Hebrew as a discrete language corresponded to the emergence of Israel as a discrete polity in the central hill country of Palestine in the last centuries of the second millennium BC. By the tenth century BC, two Hebrew-speaking states had been established, Israel to the north in the Samarian hills and portions of central Transjordan and Galilee, and Judah to the south in the Judaean hills with its capital at Jerusalem. The modest corpus of surviving inscriptions from the northern kingdom is sufficient to show that its dialect displayed features that were significantly different from that of Judah, as it is known from a more generous inscriptional corpus and, indeed, from the Hebrew Bible itself.

The two Iron Age states survived until 722 BC in the case of Israel, when its capital, Samaria, fell to the Assyrians (precipitating the extinction of the northern dialect), and until 586 BC in the case of Judah, when Jerusalem was destroyed by the Babylonians. Despite these catastrophes, Hebrew endured as a spoken and literary language in Palestine throughout the second half of the first millennium BC. During this period the use of Aramaic increased steadily in the larger region, becoming the regnant language of both Samaria and Galilee, and, beginning in the third century BC, Greek was introduced to many of the major cities of Palestine. Nevertheless, Hebrew persisted, alongside Aramaic, as a spoken language in Judah (or Judaea) proper into the rabbinic period.

Although Biblical Hebrew, Late Biblical Hebrew and the Hebrew of the literary manuscripts from Qumran constitute a unilinearly evolving dialect, descended from the language of pre-exilic Judah, Rabbinic Hebrew exhibits features that set it apart from this development. Since most of the literature of Rabbinic Hebrew is highly technical in character, it was once supposed that it was a language spoken only by scholars or even an artificially confected language that was never spoken at all. But the discovery and linguistic analysis of the nonliterary or quasi-literary documents from Qumran – especially the Copper Scroll and the Halakhic Letter (MMT) – and of the Bar Kochba correspondence from the Wadi Murabbaʿat and the Nahal Hever show that Rabbinic Hebrew was a popularly spoken language in the early centuries of the Common Era. Although many of the features of Rabbinic

Hebrew that diverge from Biblical Hebrew can be traced to contemporary influences, such as the prevalence of Aramaic and Greek, many others seem to be dialectal survivals from a much earlier period, when an ancestral form of Rabbinic Hebrew existed alongside Biblical Hebrew. The beginning of the demise of Rabbinic Hebrew as a spoken language is probably to be traced to the Roman suppression of the Second Jewish Revolt in AD 135 and the accompanying depredations, including the deportation of many Jews and the flight of others into the Aramaic-speaking Galilee. Even under these conditions Hebrew continued to be heard in some circles, but the primary language of Jews in the Roman diaspora was Greek just as the primary language of the long-established Babylonian diaspora was Aramaic. In Palestine, too, Rabbinic Hebrew was eventually replaced by Aramaic as a spoken language and survived only as the scholarly language of the Galilean exile community.

2. WRITING SYSTEMS

2.1 The Hebrew consonantal script

The earliest inscriptions unambiguously identifiable as Hebrew are written in a distinctive form of the consonantal writing system that served as the national script of both Israel and Judah in the Iron Age. This Hebrew script arose as a branch of the Phoenician, through which it was descended from the archaic consonantal script of the second millennium BC. The intermediary role of Phoenician is shown by the fact that the two scripts share a sign inventory that is fully representative of the consonantal phonology of Phoenician but insufficient to represent all the consonantal phonemes of Hebrew. In particular, only one sign corresponds to the Proto-Semitic phonemes /š/ and /ś/, a situation that is adequate for Phoenician, where the two consonants have merged (see Ch. 4, §3.1), but not for Hebrew, where they remain distinct (see §3.1 below).

After the Babylonian destruction of Jerusalem in 586 BC, the Hebrew script fell into disuse. Hebrew came to be written primarily in the Aramaic script, which, like the Aramaic language, was widely used in both the Neo-Babylonian and Persian Empires. Like the Hebrew writing system, the Aramaic had arisen as an early branch of Phoenician, so that it provided the same consonantal inventory as the old Hebrew script, and its adoption for writing Hebrew was straightforward. It was out of the Aramaic script tradition that the standard biblical book hand, known as the "square script" or simply the Jewish script, eventually developed. This writing system is shown in Table 3.1.

2.2 Vowel representation

Whereas Phoenician orthography was purely consonantal, the earliest Hebrew inscriptions exhibit a rudimentary form of vowel representation, with certain letter signs (*wāw*, *yôd* and *hē'*) being assigned a secondary use as vowel markers. At first this use of *matres lectionis* ("mothers of reading") was confined to final long vowels, with *wāw* representing final *ū*, *yôd* representing final *ī*, and *hē'* representing final *ā*, *ē* or *ō*. Eventually, internal vowel letters began to be indicated on a sporadic basis, with *wāw* representing internal *ō* (contracted from **aw*) or *ū*, and *yôd* representing internal *ē* (contracted from **ay*) or *ī*. During the second half of the first millennium BC, *wāw* gradually replaced *hē'* as the marker of final *ō*.

By the last century before the Common Era, the tendency to represent vowels *plene* (i.e., "fully" or with *matres*) reached its most elaborate development. Nevertheless, this development, though observable in the Samaritan Pentateuch and numerous biblical manuscripts

Table 3.1 The Hebrew alphabet

	Letter name	Transcription	Phonetic value
א	*'ā́lep*	*'*	[ʔ]
ב	*bêt*	*b*	[b], [v]
ג	*gîmel*	*g*	[g], [ɣ] or [ʁ]
ד	*dā́let*	*d*	[d], [ð]
ה	*hē'*	*h*	[h]
ו	*wāw*	*w*	[w]
ז	*záyin*	*z*	[z]
ח	*ḥêt*	*ḥ*	*[ħ], [H]
ט	*ṭêt*	*ṭ*	*[t'], [t]
י	*yôd*	*y*	[y]
כ	*kap*	*k*	[k], [x] or [χ]
ל	*lā́med*	*l*	[l]
מ	*mēm*	*m*	[m]
נ	*nûn*	*n*	[n]
ס	*sā́mek*	*s*	[s]
ע	*'áyin*	*'*	[ʕ]
פ	*pēh*	*p*	[p], [f]
צ	*ṣādēh*	*ṣ*	*[s'], [t͜s] or [t^{s}]
ק	*qôp*	*q*	*[k'], [k]
ר	*rēš*	*r*	[r]
שׂ	*śîn*	*ś*	*[ɬ], [s]
שׁ	*šîn*	*š*	[ʃ]
ת	*tāw*	*t*	[t], [θ]

from Qumran, is not reflected in the Hebrew Bible as transmitted in rabbinic tradition. In their efforts to standardize the sacred text, the rabbis elected a conservative tradition, giving authority to older manuscripts with "defective" spelling, so that the biblical books were preserved in an archaic orthography. In this way, rabbinic authority gave rise to the manuscript tradition that, in essential form, has survived into modern times. Although this tradition can safely be regarded as a faithful representation of the Hebrew language of the first millennium BC, the linguistic information it provides is accurate and complete only within the limits of the orthography of the Hebrew-Aramaic consonantal script.

2.3 Systems of biblical vowel notation

Because of its many ambiguities with regard to pronunciation, the biblical manuscript tradition was reinforced from an early date by an oral tradition that provided a guide to vocalization for use in liturgy and study. As Hebrew continued to develop regionally, the pronunciation traditions in the eastern (Babylonian) and western (Palestinian) Jewish communities began to diverge. By the second half of the first millennium AD these oral traditions had given rise to distinctive systems of "pointing" (*nîqûd*), graphic conventions for representing pronunciation fully by placing diacriticals above or below the text. The Babylonian tradition was fixed by a superlinear system developed in the sixth century AD and refined in the eighth–ninth centuries. The original Palestinian system, which was developed in the

Table 3.2 The Tiberian representation of the principal Hebrew vowels

Masoretic diacritical	Probable phonetic realization	Tiberian representation without *mater*	Tiberian representation with *mater*	Tiberian representation with final *mater*
hîreq	[i]	בִ, *bi* or *bī*	בִי, *bî*	
ṣērê	[e]	בֵ, *bē*	בֵי, *bê*	בֵה, *bēh*
səgōl	[ɛ]	בֶ, *be*	בֶי, *bê*	בֶה, *beh*
pataḥ	[a]	בַ, *ba*		
qāmeṣ	[ɔ]	בָ, *bā* or *bo*		בָה, *bâ*
ḥōlem	[o]	בֹ, *bō*	בוֹ, *bô*	בֹה, *bōh*
qibbûṣ	[u]	בֻ, *bu* or *bū*		
šûreq			בוּ, *bû*	

sixth–eighth centuries, was also superlinear. The extant documents using both of these systems provide important information about the development of Hebrew in late antiquity, although only a few manuscripts with Palestinian vocalization have survived. The older Palestinian system was superseded by a primarily infralinear and especially rigorous system developed in Tiberias, which enjoyed its most creative period between the late eighth and early tenth centuries AD. The Tiberian system of vowel notation is the only one that survives in active use, and it is regarded as authoritative in Jewish tradition, though a superlinear system developed for the Samaritan Pentateuch has a similar role in the Samaritan community. The Tiberian pointing is reinforced in its mission of safeguarding the integrity of the text by the Masora, a body of detailed annotations produced by scholars known as Masoretes (*ba'ălê hammāsôret*, literally, "masters of the tradition"); the text of the Hebrew Bible, when equipped with this apparatus, is called the Masoretic Text.

2.4 Tiberian vowel signs and modern transliteration

The representation in the Masoretic Text of the vowels and their morphophonemic varieties (see §3.2.1) was accomplished by the introduction of the Tiberian diacriticals into a text that, as explained in §2.2 above, already contained a minimal indication of vowels in the form of the *matres lectionis*. The present system of vowel representation is thus composite, and it is necessary in transliteration to indicate, as far as possible, both the *matres* and the diacritical marks of the Masoretes. It is also desirable to indicate vowel quantity because of the important light it sheds on the character of the ancient language and its historical, pre-Tiberian development. Information about vowel quantity cannot be deduced on the sole basis of the Tiberian vowel signs, however, since their purpose was to indicate quality rather than quantity. Nor are the *matres* a fully reliable guide. There was, to be sure, a tendency in the text to mark the ancient long vowels with *matres*, but in the conservative orthography of the Bible this was not carried through consistently or systematically. When vowels are marked for length in transliteration, therefore, they represent an interpretation made on the basis of an analysis of word structure and stress in light of modern research into the pre-Tiberian history of the language.

Table 3.2 lists the Tiberian spellings of the principal varieties of the seven vowels identified below in §3.2.1 together with their corresponding transliterations (for purposes of illustration the vowels are attached to the consonant *b*).

When using this type of transliteration it is important to keep its limitations and shortcomings in mind. Though it has the merit of highlighting information about the length of vowels, it can be misleading in this regard, since it gives the impression, for example, that *ṣērê*, transliterated <ē>, is the lengthened form of *səgōl*, <e>, when in fact *ṣēre* is an altogether different, higher vowel than *səgōl* ([e] ~ [ɛ]). The chief purpose of the transliteration system is to permit the reader to reconstruct the Tiberian spelling, but here, too, there are a few imperfections and unavoidable ambiguities. For example, both *ṣērê-yôd* (י..) and *səgōl-yôd* (י.:) are transliterated <ê> (in some systems the latter is rendered <e(y)> or <ệ> to avoid the ambiguity), and final *ṣērê-hē'* (ה..) is transliterated <ēh> to distinguish it from *ṣērê-yôd* (י..) even though the *hē'* is a *mater* (see §2.2), that is, non-consonantal (in some systems *ṣērê-hē'* is rendered <ê> like *ṣērê-yôd* and *səgōl-yôd*, eliminating the misrepresentation but compounding the ambiguity).

3. PHONOLOGY

3.1 Consonants

Table 3.3 illustrates the consonantal phonemes of Hebrew. As shown, the consonantal system consists of seventeen obstruents, including nine oral stops and eight fricatives; and six sonorants, including four approximants (glides and liquids) and two nasals.

3.1.1 Obstruents

The set of stops comprises, in addition to the glottal stop /ʔ/, a symmetrical group of six consonants produced in two manners of phonation (voiced and voiceless), at three points of articulation (bilabial, alveolar and velar). This set is supplemented by two (dental and velar) ejective stops, the so-called "emphatics." In Tiberian Hebrew the six non-emphatic stop phonemes, /b/, /p/, /d/, /t/, /g/ and /k/, possess a complete set of conditioned spirantized allophones, [v], [f], [ð], [θ], [ɣ] or [ʁ], and [x] or [χ], conventionally transliterated as *ḇ*, *p̄*, *ḏ*, *ḡ* and *ḵ*, the development of which is discussed below (see §3.3).

The fricative group includes three voiceless, nonemphatic sibilants, /s/, /š/, and the sound conventionally transcribed as *ś*. Though the three were originally distinct, they were later reduced to two when *ś* lost its primitive character as a lateral (i.e., /ɬ/), and merged with the other voiceless alveolar sibilant, /s/ (confusion of /s/ and *ś* is already present in Late Biblical Hebrew and becomes increasingly common at Qumran and in Rabbinic Hebrew). The sibilant inventory is completed by two other fricatives, voiced /z/ and emphatic /s'/ (conventionally written *ṣ*). All of these are alveolars except the post- or palato-alveolar /š/.

Biblical Hebrew has lost all three Proto-Semitic interdentals, **ð*, **θ* and **θ̣* as well as the emphatic lateral **ṣ́* or **ð̣* and the velar or uvular fricatives **ǵ* and **ḫ* (see §3.6.1), though the interdentals **ð* and **θ* ([ð] and [θ]) and the velars **ǵ* and **ḫ* ([ɣ] and [x]) have been "revived" in the form of the spirantized allophones of /d/, /t/, /g/ and /k/, as noted above.

The original pronunciation of the three Hebrew ejectives or emphatics, *ṭ*, *ṣ* and *q*, is unknown. Although the nature of the emphatics in Ethiopic and Arabic is itself debated, it is usually argued on the basis of these cognate languages that the Hebrew emphatics were originally glottalic, as in Ethiopic and (probably) Old South Arabic – thus [t'], [s'] and [k'], the presumed Proto-Semitic situation – but later became pharygealized ([tˤ], [sˤ] and [kˤ]) among Jews living in Arabic-speaking communities, and simplified to [t], [ts̩] or [tˢ]

Table 3.3 The consonantal phonemes of Hebrew

Manner of articulation	Place of articulation: Bilabial	Dental/ Alveolar	Palato-alveolar	Palatal	Velar	Pharyngeal	Glottal
Stop							
Voiceless	p (פ)	t (ת)			k (כ)		ʼ(/ʔ/, א)
Voiced	b (ב)	d (ד)			g (ג)		
Emphatic		ṭ (/t'/, ט)			q (/k'/, ק)		
Fricative							
Voiceless		s (ס)	š (שׁ)			ḥ(/ħ/, ח)	h (ה)
Voiced		z (ז)				ʻ (/ʕ/, ע)	
Emphatic		ṣ (/s'/, צ)					
Lateral		ś (/ɬ/, שׂ)					
Approximant							
Glide	w (ו)			y (י)			
Rolled		r (ר)					
Lateral		l (ל)					
Nasal	m (מ)	n (נ)					

and [k] among European Jews. As shown by Tiberian tradition and confirmed by earlier Greek transcriptions, the emphatic stops, *ṭ* and *q*, did not share the secondary spirantized realization acquired by the six nonemphatic stops noted above.

Hebrew distinguishes four "guttural" consonants: two pharyngeals, one voiced /ʕ/ (conventionally transcribed as ʻ) and one voiceless /ħ/ (*ḥ*), both of which are composite in origin (see §3.6.1), and two voiceless glottals, one stop /ʔ/ (ʼ) and one fricative /h/. As the language evolved, there was a tendency for these consonants to weaken and/or coalesce, a development with important secondary phonological consequences (see §3.3). While the glottals participated in this general pattern of weakening, they underwent, in addition, important changes of their own. In particular, the glottal stop, /ʔ/, was lost in syllable-final positions, a phenomenon that began very early and seems to have proceeded in stages (see §3.6.1) and in which the other glottal, /h/, may have participated in part.

3.1.2 Sonorants

Hebrew has two nasals, bilabial /m/ and alveolar /n/, both voiced. The tendency in Rabbinic Hebrew for these two consonants to alternate when final (especially **-m* > *-n*) is already in evidence in Septuagint transliterations and Qumran manuscripts but lacking in Biblical Hebrew itself, unless **šāllûm* is intended by the name *šāllûn* in Nehemiah 3:15 (for the related question of the replacement of the plural ending *-îm* with *-în*, see §4.2.2). When immediately followed by a non-guttural consonant, /n/ undergoes regressive assimilation (**nC* > *CC*), unless it follows the preposition *lə-* or is the third consonant in the stem: for example, *zākántā*, "you have grown old" (1 Samuel 8:5).

Hebrew has four approximants, all voiced. Two of these, the bilabial and palatal semivowels /w/ and /y/, are glides. The other two are liquids; they include /r/, a rolled consonant, probably realized as either an alveolar [r] or uvular [ʀ] trill, and /l/, a lateral alveolar liquid.

	FRONT	*CENTRAL*	*BACK*
HIGH	i		u
	e		o
MID			
	ɛ		ɔ
LOW		a	

Figure 3.1 The seven full vowels of Tiberian Hebrew

3.2 Vowels

3.2.1 The quality of the Tiberian vowels

As explained below (see §3.2.2), ancient Hebrew in its early development probably preserved the basic triad of Proto-Semitic vowels, **i*, **a* and **u*, each of which could be long or short, and two "diphthongs" or vowel-glide sequences, **ay* and **aw*. The Tiberian system by which Biblical Hebrew is represented is much more complex, however, reflecting the medieval pronunciation that had evolved over the centuries from numerous phonological changes. There are Masoretic diacriticals for seven full vowels (*ḥîreq* [i], *ṣērê* [e], *səgōl* [ɛ], *pataḥ* [a], *qāmeṣ* [ɔ], *ḥōlem* [o] and *qibbûṣ*/*šûreq* [u]), and when vocal *šəwā* [ə] and the three other ultrashort or reduced vowels (the *ḥāṭēp* vowels) are added, the number of vowels rises to eleven. The approximate phonetic realization of the seven full vowels is illustrated in Figure 3.1, which presents Tiberian Hebrew as possessing a complete inventory of primary vowels.

3.2.2 The origin of the Tiberian vowels

As noted above (§3.2.1), Hebrew, in the early stages of its development, probably preserved the Proto-Semitic system of three vocalic phonemes, high front **i* and back **u* and low central **a*, which could occur either long or short, and two "diphthongs" or vowel-glide sequences, **ay* and **aw* (see Appendix 1, §§3.2.2 and 3.2.3). Though the phonological changes by which these sounds gave rise to the Tiberian system described above are numerous and often complex, constrained by the rules of syllabification and stress (see §§3.4 and 3.5 below), it is possible to describe the Masoretic vowels and diphthongs in relation to their ancient antecedents by taking historical and structural considerations into account.

3.2.2.1 The development of the originally long vowels

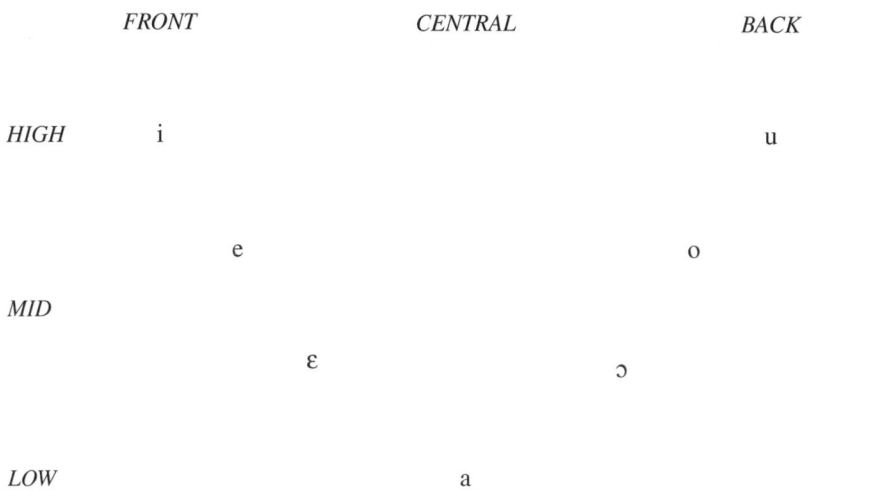

The Proto-Semitic long vowels, **ī*, **ū*, and **ā*, undergo no special development in Hebrew. Proto-Semitic **ā* is realized as [o], but this is not an inner-Hebrew development but the result of a sound change (**ā* → *ō*) that Hebrew inherited from Proto-Canaanite (see §3.6.2). Proto-Semitic **ī* and **ū* remain unchanged, and they are most often represented orthographically in the the Masoretic Text with *plene* spellings, *î* (י .) and *û* (וּ), though this is by no means consistent (see §§2.2 and 2.4). In terms of their phonological behavior, the Hebrew vowels derived from the Proto-Semitic long vowels may be described as unchangeably long to distinguish them from reducible long vowels derived from originally short vowels (§3.2.2.2); they are not subject to reduction to *šĕwā* (ə), regardless of position.

3.2.2.2 The development of the originally short vowels

The development of the Hebrew short vowels is much more complex. Because of changes that occurred during the evolution of the language, an originally short vowel may be realized as long, short (not necessarily the same short vowel as the original) or reduced (*šəwā* or one of the *ḥāṭēp* vowels). The possible morphophonemic variants of each of the short vowels are shown in (1):

(1)

Original short vowel	*Lengthened*	*Short*	*Reduced*
*i	ē	i, a, e	ə, ă, ĕ
*u	ō	u, o	ə, ŏ
*a	ā	a, i, e	ə, ă, ĕ

The potential for an originally short vowel to lengthen or reduce is constrained by the type and position of the syllable in which it appears. To lengthen, it must be in an open syllable (CV) or an accented closed syllable (CV′C). To reduce, it must be in an unaccented open syllable (CV), since a closed syllable (CVC), like an open syllable containing an originally long vowel (CV:), is irreducible (for syllabification, see §3.4). In general, therefore, an originally short vowel tends to lengthen in a tonic syllable or in an open pretonic syllable, it tends to remain short in a closed unaccented syllable (though its quality may change), and it tends to reduce in an open propretonic syllable. In practice, however, the operation of these very general rules differs for nouns (including adjectives and verbal nouns) and finite verbs with pronominal suffixes, on the one hand, and finite verbs without pronominal suffixes, on the other. The rule of thumb for nouns and finite verbs with pronominal suffixes is that an originally short vowel reduces in a propretonic syllable if possible – that is, if a propretonic syllable is present and its vowel is reducible – while it lengthens in a pretonic syllable. The rule of thumb for finite verbs without pronominal suffixes is that an originally short vowel reduces in a pretonic syllable if possible, while it lengthens in a propretonic syllable. These rules, too, are generalizations, however, and a clearer picture emerges when the situation is reviewed for vowels in each of the three common syllabic stress positions: tonic, pretonic and propretonic.

Originally short vowels in *tonic* syllables are, in most circumstances, lengthened in both nouns and verbs. That is, the high vowels **i* and **u* are lowered to *ē* ([e]) and *ō* ([o]), and the low vowel **a* is backed to *ā* ([ɔ]). With certain exceptions, this pattern holds for tonic syllables of all kinds in nouns and finite verbs with pronominal suffixes when the short vowel in question is **i* or **u*. When the vowel is **a*, the pattern holds for open and singly closed (word-final) syllables but not for originally doubly closed syllables (-C_1C_1# or -C_1C_2#). Since lengthening took place prior to the simplification of final doubled consonants, the vowel **a* before a final, originally doubled consonant (-CC#) remains: thus, **ʿamm* → *ʿam* "people" (note, however, that **i* and **u* both lengthen before -CC#: **libb* → *lēb* "heart"; **ʿuzz* → *ʿōz* "strength"). Also, in an originally word-final doubly closed syllable (see §3.4), when the tone vowel has become penultimate because of the insertion of an anaptyctic vowel to resolve the consonant cluster (-C_1C_2# → -C_1VC_2#), an accented short *a is not lengthened (except in pause; see §3.5), though it retains its stress and is raised to *e* ([a] → [ɛ]). This pertains especially to nouns of the type *CaCC – thus, *málk → *mélek*, "king" (pausal *mā́lek*). Note that with the high vowels there is no exception here (i.e., they usually lengthen in this situation), but sometimes, not consistently, before a word-final consonant cluster *i ([i]) → *e* ([ɛ]) instead of *ē* ([e]), especially in some nouns of the type *qitl: for example, *ṣídq → *ṣédeq*, "righteousness," in contrast to *sípr → *sḗper*, "book."

Similarly, the lengthening of *a does not take place in the tonic syllable as a result of the triphthongization of some diphthongs, as in *báyt → *báyit* (contrast *máwt → *mā́wet*), or the formation of the dual ending *-áym → *-áyim*. One other important exception where stressed *a is not lengthened is the verbal suffix of the first-person singular: *-ánî* "me" (but, again, pausal *-ā́nî*).

The pattern of lengthening of originally short vowels in tonic syllables also holds true for finite verbs without pronominal suffixes, but only for *i and *u – thus, *yittín → *yittḗn* "he gives"; *tiktúb → *tiktṓb* "she writes." Originally short *a remains short in these circumstances – *yišmáʿ* "he hears." Again, however, the situation is different when an originally word-final doubly closed syllable is involved. In these cases, the original short vowel is retained without lengthening in the tonic syllable after anaptyxis (*yírb → *yíreb* "may he become numerous"), though *a ([a]) is raised to e ([ɛ]) (*yárb → *yéreb* "may he make numerous").

Finally, mention should be made here of the vowel shift described by F. W. M. Philippi, according to which *i becomes *a* in originally closed accented syllables (*íCC# → áCC#) – in short, "Philíppi → Philáppi." Though this "law" seems to explain many Hebrew forms – such as (*bint →) *bitt → *batt (→ *bat*) "daughter"; (*ʿāmídt →) *ʿōmídt → *ʿōmádt (→ *ʿōmédet) "standing" (fem. sg. active participle); *zāqíntī → *zāqántî* "I am old" – its application admits of a very large number of exceptions, and it is inoperative in some witnesses (e.g., the Hexaplaric) to the developing Hebrew tradition.

Originally short vowels in open *pretonic* syllables are, in general, lengthened in nouns and reduced in unsuffixed verbs. More specifically, in nouns and finite verbs with pronominal suffixes, *i and *u are lengthened pretonically if there is a reducible propretonic (*šākinīm → *šəkēnīm* "neighbors"). If the propretonic is lacking or irreducible, however, the behavior of pretonic *i and *u depends on the quality of the tonic vowel. If the tonic vowel is also high, pretonic *i and *u reduce to *šəwā*: for example, *gibūl → *gəbûl* "boundary"; *šōmirīm → *šōmərîm* "guards"; *yišmurihū → *yišmərēhû* "he guards him." If the tonic vowel is not high, pretonic *i and *u lengthen (*i → *ē*, *u → *ō*): thus, *libáb → *lēbā́b* "heart"; *maṣṣibā → *maṣṣēbâ* "pillar." Pretonic *a always lengthens (*a → *ā*) in nouns and suffixed verbs, whether the propretonic is reducible (*dabarīm → *dəbārîm* "words") or not ((*kawkabīm →) *kōkabīm → *kôkābîm* "stars").

In contrast to the situation with nouns and suffixed verbs, the originally short vowels are usually reduced pretonically in finite verbs without pronominal suffixes – thus, for example, *yignubū → *yignəbû* "they steal"; *yittinū → *yittěnû* "they give"; *yikbadū → *yikbědû* "they are heavy." An important exception is when the pretonic is the first syllable in a word; in such a case the vowel is lengthened: thus, *himítū → *hēmíʾtû* "they killed."

Originally short vowels in *propretonic* syllables are, when possible, reduced in nouns and lengthened in unsuffixed verbs. The specific rule for nouns and finite verbs with pronominal suffixes is that an originally short vowel reduces propretonically if it is reducible, that is, if it appears in an originally open syllable. If the propretonic is irreducible, however, the pretonic reduces according to the rules (and exceptions) given above. In finite verbs without pronominal suffixes, an originally short vowel reduces when possible in a pretonic syllable, as also explained above, and if this happens, **i*, **u*, or **a* in the propretonic syllable lengthens: for example, **napalā* → *nāpəlâ* "she fell." If, however, the pretonic is not reducible (that is, if it is closed or contains an originally long vowel), the propretonic vowel reduces: **yudabbir* → *yədabbēr* "he speaks."

To this point the discussion of the originally short vowels has been concerned primarily with their behavior in open syllables or closed accented syllables, both of which permit the lengthening or reduction of the vowel. In closed unaccented syllables, however, **i*, **u*, and **a* remained short despite occasional changes of vowel quality. This is true whether they appear in originally closed pretonic or propretonic syllables, and it applies to both nouns and verbs. Examples of the former (pretonic) include the nouns **šibṭuh* → *šibṭô* "his tribe"; **kulluh* → *kullô* "all of it" (cf. **ḥudšah* → *ḥodšāh* "her new moon"); and **gapnī* → *gapnî* "my vine"; and the verbs **yimṣa'* → *yimṣā'* "he finds"; **yuggad* → *yuggad* "it is reported"; and **yašbīt* → *yašbît* "he causes to cease." Examples of the latter (propretonic) include the noun **milḥamāt* → *milḥāmôt* "wars" and the verb **yišmurū* → *yišmərû* "they watch."

While the *quantity* of an originally short vowel remains the same in a closed unaccented syllable, however, its *quality* may be altered. Although a number of situations in which this occurs could be listed, the attenuation of **a* to *i* in the sequence *$CaC_1C_2āC$ → $CiC_1C_2āC$ (where C_1 is not a guttural) is especially noteworthy. This phenomenon, commonly known as "*qatqat* → *qitqat* dissimilation," operates in *m*- prefix nouns, such as **madbā́r* → *midbā́r* "wilderness" and **malḥāmā́* → *milḥāmâ* "battle" (see §4.2.5.4), and especially (with short *a* in the second syllable) in construct forms, such as **ṣadqat´* → *ṣidqat´* "righteousness (of)" and **mazbaḥ´* → *mizbaḥ´* "altar (of)." The historical distribution of *m*-prefix nouns with the form *miqtal* suggests that *qatqat* → *qitqat* dissimilation took place at a relatively late date, since forms like *midbār* are found only in Tiberian Hebrew, in contrast to Hexaplaric and Babylonian *madbār*. On the other hand, verbal forms like *yiqtal* (<**yaqtal*) – for example, **yalmad* → *yilmad* "he learns" – and *niqtal* (<**naqtal*), the *Nip'al* perfect, developed much earlier, as shown not only by their attestation in all traditions of Hebrew vocalization but also by the presence of **yiqtal* in cognate languages like Aramaic and Ugaritic. This suggests that the various forms that are often explained by appeal to *qatqat* → *qitqat* dissimilation are not in fact the result of a single phenomenon (for **yiqtal* and the so-called Barth–Ginsberg Law, see §3.6.2).

3.2.2.3 The development of "diphthongs"

As noted above (see §3.2.2), it is customary to state that Proto-Semitic possessed two diphthongs, **aw* and **ay*, both of which were preserved, with modifications, in Hebrew. But since Proto-Semitic did not permit sequences of two (or more) vowels within a syllable (see Appendix 1, §3.2.3), the glides or semivowels, **w* and **y*, must be interpreted as consonants, and the two sequences (both [a + glide]) cannot be classified as true diphthongs. This sheds light on their realization in Tiberian Hebrew. When either of the "diphthongs" occurs in an accented syllable, CáwC or CáyC, it is "triphthongized," or disyllabically resolved, before a final consonant by the insertion of an anaptyctic vowel, *e* in the case of *áw* (CáwC → Cā́weC) and *i* in the case of *áy* (CáyC → CáyiC) – thus, **máwt* → *mā́wet* "death," and **báyt* → *báyit* "house." In other words, the syllable containing the diphthong behaves like other syllables with final consonant clusters (see §3.4). Note, however, that when stressed **áy* occurs immediately before a syllable with the form Cā, it dissimilates to [ɛ], spelled *səgōl-yôd* (ֶי) in the Masoretic Text – thus *-*áyCā* → -*ḗCā*, as in **ḥuqqáykā* →**ḥuqqḗ'kā* "your statutes." In an unstressed syllable either diphthong is "monophthongized" or contracted: **aw* → *ô* or **ay* → *ê* – thus, **mawtṓ* → *môtṓ* "his death," and **baytṓ* → *bêtô'* "his house." The vowels thus contracted merged phonetically with other long *ō*- and *ē*- vowels, regardless of their historical origin, including *ō* < **ā* (see §3.6.2) and *ō* < **u* and *ē* < **i* (see §3.2.2.2 and [1]; for the behavior of diphthongs in the dialects of Iron Age Hebrew, see §3.6.2).

3.3 Allophonic and morphophonemic variants

3.3.1 Fricative allophones

At some point in the development of Tiberian Hebrew the six nonemphatic stops, /b/, /p/, /d/, /t/, /g/ and /k/, acquired a second, continuant realization, giving rise to six fricative allophones, [v], [f], [ð], [θ], [ɣ] or [ʁ], and [x] or [χ], conventionally transliterated as *ḇ*, *p̄*, *ḏ*, *ṯ*, *ḡ* and *ḵ*. These forms arose as subphonemic or phonetic variants, originally restricted to nongeminated consonants in postvocalic positions. This development, which was shared by and probably influenced by Aramaic, is widely assumed to have taken place in the second half of the first century BC, but its precise chronology is unknown. The fricative allophones are fully represented in the Tiberian Masora, and there is evidence for their presence in the time of Rabbinic Hebrew, but their existence before the Common Era is not unambiguously documented.

3.3.2 Gutturals

The so-called gutturals (pharyngeals and glottals or laryngeals) underwent a pattern of progressive but dialectically heterogeneous weakening that resulted in a special set of rules in Tiberian grammar governing these consonants, /ʕ/ (ʿ), /ħ/ (*ḥ*), /ʔ/ (ʾ), /h/, and the vowels in their environment. Though these rules are extensive and complex, three basic stipulations may be mentioned here. First, a guttural cannot be doubled (a rule that also applies to the liquid /r/), so that a doubled guttural was simplified (*GG → G), either with lengthening of the vowel in the newly opened preceding syllable (compensatory lengthening) – as in **yiʾʾakil* → *yēʾākēl* "it is eaten"; **barrik* → *bārēk* "to bless" – or without this lengthening (so-called virtual doubling) – **biʿʿir* → *biʿēr* "he burned"; **yuraḥḥim* → *yəraḥēm* "he has compassion."

Second, a guttural cannot be followed by a simple *šəwā* ([ə]), requiring instead a "compound *šəwā*," a reduced or ultrashort variant of one of the short vowels (the *ḥāṭēp* vowels, *ĕ*, *ŏ*, and *ă*), as an auxiliary – thus, *ʾĕlōhîm* "god," *ʾohŏlî* "my tent" and *ḥălôm* "dream."

Third, when final, a guttural, other than /ʔ/ (ʾ), requires anaptyxis of *a* ("furtive *pataḥ*") following a vowel other than *a* or *ā*: for example, **rūḥ* → *rûaḥ* "wind"; **hišmīʿ* → *hišmîaʿ* "he caused to hear."

While it is difficult to date this pattern of weakening, and its progress is unlikely to have been uniform, it seems to have been well advanced by the time of the Samaritan Pentateuch and the Qumran literature, since occasional confusion of gutturals is found in both, and Qumran orthography exhibits conspicuous irregularities when the gutturals are involved, especially in nonformal manuscripts (i.e., those in which the scribes were not careful to reproduce the spelling practices of the biblical literature). On the other hand, it is clear that this development was primarily a matter of the weakening and coalescence of the gutturals rather than their disappearance, as shown by the mixed evidence of the Hexaplaric transcriptions. That the gutturals, in some configuration, were still a feature of Jewish speech *c.* AD 400 is shown by Jerome's remark that the Jews ridiculed the Christians for their inability to pronounce them. It seems clear, then, that the gutturals were preserved in some communities and lost in others, most probably where Greek influence was strongest. Thus the Talmud (*Megillah* 24b) refers to a lack of distinction (coalescence) among the gutturals in the speech of certain Galilean villages, but not others (on the quiescence of /ʔ/, which, though it played a part in the general phenomenon of guttural weakening, was of much earlier origin, see §3.6.1).

3.3.3 Vowel variation

For the development of vowel morphophonemic variation in Tiberian Hebrew, see §§3.2.2.1–3.2.2.2.

3.4 Syllable structure and phonotactic constraints

A Hebrew syllable must begin with a consonant. There is a single but important exception to this rule in Tiberian grammar, according to which the conjunction *wə-* "and" becomes *û-* before a syllable beginning with a consonant (not *y-*) plus *šəwā* – as in *ûd(ə)bārîm* "and words" – or a syllable beginning with a labial – such as *ûmélek* "and a king" (the Babylonian vocalization tradition also reflects the former situation, but not the latter, preserving the equivalent of *wə-* before a labial followed by a full vowel).

A syllable may contain only one vowel sound. The Hebrew diphthongs do not constitute an exception to this rule, since, as noted above (§3.2.2.3), they are not true diphthongs but vowel–glide combinations, and since, in any case, they are always either monophthongized to single vowel sounds – as in **baytuh* → *bêtô* "his house" – or triphthongized to vowel–glide–vowel combinations, thus forming parts of two distinct syllables – **bayt* → *báyit* "house."

A syllable may be open or closed. A syllable ending with a vowel (long, short, or reduced) is described as open, while a syllable ending with a consonant is described as closed. Occasionally a syllable ends in two consonants, and in this case it is called doubly closed: for example, *kātábt* "you (fem. sg.) wrote." Doubly closed syllables occur only at the ends of words, having arisen when a final vowel was lost (*kātábt* < **katabtī*). Such consonantal clusters were not permitted by the phonotactic rules of Proto-Semitic (see Appendix 1, §3.2.3), and Hebrew grammar exhibits a tendency to avoid them. When they do occur, the preceding vowel may be short (*wayyišb* "and he captured"; *wayyašq* "and he watered") or, with [i] lowered to [e] under the stress, long (*wayyēbk* "and he wept"; *wayyēšt* "and he drank"); but the medieval grammarians disagreed whether the final *šəwā* in such words was silent or vocal, and the Masoretes most often eliminated the problem by inserting an anaptyctic vowel, usually *səgōl* (**wayyipn* → *wayyípen* "and he turned"; **yibn* → *yíben* "let him build"), but *pataḥ* before or after gutturals (**wayyiḥr* → *wayyíḥar* "and he was angry") and *ḥîreq* after *y* (**ʿayn* → *ʿáyin* "eye"). "Segholation," as this phenomenon is sometimes called, is most characteristic of nouns of the common type *CVCC ("segholates"; see §4.2.5.2) – **ʾarṣ* → *ʾéreṣ* "earth"; **ʿizr* → *ʿḗzer* "help"; **buqr* → *bṓqer*" "morning"; and with gutturals, **naḥl* → *náḥal* "wadi" and so forth. Though anaptyxis in segholates is reflected in both the Babylonian and Tiberian traditions, its absence in the Hexaplaric materials suggests that it was a late phenomenon.

A syllable may be accented or unaccented (see §3.5). An accented syllable may be open or closed and contain a long or short vowel (CV(:), CV(:)C), though an accented syllable may not contain a reduced vowel. With rare exceptions, an unaccented syllable containing a long vowel will be open, while an unaccented syllable containing a short vowel is always closed (for the specific distribution of vowels in various types of syllables, which depends on rules of syllable formation deriving from the historical development of the language, see §3.2.2.2). In the Masoretic Text, when a closed unaccented syllable occurs in the middle of a word, the end of the syllable is indicated by the *šəwā* sign (ְ). The Masoretic diacritical for this syllable-dividing silent *šəwā* (*šəwā quiescens*) is the same as for the vocal *šəwā* (*šəwā mobile*). In most cases, this will cause no difficulty for the reader since a consonant following an unaccented short vowel must be syllable final, so that it must close the syllable and the *šəwā* standing under it must be silent. Ambiguity arises only when the diacritical is *qāmeṣ*, which can indicate either long *ā* or short *o*. To resolve the ambiguity the Masoretes usually inserted the accent called *meteg*, a small perpendicular line (ֽ), to the left of the *qāmeṣ* in an accented syllable, indicating that the *qāmeṣ* should be read as *ā* and thus that the following *šəwā* was vocal. In the absence of the *meteg*, the syllable should be read as unaccented and closed. Contrast *'ākəlâ* (אָֽכְלָה) "she ate" and *'oklâ* (אָכְלָה) "food."

According to the phonotactic rules of Tiberian grammar, only a consonant or a *full* vowel could constitute the coda of a syllable. In Masoretic sources, therefore, a consonant followed by a reduced vowel (simple or compound *šəwā*) was not regarded as an independent syllable. Thus, contrary to the guidelines given above, a word like *məlākîm* "kings" would be analyzed as containing two syllables – *məlā-kîm* – rather than three – *mə-lā-kîm*. This rule explains, among other things, why the Masoretes chose the same sign (ְ) to represent both vocal and silent *šəwā*. Since most reduced vowels developed from vowels that were previously full, however, the medieval rule has the disadvantage of obscuring the historical development of the language, and it is not followed as a convention of syllabification by most modern grammarians.

Tiberian Hebrew does not tolerate two successive open syllables with the vowel /ə/. When such a sequence is produced in inflection or from a combination of morphemes, such as the prefixation of a preposition or suffixation of a pronoun to a noun, the phenomenon commonly called "the rule of *šəwā*" occurs. The sequence is simplified to a single closed syllable containing the vowel /i/ (*CəCə → CiC) – thus, **dəbərê´ → dibrê´* "words (of)," **bədəbārîm → bidbārîm* "with words," and **dəbərêhem → dibrêhem* "their words."

3.5 Stress

In Hebrew the principal tone is usually, but not always, on the ultima – thus, *dābā́r* "word," *dəbārī́m* "words." This situation is the result of a shift of stress to the ultima that took place in two phases early in the history (or prehistory) of the language. The original position of the stress in Proto-Hebrew is disputed. It seems clear, though, that it shifted to the ultima in two stages. The first shift affected all words except finite verbs without pronominal suffixes, and the second shift occurred in these verbs. This two-stage development gave rise to several distinctive features of Hebrew grammar, including some of the phonological features already noted, such as the tendency of vowels in open pretonic syllables to lengthen in nouns but reduce in unsuffixed verbs (see §3.2.2.2), as well as important morphological features to be noted, such as stem allomorphism for many noun-types (§4.2.6). Both of these shifts are reflected in the Hexaplaric, Babylonian, and Tiberian traditions of vocalization, and, in fact, they are likely to have been very early. In all likelihood the first, major shift closely followed the loss of final short vowels, which was shared by most of the Northwest Semitic languages, so that it was probably pre-Hebrew. Note in this regard that ultimate stress is also characteristic of Aramaic, as indicated, for example, by the Masoretic accentuation of Biblical Aramaic, and Phoenician, as can be inferred from vowel changes in the ultima that are likely to have been caused by stress.

Despite the preference for stress on the ultima, the penult receives the tone in a number of situations. For example, segholate nouns, as already noted, are characteristically paroxytonic – as in *'ḗmeq* "valley" – and the ultimate stress of the imperfects of certain types of verbs retreats in the production of jussives and the so-called "converted" or *wāw*-consecutive imperfects – *yiglḗh* "he will uncover" ∼ *yígel* "let him uncover" ∼ *wayyígel* "and he uncovered." Also, a number of word-ending elements are for historical or structural reasons toneless. These include several verbal sufformatives (e.g., *ḥāšábtā* "you thought"), several nominal and verbal pronominal suffixes (*šāmərḗnî* "protect me"), and the so-called locative *-h* (*báytāh* "to the house, homeward"; *'árṣāh* "to the earth").

Both stress and consequent vowel quantity can be significantly affected by the so-called pause, a term for the increased stress placed on the tonic syllable of a word in the Hebrew Bible marked by one of the major accent diacritics, usually at the end of a verse or half-verse. In cases of the type just described, for example, where the stress of some imperfect verbs retreats from the ultima to the penult in the formation of converted imperfects, the tone returns under the pause to the ultima, which is lengthened accordingly – thus, *tāmû́t* "she will die" ~ *wattā́mot* "and she died" ~ *wattāmṓt* "and she died." Similarly, the tone may be restored under the pause to a vowel that lost its stress and was reduced to *šəwā* in the process of syllable formation according to one of the rules described above in §3.2.2.2, with the result that the original quality of the vowel returns and, if short, lengthens under the tone: thus, **yittinū* → *yittĕnû* → *yittḗnû* "they give." In general, short vowels tend to lengthen under the pause (**qātáltā* → *qātā́ltā*), and often their newly lengthened status gives a clue to the pre-Masoretic quality of the underlying vowel, as in the case just cited of *yittḗnû* (*ē* < **i*) and especially of segholate nouns, where, for example, an original */a/* realized as [ɛ] may be restored and lengthened under the pause (**gabr* → *géber* → *gā́ber* "man").

Numerous minimal pairs can be cited to show that stress is phonemic in Hebrew: for example, *bā́'â* ['bɔʔɔ] "she came" ~ *bā'â'* [bɔ'ʔɔ] "coming" (feminine singular active participle); *bān'û* "they built" ~ *bā́nû* "in us."

3.6 Diachronic phonological developments in relation to Proto-Northwest Semitic and Proto-Semitic

3.6.1 Consonants

Of the twenty-three consonantal phonemes represented in Table 3.3, eighteen preserve Proto-Semitic consonants unaltered, and five – all fricatives – are the result of unconditioned mergers of two or three Proto-Semitic phonemes. These five include:

1. *z* (/z/), which arose from the merging of the voiced dental **z* (/z/) and the voiced interdental **ð* (or **ḏ*) (/ð/) – compare *zā'aq* (<**za'aq* < **za'aqa*) "he cried" to *zāhāb* (<**zahab* < **ðahab-*) "gold."
2. *ḥ* (/ħ/) from the voiceless pharyngeal **ḥ*(/ħ/) and the voiceless velar **ḫ* (/x/) – compare *ḥēn* (<**ḥínn* < **ḥinn-*) "favor" to *ḥārēš* (<**ḥariš* < **ḫariš-*) "he is silent."
3. *'*(/ʕ/) from the voiced pharyngeal **'*(/ʕ/) and the voiced velar **ǵ* (/ɣ/) – compare *'áyin* (<**'áyn* < **'ayn-*) "eye" to *'almâ* (<**'almā* < **ǵalmat-*) "young woman."
4. *ṣ* (/s'/) from the emphatic dental **ṣ* (/s'/, the emphatic interdental **θ̣* (/θ'/) and the emphatic lateral **ṣ́* (or **ŝ*) (/ɬ'/) – compare *ṣédeq* (<**ṣídq* < **ṣidq-*) "righteousness," to *ṣēl* (<**ṣíll* <**θ̣ill-*) "shadow," and *ṣémer* (<**ṣámr* < **ŝamr-*) "wool."
5. *š* (/š/) from the voiceless palatal **š* (/š/) and the voiceless interdental **θ* (or **ṯ*) (/θ/) – compare *šēm* (<**ším* < **šim-*) "name" and *šōpēṭ* (<**šōpiṭ-* < **θāpiṭ-*) "judge."

Proto-Semitic possessed a triad of dental/alveolar affricates: voiced *$*d^z$*, voiceless *$*t^s$* and ejective *$*t^{s}$'*; see Appendix 1, §3.2.1.1. At an early date, these were deaffricated and merged with phonemes ancestral to the dental fricative triad in Hebrew – *$*d^z$* with **z*, *$*t^s$* with **s*, and *$*t^{s}$'* with **θ̣* – so that it is not necessary to take them into account in a description of the Hebrew phonological system.

As noted in §3.3.2, *' (/ʔ/) participated in the general pattern of weakening that affected the other gutturals. In addition, however, it exhibits certain special characteristics suggesting that it lost consonantal force in certain conditions at a very early date. Though stable in initial positions, *' is lost frequently in syllable-closing positions, and always at the end of words. Quiescence of *' is attested for nouns of the type *Ca'C- in Canaanite dialects as early as the fourteenth-century BC Amarna documents, as shown by the cuneiform spellings *ru-šu-nu* =*rōšunu (< *rāšunu < *ra'šunu) "our head" (EA 264:18), and *ṣu-ú-nu* = *ṣōnu (< *ṣānu < *ṣa'nu) "flock" (EA 263:12). These glosses show that, at least in some Canaanite dialects, syllable-final *' was lost prior to the Canaanite Shift (*ā → ō; see §3.6.2), and the participation of Hebrew in this development is demonstrated by the noun forms *rō(')š* "head," and *ṣō(')n* "flock," in which the long vowels show that the /ʔ/, though preserved orthographically, has quiesced. When *' is lost in the related Hebrew sequences *Ci'C- and *Cu'C-, *i and *u are lengthened (lowered) to ē and ō, as in *(lā)śē(')t* (< *śi't) "to carry" and *bō(')r* (<*bu'r) "pit." When syllable-final *' is lost in Hebrew verbs in which the third root consonant is ' (III-'), a preceding *a* is lengthened to *ā*, but it does not shift to *ō*, showing that in this environment *' quiesced after the Canaanite Shift was completed: thus, *māṣā(')* (< *māṣa') "he found"; *nāśā́(')tā* (< *nāśá'tā) "you carried." In the same situation, a preceding *i* is, again, lengthened to *ē* – as in *yārḗ(')tî* (< *yārí'tī) "I was afraid." Though, in most cases, quiescent *' is preserved orthographically in Tiberian Hebrew, it is sometimes omitted altogether, as in *māṣā́tî* for *māṣā́(')tî "I found" in Numbers 11:11. In other cases, the consonantal force of *' has been restored by Masoretic hypercorrection, leading to grammatically artificial vocalizations, such as *zə'ēb* for *zē(')b (< *zi'b) "wolf."

3.6.2 Vowels

As noted in §3.2.2.1, Proto-Semitic *ā is realized in Hebrew as /o:/ as the result of an unconditioned sound change (*ā → ō) shared by the Canaanite languages. The *Canaanite Shift*, as it is called, is attested in Amarna glosses, such as those cited in §3.6.1 as well as *sú-ki-ni* for *sōkini* (cf. Hebrew *sōkēn* "steward"), glossing Akkadian *rābiṣi* "inspector" (genitive), in EA 256:9 (cf. EA 362:69).

As noted in §3.2.2.3, the Hebrew diphthongs, *aw and *ay, are preserved and triphthongized under the tone but contracted in unaccented positions – thus, *yáyin* (< *yayn) "wine," but *têmān* (< *taymā́n*) "Teman, Southland." Epigraphic evidence, however, shows that the diphthongs behaved differently in the northern and southern dialects of Hebrew. In Israelite or Northern Hebrew, *aw and *ay contracted in all positions (i.e., stressed or unstressed) – thus, *yn* (*yēn ~ Biblical Hebrew *yáyin*) "wine"; *tmn* (*tēmān ~ Biblical Hebrew *têmān*) "Teman, Southland" – while in Judahite or Southern Hebrew, *aw and *ay were preserved in all positions – *yyn* (*yayn ~ Biblical Hebrew *yáyin*) "wine"; *tymn* (*taymān ~ Biblical Hebrew *têmān*) "Teman, Southland." It is clear that, as expected, the biblical pattern developed from that of the southern dialect of Jerusalem, in which diphthongs began to contract in unstressed positions during the last half of the first millennium BC.

As pointed out in §3.2.2.2, in the discussion of the phenomenon known as *qatqat → qitqat dissimilation*, which was generalized relatively late in the development of Hebrew, a change with this pattern (change of *a to *i in a closed unaccented syllable) occurred in prefixed verbal forms at an early date (*yaqtal → yiqtal*). When final short vowels were lost in Proto-Hebrew, and the stress shifted to the ultima, the prefix vowels of singular and first-person plural verbs were most often left in closed, unaccented syllables – that is, *yáqtulu → *yáqtul → *yaqtúl. Whereas in Proto-Semitic the (indicative) verbal prefixes contained an *a*-vowel regardless of which of the three theme-vowels (*a*, *i*, *u*) the verb had – thus,

yaqtal-*, **yaqtil-*, **yaqtul-* – in Proto-Hebrew, and Northwest Semitic generally, the prefix-vowel of the *yaqtal*-type changed from *a* to *i*. This phenomenon was first described by Jacob Barth, and it was confirmed by H. L. Ginsberg, who showed that it was "fully operational" for Ugaritic. Thus according to the *Barth–Ginsberg Law*, as it is now commonly called, the prefix of *yqtl* in the simple active conjugation is vocalized with *i* when the thematic vowel is *a*; otherwise it is vocalized with *a* – thus *yiqtal*, but *yaqtul* and *yaqtil*. This is illustrated by Hebrew forms like **yakbad* → *yikbad* "he is heavy," **yašlaḥ* → *yišlaḥ* "he sends" and so forth. In Hebrew, however, the **yi-* prefix is not limited to verbs with *a* as theme vowel, as shown by forms like *yišpōṭ* (< **yišpuṭ* < **yašpuṭ*) "he judges." In contrast to **yaqtal* → *yiqtal*, this change (yaqtul* → **yiqtul* (→ *yiqtōl*)) was not inherited from Proto-Northwest Semitic, as shown by syllabically written Ugaritic forms like *ia-aš-pu-ṭú-* for **yašpuṭu*, corresponding to consonantal *yṯpṭ* (**yaθpuṭu*) "he judges." In Hebrew, then, the form should probably be explained by simple pattern-leveling. That is, at an early stage the prefix vowel was *i* only in verbs with the stem-vowel *a*, as in Ugaritic. Subsequently, however, the *yi-* prefix was leveled through for other Hebrew verbs, namely, those with the stem-vowels *i* and *u*.

4. MORPHOLOGY

4.1 Morphological-type and word structure

Hebrew, like the other members of the Semitic family, is a fusional language. The meaning of a word is derived by inflection of a simple stem, commonly called the *root* on the basis of medieval usage – *šōreš* "root," rendered into Latin as *radix*, hence *litterae radicales* "root letters" or "radicals," as the individual consonants of the root (√) are still commonly called. As a rule, Hebrew words, whether verbs or nouns, are based on roots consisting of (usually) three radicals with a fixed sequence, which are inflected by affixes and/or some variation of additional morphological features, such as gemination and especially vowel patterning (*vowel gradation* or *ablaut*). The most important of these inflectional patterns are described below in subsequent sections.

Hebrew roots are predominantly triradical. Some evidence of originally biradical forms seems to survive, as in the case of certain verbs with *y* as first radical (I-*y*), which were originally *I-*w*, a group having root allomorphs √wCC and √CC in Proto-Semitic and Afro-Asiatic (see Appendix 1, §3.3.1). As explained below in §4.5.4.2, this accounts for Hebrew forms like *šēb* (< **šíb*) "sit!" the masculine singular imperative of √*yšb* (< *√*wšb* < *√[*w*]*θb*). Other Hebrew stem-types are sometimes interpreted as artificially triradical, altered from original biradicals, such as the so-called geminate roots (i.e., those with identical second and third radicals). At the same time, roots containing a glide as one of the stem consonants are often regarded as essentially biradical; these include not only the *I-*w* and (less often) *I-*y* roots, but also the so-called hollow or middle-weak roots (II-*w* and II-*y*) and the final-weak roots (III-*w* and III-*y*). Nevertheless, these "weak" types can also be explained as originally triradical, having developed from the partial or complete loss of one of the stem consonants by some process such as the elision of a glide in an intervocalic position. In short, the degree of biradicalism that is operative in Hebrew remains a debated point. What can be stated confidently is that, whatever the degree of biradicalism in its antecedent stages, Hebrew has been strongly conformed to a predominant triradical pattern.

Most of the small number of ostensible quadriradicals in Hebrew can be explained as products of augmentation or reduplication – for example, *garzen* "ax" (from √*grz* "cut");

galgal "wheel" (from √*gll* "roll") – and the same is true of the even rarer quinqueradicals – *səḥarḥar* "it palpitates" (from √*sḥr* "move around") – when they are not in fact loanwords.

4.2 Noun morphology

Hebrew nouns have two genders, masculine and feminine; three numbers, singular, dual, and plural; and two states, free or absolute and bound or construct. Hebrew nouns are not marked inflectionally for case (see §4.2.3). In general, Hebrew adjectives (including verbal adjectives) are inflected like nouns.

The basic nominal paradigm is given in (2), using the nouns *yôm* "day" and *šānâ* "year" as examples. Note that the plural *yāmîm* "days" is formed from a different root from that of the singular and dual, and that *šānôt* "years" has a more common alternative form – *šānîm*; these peculiarities do not obscure the inflection.

(2)

		Masculine	*Feminine*
Singular	*Absolute*	yôm	šānâ
	Construct	yôm′	šənat′
Dual	*Absolute*	yômáyim	šənātáyim
	Construct	yômê′	šənātê′
Plural	*Absolute*	yāmîm	šānôt
	Construct	yəmê′	šənôt′

4.2.1 Gender

As a rule, if the referent of a noun is naturally masculine, the noun will be masculine (*par* "bull") and if the referent is naturally feminine, the noun will be feminine (*pārâ* "heifer"). Nouns designating things without natural gender, such as inanimate objects or abstract ideas, may be either masculine or feminine – thus, *géšem* "rain" (masculine), and *gibʿâ* "hill" (feminine).

Though there are numerous exceptions, masculine nouns are, as a general rule, unmarked, while feminine nouns are marked. The feminine is marked by one of two endings, *-â* (bound form *-at*) and *-t*. Although these two endings seem to have existed from an early stage in the language as unconditioned morphemic alternants, there are certain environments in which one or the other is preferred. Thus, feminine noun stems ending in a consonant cluster or a consonant preceded by a long vowel (-CC- or -V:C-) are marked by *-â* – as in *ʾiššâ* "woman" and *ʿēṣâ* "counsel" – while *-t* follows forms ending with a vowel – *miṣrît* "Egyptian" – and, very characteristically, is preferred on active participles, often leading to a "segholated" (cf. §3.4) ending – thus **yāšibt* → *yōšébet* "sitting" (the *-t* ending is used much more widely in Rabbinic Hebrew than in Biblical Hebrew). There are also many unmarked feminine nouns, including some with naturally feminine meaning, such as *ʾēm* "mother," and others designating inanimate objects, such as *ʾében* "stone" and *ʿîr* "city."

4.2.2 Number

Plural nouns and adjectives in the unbound state are most often marked by the endings *-îm* and *-ôt* (for nouns in the bound state, see §4.2.4). The great majority of the former are masculine and the latter feminine, as suggested by (2). There are, however, numerous masculine nouns with the *-ôt* plural ending – thus, *ʾāb* "father," *ʾābôt* "fathers," and *māqôm* "place," *məqōmôt* "places" – and a few that have both *-îm* and *-ôt* – for example, *nāhār* "river," *nəhārîm* and (more often) *nəhārôt* "rivers." Similarly, several feminine nouns, whether or not they are marked as feminine in the singular (see §4.2.1) and whether or not they have natural feminine referents, take the *-îm* plural ending. Examples of marked feminine singular nouns with *-îm* plural endings include the natural feminine *'iššâ* "woman," *nāšîm* "women," but also *ḥiṭṭâ, ḥiṭṭîm* "wheat" (see also [2] above for *šānâ*, which usually forms its plural as *šānîm* but frequently as *šānôt*). Examples of unmarked feminine singular nouns with *-îm* plural endings include the natural feminine *rāḥēl* "ewe," *rəḥēlîm* "ewes," but also *'îr* "city," *'ārîm* "cities." Examples of unmarked feminine singular nouns with *-ôt* plural endings include the natural feminine *'ēm* "mother," *'immôt* "mothers," but also *'éreṣ* "land," *'ărāṣôt* "lands." Certain unmarked nouns that are construed sometimes as masculine and sometimes as feminine may have both plural endings – thus *'āb* "cloud" (usually masculine, but feminine in 1 Kings 18:44), *'ābîm* and *'ābôt* "clouds."

In Late Biblical Hebrew the plural ending *-în* alternates with *-îm* (cf. *yāmîn* "days," in Daniel 12:13), and in Rabbinic Hebrew *-în* is increasingly preferred. Though this development may have been influenced by Aramaic, it probably had its origin in dialect variation within Hebrew, since its distribution in the Bible is not exclusively confined to the latest literature and, in fact, occurs once in the most archaic poetry (*middîn* "carpets," in Judges 5:10). Its ultimate explanation is the existence in Proto-Northwest Semitic of **-m* and **-n* allomorphs of the Proto-Semitic plural/dual boundness marker **-n* (see §4.2.4).

Although the dual is used in some Semitic languages, such as Ugaritic and Arabic, to refer to two of anything, its use in Biblical Hebrew is largely confined to natural pairs, such as *'oznáyim* "ears," or *na'ăláyim* "sandals," or to numerals (*šənáyim* "two") and double units of measurements of time or quantity: for example, *šəbû'áyim* "two (successive) weeks, a fortnight"; *'ammātáyim* "two cubits." Probably as the result of a dialectal survival, the original broader use of the dual returns in Rabbinic Hebrew, where it can denote a pair of anything.

With unmarked nouns, the unbound dual ending, *-áyim*, is added directly to the base of the singular – thus, *ragláyim* ((*régel* <) **ragl-* + *-áyim*) "feet" (masculine); and *yādáyim* ((*yād* <) **yad* + *-áyim*) "hands" (feminine). With nouns marked as feminine, the ending is added to the singular base following one of the two types of marker (see §4.2.1), as follows. Nouns ending in *-â* (bound form *-at*) follow the pattern of *śāpâ* (bound form *śəpat*) "lip," *śəpātáyim* "lips." Nouns ending in *-t* follow the pattern of *nəḥőšet* (bound form *nəḥőšet* < **nuḥušt*) "bronze," *nəḥuštáyim* "bronze fetters," unless assimilated to the preceding pattern, as evidently in the case of *délet* (< **dalt*, but bound form *dəlat'*) "door," *dəlātáyim* "(double) doors."

Adjectives follow more restricted rules with regard to number. The kind of variety displayed by nouns in forming *-îm* and *-ôt* plural, as described above, is lacking in adjectives (including participles), the masculine plurals of which are consistently marked by *-îm* and feminine plurals by *-ôt*. Also, dual endings do not occur with adjectives.

4.2.3 Case

In Proto-Northwest Semitic, the three short vowels were used to indicate case in singular nouns – **-u* for nominative, **-i* for genitive, and **-a* for accusative – and, following **-āt-*, in feminine plural nouns – **-ātu* for nominative and **-āti* for oblique. The loss of final short vowels and the leveling of the **-īm* ending on masculine plurals (see §4.2.2) left Hebrew nouns with no inflectional indication of case, except perhaps the bound–unbound opposition in genitive constructions. As a result, the case of nouns may be identified only from syntactical criteria.

4.2.4 State

In Biblical Hebrew, as in other Semitic languages that have lost the Proto-Semitic system of case endings, the chief way to express a genitive relationship is the so-called construct chain (on the role of the construct chain in the determination of substantives, see §5.4). A construct chain consists of the juxtaposition of two or (rarely) more nouns in a sequence such as *dəbar hammélek* "the word of the king." In this example, *hammélek* "the king" is free in form like other nouns not forming parts of construct chains. It derives a genitive force, however, from its relationship to the preceding bound form *dəbar'*. In traditional terminology, *dəbar'*, the *nomen regens*, is said to "govern" *hammélek*, the *nomen rectum*.

The two parts of a construct chain are closely associated accentually, with the principal stress moving ahead to the *nomen rectum*, which therefore remains morphologically unchanged and in what is called the *absolute state*. The *nomen regens*, however, becomes proclitic and often undergoes changes (especially including vowel shortening or reduction) in consequence of the loss of stress, so that it is said to be in the *construct state* – compare *dābār* "word" (absolute state) to *dəbar'* (construct state). The changes that affect singular nouns in the construct state include vowel reduction in newly unstressed syllables (*ā* → ə and *ē* → ə) and the shift of *ā* to *a* in final closed syllables (both illustrated, again, by the contrast *dābār* ∼ *dəbar'*). Nouns ending in a final stressed *səgôl* (*-eh* = ֶה) become final *ṣērê* (*-ēh* = ֵה) in construct: for example, *maḥăneh* "camp" (absolute) ∼ *maḥănēh'* (construct).

As noted in §4.2.2, plural nouns in the absolute state normally end in *-ôt* (usually feminine) or *-îm* or, in Rabbinic Hebrew, *-în* (usually masculine). The *-îm* and *-în* endings are survivals of a Proto-Semitic boundness marker for plural and dual nouns, *-*n(a)*. That is, free or unbound Proto-Semitic nouns ended in *-*m* following short vowels and *-*n(a)* following long vowels and diphthongs, so that nouns lacking these endings were "marked" as bound or construct (see Appendix 1, §3.3.2.1). In the evolution of the descendant languages the two endings were leveled and otherwise simplified. In the Northwest Semitic group the short-vowel ending, *-*m*, disappeared, so that the bound–unbound contrast was lost in singular and feminine plural nouns until the later sound changes already described developed as the result of the proclisis of bound forms. On the other hand, the long-vowel ending, *-*n(a)*, survived as a marker of the absolute plural and dual. Original *-*n(a)* was realized, however, as *-n* in some Northwest Semitic languages (Aramaic, Moabite, the Deir ʿAlla dialect, and Rabbinic Hebrew) and as *-m* in others (Ugaritic, Phoenician, Ammonite, and Biblical Hebrew).

The bound or construct endings of plural nouns are *-ê* (ֵי) corresponding to *-îm* in the absolute state, and *-ôt* corresponding to *-ôt* in the absolute. When pronominal suffixes are added to plurals ending in *-ôt*, the plural bound-form ending *-ê-* (<*-*ay*-) is interposed – thus, *miṣwôtê'kā* "your commandments." Not all of these forms can be readily explained in relation to the antecedent forms reconstructed for Proto-Northwest Semitic.

The Proto-Northwest Semitic forms of the unmarked, usually masculine, unbound plural were **ūn* in the nominative and *-*īn* in the oblique, corresponding to *-*u* nominative, *-*a* accusative, and *-*i* genitive in the singular (see §4.2.3). When the loss of final short vowels caused the case system to collapse in the singular, the endings were leveled in the plural as well, and the oblique form, *-*īn*, was generalized (as *-īn* or *-īm*, as explained above). At this point, the corresponding bound form in the plural must have been *-*ī*, but for unknown reasons this form was abandoned in favor of the corresponding dual form, *-*ay* (→ *-ê*; see below).

The Proto-Northwest Semitic forms of the marked, usually feminine, unbound plural were *-*ātu* in the nominative and *-*āti* in the oblique. With the loss of final short vowels these fell together as *-*āt*, the expected antecedent form of *-ôt*. It is unknown, however, why the newly formed masculine plural bound form *-ê-* (<**-ay-*) came to be inserted before suffixes added to these nouns.

For dual nouns the construct ending is *-ê* (ֵי), originally **-ay*, corresponding to *-áyim* in the absolute state. In unmarked nouns *-ê* is added directly to the end of the base – thus *raglê'* "feet" (masculine), and *yədê'* "hands" (feminine). With nouns marked as feminine, the endings are added following the marker, as explained in connection with the dual absolute endings in §4.2.2 above – as in *śiptê'* "lips."

In Rabbinic Hebrew, though the construct chain is still used frequently to express the genitive, it is increasingly replaced by a construction in which nouns are joined by the genitive particle *šel*, which arose from a combination of the relative particle *še-* (see §4.3.3) and the proclitic preposition *lə-* "belonging to, of" – thus, *haddābār šellamélek* or, more commonly, *haddābār šel hammélek* "the word of the king." The *nomen regens* in such a construction is not in the construct state, and it may have an anticipatory pronominal suffix – thus already in Late Biblical Hebrew, *hinnēh miṭṭātô šellislōmōh* "There is the couch of Solomon" (Song of Songs 3:7).

4.2.5 Noun formation

The various Hebrew noun- and adjective-types are derived from the application of several kinds of operations to verbal roots, including vowel patterning, root consonant gemination and affixation. Though several noun-types have general or specific semantic associations, there are many others for which such associations cannot be identified. The following tabulation provides a selection of some of the most important noun-types. In arrangement it proceeds from the simpler to the more complex forms, and the paradigm root used is √*qtl* (√*ql* for biradical types). Except where indicated, the examples come from Biblical Hebrew.

4.2.5.1 Biradical types

The pattern CV:C (<*CVC) includes a number of common nouns of the types *qāl* (<**qal*) – thus, *dām* "blood"; *dāg* "fish." The associated feminine forms are *qālâ* (<**qalat*; e.g., *bāmâ* "high place," *šānâ* "year") and *qélet* (<**qalt*; e.g., *qéšet* "bow"; cf. Northern Hebrew *št*=**šatt* (<**šant*) "year"). The active participle of roots II-*w*/*y* is formed from this pattern – thus, *bā'* and (feminine) *bā'â* "coming"; *śām* and (feminine) *śāmâ* "placing." Two members of this group, *'āb* "father" and *'āḥ* "brother" (plural *'aḥim* <**'aḥḥīm*), have their construct form in *-î* (*'ăbî*), suggesting that these words had (anomalously) long singular case vowels in Proto-Semitic, the vowel of the genitive (**-ī*) having been leveled through the paradigm after the collapse of the case system. The CV:C pattern also includes nouns of the type *qēl* (<**qil*): thus, *'ēl* "god," *'ēṣ* "tree." Again there are two associated feminine forms, namely, *qēlâ* (<**qilat*; e.g., *bēṣâ* "egg," *mē'â* "hundred") and *qélet* (<**qilt*), which forms the infinitive construct of roots *I-*w* and some roots I-*n*: for example, *šébet* (√*yšb* < √**wθb*) "to sit"; *réšet* (< √*yrš* < √**wrθ*) "to take possession of"; *géšet* (√*ngš*) "to approach." Though *qēl* is the absolute, presuffixal, and construct form for most members of this group, the common nouns *šēm* "name" and *bēn* "son" have the presuffixal forms *šəm-* and *bən-* and (sometimes) the construct forms *ben-* and *šem-* (the latter is rare). Another common noun, *bat* "daughter," belongs to this pattern (**qilt*): **bint* → **bitt* → **batt* (by Philippi's Law, see §3.2.2.2) → *bat.*

Nouns of similar form but deriving from a biradical type containing an originally *long* vowel, CV:C (<*CV:C), include the patterns *qôl* (<**qōl* < **qāl*; e.g., *qôl* "voice," *ḥôl* "sand"); *qîl* (<**qīl*; e.g., *šîr* "song," *qîr* "wall"); and *qûl* (<**qūl*; e.g., *sûs* "horse," *rûaḥ* "wind"). From *qîlâ*, the feminine corresponding to *qîl*, come the nouns *bînâ* "understanding" and *qînâ* "dirge." The infinitive construct of roots II-*w* is formed from the *qûl* pattern – thus, *qûm* "to arise" – and that of roots II-*y* is formed from the *qîl* pattern – thus, *dîn* "to judge," *rîb* "to contend."

4.2.5.2 Triradical types without a doubled radical

The pattern CVCeC (< *CVCC) constitutes an important group of nouns (the "segholates," see §§3.4–3.5), which, when derived from sound roots, take the forms *qétel* (< **qatl* or **qitl*), *qḗtel* (< **qitl*) and *qṓtel* (< **qutl*). A distinctive feature of the segholates, including their feminine forms (*CVCCat), is the formation of the plural from the base *CVCaC (feminine *CVCaCat); i.e., with *-a-* interposed between the second and third radicals. A large number of common nouns belong to the group *qétel* (< **qatl*): *mélek* "king," *késep* "silver," *'éreṣ* "earth," *gépen* "vine," *kéleb* "dog," *'ébed* "slave," and so forth. Almost as large is the group **qitl*, including *qḗtel* (< **qitl*; e.g., *sḗper* "book," *šḗbeṭ* "rod") – and *qétel* (< **qitl*; e.g., *ṣédeq* "righteousness," *qéreb* "midst"). The corresponding feminine is *qitlâ* (< **qitlat*): for example, *šipḥâ* "maidservant," *gib'â* "hill," *yir'â* "fear," but also *ḥerpâ* "reproach," *'erwâ* "nakedness." When based on an active verbal root, **qitl(at)* nouns frequently have a passive sense – thus, *šḗma'* "report" (something heard) from √*šm'* "hear"; *zḗker* "memory" (something remembered); *zéba* "sacrifice" (something sacrificed); compare *'ḗmeq* "valley" (something deep), from the stative verb √*'mq* "be deep." (Note: the presence of two types, *qḗtel* and *qétel*, from **qitl*, and the convergence of *qétel* < **qitl* with *qétel* < **qatl* present problems in interpreting the Tiberian tradition, and when the evidence of the Babylonian [e.g., *málak* ~ Tiberian *mélek* and *qárab* ~ Tiberian *qéreb*] and Hexaplaric traditions is added, a number of ambiguities involving nouns of the type *qatl* and *qitl* emerge.) The third group of segholates, *qṓtel* (< **qutl*), also includes some common nouns: for example, *bṓqer* "morning," *ḥṓdeš* "month," *šṓreš* "root"; *'ṓraḥ* "path." Nouns of this group are frequently abstract (e.g., *qṓdeš* "holiness"), especially when derived from stative roots – thus, *rṓḥab* "width," *gṓbah* "height," *ḥṓšek* "darkness."

Another large, important group is represented by the pattern CV:CV:C (< *CVCVC). This pattern is especially characteristic of adjectives, but it produces many common nouns as well. The group *qātāl* (< **qatal*) includes a number of primary nouns having the form *qātāl* – such as *zāhāb* "gold," *nāhār* "river" – but some of the nouns in this group are clearly collectives, such as *qāhāl* "assembly" and *bāqār* "cattle," and it is possible to interpret many of the others in this way, including *'āpār* "dust," *'ānān* "cloud," *māṭār* "rain," and possibly *'ādām* "man, person, humanity"; it has been suggested that some of these derive from a Proto-Semitic **qatal* plural morpheme. The same type (*qātāl*) is especially productive of abstract nouns derived from verbs, which may be active (e.g., *ḥāmās* "distortion," *nāqām* "vengeance") or stative (e.g., *'āšām* "guilt," *śābā'* "satiety," *rā'āb* "hunger," *ṣāmā'* "thirst"). The corresponding feminine form is *qətālâ* (< **qatalat*) – for example, *'ădāmâ* "soil" – which, like *qātāl*, is characteristic of abstract nouns, such as *ṣədāqâ* "righteousness" and *bərākâ* "blessing." Finally, and most typically, the group *qātāl* (< **qatal*) contains numerous adjectives from stative roots, such as *ḥādāš* "new," *rāšā'* "evil," *ḥāzāq* "strong," *lābān* "white," *šāpāl* "low," and so forth. This is also true of the groups *qātēl* (< **qatil*) – such as *zāqēn* "old," *śāmēaḥ* "joyous," *ṭāmē'* "unclean" – and *qātôl* (< **qatul*): thus, *gādôl* "big," *'āmōq* "deep," *mātôq* "sweet," *ṭāhôr* "clean," *qārôb* "near," *rāḥôq* "distant."

The pattern CV:CV:C (< *CVCV:C) is especially productive of adjectives, many of which are substantivized as nouns. The type *qātôl* (< **qatāl*), however, is primarily nominal. Though it includes a few primary nouns – such as *šālôš* "three," *'ātôn* "jenny" – it specializes as the form of the infinitive absolute of the simple verbal stem (Qal) – thus, *kātôb* "to write." Other well-known nouns with this form, such as *šālôm* "peace" and *kābôd* "glory," are like the infinitive in expressing the abstract idea of the verb. The type *qātîl* (< **qatīl*), though it includes few primary substantives, frequently forms adjectives from verbs, whether from stative roots (*ḥāsîd* "pious," *ṣā'îr* "little") or active roots. Adjectives formed in this way from active roots tend to be passive in meaning and may be substantivized, such as *'āsîr* "bound," substantivized as "prisoner," and *śākîr* "hired," substantivized as "hireling." Many of these adjectives, when substantivized as passive, function as nouns of office – thus, *nāgîd* "prince" (i.e., "designee"); *māšîaḥ* "messiah" ("anointed one"); *nāśî'* "chief" ("one who is lifted up"); *pāqîd* "commissioner" ("one who is appointed"). The type *qātûl* (< **qatūl*), though again it includes few primary nouns, is a common adjectival pattern from stative roots – thus, *'ārûm* "clever," *'āṣûm* "strong." Most importantly, *qātûl* is generalized as the passive participle for active roots of the simple verbal stem (Qal) – thus, *kātûb* "written"; *pātûaḥ* "open."

The particular importance of the pattern CōCVC (< *CāCVC) is the role of the type *qôtēl* (< **qātil*), feminine *qōtəlâ* (< **qātilat*) and *qōtélet* (< **qātilt*), in forming the active participle of the simple verbal stem (Qal): for example, *yôrēd, yōrədâ, yōrédet* "going down." These are often substantivized – thus, *kōhēn* "priest," *sōpēr* "scribe," *yô'ēṣ* "counsellor," *gō'ēl* "kinsman," *ḥōtēn* "father-in-law," *yôlēdâ* "woman in labor" (with retention of *ē* in the substantive).

4.2.5.3 *Triradical types with doubling of the second radical*

The pattern CVCCV:C (< *CVCCVC) includes mostly adjectives, many of which may be substantivized. The type *qattāl* (< **qattal*) is an adjectival pattern that usually denotes habitual action – thus, *qannā'* "jealous," *ḥaṭṭā'* "sinful," *naggāḥ* "accustomed to gore" (of the ox in Exodus 21:29 and 36), and *'awwāl* "unjust," substantivized as "unjust person." When substantivized, this form is especially characteristic of nouns of occupation – thus *dayyān* "judge," *ṭabbāḥ* "cook," *gannāb* "thief," *ḥārāš* (< **ḥarrāš*) "craftsman" (Rabbinic Hebrew adds to this category a number of examples not found in Biblical Hebrew: e.g., *baqqār* "cattle rancher," *hārāg* (< **harrāg*) "murderer," *gammāl* "camel driver"). The type *qittēl* (< **qattil* by a pre-Hebrew sound change) belongs to a number of adjectives denoting physical conditions: thus, *'iwwēr* "blind," *ḥērēš* (< **ḥirrēš*) "deaf," *gibbēaḥ* "bald," *'iṭṭēr* "disabled" (of the right hand → "left-handed" in Rabbinic Hebrew).

4.2.5.4 *Types with derivational affixes*

Nouns with preformative mV- constitute a large group with a wide variety of meaning. Two of the most important types, **maqtal* and **miqtal*, have fallen together by *qatqat → qitqat dissimilation* (see §3.2.2.2) as *miqtāl*, with its feminine forms *miqtālâ* and *miqtélet*. Examples include *midbār* "pasture land," *mišpāṭ* "judgment," *mišpāhâ* "clan," and *milḥāmâ* "battle." In phonological situations involving a guttural, liquid, or nasal as the first root consonant, however, initial *ma-* may occur in nouns of either original type (**maqtal* or **miqtal*) – thus, *ma'ăkāl* "food," *ma'ărāb* "west," *mal'āk* "messenger," *mamlākâ* "kingdom," *mattān* (< **mantan*) "gift," *maśśā'* (< **manśa'*) "burden, oracle."

Among sufformatives may be mentioned (i) *-ôn* (< **-ān*), which forms a number of substantives, especially from roots III-*w*/*y* – for example, *ḥāzôn* "vision," *gā'ôn* "pride," *hāmôn* "sound" – as well as adjectivals, such as *'aḥărôn* "behind, latter," and *ḥîṣôn* "outer"; (ii) *-ût* (< **-ūt*), which forms abstracts from concrete nouns – *malkût* "kingdom" (from **malk* "king"), *'almānût* "widowhood" (cf. **'alman(at)* "widow"), *yaldût* "youth" (from **yald* "child"), and (iii) *-î* (< **-īy*), a common affix for forming adjectives from nouns, which is used especially to generate ordinals – such as *šəlîšî* "third" – and gentilics, which may be substantivized – thus, *raglî* "on foot," substantivized as "footman, foot-soldier" (from **ragl* "foot"), *yəhûdî* "of Judah, Jewish," substantivized as "Judahite, Jew."

4.2.6 Stem allomorphism

The early shift of stress to the final syllable (see §3.5) and the subsequent vowel changes that resulted in the course of inflection and suffixation (see §3.2.2.2) led to a wide variety in stem-form in many Hebrew nouns and adjectives. This stem allomorphism is among the most distinctive characteristics of the language in its later development. Note, for example, the variety of nominal stems found in the inflection of *dābār* "word": unbound singular stem *dābār*; bound singular stem (with forward shift of stress) *dəbar'*; presuffixal singular stem *dəbār-* (light suffixes; see §4.3.1) or *dəbar-* (heavy suffixes); unbound plural stem (with forward shift of stress) *dəbār-*; bound plural stem *dibrê'*; presuffixal plural stem *dəbār-* or *dibrê-* (see §4.3.1).

4.3 Pronominal morphology

Hebrew has personal, demonstrative, relative, interrogative, and indefinite pronouns. There is no separate reflexive or resumptive pronoun, though the oblique cases of the pronominal suffixes may be used reflexively or resumptively (retrospectively) – the latter very commonly in relative clauses.

4.3.1 Personal pronouns

Hebrew personal pronouns occur in two forms, independent and enclitic (the pronominal suffixes). Both types are inflected for number, person, and gender. There are complete paradigms of singular and plural forms, but the Proto-Semitic dual forms, which may be reconstructed for the oblique cases at least (see Appendix 1, §3.3.3), have been generally lost (but see below). First-person personal pronouns have common gender, while second- and third-person personal pronouns have distinct masculine and feminine forms.

The standard forms of the independent personal pronouns, which serve as the nominative case (i.e., as subject or predicate nominative), are as follows.

(3)

		Number	
Person	*Gender*	*Singular*	*Plural*
First	*Common*	'ānōkî, 'ănî	'ănáḥnû
Second	*Masculine*	'attâ	'attem
	Feminine	'att	'atten, 'attḗnnâ
Third	*Masculine*	hû'	hḗm, hḗmmâ
	Feminine	*hî'*	hḗnnâ

Although *'ānōkî* and *'ănî* are both widely used in Biblical Hebrew, the former is more common in earlier biblical literature, while the latter is predominant in the later literature, especially Late Biblical Hebrew, and survives alone in Rabbinic Hebrew. In Biblical Hebrew *'ănáḥnû* has a rare variant, *náḥnû*; in Rabbinic Hebrew (and already in Jeremiah 42:6 and at Qumran) both are replaced by *'ānû*. The second-person singular forms exhibit some variety. Thus *'attâ* (masculine) is sometimes spelled *'t* in Late Biblical Hebrew (vocalized as *'att* or *'attā*) and Qumran, while in Rabbinic Hebrew and the Hexapla the two forms alternate; *'att* (feminine) is spelled *'ty* occasionally in Biblical Hebrew (always vocalized as **att*) and regularly in the Samaritan Pentateuch. Both *'t* (masculine) and *'ty* (feminine) are likely to have arisen under Aramaic influence, though dialectal intrusion cannot be ruled out for the earlier examples, especially in the case of *'ty*, which indicates the typologically earlier pronunciation **'attī*. As with certain verb forms (see §4.5.4.1), the masculine and feminine forms of the personal pronouns show a tendency to merge in Rabbinic Hebrew, so that *'attem* and *'atten*, on the one hand, and *hēm* and *hēn* (which has replaced Biblical Hebrew *hḗnnâ*), on the other, alternate in both the masculine and feminine.

The pronominal suffixes of the noun serve as the genitive of the personal pronoun when attached to substantives or prepositions (the latter corresponding most often to the dative or ablative in Indo-European and other languages), and the accusative when attached to verbs and certain particles:

(4) The pronominal suffixes on singular nouns

		Number	
Person	*Gender*	*Singular*	*Plural*
First	*Common*	-î	-ḗnû
Second	*Masculine*	-ĕkā	-kem
	Feminine	-ēk, ḗkî	-ken
Third	*Masculine*	-ô, -ḗhû	-ām
	Feminine	-āh, -'êhā (ָהָ-)	-ān

As noted, these suffixes are genitive. They are inflected for singular and plural number. In Biblical Hebrew, however, there seem to be isolated survivals of the Proto-Semitic dual pronouns, as preserved, for example in Ugaritic (Ch. 2, §4.3.1.2) and Arabic. These occur in passages where apparently masculine plural pronominal suffixes of the second or third person have feminine pairs as antecedents, such as 2 Samuel 6:7, 10, and 12, where *-hem* and other ostensibly masculine suffixes occur in place of *-hen*, and so forth, referring to the feminine antecedent *pārôt* "(a yoked pair of) cows"; to *-hem* compare the corresponding dual pronouns in Ugaritic, *-hm*, and Arabic, *-humā*.

The (genitive) pronominal suffixes for dual and plural nouns are presented in (5):

(5) The pronominal suffixes on plural nouns

		Number	
Person	*Gender*	*Singular*	*Plural*
First	*Common*	-ay	-ḗnû
Second	*Masculine*	-'êkā (ֶיךָ-)	-êkem
	Feminine	-áyik	-êken
Third	*Masculine*	-āyw	-êhem
	Feminine	-'êhā (ֶיהָ-)	-êhen

These suffixes are added to the noun stem, followed by the plural construct ending *-ê* (< **-ay*), originally the dual stem (see §4.2.4). This applies both to masculine (*dəbāráyik* "your (fem. sg.) words") and feminine (*ḥômôtáyik* "your (fem. sg.) walls") nouns.

In archaic and poetic contexts, the third-person masculine plural suffix has the variant *-ā́mô* on singular nouns and *-ḗmô* on plural nouns. There is also evidence of variant traditions in the pronunciation of the second-person masculine singular pronominal suffix. Although this suffix is consistently vocalized *-ḗkā* on both singular and plural nouns in Tiberian Hebrew, it is usually spelled with final *-k* (i.e., ך- not כה-), and the Hexaplaric form is consistently *-akh* (-αχ); taken together, these things point to a non-Masoretic pronunciation *-āk*, which corresponds to the Rabbinic Hebrew form. On the other hand, the antiquity of the Tiberian vocalization is confirmed by the heavy predominance of the spelling כה- at Qumran.

When one of the genitive suffixes is added to a noun, the stress in the resulting word usually shifts to the suffix, causing an alteration in the form of the noun stem as the result of vowel reduction in accordance with the rules summarized in §3.2.2.2. It follows that the form of the noun stem before suffixes is often similar or identical to the form of the noun stem in the construct state, which is typically altered by the same kind of shift of stress and consequent vowel reduction (see §4.2.4). Thus for the noun *dābār* "word," the corresponding forms are construct singular *dəbar′* "word (of)"; suffixed singular *dəbarkem* "your (masc. pl.) word"; construct plural *dibrê′* "words (of)"; and suffixed plural *dibrêkem* "your (masc. pl.) words."

In the suffixal forms of singular noun stems, variation may occur before the so-called *heavy* and *light* suffixes. The heavy suffixes are those beginning with a consonant, namely, *-kem* and *-ken*. In the case of the light suffixes, the noun ends with an open syllable, causing the stem-vowel to lengthen (cf. §3.4) – thus, *dəbarkem* "your (masc. pl.) word," but *dəbārĕkā* "your (masc. sg.) word"; *ḥômatkem* "your (masc. pl.) wall," but *ḥômātĕkā* "your (masc. sg.) wall."

In the suffixal forms of plural noun stems, the double reduction leading to *dibrê-*, the form required by the "rule of *šəwā*" (see §3.4), occurs only with the second- and third-personal plural suffixes (i.e., those which are bisyllabic and accented on the final syllable).

Although the suffixal forms of most noun stems are produced by these rules, there are numerous other variations, many predictable on historical grounds – such as, *ʿōz* (< **ʿuzz-*) "strength," suffixed form *ʿuzzəkem* "your strength" – others simply irregular – for example, *yād* (< **yad-*), heavy suffixed form *yedkem* "your hand." A few noun stems are unchanged by suffixation – thus, *sûs* "horse," suffixed form *sûsām*; *sûsîm* "horses," suffixed form *sûsḗhem*.

The attested forms of the pronominal suffixes when attached to the perfect verb are presented in (6):

(6) The pronominal suffixes on perfect verbs

		Number	
Person	*Gender*	*Singular*	*Plural*
First	*Common*	-ánî	-ā́nû
Second	*Masculine*	-əkā, -ĕkā	-kem
	Feminine	-ēk	—
Third	*Masculine*	-ô, -ā́hû	-ām
	Feminine	-āh	-an

As noted, these are object suffixes. The forms shown are those used when the suffix is stressed and follows a verbal stem ending in a consonant, such as *šəlāḥánî* "he sent me." The forms are slightly different when the suffix is unstressed and/or when following a stem ending in a vowel – thus, *šəlāḥátnî* "she sent me," *šəlaḥtî́nî* "you (fem. sg.) sent me."

The attested forms of the (accusative) pronominal suffixes when attached to the imperfect verb are presented below.

(7) The pronominal suffixes on imperfect verbs

		Number	
Person	*Gender*	*Singular*	*Plural*
First	*Common*	-ḗnî, énnî	-ḗnû, -énnû
Second	*Masculine*	-əkā, -ékkā	-kem
	Feminine	-ḗk	—
Third	*Masculine*	-ḗhû, énnû	-ēm
	Feminine	-éhā, -énnâ	-ēn

In the case of the imperfect, the object pronouns follow *-ḗ-* or *-ḗn-*, which is suffixed to the verbal stem. The forms with *-nn-* suggest a derivation from the Proto-Northwest Semitic energic (see §4.5.2).

4.3.2 Demonstrative pronouns

In Hebrew the demonstrative pronouns are inflected for gender and number. The common forms of the near ("this, these") and far ("that, those") demonstratives are listed in (8):

(8)

		Singular	*Plural*
Near demonstrative	*Masculine*	zeh	'ḗlleh
	Feminine	zō(')t	'ḗlleh
Far demonstrative	*Masculine*	hû'	hēm
	Feminine	hî'	hḗnnâ

Note that the far demonstratives are identical to the independent personal pronouns of the third person. The masculine and feminine singular far demonstratives showed an early tendency to merge, so that the feminine form is spelled *hw'* throughout the Pentateuch, though it is consistently vocalized *hî'* by the Masoretes. The forms *zōh* and *zô* appear in Biblical Hebrew as rare variants of *zō(')t*, and *zô* became the regnant form in Rabbinic Hebrew. The longer forms *hallaz* ("this," common), *hallā́zeh* ("this," masculine), and *hallēzû́* ("this," feminine), which occur in Biblical Hebrew as rare synonyms of *zeh* and *zō(')t*, constitute in Rabbinic Hebrew a full alternate paradigm of the near demonstrative, to which *hallā́lû* ("these," common) provides the plural.

The demonstratives are used as both pronouns and adjectives, and, as adjectives, they are subject to the same rules of gender agreement and definiteness as other adjectives – compare *zeh hā'îš* "this is the man," to *hā'îš hazzeh* "this man" (on the article see §4.4).

4.3.3 Relative pronouns

The common relative pronoun in Biblical Hebrew is *'ăšer*, which is indeclinable. Less often, in Archaic Hebrew and especially in Late Biblical Hebrew, the proclitic form *še-* (with gemination of the following consonant if possible) is found instead. In Rabbinic Hebrew this form replaces *'ăšer* almost entirely. Occasionally, and almost exclusively in poetry, *zeh* and *zû* are used as relatives (Psalm 74:2; Isaiah 42:24), recalling their derivation from the old relative-determinative pronoun *ð- (see Appendix 1, §3.3.4).

These forms are of disparate origin. Voiceless and voiced relative particles, *θ- and *ð-, must be posited for Proto-Northwest Semitic. The former (*θ-) is the base of the Hebrew relative *še-*, as well as Standard Phoenician and Ammonite *'š-* and Phoenician-Punic *š-* (see Ch. 4, §4.3.5). The latter (*ð-), as noted, underlies the relative use of Hebrew *z-*. Hebrew *'ăšer* and Moabite *'šr* are thought to have arisen from a form of the substantive **'aθr-* "place."

It is probable that the variation in Hebrew between *'ăšer* and *še-* was originally dialectal, the former, shared by Moabite, having been the southern (Judahite or at least Jerusalemite) form, and the latter, which has cognates in Phoenician and Ammonite, having been the northern (Israelite) form.

4.3.4 Interrogative and indefinite pronouns

The interrogative pronouns are *mî* "who?" and *mah* "what?" Neither is inflected for gender or number. In comparison to Common Semitic **man* "who," Hebrew *mî* is an innovation (**mi:y-*) shared with Ugaritic (*my*), Old Canaanite (cf. *mi-ya* in EA 85:63; 94:12 and 116:67), Phoenician (*my*), and probably Ammonite (*m-*). The first consonant of the word following *mah* is doubled when possible (otherwise the vocalization of *mah* may be affected). This suggests that although the *-h* in the Tiberian spelling of *mah* (מָה) is a *mater* (see §2.2), the primitive form may have been **mah* (with consonantal *-h*), especially in light of Ugaritic *mh* "what?" (see Ch. 2, §4.3.4.1).

Both *mî* and *mah* are used as indefinite pronouns in the sense of "whoever" and "whatever": for example, *mî yārē' wəḥārēd yāšōb* "whoever is fearful and trembling, let him turn back" (Judges 7:3). When *mî* and *mah* are used as indefinites in Rabbinic Hebrew they are usually augmented by the relative *še-* (see §4.3.3) and preceded by the proclitic substantive *kol'* – thus, *kol-mî še-* "whoever," and *kol-mah še-* "whatever."

The Proto-Semitic interrogative **'ayy-* (see Appendix 1, §3.3.4), from which a group of Hebrew interrogative adverbs is derived (*'ayy-* + pronominal suffix "where?"; *'ayyēh* "where?"; *'êk* "how?" etc.), was combined with the near demonstratives in Rabbinic Hebrew to produce another series of interrogative pronouns/adjectives: *'êzeh*, *'êzehû* "who? which?" (masculine singular); *'êzô*, *'êzōhî* "who? which?" (fem. sg.); *'êlû* "who? which? (common pl.) – compare *'ê-zeh* "which?" already in Ecclesiastes 2:3 and 11:6.

4.4 The article

The Hebrew definite article is prefixed directly to the noun it determines (on determination of substantives, see §5.4). The usual form of the article is *ha-* with gemination of the following consonant: for example, *hammélek* "the king." When gemination is not possible, as in the case of nouns with initial guttural consonants or *r* (see §3.3.2), and in certain other circumstances, there is alternation of the length or quality of the vowel of the article itself. Like other Semitic languages, Hebrew lacks an indefinite article.

4.5 Verbal morphology

Finite Hebrew verbs have two indicative forms, which contrast aspectually as perfective and imperfective (for the Proto-Northwest Semitic origins of the Hebrew indicatives, see §4.5.1). Both forms have three persons, two genders and two numbers (singular and plural). The *perfect* is inflected by the modification of a verbal stem through the addition of suffixes indicating person, gender, and number – thus, *stem* + *suffix*. The *imperfect* is inflected by modification of a related verbal stem through the addition of (i) prefixes indicating person and sometimes gender and (ii) suffixes indicating number and sometimes gender – thus, *prefix* + *stem* + *suffix*. The perfect stem for transitive-active verbs of the simple conjugation (Qal) is **qāṭal*, while the imperfect stem is **qṭōl*; both of these change slightly when inflected (for the inflections, see §§4.5.4.1–2).

Like other Semitic languages, Hebrew verbs have a number of different stem patterns with a diversity of contrasting forms that signify semantic variations in relation to the basic meaning of the verbal root. These patterns (see §4.5.5) are conventionally called *conjugations*, and, more specifically, *derived* conjugations, since they are produced by the application of certain morphological and phonological changes to the simple stem, traditionally known as Qal (*qal* "light, easy, simple") in Hebrew. Note that the term "conjugations" is retained here because of its conventional use in modern grammars, despite the lack of correspondence of the Hebrew verbal stems to the conjugations of the languages – principally Latin – from which the term derives; the term *binyānîm* "structures," used by the medieval grammarians is more descriptive.

In addition to the indicatives, Hebrew has certain modal verb forms, including a command imperative as well as a cohortative and a jussive, both of which are primarily volitional in force (see §4.5.2). There are also a number of nonfinite verbal forms (see §4.5.3).

4.5.1 The aspects of the indicative verb

The perfect verb is *punctual* in aspect, while the imperfect is *durative.* In most cases, the perfect expresses a completed action, so that it may be translated with a verb in the simple past tense – thus, *kātábtî* "I wrote." With verbs denoting dispositions or perceptions acquired in the past but still held or felt, a present-tense translation may be required – thus, *yādáʿtî* "I know" (i.e, "I have come to know"); *bāṭáḥtî* "I trust" ("I have come to trust"). With stative verbs, the best translation may employ a predicate adjective – thus, *zāqántî* "I am old" ("I have grown old, aged"). The so-called *performative* perfect, employed in indirect speech and especially when the speaker is someone with authority, is used to indicate that the action expressed in the verb is accomplished by the very fact of its utterance – thus, *ʾāmártî* "I say" ("proclaim, declare"). By contrast, the imperfect expresses an action that is incomplete and ongoing or still to be accomplished in the future, so that it may be translated with a verb in the present or future tense – thus, *ʾektōb* might be rendered "I write," "I will write," or "I keep writing" (habitually or repeatedly). In Rabbinic Hebrew the aspectual character of the verbal system has weakened substantially, moving in the direction of a true tense system, with the perfect becoming predominantly a past-tense form and the imperfect taking on a modal character, while the principal burden of expressing the present and future tenses is assumed by the participle.

A verbal feature that is especially distinctive of Biblical Hebrew (though attested in early inscriptions in other Northwest Semitic languages) is the existence of the *converted* imperfect and perfect, which form the basic fabric of the narrative sequences in Biblical Hebrew (see §5.2.1). In these sequences converted imperfects, which are marked by a distinctive form of the conjunction (*wa-* + junctural doubling), have the punctual translational value of the perfect: thus, *wattṓʾmer śāray ʾel-ʾābrām . . . wayyišmaʿ ʾābram ləqôl śāráy wattiqaḥ śāray . . .* "and Sarai said to Abram . . . and Abram listened to the voice of Sarai, and Sarai took . . . " (Genesis 16:1–3). Converted perfects, which are also joined to the conjunction (in this case with its ordinary forms), have the durative translation value of the imperfect: for example, *wəʿālâ hāʾîš* "and the man used to go up" (1 Samuel 1:3).

The converted imperfect exhibits a tendency, shared by the jussive (see §§3.5 and 4.5.2), to retract the tone from the final syllable of the verb (except in first-person forms), resulting in a shortening or collapse of the end of the word in certain forms found among the weak verbs (see §4.5.4.2) and the derived conjugations (see §4.5.5) – thus, indicative *yāqûm* "he arises"; jussive *yā́qōm* "let him arise"; converted imperfect *wayyā́qom* "and he arose." There is a tendency in the converted perfect, operative in first- and second-person singular forms, to shift the tone forward to the ultima (without a corresponding change in vocalization) – thus, perfect *kātábtā* "you wrote," converted perfect *wəkātabtā́* "and you will write."

The origin of the converted verb forms can be explained with reference to distinctive developments that took place in early Hebrew in relationship to its antecedents. The indicative verbal system of Proto-Northwest Semitic had three forms: (i) **qatala,* a perfective, which expressed completed actions, usually in the past, but which (like its descendant, Hebrew *qātal*) also had a number of present-future uses; (ii) **yaqtulu,* an imperfective, which was used for habitual or durative actions but also served to express the present and future "tenses"; and (iii) * *yaqtul*, a perfective, which functioned both as a jussive and as a preterite, in other words, to express simple past actions (a past "tense"). With the loss of final short vowels, **yaqtulu* and the two types of **yaqtul* fell together as **yaqtul*, the antecedent of Hebrew **yiqtōl* (see §3.6.2). This form became the ordinary Hebrew imperfect, retaining the present-future force of **yaqtulu*, but the jussive force of **yaqtul* was also preserved in *yiqtōl*. The preterite force was lost, however, except in certain restricted environments, most characteristically the converted imperfect *wayyiqtōl*. In most other situations the preterite role of **yaqtul* was appropriated by the perfect, *qātal* (< **qatal* < **qatala*). The converted perfect may have arisen by analogy with the converted imperfect, but it is unlikely that this would have happened were it not for the other present-future uses that *qātal* inherited from **qatala*.

Among the most important differences between Biblical Hebrew and Rabbinic Hebrew is the loss of the system of converted imperfects and perfects, completing a trend already observable in Late Biblical Hebrew.

4.5.2 Command forms (the imperative and cohortative/jussive system)

In addition to the two indicatives, Hebrew has three principal modal forms, which are based on the imperfect and, when taken together, constitute a loose system expressing command and volition. The Hebrew imperative, which exists in the second person only, is formed by distinctive suffixes indicating gender and number attached to the imperfect stem without its prefixes. The imperative expresses direct command.

Both the cohortative and jussive express volition and resolve, though the jussive can also be described as an indirect command form, and, in combination with the adverbial particle *'al* (*'al + jussive*), it serves as the negative imperative. The cohortative (first person) and jussive (second and especially third person) are formed from the imperfect stem by the addition of distinctive prefixes expressing person and sometimes gender, and suffixes expressing number and sometimes gender. As noted above (§§3.5 and §4.5.1) there is a tendency in the jussive, observable in certain forms found among the weak verbs (see §4.5.4.2) and the derived conjugations (see §4.5.5), to retract the tone from the final syllable of the verb, resulting in a shortening or collapse of the end of the word in comparison to the indicative. The jussive-imperative-cohortative system for the simple stem (Qal) of the strong verbs is shown in (9) (the second-person jussive is not included).

(9)

		Number	
Form	*Gender*	*Singular*	*Plural*
Jussive	*Masculine*	yiktōb "let him write"	yiktəbû "let them write"
	Feminine	tiktōb "let her write"	tiktóbnâ "let them write"
Imperative	*Masculine*	kətōb "write"	kitbû "write"
	Feminine	kitbî "write"	kətóbnâ "write"
Cohortative	*Common*	'ektəbâ "let me write"	niktəbâ "let us write"

In terms of their historical origin, the jussive and imperative are descended directly from the jussive and imperative of Proto-Northwest Semitic – thus, jussive *yiqtōl* < **yaqtul* and imperative *qətōl* < **qutul* (the development of the former is described in §4.5.1). The cohortative is a partial survival of a volitional subjunctive: *'eqtəlâ* < **'aqtula*. Proto-Northwest Semitic also had an energic with the form **yaqtulanna*, similar in force to the subjunctive and thus to the Hebrew jussive and cohortative. Relics of this form may survive in (i) the so-called *nûn energicum*, a tone-bearing syllable with the form *-én-* (raised under stress from **-án-*, which is sometimes preserved before the first-person singular suffix) that may be inserted before the pronominal suffixes of the imperfect (e.g., *wə'ešmərénnâ* "and I will keep it," Psalm 119:34) and (ii) the *-nā'* particle often used to strengthen cohortatives, jussives with optative force, and imperatives, especially in the rhetoric of courteous speech (e.g., *tədabbēr-nā' šipḥātəkā 'el-'ădōnî hammélek* "Let your maidservant speak to my lord the king," 2 Samuel 14:12).

In Rabbinic Hebrew the special lengthened cohortative forms and shortened jussive forms disappear almost entirely (expanding a tendency already observable in the Samaritan Pentateuch), and the feminine plural imperative *kətóbnâ* is lost, leaving *kitbû* as the common form. In general, the use of the imperative is much more restricted than in Biblical Hebrew.

4.5.3 Verbal nouns

Hebrew has two participles, active and passive. As noted in §4.2.5.2, the active participle of the simple verbal stem (Qal) has the form *qôtēl* (< **qātil*), feminine *qōtəlâ* (< **qātilat*) and *qōtélet* (< **qātilt*) – thus, *kōtēb* (etc.) "writing." The Qal passive participle is formed from active verbal roots using the form *qātûl* (< **qatūl*) – thus, *kātûb* "written."

As in certain other Semitic languages, such as Akkadian and Ugaritic, Hebrew forms an infinitive of the simple stem – the G-stem (*Grundstamm*) or Hebrew Qal – from the nominal pattern **qatāl*. By normal phonological developments this infinitive, which is known as the *infinitive absolute*, has the form *qātôl* in Hebrew. In contrast to the situation in Akkadian (though in common with Ugaritic) the Hebrew reflex of this infinitive is not inflected, and it surrenders the ordinary infinitive functions to a second infinitive, known as the *infinitive construct*, which has the form *qətôl* (though the Qal infinitive construct has the form of the construct state of the Qal infinitive absolute (*qətôl* ~ *qātôl*), it does not function as its construct, and the terminology should not lead to confusion with the construct and absolute states of ordinary nouns). Thus, the infinitive construct is the true Hebrew infinitive, while the infinitive absolute is primarily adverbial in function, serving most characteristically to emphasize the verbal idea of the finite verb that it immediately precedes or follows: for example, *dārōš dāraš mōšeh* "Moses sought diligently" (Leviticus 10:16). Otherwise, the infinitive absolute is used to suggest the verbal idea in a general way, even occasionally serving as an uninflected substitute for a finite verb, in which case it derives its "inflection" from that of preceding verbs in a sequence: thus, *ûmāṣā́'tā 'et-ləbābô ne'ĕmān ləpānêkā wəkārôt 'immô habbərît* "and you found his heart faithful before you and cut a covenant with him" (Nehemiah 9:8).

In Rabbinic Hebrew, the infinitive absolute is lost entirely, and the infinitive construct occurs almost exclusively with prefixed *lə-*.

4.5.4 Verb inflection

4.5.4.1 *The sound verb*

The perfect and imperfect verbs of the simple stem (Qal) formed from sound roots are conjugated as shown in (10) and (11). Variations in these paradigms occur when one of the root consonants is a guttural, in accordance with the special phonological rules that obtain in the environment of gutturals (see §3.3.2):

(10) The Qal perfect verb

		Number	
Person	*Gender*	*Singular*	*Plural*
Third	*Masculine*	kātab "he wrote"	kātəbû "they wrote"
	Feminine	kātəbâ "she wrote"	kātəbû "they wrote"
Second	*Masculine*	kātábtā "you wrote"	kətabtem "you wrote"
	Feminine	kātabt "you wrote"	kətabten "you wrote"
First	*Common*	kātábtî "I wrote"	kātábnû "we wrote"

(11) The Qal imperfect verb

		Number	
Person	*Gender*	*Singular*	*Plural*
Third	*Masculine*	yiktōb "he writes"	yiktəbû "they write"
	Feminine	tiktōb "she writes"	tiktóbnâ "they write"
Second	*Masculine*	tiktōb "you write"	tiktəbû "you write"
	Feminine	tiktəbî "you write"	tiktóbnâ "you write"
First	*Common*	'ektōb "I write"	niktōb "we write"

Though it is always vocalized in the Masoretic Text as shown above, the ending of the second-person masculine singular perfect is most often written without a final *hē'* in the Masoretic Text and Rabbinic Hebrew – thus, *ktbt* rather than *ktbth* (the usual Qumran form) – indicating a pronunciation **katabt*, which is also the more common form in the Hexapla (cf. the situation with the corresponding personal pronoun, §4.3.1). The second-person feminine singular perfect, though always vocalized as shown, is sometimes spelled with final *yôd*, indicating a pronunciation **katábtî* (cf., again, the corresponding personal pronoun, §4.3.1). In Rabbinic Hebrew, as part of the general tendency for final *-n* to replace final *-m* (see §3.1.2 and §4.2.2), the gender distinction in the second-person plural perfect is obscured, with *kətabten* becoming the common form. In Late Biblical Hebrew and Rabbinic Hebrew, the third- and second-person feminine imperfect forms coalesce with the corresponding masculine forms, *yiqtəlû* and *tiktəbû*, and the older form, *tiqtólnâ*, is lost.

The paradigm verb used here (*kātab* "write") belongs to the *a* ~ *u* vowel class, meaning that in its antecedent form the theme-vowel for the perfect was **a* (**kataba* → *kātab*) and the theme-vowel for the imperfect was **u* (**yaktub-* → *yiktōb*). As in other Semitic languages, however, Hebrew verbs are distributed among several vowel classes, which correspond generally to their semantic character. The principal theme-vowel patterns in Hebrew are listed in Table 3.4 (the paradigm verbs used are *kātab* "write," *nātan* "give," *šākab* "lie down," *qārab* "draw near," *zāqēn* "grow old," and *qāṭōn* "be small").

4.5.4.2 The weak verbs

The inflection of the Hebrew verb is modified under certain conditions: (i) when the second and third root consonants are identical ("geminate" verbs); (ii) when the initial root consonant is *n-* (I-*n*); (iii) when one of the root consonants is a guttural (I-, II-, or III-G); or (iv) when one of the original root consonants was a glide, **w* or **y* (*I-, *II- or *III-*w*; I-, *II- or *III-*y*). The following synopsis enumerates the most important changes that occur during the inflection of these *weak verbs*, as they are customarily called.

The distinctive feature of the perfect of geminate verbs is the interposition of *-ō-* before verbal suffixes beginning with a consonant – thus, *sābəbâ* "she went around," but *sabbṓtā* "you went around." This feature is Proto-Semitic in origin. Though the imperfect displays

Table 3.4 The vowel classes of Hebrew verbs

Theme vowels	Aspect	Hebrew form	Antecedent form	Description
a, u	PERFECT	*kātab*	**kataba*	A large class of primarily active-transitive
	IMPERFECT	*yiktōb*	**yaktub-*	verbs. III-guttural tended to become (*a, a*^{1}).
a, i	PERFECT	*nātan*	**natana*	A large class with no semantic restrictions,
	IMPERFECT	*yittēn*	**yantin-*	but lost in Hebrew except for a few verbs.
a, a^1	PERFECT	*šākab*	**šakaba*	An active-intransitive class, which falls
	IMPERFECT	*yiškab*	**yiškab-*	together formally with the stative (*a, a*) class.
a, a^2	PERFECT	*qārab*	**qaraba*	A small stative class, enlarged by original
	IMPERFECT	*yiqrab*	**yiqrab-*	(*i, a*) and (*u, a*) verbs with guttural roots.
i, a	PERFECT	*zāqēn*	**zaqina*	A large, primarily stative-intransitive class.
	IMPERFECT	*yizqan*	**yizqan-*	Many II- and III-gutturals became (*a, a*).
u, a	PERFECT	*qāṭōn*	**qaṭuna*	A small stative class, originally *(*u, u*), but
	IMPERFECT	*yiqṭan*	**yiqṭan-*	transformed by resistance to stative **yaqtul*.

wide variation, the basic forms are predictable from normal phonological changes – thus, *yāsōb* (< **yasubbu*) "he goes around."

I-*n* verbs are inflected normally in the perfect and in the imperfect indicative, except that in the latter case the expected assimilation of *n*- to the second radical occurs – thus, *yiddōr* (< **yaddur* < **yandur-*) "he vows" (*a, u*); *yittēn* (< **yittin* < **yantin-*) "he gives" (*a, i*); and *yiggaš* (< **yiggaš* < **yangaš-*) "he draws near" (*a, a*). In the (*a, a*) type, the imperative is usually shortened (*gaš*), and the "normal" form of the infinitive construct alternates with a short form with *-t* (*géšet*; see §4.2.5.1). The imperative and infinitive construct corresponding to *yittēn* are *tēn* and *tēt*. Perhaps because it is the antonym of *nātan* "give," the common verb *lāqaḥ* "take" has come to be inflected as if it were I-*n* in its imperfect and related forms – thus, *yiqqaḥ* (imperfect), *qaḥ* (imperative) and *qáḥat* (infinitive construct).

The perfect of I-G verbs presents no special problems, with the *ḥāṭēp*-vowel *ă* replacing simple *šəwā* (ə) as necessary (see §3.3.2) – thus, *ʿămadtem* "you stood." The imperfect appears in two forms according to the vowel classes of the verbal stems – thus, *yaʿămōd* "he stands" (*a, u*) and *yeḥĕzaq* "he is strong" (*a, a*). As noted in §3.6.2, the change of the imperfect prefix **ya-* → *yi-* took place first in verbs with *a* as the imperfect theme-vowel (**yaqtal* → *yiqtal*) and was subsequently extended to the other verbs. These two I-G forms reflect the intermediate stage – thus, *yaʿămōd* < **yaʿmud*, but *yeḥĕzaq* < **yiḥzaq* < **yaḥzaq*. Many I-ʾ verbs generally follow the pattern of other I-G verbs, but with *ĕ* in imperfect prefixes for (*a, u*) as well as (*a, a*) stems – as in *yeʾĕsōp* "he gathers." In some I-ʾ verbs, however, the /ʔ/ quiesced at an early date in postvocalic positions, leading to the lengthening of the prefix-vowel and the development of forms like *yō(ʾ)mar* "he says."

Despite a few peculiarities, verbs II-G and III-G present no major divergences from the strong verb paradigm. In III-ʾ verbs the quiescence of word- or syllable-final /ʔ/ has led to the lengthening of the preceding *a* to *ā* (but not *ō*, as explained in §3.6.1) in perfect forms like *bārā(ʾ)* "he created" and *bārā́(ʾ)tî* "I created." Similarly in III-ʾ imperfects, the stem vowel, which is *a* as usual in gutturals, is lengthened after the loss of /ʔ/ – thus, *yibrā(ʾ)* "he creates."

Most verbs I-*y* were originally *I-*w*. As noted in §4.1, some of these, such as √*yšb* "sit" (*a, i*), have very ancient root allomorphs, with and without *w*- – thus, √**wθb* and √**θb*, leading to a mixture of forms like perfect *yāšab* (< **waθaba*) "he sat," imperfect *yēšēb* (< **yiθib-*) "he sits," and imperative *šēb* (< * *θib*) "sit." In general, however, I-*y* verbs are regular in their inflection. As in I-*n* verbs of the (*a*, *a*) type, there is usually shortening of the imperative – thus, *rēd* "go down"; *ṣē'* "go forth"; *dāʿ* "know" – and the infinitive construct, which is augmented with -*t* – thus, *rédet* "to go down"; *ṣē(')t* "to go forth"; *dáʿat* "to know" (see §4.2.5.1).

When inflected, verbs II-*w/y*, the so-called hollow roots, behave as if biradical. In the perfect the inflectional endings are added to a biconsonantal stem – thus, *qām* "he arose," *qā́mâ* "she arose," *qámtā* "you arose," and so forth. In the imperfect, the distinction between verbs II-*w* and II-*y* becomes evident – thus, *yāqûm* "he arises," but *yāśîm* "he places." The jussive forms of these verbs are distinctive – *yāqōm* and *yāśēm* – and the converted imperfect employs the same forms, with retraction of the stress – *wayyā́qom* and *wayyā́śem*. The imperfect–jussive contrast is probably a survival of the Proto-Northwest Semitic situation (see §4.3.1 and §4.3.2), later vowel length being determined by whether the syllable was open or closed – thus, imperfect **yaqūmu* → *yāqûm*, but jussive **yaqum* → *yāqōm*. In later periods the hollow verbs tend to assimilate to triradical patterning, giving rise to forms like Late Biblical Hebrew Piʿel *qiyyam* "it established" (Esther 9:32) and Rabbinic Hebrew Piʿel *qiyyêm*.

III-*w*/*y* verbs are inflected according to a single paradigm regardless of the original final consonant (**w* or **y*) or vowel class. Thus, for example, the III-*y* (*a*, *i*) verb *bānâ* "build" – *bānâ* (< **banaya*) "he built," and *yibneh* (< **yabniyu*) "he builds" – has the same Hebrew forms as the III-*w* (*i*, *a*) verb *ḥāyâ* "live" – *ḥāyâ* (< **ḥayiwa*) "he lived," and *yiḥyeh* (< **yiḥyawu*) "he lives." The jussive (and converted imperfect) form is apocopated with retracted stress and (variable) anaptyxis – thus, *yíben* (< **yibn* < **yabni* < **yabniy*) "let him build"; and *tíreṣ* (< **tirṣ* < * *tirṣa* < **tarðaw*) "let her be pleased"; but *yēbk* (< **yibk* < * *yabki* < **yabkiy*) "let him weep"; and *yēšt* (< **yišt* < **yišta* < * *yištay*) "let him drink."

4.5.5 The derived conjugations

As noted in §4.5, there are several stem patterns, known as "derived conjugations" or *binyānîm*, by which semantic variety is derived from verbal roots. The most common *binyānim*, which are traditionally named for the corresponding third-person masculine singular perfect form of the verbal root √*pʿl*, are called Nipʿal, Piʿel, Puʿal, Hipʿil, Hopʿal and Hitpaʿel. Few, if any, Hebrew verbs are attested in all of these forms. In addition to these six, there is a special set used for II-*w/y* verbs, and a small additional group that occur relatively seldom. A synopsis of the forms of the derived conjugations in relation to the Qal verb is given in (12):

(12) Synopsis of the basic conjugations

	Perfect	*Imperfect*	*Imperative*	*Infinitive absolute*	*Infinitive construct*	*Participle*
Qal	qātal	yiqtōl	qətōl	qātôl	qətōl	qōtēl
Nipʿal	niqtal	yiqqātēl	hiqqātēl	niqtōl	hiqqātēl	niqtāl
Piʿel	qittēl	yəqattēl	qattēl	qattōl	qattēl	məqattēl
Puʿal	quttal	yəquttal	—	quttōl	—	məquttāl
Hipʿil	hiqtîl	yaqtîl	haqtēl	haqtēl	haqtîl	maqtîl
Hopʿal	hoqtal	yoqtal	—	hoqtēl	—	moqtāl
Hitpaʿel	hitqattēl	yitqattēl	hitqattēl	hitqattēl	hitqattēl	mitqattēl

4.5.5.1 *Nip'al*

The Nip'al is formed by the prefixation of *n-* to the verbal stem – thus perfect *niqtal* (<**naqtala*) and imperfect *yiqqātēl* (<**yanqatil-*). In addition to *niqtôl* (see [12]), which in light of the comparative Semitic evidence is probably the original form of the infinitive absolute, two other forms occur, *hiqqātôl*, the *ō* of which may have arisen by analogy with Pi'el *qattōl*, and *hiqqātēl*, which is identical to the form of the infinitive construct.

The meaning of the *Nip'al* is mediopassive. In origin it may have served to give intransitive-stative force to transitive-active verbs in Qal, to which it remains close inflectionally, and this early meaning is preserved in its frequently fientic character – as in Qal *rā'â* "he saw" ~ Nip'al *nir'â* "he appeared" (i.e., "he became visible"). With the loss or obscuration of the Qal passive, however, the Nip'al absorbed the role of the primary passive correspondent of Qal – thus, Qal *'āsar* "he bound, imprisoned" ~ Nip'al (imperfect) *yē'āsēr* "he will be bound, imprisoned" (Genesis 42:19). With other transitive Qal verbs, the voice of the corresponding Nip'al may be middle rather than passive: for example, Qal *'āsap* "he gathered" (transitive) ~ Nip'al (plural) *ne'ĕspû* "they gathered"; compare *ûpəlištîm ne'ĕspû ləhillāḥēm 'im-yiśrā'ēl* "And the Philistines gathered to fight with Israel" (1 Samuel 13:5). Finally, the Nip'al sometimes has reflexive force – thus, Qal *mākar* "he sold" ~ Nip'al *nimkar* "he sold himself."

4.5.5.2 *Pi'el*

The Pi'el is formed by doubling of the second radical – *qittēl* (< **qattila* or **qattala*), *yəqattēl* (<**yuqattil-*). Predictable phonological changes occur when the second radical cannot be doubled because it is a guttural (see §3.3.2), and there is a special conjugational system for verbs II-*w/y* (see §4.5.5.7).

The basic and original meaning of the Pi'el is factitive (transitivizing), as applied to verbs that are intransitive or stative in the Qal – thus, Qal *ḥāzaq* "be strong" ~ Pi'el *ḥizzaq* "strengthen, fortify." With active-transitive verbs, the Pi'el may pluralize the Qal meaning, so that the effect is intensive or iterative – thus, Qal *nātaq* "tear away, pull off" ~ Pi'el *nittēq* "tear apart, rip out"; Qal *šābar* "break" ~ Pi'el *šibbar* "shatter." For many verbs that occur in both Qal and Pi'el, however, the difference in meaning is subtle or unclear, though the lexicons tend to try to specify an intensifying nuance for the Pi'el. With certain active-transitive verbs, the Pi'el seems to be the causative of the Qal: for example, Qal *lāmad* "learn" ~ Pi'el *limmad* "cause to learn, teach." This is the role of the Hip'il with active-transitive verbs, however, and most such Pi'els may in fact be denominative. In any case, the Pi'el is especially productive of denominatives: thus, *qinnē'* "be jealous" (from *qin'â* "jealousy"); *'ippēr* "cast dust on" (from *'āpār* "dust").

4.5.5.3 *Pu'al*

The Pu'al, like the Pi'el, is formed by doubling of the second radical, but it is distinguished from the Pi'el by its *u-a* vowel patterning, which persists throughout the paradigm – thus, *quttal* (<**quttala*), *yəquttal* (<**yuquttal-*), and so forth. When the second radical cannot be doubled, the changes that occur are the same as those for the Pi'el (see §4.5.5.2).

The Pu'al functions as the passive of the Pi'el. It is used relatively infrequently except in its participial form, which serves as the passive participle of the Pi'el: for example, Pi'el infinitive construct *qaddēš* "to consecrate" ~ Pu'al participle *məquddāš* "consecrated." In Rabbinic Hebrew the Pu'al survives only as a participle.

4.5.5.4 *Hitpa'el*

The Hitpa'el is distinguished by prefixed *t*- and, like the Pi'el and Pu'al, the doubling of the second radical. In contrast to the other conjugations, however, the Hitpa'el seems to follow the pattern of the imperfect in the inflection of the perfect, imperative, and infinitives. In these same forms the preformative takes the shape *hit*-, the *hi*- possibly having arisen under the influence of the Hip'il. When the first root consonant is one of the dental stops (see §3.1.1), the prefixed *t*- is assimilated – as in *yiṭṭāmē'* (< **yitṭāmē'*) "he defiles himself." When the first root consonant is a sibilant (see §3.1.1), the *t*- metathesizes with it for the sake of euphony – *yištakkəḥû* (< **yitšakkəḥû*) "they were forgotten" (Ecclesiastes 8:10). When the second radical cannot be doubled, the changes that occur are the same as those for the Pi'el (see §4.5.5.2).

The Hitpa'el is intransitive in meaning. Most characteristically, it gives reflexive (or reciprocal) force to an active form of same verb – thus, Pi'el *qiddēš* "consecrate" ~ Hitpa'el *hitqaddēš* "sanctify oneself." In addition, it is often iterative – as in Qal *hālak* "walk" ~ Hitpa'el *hithallēk* "walk back and forth" – and sometimes denominative – *hitnabbē'* "prophesy" (from *nābî'* "prophet").

Though the Hitpa'el is morphologically related to the Pi'el and Pu'al by the common feature of the doubled second radical, the active verbs to which it corresponds are not always Pi'el but may be Qal or Hip'il as well. This points to the likely historical background of the Hitpa'el as a composite conjugation produced by the merger of the prefixed *t*-forms of verbal roots of the simple, factitive, and causative stems. Remnants of an original *t*-form of the simple stem are recognizable in a few Hitpa'els that lack doubling of the second radical: for example, *hitpāqədû* "they mustered" (Judges 20:17)

In Rabbinic Hebrew the Hitpa'el was largely replaced, at least in the perfect, by the Nitpa'el (properly Nitpa'al), a new conjugation created by fusion of the Hitpa'el with the Nip'al, which could also have reflexive meaning (see §4.5.5.1).

4.5.5.5 *Hip'il*

The formal marker of the Hip'il, found on the perfect, imperative, and infinitives, is prefixed *h*-. The long stem-vowel -*î*- is characteristic of both the perfect and imperfect, but the jussive has the expected -*ē*- (*yaqtēl* < **yaqtil* < **yuhaqtil*), and the -*î*- must have arisen by analogy with the Hip'il of verbs II-*w/y* – compare jussive *yāsēr* (< **yasir* < **yuhasir*) "let him remove," to imperfect *yāsîr* (< **yasīr* < **yuhasīr-*) "he removes."

In general the Hip'il serves as the causative of the Qal. With intransitive or stative verbs it is singly causative: for example, Qal *lābēš* "be dressed" ~ Hip'il *hilbîš* "cause to be dressed, clothe." This is especially characteristic of verbs of motion – Qal *hālak* "go, walk" ~ Hip'il *hôlîk* "bring, lead." When the Qal is transitive, the Hip'il may be doubly causative: for example, Qal *yāda'* "know" ~ Hip'il *hôdîa'* "cause (someone) to know (something)" (cf. *wənôdî'â 'etkem dābār* "and we will apprise you of something" [1 Samuel 14:12]); Qal *rā'â* "see" ~ Hip'il *her'â* "cause (someone) to see (something)" (cf. *wayyar'ēm 'et-məbô' hā'îr* "and they showed them the entrance to the city" [Judges 1:25]). Sometimes, especially when the Qal is stative, the Hip'il may be fientic or otherwise intransitive, even in verbs that also have causative Hip'ils: Qal *'ārēk* "be long" ~ Hip'il *he'ĕrîk* "become long," but also "make long, prolong." Many of these Hip'ils are inchoative or inceptive – such as Qal *bā'aš* "stink"; Hip'il *hib'îš* "begin to stink, become stinking," but also "cause to stink." Like the Pi'el, though less characteristically so, the Hip'il may form denominatives: for example, *he'ĕzîn* "listen" (from *'ṓzen* "ear").

4.5.5.6 *Hopʿal*

Like the Hipʿil, its active counterpart, the Hopʿal is characterized by *h-* prefixed to the perfect. In contrast to the *hi-* preformative of the Hipʿil, however, the Hopʿal has the variants *ho-* and *hu-*; in Rabbinic Hebrew the option has been resolved in favor of the latter (often written plene, i.e., -הוּ), probably by analogy with the Puʿal (Piʿel : Puʿal :: Hipʿil : Hupʿal).

Semantically, the Hopʿal is the passive of the Hipʿil – thus, Hipʿil *hišlîk* "he threw" ~ Hopʿal *hošlak* "he was thrown."

4.5.5.7 *Polel, Polal, and Hitpolel*

Because most "hollow" verbs (II-*w/y)* are inflected as if they were biconsonantal (see §4.5.4.2 and note exceptions in Rabbinic Hebrew), they do not accept doubling of the second radical, the chief marker of the factitive conjugation group, Piʿel, Puʿal, and Hitpaʿel. In hollow verbs like √*qwm* "rise up," therefore, the functions of these conjugations are taken over by a group consisting of the Polel (active), Polal (passive), and Hitpolel (reflexive) conjugations. These are characterized formally by reduplication of the final stem consonant and *ō* in the first stem syllable – thus, Polel perfect *qômēm* "he raised up," and imperfect *yəqômēm* "he raises up"; Polal *qômam* "he was raised up," and *yəqômam* "he is raised up"; and Hitpolel *hitqômēm* "he raised himself up," and *yitqômēm* "he raises himself up." Geminates (§4.5.4.2) employ these forms on occasion, too, even in verbs for which the Piʿel group is also attested: for example, Piʿel imperfect *yəḥannēn qôlô* "he speaks favorably" (i.e., "makes his voice favorable"; Proverbs 26:25) ~ Polel imperfect *yəḥōnēnû* "they will treat favorably" (Psalm 105:15).

4.5.5.8 *Other conjugations*

There are several other *binyānîm*, some very sparsely attested. Some of the more important and better understood are listed here.

The series Poʿel (active), Poʿal (passive), and Hitpoʿel (reflexive) is similar to the Polel group (see §4.5.5.7), except that it forms verbs from sound roots – thus, Hitpoʿel *yitgōʿăšû máyim* "the waters surge" (√*gʿš* "shake") in Jeremiah 46:8, a duplicate of the preceding line with Hitpaʿel *yitgāʿăšû* "[its waters] surge"; also, *šōrēš* "he took root" (Isaiah 40:24), a Poʿel denominative from *šṓreš* "root" (contrast the meaning of the Piʿel denominative *wəšēreškā* "and he will uproot you," Psalm 52:7).

The series Pilpel (active), Polpal (passive), and Hitpalpel (reflexive) is characterized by reduplication of the two strong consonants of geminate and "hollow" verbs (II-*w/y*). Like the Polel and Poʿel groups, they correspond in meaning to the factitive (Piʿel) group – thus, *gilgēl* "roll" (√*gll* "roll"); *kilkēl* "maintain" (√*kwl* "hold").

The Paʿlal (active) and Puʿlal (passive) are quadriliterals formed by the reduplication of the third radical. Their meaning in either voice is stative – thus, *šaʾănan* "he has been at ease" (Jeremiah 48:11); *ʾumlal* "it is withered" (Joel 1:10).

4.6 Numerals

The Hebrew cardinals 1–10 are listed in (13).

(13)

	Modifying a masculine noun		Modifying a feminine noun	
	Absolute	*Construct*	*Absolute*	*Construct*
1	ʾeḥad	ʾaḥad	ʾaḥat	ʾaḥat
2	šənáyim	šənê	štáyim	štê
3	šəlōšâ	šəlṓšet	šālōš	šəlōš
4	ʾarbāʿâ	ʾarbáʿat	ʾarbaʿ	ʾarbaʿ
5	ḥămiššâ	ḥămḗšet	ḥāmēš	ḥămēš
6	šiššâ	šḗšet	šēš	šēš
7	šibʿâ	šibʿat	šébaʿ	šəbaʿ
8	šəmōnâ	šəmōnat	šəmōneh	šəmōneh
9	tišʿâ	tišʿat	tḗšaʿ	təšaʿ
10	ʿăśārâ	ʿăśéret	ʿéśer	ʿéśer

The cardinals may be associated with the nouns they modify in one of two ways: (i) appositionally, using the absolute form; or (ii) genitivally, using the construct form. The first two cardinals agree with the modified noun (the counted item) in gender. In the case of the cardinals 3–10, however, the form that is usually feminine elsewhere – that is, the form marked with *-â* (bound form *-at*) or *-t* (see §4.2.1) – modifies masculine nouns, while the unmarked form modifies feminine nouns, a peculiarity shared with most other Semitic languages (cf. Ch. 6, §3.3.7). The ʾteens are formed by placing the unit, which follows the gender rules stated above, before the word for ten (with special forms): for example, *šəlōšâ ʿāśār pārîm* "thirteen bulls" (Numbers 29:14).

The cardinal 20 is expressed by the plural of 10 (*ʿeśrîm*), and the other tens by the corresponding plurals of the units – thus, *šəlōšîm* "30," *ʾarbāʿîm* "40," *ḥămiššîm* "50," *šiššîm* "60," *šibʿîm* "70," *šəmōnîm* "80," and *tišʿîm* "90." Note that the tens are not inflected for gender and occur only in the absolute state. The numbers 21 to 99 are formed by placing the unit, which follows the gender rules stated above, before or after the ten – thus, *šəlōšâ wəʿeśrîm ʾîš or ʿeśrîm ûš(ə)lōšâ ʾîš* "23 men." The higher numbers include the following substantives: *mēʾâ* (bound form *mēʾat*) "(one) hundred"; *mā(ʾ)táyim* "200"; *šəlōš mēʾôt* "300"; *ʾélep* "(one) thousand"; *rəbābâ* "10,000."

The ordinal "first" is expressed by the adjective *rī(ʾ)šôn* (fem. *rī(ʾ)šōnâ*). The ordinals from "second" to "tenth" are formed by adding the sufformatives *-î* (masc.) and *-ît* (fem.) to the cardinal (cf. §4.2.5.4), following the general pattern **qətîlî* – thus, *šēnî* "second," *šəlîšî* "third," *rəbîʿî* "fourth" (without the prothetic *ʾa-* of *ʾarbaʿ*, "4"), *ḥămîšî* "fifth," *šiššî* "sixth," *šəbîʿî* "seventh," *šəmînî* "eighth," *təšîʿî* "ninth" and *ʿăśîrî* "tenth."

5. SYNTAX

5.1 Word order

The usual word order in the Hebrew verbal clause is Verb–Subject–Object (VSO) followed by prepositional phrases or other adverbial elements – thus:

(14) wayiṭṭaʿ yhwh ʾĕlōhîm gan-bəʿḗden
and-he planted Yahweh God garden-in-Eden
"And Yahweh-God planted a garden in Eden" (Genesis 2:8)

Although this generalization applies to subordinate as well as independent verbal clauses, exceptions are quite common, especially when some kind of emphasis is placed on the subject (→ SVO), for example,

(15) hannāḥāš hiššî'ánî
the-serpent deceived-me
"The serpent deceived me" (Genesis 3:13)

or on the object (→ OVS or VOS), as in:

(16) 'et-qōləkā šāmá'tî baggā́n,
DIR. OBJ.-voice-your I heard in-the-garden
"I heard your voice in the garden" (Genesis 3:10)

As the preceding example shows, a pronominal subject, since it is inherent in the verb, is not usually expressed, except, again, for emphasis:

(17) hî' nātənâ-lî min-hā'ēṣ
she she gave-me from-the-tree
"She gave me [fruit] from the tree" (Genesis 3:12)

As a rule, finite, indicative verbs are negated by *lō'*, while modal (cohortative or jussive) verbs are negated by *'al*. Regularly in prose and sometimes in poetry, the direct object is marked by the accusative particle *'ēt* (most often proclitic *'et-*), which precedes the accusative word or pronominal suffix (with the form *'ôtî*, etc., but *'etkem* and *'ethen*). An indirect object, marked by the preposition *lə-*, normally follows the direct object, though this order is usually reversed when the indirect object is a pronoun and the object a noun.

In verbless clauses, in which the subject is nominal (a noun or pronoun) and the predicate is nominal, adjectival, or adverbial, the order, as a general rule, is subject–predicate in clauses identifying the subject (18A) but predicate–subject in clauses classifying the subject (18B):

(18) A. šēm- hannāhār haššēnî gîḥôn
the name of the river second Gihon
"The name of the second river was Gihon" (Genesis 2:13)
B. 'ărûrâ hā'ădāmâ ba'ăbûrékā
cursed the soil because of you
"The soil is cursed because of you" (Genesis 3:17)

These rules operate fairly consistently in independent verbless clauses, whether they are declarative or interrogative, but less predictably if the clause is volitional; the word order of subordinate verbless clauses is not as consistent. The far demonstrative or third-person personal pronouns (see §4.3.2) are often used pleonastically to coordinate the two parts of a verbless clause – thus:

(19) hannāhār hārəbî'î hû' pərā́t
the river fourth COPULA Euphrates
"The [name of the] fourth river was Euphrates" (Genesis 2:14)

5.2 Coordination and subordination

Like other Semitic languages, Hebrew exhibits a strong preference for paratactic constructions (coordination) over hypotactic constructions (subordination). Thus, in Hebrew prose narrative the great majority of clauses are joined with the conjunction *wə-*. This is true of coordinate clauses whether the relationship between the clauses being coordinated is one of conjunction or disjunction. Though subordinating conjunctions do exist, *wə-* is most often used even in the case of subordinate clauses, with subordination being signaled by word order and clause formation.

5.2.1 Conjunctive clauses

Conjunctive clauses describing sequential events most often employ the distinctive Hebrew narrative sequences, which are made up of clauses containing the so-called converted imperfect and perfect verbal forms (see §4.5.1). The converted imperfect, which is used for past narration, occurs in a sequence that typically begins with a clause containing a perfect verb followed by from one to several clauses introduced by converted imperfects, each of which requires a perfective (usually punctual) translation, as in:

(20) wəhannāḥāš hāyâ ʿārûm mikkōl ḥayyat haśśādeh . . .
and the serpent was shrewd more than any living thing of the field
wayyṓ'mer el- hā'iššâ . . . wattṓ'mer hā'iššâ el- hannāhāš . . .
and it said to the woman and said the woman to the serpent
"Now the serpent was shrewder than any of the other wild animals . . . and it said to the woman . . . and the woman said to the serpent . . . " (Genesis 3:1–2)

The converted perfect, which is used for present-future narration, operates in a reciprocal manner. It occurs in a sequence typically beginning with a clause containing an imperfect verb followed by from one to several clauses introduced by converted perfects, each of which requires an imperfective (present, future, or habitual-iterative) translation, for example:

(21) ʿal-kēn yaʿăzob- 'îš 'et-'ābîw wə'et-'immô wədābaq bə'ištô
therefore abandons a man his father and his mother and unites with his wife
wəhāyû ləbāśār 'eḥād
and they become flesh one
"Therefore a man abandons his father and mother and unites with his wife, and they become one flesh" (Genesis 2:24)

In sequences belonging to either of these categories, the introductory verbal clause may be replaced by any of a variety of other clause types or, owing to the ubiquity of such sequences, it may be omitted altogether.

5.2.2 Disjunctive clauses

Disjunctive clauses are also coordinated most often with *wə-*, but they differ from conjunctive clauses in that they begin with a nonverbal element. These include (i) simple negative clauses, which typically begin with *lō'*,

(22) wayyihyû šənêhem ʿărûmîm . . . wəlō' yitbōšāšû
"And the two of them were naked . . . but they were not ashamed" (Genesis 2:25)

(ii) contrastive clauses,

(23) mikkōl ʿēṣ- haggān 'ākōl tō'kēl ûmēʿēṣ haddáʿat
from any tree of the garden you may eat but from the tree of the knowledge of
ṭôb wārāʿ lō' tō'kal mimménnû
good and evil you may not eat from it
"From any of the trees of the garden you may eat, but from the tree of the knowledge of good and evil you may not eat!" (Genesis 2:16–17)

as well as various kinds of (iii) explanatory and circumstantial clauses, which may be nominal or verbal. Note, for example, the three circumstantial clauses embedded in the following narrative sequence:

(24) bəyôm ʿăśôt yhwh ʾĕlōhîm" ʾereṣ wəšāmáyim wəkōl śîaḥ
on the day of making Yahweh-God's earth and sky and any shrub of
haśśādeh ṭerem yihyeh bāʾāreṣ wəkol- ʿēśeb
the field not yet was on the earth and any herb of
haśśādeh ṭerem yiṣmáḥ . . . wəʾādām ʾáyin laʿăbōd
the field not yet had sprouted and a man there was not to till
ʾet-hāʾădāmâ . . . wayyíṣer yhwh ʾĕlōhîm ʾet-hāʾādām
the soil and formed Yahweh-God man
"When Yahweh-God made the earth and the sky, no wild shrub was yet on the earth, and no wild herb had yet sprouted . . . and there was no man to till the soil . . . and Yahweh-God formed man" (Genesis 2:4–7)

5.2.3 Subordinate clauses

Although clause subordination may also be expressed by word order and clause formation in clauses joined with *wə-*, there are, as noted, special subordinating conjunctions as well as a number of special constructions indicating subordination. Three of the most important types of subordinate clauses are discussed below.

5.2.3.1 Conditional clauses

Conditional clauses may begin with the conjunction *ʾim*, *hēn* or *kî*:

(25) kî taʿăbōd ʾet-hāʾădāmâ lōʾ-tōsēp tēt- kōḥāh lā́k
though you till the soil it will not again yield its strength to you
"Though you till the soil, it will not yield its strength to you again" (Genesis 4:12)

When conditional clauses lack one of the subordinating conjunctions and are joined to the preceding clauses by *wə-*, they are often susceptible to either conditional or nonconditional translation, as in the following:

(26) wĕhāyâ kol-mōṣĕʾî yahargēnî
"If anyone finds me, he will kill me"
or
"And whoever finds me will kill me" (Genesis 4:14)

5.2.3.2 Temporal clauses

Though temporal clauses often stand in simple coordination after the clause they modify –

(27) wayyíqeṣ nōaḥ miyyênô wayyḗdaʿ ʾēt ʾăšer- ʿāśâ-lô
and awoke Noah from his wine and he realized that which had done to him
bənô haqqāṭān
his son young
"When Noah awoke from his wine, he realized what his youngest son had done to him" (Genesis 9:24)

they are very frequently placed before the modified clause and introduced by a converted form of the verb "to be":

(28) wəhāyâ kî- yir'û 'ōtāk hammiṣrîm wə'āmərû 'ištô
and it will be that will see you the Egyptians and they will say his wife
zō't
this
"When the Egyptians see you, they will say, this is his wife" (Genesis 12:12)

This construction is also used routinely for temporal phrases, such as the following:

(29) wayhî miqqēṣ 'arbā'îm yôm wayyiptaḥ nōaḥ 'et-ḥallôn
and it was at the end of forty days and opened Noah the window of
hattēbâh
the ark
"At the end of forty days Noah opened the window of the ark" (Genesis 8:6)

5.2.3.3 *Relative clauses*

Relative clauses, which are usually introduced by *'ăšer* (see §4.3.3), follow and further define nouns or their equivalent:

(30) hā'ā́reṣ 'ăšer 'ar'ékā
the-land which I will show-you
"The land that I will show you" (Genesis 12:1)

They may contain resumptive (retrospective) pronominal or adverbial elements. Although *'ăšer* itself is indeclinable, the resumptive pronouns in a relative clause are declined in agreement with the noun modified by the clause:

(31) A. wə'ēṣ 'ōśeh pərî 'ăšer zar'ô- bô
and trees making fruit which their seed in it
"And trees making fruit in which is their seed" (Genesis 1:13)
B. ûmin-habbəhēmâ 'ăšer lō' ṭəhōrâ hî'
"And from the animal which is not pure" (Genesis 7:2)

Resumptive adverbials include especially *šām* "there," and related forms:

(32) hā'ădāmâ 'ăšer luqqaḥ miššām
the soil which he was taken from there
"The soil from which he was taken" (Genesis 3:23)

The so-called *independent* relative clauses are not true relatives. Rather than further define a governing substantive, they serve as one of the elements in a larger clause, as in the following.

(33) wayiššā́'er 'ak- nōaḥ wa'ăšer 'ittô battēbâ
and was left only Noah and those who with him on the ark
"Only Noah and those that were with him in the ark were left" (Genesis 7:23)

5.3 Agreement

In general, a predicate agrees with its subject in gender and number, and if the predicate is a verb, it agrees with its subject in gender, number, and person. There are, however, numerous exceptions to this general pattern. A collective subject, for example, is often construed with a plural verb. When the subject is a construct chain (see §4.2.4), the predicate may agree in number and gender with the *nomen rectum* rather than the *nomen regens*, which is properly the subject.

A verb preceding a compound subject, though often plural, may be singular, agreeing with the first member in the series:

(34) wayyitḥabbē' hā'ādām wə'ištô
and he hid himself the man and his wife
"And the man and his wife hid themselves" (Genesis 3:8)

Perhaps in extension of the last category, a verb in the initial position is sometimes masculine singular regardless of the gender and number of the subject, so that the masculine singular performs, in effect, as an uninflected verbal form, as in the following:

(35) yəhî mə'ōrōt
let there be-MASC. SG. luminaries-FEM. PL.
"Let there be luminaries" (Genesis 1:14)

Since there are no dual forms of verbs (see §4.5), adjectives (see §4.2.2), and pronouns (at least in the active language, see §4.3.1), dual subjects are construed with plural predicates.

5.4 Determination

Hebrew substantives are either definite or indefinite. Certain substantives, including proper nouns and most pronouns, are intrinsically definite. Common nouns are determined (become definite) when prefixed by the definite article (see §4.4) or when followed by a pronominal suffix or another definite noun in a genitive construction (i.e., when in construct state before another definite noun; see §4.2.4). According to the grammatical rules of Biblical Hebrew, a noun can be determined in only one of these ways, so that a proper noun cannot stand as the *nomen regens* in a construct chain, and neither a proper noun nor a noun in the construct state can have an article or a pronominal suffix. Although these rules apply generally to Northwest Semitic as a whole, they are by no means universal – the restrictions are much less severe in Ugaritic, for example. Iron Age inscriptional Hebrew provides clear exceptions, such as *yhwh šmrn* "Yahweh of Samaria," at Kuntillet 'Ajrud, and several possible or certain exceptions are found in Biblical Hebrew itself: for example, *maḥăsî ʿōz* "my refuge of strength" (Psalm 71:7).

6. LEXICON

The core vocabulary of ancient Hebrew is an inventory of words shared with other Iron Age Canaanite languages – Phoenician, Ammonite, Moabite, and Edomite. Many are common Semitic, and most are common Northwest Semitic, though several characteristic entries in the lexicon represent preferences in Hebrew that were distinct from their Aramaic equivalents. Verbal examples include Hebrew √*ʿly* versus Aramaic √*slq* "ascend"; Hebrew √*yṣ'* versus Aramaic √*npq* "go out"; Hebrew √*bw'* versus Aramaic √*ʿll* "enter"; Hebrew √*ʿzb* versus Aramaic √*šbq* "leave"; and Hebrew √*dbr* versus Aramaic √*mll* "speak"; among many others. In most of these cases, the Hebrew preference seems to have been shared by the other members of the Canaanite family, though the evidence for the lexicons of these languages, especially those spoken in Transjordan, is scant. Within the Canaanite group itself, there are also examples of lexical specialization, which, taken together, suggest an isogloss between North and South Canaanite – thus Hebrew √*hyy* versus Ugaritic-Phoenician √*kwn* "to be" (narrowed to "be firm" in Hebrew); Hebrew *zāhāb* versus Ugaritic-Phoenician *ḥrṣ* "gold" (rare in Hebrew); Hebrew √*ʿśy* versus Phoenician √*pʿl* "do, make" (relatively rare and chiefly poetic in Biblical Hebrew; Moabite also prefers √*'śy*, though Ammonite seems allied with Aramaic √*'bd*). Note also the retention in South Canaanite (Hebrew, including the Northern or Israelite dialect, and Ammonite) of √*ntn* "give" (cf. Amorite **ntn* and Akkadian *nadānu*) versus the North Canaanite (Ugaritic and Phoenician) innovation √*ytn*.

Throughout the history of ancient Hebrew there was a profound penetration of Aramaic vocabulary into the lexicon, a phenomenon that began to gain momentum in the period of Late Biblical Hebrew and steadily increased as Hebrew continued to be studied and spoken while Aramaic became the language of everyday discourse. The result is that, from an early date, there is a substantial Aramaic component to the Hebrew lexicon.

Less far-reaching but still significant is the number of loanwords that entered Hebrew from the speech of the peoples who dominated or controlled Judah (or Judaea) in antiquity. Biblical Hebrew contains a number of words derived from the languages of the major international powers of the Iron Age. There is a scattering of Egyptian words, such as *šēš* "linen" (Egyptian *šś* < **šśr* "linen") and *ṭabbá'at* "sealing ring" (Egyptian *ḏb'wt* "signet, seal"). A number of words reflect Judah's experience as a tributary of the Assyrian Empire. These include not only names of imperial institutions and officials, as found in the list in 2 Kings 18:17 – *tartān* (Neo-Assyrian *turtānu* "viceroy"), *rab-sārîs* (Neo-Assyrian *rab ša rēši* "chief eunuch") and *rab-šaqēh* (Neo-Assyrian *rab šaqê* "chief butler"), but also words that became part of the general Hebrew vocabulary, such as *šōṭēr* "official, magistrate" (originally "scribe, registrar"?) from the Akkadian verb *šaṭāru* "write."

In Late Biblical Hebrew many more Akkadian words entered the Hebrew lexicon from the Neo-Babylonian administration: for example, *'iggéret* "letter" (Neo-Babylonian *egirtu*), *mékes* "tax" (Neo-Babylonian *miksu*), *middâ* "tribute" (Neo-Babylonian *mandattu*), and **ségen* "prefect" (Neo-Babylonian *šaknu* "provincial governor"). Other words were introduced from the bureaucracy of the Persian Empire: for example, *'ăḥašdarpān* "satrap" (Old Persian *ḫšaçapāvan*; cf. Neo-Babylonian *aḫšadrapannu*), *dāt* "edict, law" (Old Persian *dāta*), and *pardēs* "park" (Old Persian; cf. Avestan *pairi-daēza* "enclosure").

With the spread of Hellenization after Alexander's conquest in the fourth century BC, Greek words began to appear in the Hebrew lexicon. Though at first the impact of Greek was felt primarily in the technical terminology of government, law, and commerce – *hipparkəyâ* "provincial government" (ἐπαρχία), *bûlê* "(city) council" (βουλή "council, senate"), *sanhedrîn* "Sanhedrin" (συνέδριον "council, congress") – it expanded into the general Hebrew vernacular as Rabbinic Hebrew evolved – thus, *qāmîn* "furnace" (κάμινος), *pîlôn* "gateway" (πυλών), *zûg* "pair" (ζεῦγος "yoke, pair"; cf. the denominative verb *ziwwēg*, "join"), and so forth. Under Roman administration, Hebrew-speaking Jews also adopted numerous Latin words, including especially, but not exclusively, military terms: for example, *qasṭrâ* "camp" (*castra*), *ligyôn* "legion" (*legiō*), *mônîṭâ* "coinage" (*monēta*), and so forth.

Bibliography

Anderson, F. 1970. *The Hebrew Verbless Clause in the Pentateuch.* Journal of Biblical Literature Monograph Series 14. Nashville/New York: Abingdon.

______. 1974. *The Sentence in Biblical Hebrew.* Janua Linguarum Series Practica 231. The Hague/Paris: Mouton.

Bauer, H. and P. Leander. 1918–1922. *Historische Grammatik der hebräischen Sprache des alten Testamentes* (2 vols.). Halle: Niemeyer. Reprint 1962, Hildesheim: Olms.

Bergsträsser, G. 1918–1929. *Hebräische Grammatik.* Wilhelm Gesenius' *Hebräische Grammatik* (29th edition, 2 vols.). Leipzig: Vogel. Reprint 1986, Hildesheim: Olms.

______. 1928. *Einführung in die semitischen Sprachen: Sprachproben und grammatische Skizzen.* Munich: Max Hueber. Translated by P. Daniels as *Introduction to the Semitic Languages: Text Specimens and Grammatical Sketches.* 1983. Winona Lake, IN: Eisenbrauns.

Blau, J. 1993 *A Grammar of Biblical Hebrew* (2nd edition). Porta Linguarum Orientalium 12. Wiesbaden: Otto Harrassowitz.

______. 1998. *Topics in Hebrew and Semitic Linguistics.* Jerusalem: Magnes Press.

Brockelmann, C. 1956. *Hebräische Syntax.* Neukirchen: Buchhandlung des Erziehungsvereins.

Garr, W. 1985. *Dialect Geography of Syria-Palestine, 1000–586 BC.* Philadelphia: University of Pennsylvania.

Harris, Z. 1939. *Development of the Canaanite Dialects.* American Oriental Society 16. New Haven: American Oriental Society.

______. 1941. "Linguistic structure of Hebrew." *Journal of the American Oriental Society* 61: 143–167.

Huehnergard, J. 1992. "Languages (Introductory)." In D. N. Freedman (ed.), *Anchor Bible Dictionary,* vol. IV, pp. 155–170. New York: Doubleday.

Joüon, P. 1923. *Grammaire de l'hébreu biblique.* Rome: Pontifical Biblical Institute. Translated and revised by T. Muraoka as *A Grammar of Biblical Hebrew* (2 vols.). Rome: Pontifical Biblical Institute, 1991.

Kautsch, E. (ed.). 1909. *Wilhelm Gesenius' Hebräische Grammatik* (28th edition). Leipzig: Vogel. Translated by A. Cowley as *Gesenius' Hebrew Grammar* (2nd edition). Oxford: Clarendon Press, 1910.

Khan, G. 1997. "Tiberian Hebrew phonology." In A. Kaye (ed.), *Phonologies of Asia and Africa,* vol. I, pp. 85–102. Winona Lake, IN: Eisenbrauns.

König, F. 1881–1897. *Historisch-kritisches Lehrgebäude der hebräischen Sprache* (3 vols.). Leipzig: Hinrichs.

Kutscher, E. 1982. *A History of the Hebrew Language.* Jerusalem: Magnes Press; Leiden: Brill.

Lambdin, T. 1971. *Introduction to Biblical Hebrew.* New York: Scribners.

Lambdin, T. and J. Huehnergard. 1998. *The Historical Grammar of Classical Hebrew: An Outline.* Cambridge, MA: Harvard University.

Lambert, M. 1946. *Traité de grammaire hébraïque* (2nd edition). Paris: Presses Universitaires. Reprint 1972, Hildesheim: Gerstenberg.

Meyer, R. 1966–1972. *Hebräische Grammatik* (3rd edition, 4 vols.). Berlin: de Gruyter.

Moran, W. 1961. "The Hebrew language in its Northwest Semitic background." In G. E. Wright (ed.), *The Bible and the Ancient Near East: Essays in Honor of William Foxwell Albright,* pp. 54–72. New York: Doubleday.

Murtonen, A. 1986–1990. *Hebrew in its West Semitic Setting: A Comparative Survey of Non-Masoretic Hebrew Dialects and Traditions* (4 vols.). Leiden: Brill.

Pérez-Fernández, M. 1997. *An Introductory Grammar of Rabbinic Hebrew.* Translated by J. Elwolde from Spanish. Leiden: Brill, 1992.

Polzin, R. *Late Biblical Hebrew: Toward an Historical Typology of Biblical Hebrew Prose.* Harvard Semitic Monographs 12. Missoula, MT: Scholars Press.

Qimron, E. 1986. *The Hebrew of the Dead Sea Scrolls.* Harvard Semitic Studies. Atlanta: Scholars Press.

Rabin, C. 1970. "Hebrew." In T. A. Sebeok (ed.), *Current Trends in Linguistics.* Vol. VI, *Linguistics in South West Asia and North Africa,* pp. 304–346. The Hague: Mouton.

______. 1973. *A Short History of the Hebrew Language.* Jerusalem: Orot.

______. 2000. *The Development of the Syntax of Post-Biblical Hebrew.* Studies in Semitic Languages and Linguistics 29. Leiden/Boston: Brill.

Rendsburg, G. 1997. "Ancient Hebrew phonology." In A. Kaye (ed.), *Phonologies of Asia and Africa,* vol. I, pp. 65–83. Winona Lake, IN: Eisenbrauns.

Richter, W. 1978–1980. *Grundlagen einer althebräischen Grammatik* (3 vols.). St. Ottilien: EOS.

Sáenz-Badillos, A. 1993. *A History of the Hebrew Language.* Translated by J. Elwolde from Spanish. Cambridge/New York: Cambridge University Press, 1998.

Schramm, G. and P. Schmitz. "Languages (Hebrew)." In D. N. Freedman (ed.), *Anchor Bible Dictionary,* vol. IV, pp. 203–214. New York: Doubleday.

Segal, M. 1927. *A Grammar of Mishnaic Hebrew.* Oxford: Clarendon Press.
Speiser, E. 1925–1934. "The pronunciation of Hebrew according to (based chiefly on) the transliterations in the Hexapla." *Jewish Quarterly Review* 16:343–382; 23:233–265; 24:9–46.
Sperber, A. 1937–1938. *Hebrew Based on Greek and Latin Transliterations.* Hebrew Union College Annual 12–13: pp. 103–274.
_______. 1966. *A Historical Grammar of Biblical Hebrew.* Leiden: Brill.
Steiner, R. 1992. "Hebrew." In *International Encyclopedia of Linguistics,* vol. II, pp. 110–118.
_______. 1998. "Ancient Hebrew." In R. Hetzron (ed.), *The Semitic Languages,* pp. 145–173. London: Routledge.
Waldman, N. 1989. *The Recent Study of Hebrew.* Bibliographica Judaica 10. Cincinnati: Hebrew Union College.
Waltke, B. and M. O'Connor. 1990. *An Introduction to Biblical Hebrew Syntax.* Winona Lake, IN: Eisenbrauns.
Yeivin, Y. 1985. מסורת הלשון העברית המשתקפת בניקוד הבבלי. Text and Studies 12. Jerusalem: Academy of the Hebrew Language.

CHAPTER 4

Phoenician and Punic

JO ANN HACKETT

1. HISTORICAL AND CULTURAL CONTEXTS

Phoenician is a member of the Semitic language family, specifically the Northwest Semitic branch of Central Semitic. Within Northwest Semitic it is a Canaanite language, the closest relatives of which are Hebrew, Moabite, Ammonite, and Edomite.

1.1 Phoenicia

A description of the sources for the Phoenician language depends to a certain extent on what "Phoenician" is held to mean. The term "Phoenicia" is generally reserved for the strip of land sixty miles long (from Acco in the south to Tell Sukas in the north) and at most thirty miles wide, on the northern coast of the Levant, bounded on the west by the Mediterranean and on the east by the Lebanon Mountains – that is, the modern coast of Lebanon and part of the northern coast of modern Israel. As a scholarly convention, this area is referred to as *Phoenicia* after 1200 BC, the beginning of the Iron Age. In the early Iron Age, the ravages of the so-called Sea Peoples along the coast of ancient Canaan and into Egypt forced the withdrawal of Egyptian control over Canaan. This withdrawal allowed the Philistines and other Sea Peoples to gain control over the southern coastal plain, and even to expand eastward, where they met a westward-expanding Israel. The northern coastal plain, however, does not seem to have been invaded from the outside, nor do any disenfranchised or other "settling" peoples seem to have taken over, so that once Egyptian control was gone, the cities in this last remaining part of what had earlier been called Canaan flourished. It is this loose assembly of coastal cities that was called Phoenicia by the Greeks and by modern scholars. The cities were never united into a political entity, although in various periods one or another city was ascendant over the others; the people of Phoenicia continued to think of themselves as Canaanites, or to identify themselves according to their native city.

1.2 Textual evidence

Phoenician inscriptions have been found in and around the ancient Phoenician cities, but also throughout the Mediterranean world. The first inscriptions of any length are a series of royal inscriptions from tenth-century BC Byblos, but beginning in the ninth and lasting until the first century AD, there are inscriptions from Asia Minor, Cyprus, Sicily, Sardinia, Malta, Rhodes, Egypt, Greece, the Balearic Islands, and Spain.

A few texts dating even earlier than 1000 BC might be called Phoenician. Several dozen inscribed arrowheads come apparently from the Beqaᶜ, the valley between the Lebanon and Antilebanon Mountains, and from farther south in Palestine (twelfth–eleventh centuries BC); and inscribed clay cones from Byblos date to the middle of the eleventh century. In both cases, the texts are almost entirely personal names and patronymics, so linguistic classification is difficult. The inscription on an eleventh-century fragmentary stela from Nora on Sardinia is most reasonably, given script and provenance, identified as Phoenician. Although the extant inscription contains parts of only four words, the stance of the letters indicates boustrophedon writing. The archaic Nora inscription is an artifact important for tracing the history of Phoenician expansion into the Mediterranean, but it is unfortunately not useful in a survey of the language.

The dialect of the Phoenician colony at Carthage and of inscriptions found throughout the Carthaginian empire is referred to as *Punic*, for which we have evidence beginning in the sixth century BC. Inscriptions dating after the fall of Carthage in 146 BC are said to be written in *Late Punic* or *Neopunic*, although the distinction is more one of script than of dialect. Neopunic inscriptions will be treated in this chapter as simply a late form of Punic that shows the drift that occurred, especially in phonology, after the stabilizing effect that Carthage's hegemony had had on the language was removed. Punic inscriptions date as late as the second century AD, and there are even later *Latino-Punic* inscriptions, Punic written in Latin script, that date to the fourth–fifth centuries AD. Punic inscriptions have been found in North African sites in modern Tunisia, Algeria, and Libya, as well as in Malta, Sardinia, Sicily, France, Spain, and the Balearics.

Besides Phoenician and Punic inscriptions proper, we have names transliterated into Hebrew, Akkadian, Greek, and Latin, plus a few transliterated lexemes found in Greek and Latin inscriptions and in classical sources, notably in Augustine (fourth century AD). Objects inscribed with personal names include seals, bowls, and ostraca. The *Poenulus* of Plautus includes some passages in Punic, but the process of transmission has garbled these passages badly enough that they must be used with circumspection.

Most of the Phoenician and Punic inscriptions can be described as royal inscriptions, tomb inscriptions (both royal and nonroyal), and cultic inscriptions (dedications of buildings or paraphernalia, votive inscriptions). The largest corpus consists of the hundreds of Punic child sacrifice (votive) inscriptions from North Africa, stelae which report that a *mulk*-sacrifice is presented to the god or gods who answered the prayer of the supplicant. Most of the stelae are no longer *in situ*, but beneath some of the stelae the burned remains of children, usually newborns, are found, and sometimes the remains of a substitute lamb or other animal.

1.3 Dialectal variation within Phoenician

In the linguistic discussion which follows this section, the focus will be on *Standard Phoenician*, with dialectal variants noted. In addition, a brief overview of dialectal differences occurring within Phoenician is presented here.

Even the earliest Phoenician inscriptions of the tenth–ninth centuries BC show evidence of dialectal differences. The dialect of Byblos is especially distinct from the other early inscriptions (said to be written in Standard Phoenician) and is treated separately in the grammars. Common Phoenician, then, must antedate the first millennium BC.

Old Byblian inscriptions from the tenth–ninth centuries retain the *-y* of III-*y* verbs (a type of "weak verb" in which the third consonant of the root was **y*; see §4.1); use *z* (proclitic on the verb) as the relative pronoun (see §4.3.5); and show *zn* as the masculine singular demonstrative (see §4.3.2). In the earliest of these inscriptions, the sarcophagus inscription of Aḥiram, the third masculine singular possessive suffix on a genitive noun is *-h*, presumably /-ihu(:)/ (see §4.3.1.2).

After the Old Byblian period, our evidence for Byblian is lacking until the fifth century. At this point, however, Byblian looks more like Standard Phoenician, with relative *ʾš* and demonstrative *z*. The III-weak verbs have lost the third root consonant altogether.

Standard Phoenician inscriptions from the ninth century forward are reasonably homogeneous, with some local variants, especially in inscriptions from Cyprus, where consonant mergers seem to have taken place and the use of "prothetic ʾ" is more pronounced than elsewhere.

Punic, the dialect of the western colonies, is extant from the sixth century onwards, but only begins to diverge from Standard Phoenician in late texts, especially after the fall of Carthage in 146 BC. These divergences are largely phonological: modification and loss of the four pharyngeal and glottal obstruents /ħ/(<ḥ>), /ʕ/, (<ʿ>), /h/, and /ʔ/(<ʾ>); and confusion of sibilants (see §3.1). The Punic lexicon is also affected by the number of loanwords and foreign names that make their way into the inscriptions from Greek, Latin, and Numidian. The third masculine possessive suffix on nouns that end in a vowel is *-y* in Standard Phoenician, but *-m* in late Punic texts (see §4.3.1.2).

2. WRITING SYSTEM

Phoenician inscriptions are written in a consonantal alphabet, the form of which indicates that it actually developed in Phoenicia, whence it was borrowed by the Hebrews and Arameans, and eventually the Greeks. The Phoenician stage of the script is part of a long history of alphabetic development that can be traced in inscriptions from earlier Canaanite-speaking peoples.

The earliest known inscriptions using this alphabet are two graffiti recently found near Luxor that date from *c.* 1800 BC. That we have material from Serabit al-Khadem in the Sinai peninsula that is perhaps only slightly later, and other exemplars of fairly high date from Palestine (seventeenth–fifteenth centuries), suggests a date for the invention of the alphabet as far back as 2000 BC.

This writing system was entirely consonantal in origin and operated according to the acrophonic principle: drawing a picture, or pictogram, to represent the first consonant of the word which the picture depicts (such as drawing a bee to represent [b], and so on). In this early form of the alphabet the original *b* depicts a house, as the Canaanite word for house, **bayt*, begins with [b]; "(palm of) hand" is **kapp*, a word that begins with [k], and so the *k* symbol is a pictogram depicting a hand. The Canaanite-speaking people who invented this writing system would have been familiar with Egyptian writing (see *WAL* Ch. 7, §2.1), but they simplified the process dramatically so that each of the original symbols corresponded to only one distinct consonantal phoneme.

Throughout the second millennium the consonantal script continued to develop. Whereas the earliest inscriptions were written both vertically and horizontally, horizontal came to predominate. A given early inscription could be written dextrograde, sinistrograde, or boustrophedon, but by 1000 BC, the direction of Phoenician writing had stabilized as sinistrograde. Since several of the pictograms changed stance according to the direction of the line of writing, when the direction stabilized, so did the stance of the characters.

Table 4.1 The Phoenician consonantal script

Character	Transcription	Character	Transcription
𐤀	ʾ	𐤋	l
𐤁	b	𐤌	m
𐤂	g	𐤍	n
𐤃	d	𐤎	s
𐤄	h	𐤏	ʿ
𐤅	w	𐤐	p
𐤆	z	𐤑	ṣ
𐤇	ḥ	𐤒	q
𐤈	ṭ	𐤓	r
𐤉	y	𐤔	š
𐤊	k	𐤕	t

By the eleventh century BC, virtually all of the pictographic forms had developed into stylized "linear" descendants. This linear script is used through the first millennium to write Phoenician and Punic, while the Hebrew and Aramaic scripts had begun to follow separate paths by the tenth century. We know that both Hebrew and Aramaic borrowed their writing systems from elsewhere because the scripts they use do not provide an exact match for the consonant repertoire of either Hebrew or early Aramaic. Moreover, the letter names that we know from Hebrew and Aramaic actually correspond to the pronunciation of those words in Phoenician, another clue that the source script was Phoenician.

Though the linear Phoenician script was purely consonantal, a means was eventually developed, as in other consonantal Semitic scripts, to signal the presence of certain vowels consonantally. Consonants so used are conventionally termed the *matres lectionis* ("mothers of reading"). Thus, in late Punic inscriptions we see an inconsistent "vowel notation"; in fact, two systems of *matres lectionis* had merged by this time. The earlier system of Punic *matres lectionis*, named the "Domestic Orthography" by Menken (1981), was used for Semitic words in Punic inscriptions (sporadically from the third century BC): the character ʾ on the end of a word indicated that the word ended in some vowel; occasionally *y* was used explicitly for final /-ī/. In Phoenician, a final vowel usually marks a morphologically significant addition to a simpler form of the word in question – a pronominal suffix on a noun or verb, for example – with the result that this ʾ often served as a morpheme marker as well. A second system of *matres lectionis*, Menken's "Foreign Orthography," came into use slightly later than the Domestic Orthography (i.e., late second century BC). This system was used in Punic for spelling foreign names and words, then consistently in later inscriptions for many words, both foreign and Punic: ʾ for *o*-vowels and *e*-vowels; ʿ for *a*-vowels; *w* for *u*-vowels; *y* for *i*-vowels.

Because of their limited land resources, the people of the coastal cities who would eventually be called the Phoenicians early on turned to the sea and to mercantile activities, and it was such maritime occupation that brought the Phoenician people and script into contact with the Greek world. The Greek adaptation of the Phoenician writing system is generally dated at *c.* 800 BC, on the basis of the variety of scripts already evident in the earliest Greek inscriptions of the late eighth century, indicating both a common origin and some period of development to account for differences. But the antiquity of some Greek letter-forms and the amount of development beyond Phoenician forms suggest a long period of contact between Phoenicians and the West before the final form of the Greek alphabet emerged. Like the early Canaanite inscriptions, the direction of writing of early Greek inscriptions can be dextrograde, sinistrograde, or boustrophedon; Greek eventually settled on dextrograde, in contrast to Phoenician from 1000 BC onward. All of these features argue for a complicated and extended process of the Greeks' acquiring their alphabet from the Phoenicians, rather than one date that can be proposed as the moment of transmission.

3. PHONOLOGY

Since Phoenician is no longer spoken, its phonology must be reconstructed on the basis of (i) transcriptions found in Hebrew, Assyrian, Greek, and Latin writings; and of (ii) comparative phonology of the Semitic languages.

3.1 Consonants

In this chapter, the transliteration scheme commonly utilized in the philological study of Phoenician will be followed, for both consonants and vowels. In Table 4.2 these conventional symbols are used, but are followed by a phonetic transcription within parentheses, where such transcription differs from the conventional representation.

Twenty-nine consonants are reconstructed for Proto-Semitic (see Appendix 1, §3.2.1). Proto-Central Semitic retains all of them, as does Proto-Northwest Semitic. The following consonant mergers occur between Proto-Northwest Semitic and Canaanite (conventional transcription is given in parentheses):

Table 4.2 The consonantal phonemes of Standard Phoenician

	Place of articulation					
Manner of articulation	Bilabial	Dental/ Alveolar	Palatal	Velar	Pharyngeal	Glottal
Stop						
Voiceless	p	t		k		ʾ(/ʔ/)
Voiced	b	d		g		
Emphatic		ṭ (/t'/)		q (/k'/)		
Affricate						
Voiceless		s (/^{t}s/)				
Voiced		z (/^{d}z/)				
Emphatic		ṣ (/^{t}s'/)				
Fricative						
Voiceless		š (/s/)			ḥ (/ħ/)	h
Voiced					ʿ(/ʕ/)	
Approximant						
Voiced	w	r ?	y			
Lateral approximant						
Voiced		l				
Nasal						
Voiced	m	n				

(1) *Proto-Northwest Semitic* → *Canaanite*
*θ and *s (š) → /s/ (š)
*ð and *^{d}z (z) → /^{d}z/ (z)
*θ' (θ̣) and *^{t}s' (ṣ) and *ɬ' (ṣ́) → /^{t}s'/ (ṣ)

The following mergers then occur between Canaanite and Phoenician:

(2) *Canaanite* → *Phoenician*
/ʕ/ (ʿ) and /γ/ → /ʕ/ (ʿ)
/ħ/ (ḥ) and /x/ (ḫ) → /ħ/ (ḥ)
/ɬ/ (ś) and /s/ (š) → /s/ (š)

Throughout Northwest Semitic, *n* assimilates to a following consonant, producing a geminate cluster. Geminate consonants are not indicated in the Phoenician script, however, and must be reconstructed, as with other features of the language, on the basis of Phoenician transcriptions into languages with scripts which do indicate gemination and by comparison with other Semitic languages.

There is no evidence for the spirantization of voiced and voiceless stops that is evident in Aramaic and Hebrew from the middle of the first millennium BC onward.

In Phoenician and Punic /ʔ/ (<'>) is often elided. In Punic, /h/ is modified (e.g., the definite article is sometimes written <'> rather than <h>) or omitted altogether. Pharyngeals and glottals are generally modified and eventually confused or lost.

3.2 Vowels

The vowels of Phoenician are less well understood than the consonants, since Phoenician inscriptions do not include any vowel notation until very late. Judging from related languages and from transcriptions into other scripts, the vowel phonemes of Figure 4.1 are identified for Standard Phoenician:

	FRONT		*CENTRAL*		*BACK*
HIGH	i:				u:
		i		u	
MID		e:		o:	
LOW			a		

Figure 4.1 Vowel phonemes of Standard Phoenician

The vowels reconstructed for Proto-Semitic are **a*, **i*, **u*, **ā*, **ī*, **ū* (see Ch. 6, §3.2.2), as well as the diphthongs **ay* and **aw* (see Ch. 6, §3.2.3). In the development of Phoenician, however, the Proto-Semitic diphthongs became long mid vowels: **ay* > /e:/ and **aw* > /o:/.

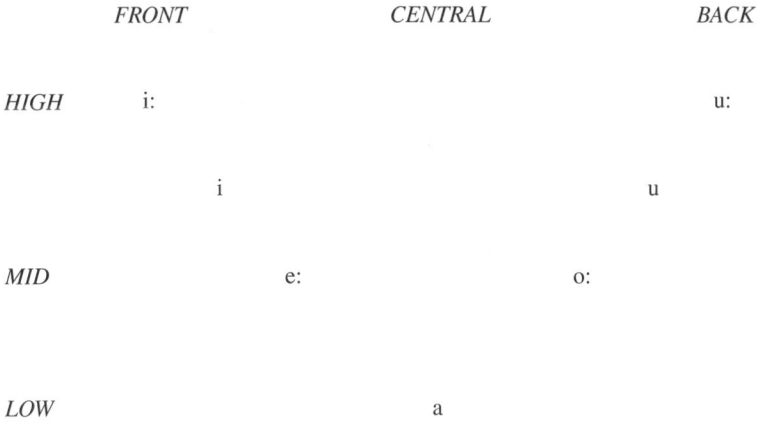

3.2.1 High vowels

High vowels undergo several changes within the history of Phoenician. The short high-front /i/ (from PS *i) shows three developments:

1. In syllables which had been originally open (see §3.2.5), accented /i/ > [ē]. Note the name βαλσιλληχ = *Balsilech* (*CIL* VIII 16) for /baʕl-sillík/ "Baal has sent," among other evidence, all of which is late (Hellenistic or beyond).
2. In syllables which had been originally open (see §3.2.5), unaccented /i/ > [ɛ]. Consider the name Γεραστρατος (Josephus, *C. Ap.* 1, 157) for /gir-ʕastart/ "one bound to Astarte," among other evidence, all late.
3. Elsewhere *i is preserved (but see §3.2.3). Thus, Assyrian *ú-ru-mil-ki* (Senn. OI Prism, col. II, line 53, 8th century BC) for Phoenician /ʔo:r-milk/ "the [divine] king is light."

The long vowel *ī remains stable; we assume the length in names such as αβιβαλος (Josephus, *Ant.* 8, 5) for /ʔabī-baʕl/ "Baal is my [divine] father."

Both the short and long high-back vowels, *u and *ū, were preserved, though appear to have been eventually fronted, and perhaps unrounded, in certain environments. The evidence for the shift is, however, meager, late, and rather unreliable (*Poenulus*), but it forms one end of a proposed chain (Fox 1996) that is otherwise well grounded. Thus, in *Poenulus*, we see evidence of /u/ > [ü] in the Latin transcription *chyl*, representing /kull/ "all," and even perhaps of [ü] > [i] in *chil*, a transcription of the same word. For the fronting of /u:/ to [ü:]/[ī:], *Poenulus* provides the (perhaps equally unreliable) evidence of the spellings *li* for /lu:/ "O that . . . !"; *hy* for /huʔ/ "he."

3.2.2 Low-central vowels

The observed Phoenician development of Proto-Semitic *ā > /o:/ (possibly with intermediate stage of */ɔ/) is actually a broader phenomenon known as the *Canaanite Shift*. This process occurs early in Canaanite, as is evidenced by the fourteenth-century Canaanite glosses in the Akkadian texts found at el-Amarna in Egypt (see *WAL* Ch. 8, §1.1). The resulting /o:/ merges with the /o:/ reflex of Proto-Semitic *aw, and both were eventually raised to /u:/ – note the Punic divine name in Greek transcription, χουσωρ for earlier /ko:sar/ (< *kawθar; Eusebius *PE* 1.10.11), and feminine plural SANUTH for /sano:t/ "years" (*KAI* 180 c, e).

In syllables which had been originally open (see §3.2.5), Phoenician accented short /a/ (from PS *a) > [o]. There is evidence that this change, known as the *Phoenician Shift*, had occurred by at least the eighth century BC. Note the eighth-century Assyrian transcription of the name *ḫi-ru-um-mu* for [ħi:rom] < /ʔaħi:rám/ "My [divine] kinsman is exalted" (T-P Annal 27, line 2; T-P Summary Inscription 9, reverse, line 5, has a variant difficult to assess: *[ḫi-r]i-mu*) and seventh-century *ba-ʾa-al-ma-lu-ku* for [baʕl-malok] < /baʕl-malák/ "Baal has ruled" (Assurb. Rassam, col. II, line 84). The [o] that was the result of the Phoenician Shift did not merge with /o:/ < *ā and < *aw and therefore was not raised to /u:/; recall the above χουσωρ < *kōšár < *kawθar, Eusebius, *PE* 1.10.11. The feminine of this same word, χουσαρτις for /ko:sart/ (Eusebius *PE* 1.10.43), provides evidence that the /á/ > [o] shift did not take place in originally closed syllables.

Elsewhere, Proto-Semitic short *a is preserved in Phoenician (but see §3.2.3).

3.2.3 Vowel reduction

There is some evidence (again, *Poenulus*) that short vowels in open syllables are reduced to schwa pretonically in verbs and propretonically in nouns and adjectives, as in Biblical Hebrew.

3.2.4 Syllable structure

Syllables in Phoenician (again to the extent that such information can be reconstructed) appear to have the standard Semitic syllable shape: CV or CVC.

3.2.5 Accent

Accent also must be reconstructed, but there are clues. Earlier Northwest Semitic had short final case-vowels: **-u* for nominative, **-i* for genitive, and **-a* for accusative. At some point, short final vowels were lost in the Canaanite languages, although there is evidence (see §4.3.1.2) that the genitive case ending remained in Phoenician. As we saw in §§3.2.1–2, lengthening or raising of certain vowels occurred in the (newly) final syllable, as long as the syllable had been originally open. This situation suggests that the accent in Phoenician, as in Hebrew, was on the syllable preceding the case-vowel; then with loss of the case-vowel, it fell on the new final syllable of the word.

4. MORPHOLOGY

4.1 Word structure

Most Phoenician words, like those in all Semitic languages, are built around a triconsonantal root, which denotes a semantic field. The words themselves are discontinuous morphemes composed of a sequence of three consonants (the *root*) and the vowels and affixes that are morphologically significant. For instance, if the root *k-t-b* means "to write," the Proto-Central Semitic (and Arabic) **katabat* would mean "she wrote," **yaktubu* would mean "he will write," **kātibūna* would mean "those who write," and so forth. There is evidence for biconsonantal roots in Afro-Asiatic, the family of which Semitic is one branch; there are, furthermore, "weak" verbal roots, roots with first, second, or third root consonants which were originally *w* or *y*, and which had dropped out of the root (usually elided intervocalically) in many of the languages, including Phoenician. But for most words, the triconsonantal root is still recoverable.

4.2 Nominal morphology

Many nouns are derived from verbal bases, such as participles, infinitives, agent nouns, nouns of place, time, instrument, *inter alia*. Such nouns are often formed with affixes and vocalic patterns that carry specific meanings.

4.2.1 Case, gender, and number

Nominals in Phoenician are marked for gender and number: masculine singular (masc. sg.), masculine plural (masc. pl.), feminine singular (fem. sg.), feminine plural (fem. pl.). There is some slight evidence of the retention of the Semitic dual. Proto-Northwest Semitic retained the three cases of Proto-Semitic (nominative, genitive, accusative), and there is evidence of at least the genitive in Phoenician (see §4.3.1.2), and possibly the accusative (see §4.4).

4.2.2 State

Nouns occur in two states, the *absolute state* and the *construct state.* A noun in the construct state (called *nomen regens*) is "in construct" with (governs) a following noun in the genitive case (the *nomen rectum*). Together they make up a *construct chain.* If the *nomen rectum* is definite – that is, it includes the definite article; is written with a possessive pronominal suffix; or is a proper noun – the entire chain is definite. If *hbrk bʕl* in *KAI* 26 A I 1 means "the one blessed by Baal," then we have an example of a construct chain modified in its entirety by one definite article written on the *nomen regens* (see Lambdin 1971).

4.2.3 Noun endings

Masculine singular nouns have -Ø ending, in both the absolute and construct states.

Feminine singular nouns end in *-t*, in both absolute and construct states. This ending represents either *-t* or *-ot* (< /-at/): both occur in Semitic, and the unvocalized inscriptions do not allow us to make a distinction, except in rare cases such as *št* (/satt-/ < */sant-/; /sanat-/ would be written *šnt*). Note the original **-at* ending on the personal name *ab-di-mi-il-ku-ut-ti* (Esarh., p. 48, line 65) for /ʕabd-milkot/ "servant of the [divine] queen." In late Punic, the final *-t* is apparently lost; witness the Latin transcription *Himilco* (*CIS* I 149; *CIL* VIII 10525) for /(ʔa)ħi:-milkot/ "brother of the [divine] queen," and Punic *ḥṣdyqʿ* (*KAI* 154, 3) "the righteous one," a feminine noun, and so vocalized [ᵗs'addi:k'o] < [ᵗs'addi:k'ot] < /ᵗs'addi:k'at/.

Masculine plural nouns end in *-m* in the absolute state: *-īm*, as in *gubulim* "boundaries" and *alonim* "gods" in *Poenulus*; note also a rare late Punic *mater lectionis* in the ending, *-ym* of *khnym*, *KAI* 161, 6, meaning uncertain. Dual nouns apparently end in *-ēm* as in *iadem* "hands," *KAI* 178, 1. Masculine dual and plural nouns in construct end in *-ē*, as in the goddess Tanit's epithet φανηβαλος for /pane:-baʕl/ "face of Baal."

Feminine plural nouns end in *-t*, in both absolute and construct states. This ending represents *-ūt* < /-ōt/ < **-āt*, as in *alonuth* "goddesses" (in *Poenulus*). In the late Latino-Punic inscriptions, the *-t* is sometimes missing. *KAI* 180 a and d have *sanu*, while c and e in the same inscription have *sanuth*, all meaning "years." The feminine dual absolute *mʾtm* for the numeral 200 is probably *miʾatēm*, with ending *-tēm* (cf. the masculine dual absolute; colloquial modern Arabic *-tēn*).

4.2.4 Adjectives

Adjectives in Semitic have the same external morphology as nouns. In Phoenician, then: masculine singular -Ø, feminine singular *-t*, masculine plural *-m*, feminine plural *-t.*

4.3 Pronouns

Phoenician attests personal pronouns, as well as demonstratives, interrogative pronouns, and relative pronouns.

4.3.1 Personal pronouns

Personal pronouns in Phoenician are of two kinds: independent and suffixed. Both sets occur in singular and plural forms, and both lack a gender distinction in the first person (but not in the second and third). There are also sometimes case distinctions, as we will see.

4.3.1.1 Independent personal pronouns

Because Phoenician verbs are conjugated for person, number, and gender, a pronominal subject in a verbal clause is usually not expressed outside the verb itself; that is, an independent pronoun is not necessary, and when used is meant to emphasize the function of the pronominal subject. Independent pronouns can, in fact, be used to emphasize any nominal form in a sentence, such as the direct object of a verb, a pronominal suffix on a noun, or the object of a preposition. The standard forms of the independent personal pronouns and their reconstructed pronunciations are given in (3):

(3)

Singular		
1st com.	’nk	/ˀano:ki:/ (occasionally in Punic ’nky, with -y for /-i:/)
2nd masc.	’t	/ˀatta(:)/
2nd fem.	’t	/ˀatti(:)/
3rd masc.	h’	/huˀ/
	h’t	/huˀat/
3rd fem.	h’	/hiˀ/
Plural		
1st com.	’nḥn	/ˀanaħn(V)/
2nd masc.	not attested	
2nd fem.	not attested	
3rd masc.	hmt	/hummat/
3rd fem.	hmt	/himmat/

4.3.1.2 Enclitic personal pronouns

The standard forms of the personal pronouns suffixed to nouns (as possessive) and to prepositions are presented in Table 4.3. The form of the enclitic pronouns attached to nouns shows some variation according to their morphophonetic context, those contexts being: (i) a nominative/accusative singular noun, or a feminine plural noun (i.e., occurring after a consonant); (ii) a genitive singular noun (i.e., occurring after *-i-*); and (iii) a masculine plural noun (i.e., occurring after some other vowel). Recall that the genitive singular ending was retained when other case endings were lost, so that the nominative/accusative enclitics are in effect forms following a consonant, while enclitics attached to genitives are forms occurring after a vowel.

Byblian third-person pronouns are different from the Standard Phoenician forms of Table 4.3. The attested Byblian forms are given in (4):

(4)

	Enclitics on singular nouns and prepositions		*Enclitics on plural nouns*	
3rd masc. sg.	h			
	w	/-o:/	w	/-e:u/
3rd fem. sg.	h	/-aha(:)/		
3rd masc. pl.	hm	/-hum(ma)/		

Table 4.3 The enclitic personal pronouns of Standard Phoenician

	C__		-i-__		-V__	
Singular						
1st com.	Ø	/-i:/	y	/-iya(:)/	y	/-ayy/
	y	/-i:/[1]				
2nd masc.	k	probably /-ka(:)/				
2nd fem.	k	/-ki(:)/				
3rd masc.	Ø	/-o:/[2]	y	/-iyu(:)/[3]	y	/-e:yu(:)/[3]
3rd fem.	Ø	probably /-a:/[4]	y	/-iya(:)/[3]	y	/-e:ya(:)/[3]
Plural						
1st com.	n	[-o(:)n][5]				
2nd masc.	not attested					
2nd fem.	not attested					
3rd masc.	m	/-o:m/[6]	nm	/-no:m/	nm	/-no:m/[7]
3rd fem.	m	/-e:m/[8]	nm	/-ne:m/[9]		

Notes to Table 4.3
[1]The variant *-y* may be a *mater lectionis* (see §2) or by analogy with the genitive singular *-y*.
[2]We assume the nominative/accusative form is patterned on the accusative: */-ahu(:)/ > */-au(:)/ > /-o/.
[3]In these cases, /y/ arises as a palatal off-glide following a front vowel. The genitive ending on singular nouns is /-i/ and on plural nouns is /-e:/: thus, */-ihu(:)/ > /-iyu(:)/; */-ayhu(:)/ > */-e:hu(:)/ > /-e:yu(:)/; and so forth.
[4]Again, the nominative/accusative form is patterned on the accusative: */-aha(:)/ > /-a:/.
[5]See PΥBAΘΩN "our lady" *KAI* 175, 2.
[6]Again, assuming the accusative form has been taken over by the nominative: */-ahum/ > */-aum/ > /-o:m/.
[7]From an old plural verbal ending *-*ūna*-, **yaqtulūnahum*. After loss of intervocalic /h/, **yaqtulūnaum* gives */yak'tulu:no:m/. Then /-no:m/ is extended to use on nouns as well; see Huehnergard 1991:190–194; Harris 1936:49–50.
[8]Amadasi Guzzo 1999 notes Krahmalkov's cautious approach (1993; either the 3rd masc. pl. *-m* was leveled through, or the 3rd fem. pl. comes from */-ahim/ > */-aim/ > /-e:m/), but argues that the former is less likely than the latter.
[9]Guzzo argues that /e:m/ and /ne:m/ are to be differentiated from masculine plural /o:m/ and /no:m/; cf. n. 8.

The third masculine singular *h* is the earliest form and is only attested in the genitive /-ihu(:)/. The interpretation of the third masculine singular form occurring on plural nouns, *w*, assumes a dual oblique ending before suffixes, as in Biblical Hebrew: thus, */-ayhu(:)/ > */-e:hu(:)/ > */-e:u(:)/, spelled <-w>.

Late Punic third-person forms are different in part. After a consonant, Punic shows the same enclitic forms as Phoenician proper (in third singular forms, the character ʾ functions as a *mater lectionis*; see §2):

(5) *3rd masc. sg.* ʾ /-o:/
3rd fem. sg. ʾ /-a:/
3rd masc. pl. m /-o:m/

After a vowel, early Punic texts show the same pronouns as Phoenician:

(6) *3rd masc. sg.* y /-iyu(:)/
3rd fem. sg. y /-iya(:)/
3rd masc. pl. nm /-no:m/

In later Punic texts, however, the third masculine singular usually appears as *-m* (/-im/). Huehnergard argues that /-iyu(:)/ would have been pronounced the same as /-iw/, and that the *-m* suffix simply demonstrates a nasalization of the word-final /-w/ (for details, see Huehnergard 1991).

Phoenician and Punic enclitic pronouns suffixed to verbs are like those attached to nouns and prepositions with a few exceptions:

(7) *Singular*

1st com.	n	/-ni:/	
2nd masc.	k	/-ka(:)/	
2nd fem.	k	/-ki(:)/	
3rd masc.	h	/-hu(:)/	Old Byblian
	w		later Byblian
	ø		Standard Phoenician, after a consonant
	y		Standard Phoenician, after a vowel
	ʾ		Punic *mater lectionis*
	m	/-im/	Late Punic
3rd fem.	y		Standard Phoenician
	ʾ		Punic *mater lectionis*
Plural			
1st com.	n	/-nu(:)/?	
2nd masc.	not attested		
2nd fem.	not attested		
3rd masc.	m		after a consonant
	nm		after a vowel

4.3.2 Demonstrative pronouns

The demonstratives in Phoenician are declined for person and number. They are used in conjunction with the definite article (see §4.4) only sporadically, even when modifying a definite noun; in other words, "this house" would be *hbt z* ("the house this") or *hbt hz* ("the house the this"). Occasionally, even combinations like *bt z* ("house this") are found when the phrase must be definite.

The various forms of the near demonstrative ("this, these") are presented in (8):

(8)

	Phoenician	*Byblian*	*Cypriot*	*Punic variants*
Masc. sg.	z	zn, z	ʾz	s, ʾz, hʾz, st, zt, *inter alia*
Fem. sg.	z	zʾt, zʾ	ʾz	st, zt
Pl.	ʾl	ʾl	ʾl	ʾlʾ

Standard Phoenician *z* is from Proto-Semitic **ð* and is also seen in other Semitic languages as the base for the near demonstratives. Prothetic *ʾ* is common in Cyprus before word-initial biconsonantal clusters (note that the use of prothetic *ʾ* suggests that Cypriot Phoenician *z* was pronounced as a double consonant sound, like Greek *zeta*; see Harris 1936:23–24; Woodard 1997:172); late forms with *s* indicate a confusion of sibilants. Vocalizations are unknown. The form extended with *-n* is known so far only at Byblos and on an inscribed ivory box found in Ur, origin unknown, *KAI* 29. Extension with *-n* is common on prepositions, however.

The far demonstrative ("that, those") is identical to the independent third-person pronouns (see §4.3.1.1), as in Biblical Hebrew.

4.3.3 Interrogative pronouns

The interrogative pronouns in their use at the beginning of questions are known in Phoenician only from *Poenulus*. In Phoenician proper, *my* (probably /miya/) "who?" and *m* (probably /mū/ < **mō* < **mā*) "what?" serve as indefinite relative pronouns as well: "whoever" effaces this inscription (*KAI* 24, 14); "whatever" (*m'š*) I did (*KAI* 24, 4). Note the occurrence of *ymu* in a Roman-era Punic inscription, *IRT* 873, 2, written in Latin characters, with a prothetic vowel.

4.3.4 Indefinite pronoun

Phoenician attests the indefinite pronoun *mnm*. Compare Peripheral Akkadian mīnummē.

4.3.5 Determinative-relative pronouns

The pronouns *'š*, *š*, along with late variations are probably equivalent to the Biblical Hebrew construction of *šɛ* + *gemination*, which replaces the more usual *'ăšɛr* in very early and relatively late Biblical texts (perhaps denoting a dialectal difference rather than a chronological one).

The Semitic source of this relative pronoun (and its Biblical Hebrew cognate) is obscure. It might be the reflex of **θ*-, as known from Old Akkadian *θū*- and *θūt*, and from standard Akkadian *ša* (reflex of Old Akkadian accusative masculine *θā*). Phoenician and Hebrew *š*-, however, are the only West Semitic forms that can be so explained, all other West Semitic relative pronouns being derived from the voiced counterpart **ð*. An alternate interpretation is one which posits earlier Canaanite **'ašar* or the like, which was clipped to *'aš* or even *š*- in Phoenician and some Hebrew dialects (northern?), but developed into *'ăšɛr* in the dialect of Hebrew most represented in the Bible (Judahite) (see Huehnergard forthcoming).

The Old Byblian relative pronoun *z* is, as in most other West Semitic languages, from **ð* (see §4.3.2).

4.4 Definite article

The Phoenician definite article, when written, appears as a prefixed *h*- accompanied by gemination of the ensuing consonant, as in Biblical Hebrew (in later texts, the glottal consonant sometimes appears as ', or is lost altogether). Though consonant gemination is not regularly indicated in Phoenician orthography, we know the following consonant was doubled because of the unusual spelling *'mmqm* for [ammak'u:m], earlier /hammak'o:m/ "the place" (*KAI* 173, 5). The origin of the definite article in West Semitic is, however, controversial, and the explanation for the Phoenician definite article is bound up with various theories. Of these, two theories predominate. The most common sees the West Semitic definite article as originating in a deictic particle, as in Indo-European. The second, championed by Lambdin 1971, identifies the origin of the West Semitic definite article in junctural doubling between a noun and a demonstrative, or between a noun and a relative, with the accusative ending of the noun (*-a*) leveled after final short vowels had been lost and the quality of the vowel between noun and demonstrative or relative no longer had meaning. According to Lambdin, in Arabic, Biblical Hebrew, and, we assume, Phoenician, Moabite, Ammonite, and Edomite (which we know only in consonantal texts), the chain [noun + /-a/ + doubling] is reanalyzed as [noun#] + [/a/ + doubling]. Since words in West Semitic ordinarily do not begin with a vowel, /h-/ or /ʔ-/ was added before /a/. Aramaic has a slightly different development, but one that gives Lambdin's theory its explanatory force: in Aramaic, [noun + /a/ + doubling] became [noun + /a/ + /ʔ/#], where the glottal stop simply provides a boundary between the short vowel and the next word, as can happen elsewhere in Semitic (this Aramaic sequence subsequently becomes [noun + /a:/]).

The definite article in Phoenician was lost after the inseparable prepositions *b-*, *l-*, *k-* (as in Biblical Hebrew), and after some free-standing prepositions, depending on dialect and chronology. Consider, for example, the Yeḥawmilk inscription from fifth-century Byblos (*KAI* 10), in which the definite article disappears after all prepositions; the Eshmunazor inscription from fifth-century Sidon (*KAI* 14), in which it is lost after all prepositions and after the direct object marker *ʾyt*; and the Karatepe inscription, from late eighth-century Asia Minor (*KAI* 26), for loss even after the *w-* "and" conjunction.

4.5 Verbal morphology

Phoenician verbs are inflected for person, gender, and number through the use of affixes and vowel patterns which are added to the (usually) triconsonantal root.

4.5.1 Verb-stems

All the Semitic languages have a verbal system that includes a basic stem (called the G-stem, from German *Grundstamm*), and several derived stems: passive, causative, reflexive, and so on. A general description follows, although the stems have individual histories in each of the Semitic languages (see also Appendix 1, §3.3.5.2):

1. *N-stem:* formed with a prefix *n-*, functioning as the passive of the G-stem, or as a reflexive.
2. *D-stem:* characterized by doubling of the middle root consonant; pluralizing or transitivizing (or raises the transitivity valence), or simply lexical.
3. *C-stem:* formed with a prefix *s-* (originally) or *h-* or *ʾ-*, functioning as a causative.
4. *t-stems* (Gt, tG, Dt, tD, and so on): built by either prefixing or infixing of a *t*; usually reflexive/reciprocal, and sometimes passive.

In addition, G, D, and C also have internal passives, in other words, related passive stems that are constructed by changes in the vowel pattern of the active stem. These are identified by the sigla G-, D-, C-.

The verbal morphology of Phoenician is fairly simple. The stems of which we have evidence are G, N, D, C, tG, Dt, and possibly some internal passives.

4.5.2 The Northwest Semitic system

The Northwest Semitic verbal system is characterized by the following constructions:

1. *A perfective:* the "Suffix-Conjugation".
2. *A preterite/jussive:* the "Prefix-Conjugation" A.
3. *An imperfective:* the "Prefix-Conjugation" B (the only prefix-conjugation attested in Phoenician).
4. *Active and passive participles:* verbal adjectives indicating essential features or ongoing activity.
5. *An infinitive "construct":* a verbal noun that serves as both infinitive and gerund.
6. *An infinitive "absolute":* actually an adverb, which stands with a finite verb to emphasize the verb, or stands alone and can be interpreted as any verb form required.
7. *An imperative.*

There is no evidence of the preterite use of Prefix-Conjugation A in Phoenician; in its jussive use, it is indistinguishable in attested forms from Prefix-Conjugation B. In Proto-Canaanite, Conjugation A was **yaqtul* and Conjugation B was **yaqtulu*; when short final vowels were lost, the morphological distinction between A and B consequently disappeared for most verbs.

4.5.3 The Phoenician system

The Northwest Semitic verbal system with its Phoenician reflex, as far as the latter is known, is set out below. The root *q-t-l* is used; vocalization is given when it is secure, even if known solely by reconstruction.

4.5.3.1 G-stem

The Suffix-Conjugation of the Phoenician G-stem is as follows:

(9)

	Singular	*Plural*
1st com.	*qataltŭ̄ > qataltī	*qatalnŭ̄ > qtln
2nd masc.	*qataltă̄ > qtlt	*qataltum(ū) > not attested
2nd fem.	*qataltĭ̄ > qtlt	*qataltin(ā,na) > not attested
3rd masc.	*qatala > qatal ([qatol])	*qatalū > qatalū
3rd fem.	*qatalat > qatala	*qatalā > not attested

See Krahmalkov 1979 for the third feminine singular *qatala*, rather than expected *qatalo*; note that this *-a* is not from an originally open syllable.

The Prefix-Conjugation of the Phoenician G-stem is given in (10):

(10)

	Singular	*Plural*
1st com.	*ʾaqtulu > ʾiqtul	*naqtulu > not attested
2nd masc.	*taqtulu > tiqtul	*taqtulūna > tiqtulū
2nd fem.	*taqtulīna > tqtl (tiqtulī?)	*taqtulnă̄ > tqtln (tiqtulna?)
3rd masc.	*yaqtulu > yiqtul	*yaqtulūna > yiqtulū
3rd fem.	*taqtulu > tiqtul	*yaqtulnă̄ > not attested

The imperative (second person) is as follows:

(11)

	Singular	*Plural*
Masc.	*qutul > qtl	*qutulū > not attested
Fem.	*qutulī > qtl	*qutulnă̄ > not attested

The Northwest Semitic infinitive construct **qutul* gives Phoenician *qtl*, and the infinitive absolute **qatāl* becomes Phoenician *qatōl*. There is evidence that the infinitive construct of some weak verbs ends in "feminine" *-t*, as in Biblical Hebrew: thus, *l-qḥt* (preposition *l-* marking a purpose clause, and infinitive *qḥt*), from a root *l-q-ḥ* (which, although a strong verb in the perfect, behaves like a I-*n* verb in the imperfect, imperative, and infintive construct); *l-dʿt*, from a root *y-d-ʿ*; *l-tt*, from a root *y-t-n*; *šbt*, from a root *y-š-b*.

Active and passive G-stem participles are presented in (12):

(12)

	Singular	Plural
Active participle		
Masc.	*qātil- (+ case ending) > qōtil	*qātilūma/*qātilīma > qōtilīm
Fem.	*qātilat-/*qātilt- > qtlt	*qātilāt-> not attested
Passive participle		
Masc.	*qatūl- > qatūl	*qatūlīm > qatūlīm
Fem.	*qatult-/*qatūlat- > qtlt	*qatūlāt > qatūlōt

No finite G-stem forms are attested in Phoenician.

4.5.3.2 Derived stems

In the construction of the derived stems, the prefixes and affixes used are the same as those of the G-stem. The following are the most basic forms, (third) masculine singular, when appropriate, from Northwest Semitic to Phoenician, as far as can be determined:

The *N-stem* functions as a passive in Phoenician:

1. *Suffix-Conjugation: *naqtala > nqtl*
2. *Prefix-Conjugation: *yiqqatilu > yqtl*; note that the **n-* affix assimilates and doubles the first root consonant.
3. *Participle: *naqtal- > *nqtl* (only attested as fem. sg. *nqtlt* and masc. pl. *nqtlm*).

The *D-stem* is generally not distinguishable from the G by morphology alone.

4. *Suffix-Conjugation: *qattila > qittil*
5. *Prefix-Conjugation: *yaqattilu > yaqattil*
6. *Imperative: *qattil > qattil*
7. *Infinitive construct: *qattil > qattil*
8. *Infinitive absolute: *qattāl > qattōl*
9. *Participle: *maqattil- > maqattil*

One or two D passive (D-) Suffix-Conjugation forms are perhaps attested, recognized as such by context and by comparison with usage in related languages. There is some evidence for the special form used for the D of roots that are middle weak, that is, missing the middle consonant and therefore having nothing to double in this conjugation: thus, **qālil, yaqallil* from a root *q-w/y-l*; *mtpp*, "drummer," participle from a root *t-w-p*.

Various Phoenician *C-stem* forms are attested:

10. *Suffix-Conjugation: *haqtila > yiqtil*; *ʾiqtil* in late Punic. It is assumed that the *h*-prefix was lost by palatalization, which would have taken place in a high-vowel environment. One suggestion assumes *ha- > hi-* (as in Biblical Hebrew) with the addition of the negative *ī*. **ī hiqtil > ī yiqtil* and probably > *yiqtēl*.
11. *Prefix-Conjugation: *yahaqtilu > yqtl*. Note the loss of intervocalic *h*; the Phoenician form is perhaps *yaqtil*.
12. *Infinitive: *yaqtil* > /yaqtil/, as in Karatepe's *yṭnʾ*, probably /yaṭniʾ/. There is some late evidence of a construct form with *l-*, but without *h-* or *y*-prefix, perhaps /laqtil/.
13. *Participle: *mahaqtil- > mqtl*. Note again the loss of intervocalic *h*. Phoenician perhaps has *maqtil*, although late Punic texts have a *-y-* between the *m-* prefix and the root, representing either a high vowel (*miqtil*), or the reanalysis to *mVyaqtil*, by analogy with the Prefix-Conjugation (*yqtl*).

Again, one or two C passive (C-) stem-forms are perhaps attested.

Regarding the *t-stems*, two passive tG forms are attested at Byblos (*yitqatil*?), and two reflexive Dt forms elsewhere (*yiqtattil*?).

4.6 Prepositions and particles

Phoenician, like many of the Semitic languages, has both free-standing and inseparable (proclitic) prepositions. Inseparable prepositions are *b-* "in," "consisting of"; *l-* "to/for," "at"; and *k-* "like/as." The definite article is lost after these three inseparable prepositions. The preposition **min-* "from" usually occurs as inseparable *m-*, with the *n-* assimilated to, and presumably doubling, the following consonant.

Many prepositions in Phoenician are extended, either by "prothetic ʾ", as in *ʾb* for *b-*, or by the addition of *-n* or *-t* at the end, as in *bn* for *b-*, *ln* for *l-*, *ʿlt* for *ʿl* "(up)on, over," and *pnt* "before." Prepositions are often combined with nouns to make new prepositions, such as *lpn* "in front of" from *l-* "at" and *pn* "face of"; and they are also combined with each other, even the proclitic prepositions – *lm* "from" from *l-* and *m-* < **min*; even *lmb* "in," "from," "on account of" from *l-*, *m-*, and *b-*.

In Phoenician, the marker of a definite direct object is *ʾyt* from **ʾiyyāt* > /ʔiyyōt/ ([ʔiyyūt]), and is clearly distinct from the preposition *ʾt* "with" (/ʔitt/). In Punic, the direct object marker is written *ʾt* or even *t*, indicating loss of the consonantal *y* and eventual elision of the ʾ, as well. In *Poenulus*, the Latin transcription *yth* indicates that the vowel has become rounded.

The most interesting adverbs in Phoenician are the several negative adverbs, usually modifying verbs. The most common is *bl*, presumably /bal/ as in Biblical Hebrew, usually negating a verb but also used with nouns. There is also a negative *ʾy*, presumably /ʔi:/ as in Biblical Hebrew, with *y* as a *mater lectionis* (see §2), which is used as both a particle of nonexistence and a verbal negative. The two can be combined, *ʾbl* or *ʾybl*. For negative commands and prohibitions, *ʾl* /ʔal/ is used. For a negative purpose clause, *lm* "so that not, lest" is used, a combination of preposition *l-* and negative *m-*. There is no evidence for the negative *lʾ* so common in Hebrew, Arabic, and Aramaic.

There is evidence for the use of a locative /-a/ ending (originally **-ah* with consonantal *h*), in some Punic forms with ʾ *mater lectionis* at the end of the word: *mʿlʾ* and *mtʾ* [sic] for "above" and "below," *KAI* 145, 14.

4.7 Conjunctions

The most common conjunctions in Phoenician are *w-* (/wa-/?; later /u/) "and"; *ʾm* (/ʔim/?) "if/when"; *k* (/ki:/?) "that; because; when"; and *ʾp* /ʔap/?) "moreover." Prepositions can be used as conjunctions when paired with the relative *ʾš* (see §4.3.5).

5. SYNTAX

The survey of our sources for Phoenician (see §1) makes clear that very little of what we have in Phoenician provides evidence for the syntax of the language. Our longest inscription, from Karatepe in Asia Minor, is a translation of a Luwian inscription, and so must be used with caution as evidence for Phoenician syntax. A large percentage of our inscriptions are formulaic and simply identify the object on which they are written: "that which PN vowed to DN." There are some clear features of syntax, however, that can be dealt with here.

5.1 Word order

Phoenician, like other Semitic languages, makes frequent use of verbless or "nominal" clauses. There is no verb "to be" in the present tense in Phoenician, so equational clauses/sentences are often written as subject + adverb or predicate adjective, and occasionally subject + predicate nominative. Verbal clauses – clauses that contain a conjugated verb – in Phoenician, as elsewhere in Semitic, are usually V–S–O. A switch in word order so that the subject precedes the verb is often a marker of emphasis on the subject.

5.2 Hendiadys

Verbal hendiadys is known in Phoenician, as in Biblical Hebrew. This conjoined construction takes one of two forms: (i) [finite verb A + *w-* "and" + finite verb B]; or (ii) [finite verb A + preposition *l-* + infinitive construct of verb B]. Such structural combinations, of course, need not be examples of hendiadys, but when they are, verb B is the main verb of the clause, and verb A is to be translated adverbially, as in:

(13)	w-kl	ʾdm	ʾš	ysp	l-pʿl	mlʾkt	ʿlt	mzbḥ	zn...
	and-any	person	who	would increase	to do	work	on	altar	this...

"And anyone who would do work again on this altar..." (*KAI* 10, 11–12).

The causative *ysp* is being used to denote repeated or continuous action, and is not interpreted literally.

5.3 Infinitive absolute

The infinitive absolute in Phoenician can be used to represent any verbal form if the context has made clear which form is expected (i.e., it functions as an unmarked verb form). This use of the infinitive absolute is especially pronounced in the Karatepe inscription, where infinitives absolute even take pronominal objective suffixes.

5.4 The vocative

Vocative *l-* is known in Phoenician, as in Ugaritic and Arabic, but is rare. To express a wish, Phoenician can use the particle *l-* /lu:/ "O that...!," proclitic on a verb, but that too is rare. Ordinarily a wish is conveyed by the volitive forms of the verb: (i) the first-person *cohortative*, which is indistinguishable from the imperfect (but note *ʾpqn* in *KAI* 50, 3, where the *-n* seems to be a volitive particle, like Biblical Hebrew *nāʾ*); (ii) the imperative, in most cases indistinguishable from the perfect; and (iii) the third-person *jussive*, ordinarily indistinguishable from the imperfect.

5.5 Relative clauses

Relative clauses in Phoenician are generally introduced by the relative pronoun *ʾš* (*z* in Old Byblian), and occasionally by the "interrogative" pronouns (see §4.3.3). There are rare occurrences also of a resumptive pronoun after *ʾš*:

(14)	ʾnk	yḥwmlk...	ʾš	pʿltn	hrbt	bʿlt	gbl	mmlkt	ʿl	gbl
	I	Yeḥawmilk...	who	she made me	the lady	the Lady of	Byblos	sovereign	over	Byblos

"I am Yeḥawmilk whom the lady, Lady of Byblos, made sovereign over Byblos" (*KAI* 10, 1–2).

6. LEXICON

The Phoenician lexicon is, for the most part, typically Semitic, but the Phoenicians spread throughout the Mediterranean as merchants and eventually colonists. Those Phoenicians would, of course, have had exposure to other languages and would have adopted words and names from other cultures. These loanwords come from a number of other languages and language families. The Kilamuwa inscription from Anatolia, where an Aramaic dialect is the local language, describes Kilamuwa as *br* "son of" Ḥayya', using Aramaic *br* rather than the Canaanite *bn* that is usual in Phoenician. There are also Luwian personal and place names in Phoenician inscriptions from Anatolia, such as the name Kilamuwa itself, and several in the Azatiwada inscription from Karatepe. We also see Egyptian personal and place names in Phoenician inscriptions found in Egypt.

Greek and Latin names and their (usually nominative) case endings are fairly common in later inscriptions, plus a few words like *drachma, imperator, senator, and podium.* Numidian words and personal and place names are known from the North African inscriptions: *mynkd* "ruler," from Numidian *mnkd* "head, chief"; personal names Massinissa (*msnsn*) and Micipsa (*mkwsn*); and the place name Thugga (*tbgg*).

7. READING LIST

Ward 1997 is a good, standard overview of Phoenician history and culture. Markoe 2000 also provides an overview, but stresses material culture. Moscati 1968 and Harden 1962 are classic book-length descriptions.

McCarter 1975 traces the development of the Canaanite/Phoenician alphabet, as does Naveh 1982, more generally. Woodard 1997 is an excellent source for early Greek alphabets and their relationship to the Phoenician and Phoenicians.

Amadasi Guzzo 1997 is a nice summary of the Phoenician language. Huehnergard 1992 and 1995 place Phoenician within the Semitic languages. Harris 1936 is still a useful structuralist introduction, although dating of inscriptions is especially out of date, and recent finds are, of course, not included. Segert 1976 is more up to date and includes more about the use of classical and other sources for our knowledge of Phoenician, something between an introductory and reference grammar. Friedrich, Röllig, and Amadasi Guzzo 1999 is a sound reference grammar, with abundant citations to evidence for Phoenician language and grammar outside the Phoenician corpus itself.

Abbreviations

Assurb. Rassam	Rassam Cylinder of Assurbanipal. Streck, M. *Assurbanipal und die letzten assyrischen Könige bis zum Untergang Nineveh's.* Leipzig: Hinrichs, 1916.
CIL	*Corpus Inscriptionum Latinarum.* 1862–. Berlin: Reimer.
CIS	*Corpus Inscriptionum Semiticarum.* Pars Prima, Inscriptiones Phoeniciae. 1881–. Paris: Klincksieck.
Esarh.	Borger, R. *Die Inschriften Asarhaddons Königs von Assyrien.* Archiv für Orientforschung Beiheft 9; Graz, 1956.
Eusebius *PE*	Eusebius, *Præparatio evangelica*
IRT	*The Inscriptions of Roman Tripolitania.* Edited by J. Reynold and J. Ward. Rome: British School at Rome, 1952.

Josephus *Ant.*	Josephus, *Jewish Antiquities*
Josephus *C. Ap.*	Josephus, *Contra Apion*
KAI	*Kanaanäische und aramäische Inscriften* (3rd edition, 3 vols.). Edited by H. Donner and W. Röllig. Wiesbaden: Otto Harrassowitz, 1971–1976.
Senn. OI Prism	Oriental Institute Prism of Sennacherib's Annals. Luckenbill, D. *The Annals of Sennacherib.* Chicago: University of Chicago Press, 1924.
T-P	Tadmor, H. *The Inscriptions of Tiglath-Pileser III, King of Assyria.* Jerusalem: Israel Academy of Sciences and Humanities, 1994.
DN	divine name
PN	personal name

Bibliography

Amadasi Guzzo, M. 1996. "L'accompli à la 3e personne du féminin singulier et le pronom suffixe à l'accusatif de la 3e personne du singulier: note de grammaire phénicienne." In B. Pongratz-Leisten, H. Kühne, and P. Xella (eds.), *Ana šadî Labnāni lū allik: Festschrift für Wolfgang Röllig,*
pp. 1–9. Neukirchen-Vluyn: Neukirchener Verlag.

———. 1997. "Phoenician-Punic." In Meyers 1997, vol. 4, pp. 317–324.

———. 1999. "Plural feminine personal suffix pronouns in Phoenician." *Eretz Israel* 26 (Cross volume): 46*–51*.

Cross, F., and D. Freedman. 1951. "The pronominal suffixes of the third person singular in Phoenician." *Journal of Near Eastern Studies* 10:228–230.

———. 1952. *Early Hebrew Orthography: A Study of the Epigraphic Evidence.* American Oriental Series 36. New Haven: American Oriental Society.

Fox, J. 1996. "A sequence of vowel shifts in Phoenician and other languages." *Journal of Near Eastern Studies* 55:37–47.

Friedrich, J., and W. Röllig. 1999. *Phönizisch-punische Grammatik* (3rd edition, revised by M. Amadasi Guzzo). Analecta Orientalia 55. Rome: Pontifical Biblical Institute. [Original publication: Johannes Friedrich. *Phönizisch-punische Grammatik.* 1951.]

Garr, R. 1985. *Dialect Geography of Syria-Palestine, 1000–586* BCE. Philadelphia: University of Pennsylvania.

Hackett, J. 2002. "The study of partially documented languages." In S. Izre'el (ed.), *Semitic Linguistics: The State of the Art at the Turn of the Twenty-first Century*, pp. 57–75. *Israel Oriental Studies* 20. Winona Lake, IN: Eisenbrauns.

Harden, D. 1962. *The Phoenicians.* London: Thames and Hudson.

Harris, Z. 1936. *A Grammar of the Phoenician Language.* American Oriental Series 8. New Haven: American Oriental Society.

Hetzron, R. 1974. "La division des langues sémitiques." In A. Caquot and D. Cohen (eds.), *Actes du premier Congrès international de linguistique sémitique et chamito-sémitique, Paris 16–19 juillet 1969*, pp. 181–194. The Hague/Paris: Mouton.

Huehnergard, J. 1991. "The development of the third person suffixes in Phoenician." *Maarav* 7:183–194.

———. 1992. "Languages: introductory survey." In D. N. Freedman (ed.), *The Anchor Bible Dictionary*, vol. IV, pp. 155–170. New York: Doubleday.

———. 1995. "Semitic languages." J. Sasson (ed.), *Civilizations of the Ancient Near East*, vol. 4, pp. 2117–2134. New York: Scribners.

———. forthcoming. "On the etymology of the Hebrew relative *šɛ-*." In Avi Hurvitz and Steven E. Fassberg (eds.), In *Biblical Hebrew in Its Northwest Semitic Setting: Typological and Historical Perspectives.* Jerusalem: Magnes.

Kouwenberg, N. 1997. *Gemination in the Akkadian Verb.* Studia Semitica Nederlandica. Assen: Van Gorcum.

Krahmalkov, C. 1970. "Studies in Phoenician and Punic grammar." *Journal of Semitic Studies* 15:181–188.

______. 1972. "Comments on the vocalization of the suffix pronoun of the third feminine singular in Phoenician and Punic." *Journal of Semitic Studies* 17:68–75.

______. 1974. "The object pronouns of the third person of Phoenician and Punic." *Rivista di studi fenici* 2:39–43.

______. 1993. "The third feminine plural possessive pronoun in Phoenician-Punic." *Journal of Near Eastern Studies* 52:37–41.

______. 2000. *Phoenician-Punic Dictionary.* Leuven: Peeters.

______. 2001. *A Phoenician Punic Grammar.* Leiden, Boston: Brill.

Lambdin, T. 1971. "The junctural origin of the West Semitic definite article." In H. Goedicke (ed.), *Near Eastern Studies in Honor of William Foxwell Albright*, pp. 315–333. Baltimore: Johns Hopkins University Press.

Markoe, G. 1997. "Phoenicians." In Meyers 1997, vol. 4, pp. 324–331.

______. 2000. *Phoenicians.* Berkeley, Los Angeles: University of California Press.

McCarter, P. 1975. *The Antiquity of the Greek Alphabet and the Early Phoenician Scripts.* Missoula, MT: Scholars Press.

Menken, D. 1981. "Neopunic Orthography." Dissertation, Harvard University.

Meyers, E (ed.). 1997. *Oxford Encyclopedia of the Archaeology of the Near East* (5 vols.). New York: Oxford University Press.

Moscati, S. 1968. *The World of the Phoenicians.* Translated by A. Hamilton. London: Weidenfeld and Nicolson.

Naveh, J. 1987. *Early History of the Alphabet* (2nd edition). Jerusalem: Magnes Press.

Segert, S. 1976. *A Grammar of Phoenician and Punic.* Munich: Beck.

Voigt, R. 1998. "Der Artikel im Semitischen." *Journal of Semitic Studies* 43:221–258.

Ward, W. 1997. "Phoenicia." In Meyers 1997, vol. 4, pp. 313–317.

Woodard, R. 1997. *Greek Writing from Knossos to Homer.* New York: Oxford University Press.

CHAPTER 5

Canaanite dialects

DENNIS PARDEE

1. HISTORICAL AND CULTURAL CONTEXTS

The term *Canaanite* has two primary usages: (i) to designate the dialects of Northwest Semitic spoken in the region called *Canaan* in the second half of the second millennium BC; and (ii) to differentiate the "Canaanite" dialects of the first millennium, primarily Phoenician and Hebrew, from other Northwest Semitic languages spoken in Canaan after *c.* 1000 BC, primarily the Aramaic dialects. The principal feature defining Canaanite is the so-called *Canaanite shift*, that is, Proto-Semitic **ā* realized as *ō* (e.g., Hebrew *ṭōb* "good" corresponds to Aramaic *ṭāb*).

For the Canaanite of the second millennium BC, there are two primary sources: (i) the texts written in Akkadian, the lingua franca of the time, by Canaanite scribes and which contain both Canaanitisms and explicit glosses, i.e., words written in cuneiform script as a gloss in the local language on a preceding Akkadian word; (ii) the *Proto-Canaanite* inscriptions, that is, inscriptions written in archaic linear script and apparently recording the local language.

Some controversy surrounds what "Canaan" meant, both politically and geographically, in the second millennium BC (Na'aman 1994). In the second half of the millennium, the term was used to designate the area of Asia under Egyptian control, including a number of city-states. It comprised an area stretching roughly from what is today northern Lebanon to the border of Egypt, perhaps including some of the arable lands of Transjordan. The term is already attested in the first half of the millennium (eighteenth-century BC texts from Mari) in regard to cities located in the same general area, and there is no reason to doubt that the geographical extent of Canaan was already similar to that known several centuries later. The origin of the term is, however, still unclear.

On the possibility of dividing Canaanite into *North Canaanite* and *South Canaanite*, with the former comprised by Ugaritic, see Tropper 1994 and Pardee 1997c.

For the Canaanite of the first millennium BC and later, there are nearly continuous bodies of inscriptions beginning shortly before 1000 BC. In the case of Phoenician, these inscriptions are found from Anatolia to Egypt to Mesopotamia during roughly the first half of the millennium, then throughout the western Mediterranean as late Phoenician and Punic until the latter dies out well into the Christian era. In the case of Hebrew, a long series of dialects is attested from the tenth century BC down to the present. Canaanite languages distinct from Hebrew and Phoenician were also spoken in Transjordan during the first millennium BC, i.e., Moabite, Ammonite, and Edomite. The sources for these languages are very sparse and they cease in the Persian period, replaced by Aramaic; there are thus few data by which to determine how long they survived as living languages.

Because separate articles are devoted to detailed presentations of Hebrew and Phoenician, this article will deal with the earlier manifestations of Canaanite.

2. WRITING SYSTEMS

The two principal bodies of evidence for Canaanite in the second millennium BC correspond to two writing systems.

2.1 Cuneiform

The greater number of data come from Canaanite features in Akkadian documents that date for the most part from the early fourteenth century. For the description of Akkadian cuneiform as a writing system, see *WAL* Chapter 8, §2.

The vast majority of these documents, which total nearly four hundred, were discovered at Tell el-Amarna in Egypt (see *WAL* Ch. 8, §1.1). They represent the international correspondence directed to Egyptian pharaohs of the early fourteenth century, from as far away as Hattusas, the capital of the Hittite empire (north-central Anatolia), and Babylon (southern Mesopotamia). The Akkadian of these letters varies according to the local scribal schools; that used by the scribes of the various cities of Canaan is so marked by local features that it has been described as a scribal "code," a hybrid language that, though basically Akkadian and thus incomprehensible to speakers of the local language, would have been understood only by Akkadian speakers trained in its use (Moran 1987:27; 1992:xxi–xxii; Rainey 1996, II:1–16, 31–32).

The Canaanite substratum may be derived by triangulation between the written forms, normative Akkadian of the period, and later Canaanite. The primary difficulties with this derivation are two: (i) problems stemming from the writing system itself, which permits multiple values for a given sign; and (ii) the very process of describing an unknown language by assumed parallels from other languages that are only attested half a millennium and more later. These difficulties are palliated in part by the presence of explicit glosses: an Akkadian word or a Sumerian logogram of known meaning may be followed by one or two oblique wedges (German *Glossenkeil* is the technical term for such a wedge) and then by a Canaanite word. The most famous of these is perhaps *ŠU : zu-ru-uḫ* in *EA* 287:27, where *ŠU* is the logogram for "hand/arm" and *zu-ru-uḫ* is the Canaanite gloss, corresponding to Hebrew *zərōa*^{c}, Aramaic *dərā*^{c}, and Arabic *ḏirā*^{c} and illustrating the shift of **ā* to *ō* (Sivan 1984: 29), and perhaps of **ḏ* to *z* (Sivan 1984: 41).

As fraught with difficulties as the above described derivational process is, we know much more about Canaanite from these Akkadian texts than we do from the so-called Proto-Canaanite inscriptions. That is because the latter are far fewer in number and poorly preserved.

2.2 Proto-Canaanite

The problem of the Proto-Canaanite inscriptions is directly linked with that of the *Proto-Sinaitic* inscriptions. The latter are a group of inscriptions, numbering about thirty, discovered near Egyptian turquoise mines in the Sinai, dated variously to the eighteenth or fifteenth centuries BC, which have been only partially deciphered but which seem to represent a form of early West Semitic (for a recent overview with bibliography, see Pardee 1997b). Corresponding to these texts are a group of about twenty texts discovered in southern Canaan and spread over about five centuries, from the seventeenth century BC to the twelfth (Sass 1988, 1991).

The state of preservation of these latter, Proto-Canaanite, inscriptions is even poorer than is that of the Proto-Sinaitic inscriptions. The identification of Proto-Canaanite as a West Semitic script rests on (i) formal similarity with the earlier Proto-Sinaitic script; (ii) the decipherment of a minority of these texts; and (iii) the formal evolution towards Phoenician script. Because of these difficulties, the state of decipherment of these inscriptions is even less advanced than in the case of the Proto-Sinaitic inscriptions. The principal text of one of the best-preserved of Proto-Canaanite inscriptions, that from ʿIzbet Ṣarṭah, seems not to be Semitic in spite of the fact that it contains a Hebrew/Phoenician-type abecedary. On the other hand, the well-known Lachish Ewer inscription has been very plausibly deciphered as West Semitic (for an overview, with bibliography, see Pardee 1997a). Unfortunately, the state of preservation of most of the other inscriptions and their broad geographical and temporal spread make reliable decipherment in most cases impossible. These inscriptions, to the extent that they are Semitic, are written in a purely consonantal script, with no use of *matres lectionis*; and this feature coupled with the problems posed by the paucity and state of the texts make it difficult to define the language represented. The presence of a Hebrew/Phoenician-type abecedary dating to *c.* 1200 BC in the ʿIzbet Ṣarṭah inscription may be seen as indicating, even if the actual text accompanying the abecedary is in another language, that the script was used in other cases to write texts in a language of the Canaanite type. This conclusion is borne out by the Lachish Ewer inscription.

In addition to these texts from southern Canaan, there are a group of arrowhead inscriptions discovered in southern Canaan and Phoenicia and a very limited number of archaic Phoenician inscriptions from Byblos that seem to provide a bridge between Proto-Canaanite and Phoenician. Unfortunately, the small number of texts and the states of preservation again interfere in determining origins and filiations of the scripts as well as of the languages represented.

Finally, there is at least one inscription in the Ugaritic cuneiform script that has been identified as Phoenician in nature (see Ch. 4, §2.1).

3. GRAMMAR

From inscriptions that predate the abecedaries of the ʿIzbet Ṣarṭah ostracon (twelfth century BC), some fifteen Proto-Canaanite signs representing consonantal phonemes are identifiable with some degree of certainty. As these match the Proto-Sinaitic data, as well as the data from the later West-Semitic languages, it may be assumed that the original Proto-Canaanite consonantal inventory was similar to, if not identical with, the Proto-Sinaitic inventory and that the two groups of texts represent the same language, or two or more languages/dialects descended from a common ancestor.

Virtually all other aspects of the linguistic description of Canaanite dialects are derived from the texts written in Akkadian cuneiform. After a century of research, comprehensive studies of these data have been produced by Sivan 1984 (phonology, morphology, and lexicon of the Northwest Semitic words in western Akkadian texts of the fifteenth–thirteenth centuries); Rainey 1996 (a study of the Akkadian of the Amarna texts, with special emphasis on Canaanite features, particularly verbal morphosyntax); and Moran 1987 and 1992 (comprehensive translations of the Amarna texts into French and English). Sivan spread his net a bit wider than he might have done (see Huehnergard 1987); his work is thus useful as a collection of all data furnished by texts written in Akkadian on the various Northwest Semitic languages from Antioch to the border of Egypt in the period covered, but it is more difficult to use as a source for defining Canaanite. Rainey 1996, on the other hand, is specifically a study of the Akkadian texts written by Canaanite scribes; its goal, however, was not to present exclusively the extracted Canaanite data as a grammar of Canaanite, but to present the larger picture, of which the Canaanite part is sometimes quite small. All the relevant data are, however, gathered in these two works, accompanied by expert analyses and extensive bibliographical information (including proper credit to earlier scholarship, particularly Moran's basic studies).

The following are some of the primary characteristics of Canaanite of *c.* 1400 BC:

1. The Canaanite shift of **ā* to *ō*.
2. A consonantal inventory that is smaller than that of Ugaritic and different from that of Aramaic (e.g., **ḏ* → *ṣ*).
3. A case system marked primarily by suffixed vowels, like that of Ugaritic (see Ch. 2, §4.2.2). Case-vowels have generally disappeared or acquired other functions in the first-millennium Northwest Semitic languages.
4. A verbal system of which the morphology and morphosyntax are very similar to those of Ugaritic (see Ch. 2, §4.4). The first-millennium languages have evolved beyond this stage, often retaining only remnants of the earlier systems.
5. The probable absence of a Š-causative stem (like Phoenician and Hebrew).
6. Dissimilation of the vowel *a* in *YaQTaL-* verbal forms, giving *YiQTaL*, the so-called *Barth–Ginsberg Law.*
7. Many details of the lexical inventory are known (Sivan 1984), but pieces of systems – for example, primary verbs of movement – are missing, making comparisons with later systems difficult.

One may speak of these features as defining Canaanite; it is likely, however, that constellations of less important features characterized a number of local Canaanite dialects.

References and Abbreviations

EA = text citation according to Knudtzon, J. 1915. *Die el-Amarna Tafeln mit Einleitung und Erläuterungen.* Leipzig: Hinrichs.

Huehnergard, J. 1987. Review of Sivan 1984. *Journal of the American Oriental Society* 107:713–725.

Moran, W. 1987. *Les lettres d'el Amarna. Correspondance diplomatique du pharaon.* Littératures Anciennes du Proche-Orient 13. Paris: Les Editions du Cerf.

______. 1992. *The Amarna Letters.* Baltimore: Johns Hopkins University Press.

Na'aman, N. 1994. "The Canaanites and their land – a rejoinder." *Ugarit-Forschungen* 24:397–418.

Pardee, D. 1997a. "Proto-Canaanite." In E. Meyers (ed.), *The Oxford Encyclopedia of Archaeology in the Near East*, vol. 4, pp. 354–355. Oxford: Oxford University Press.

______. 1997b. "Proto-Sinaitic." In E. Meyers (ed.), *The Oxford Encyclopedia of Archaeology in the Near East*, vol. 4, pp. 352–354. Oxford: Oxford University Press.

______. 1997c. Review of Tropper 1994. *Journal of the American Oriental Society* 117:375–378.

Rainey, A. 1996. *Canaanite in the Amarna Tablets. A Linguistic Analysis of the Mixed Dialect Used by Scribes from Canaan* (4 vols.). Handbuch der Orientalistik, 25. Leiden: Brill.

Sass, B. 1988. *The Genesis of the Alphabet and Its Development in the Second Millennium BC.* Ägypten und Altes Testament 13. Wiesbaden: Otto Harrassowitz.

______. 1991. *Studia Alphabetica. On the Origin and Early History of the Northwest Semitic, South Semitic and Greek Alphabets.* Orbis Biblicus et Orientalis 102. Freiburg: Universitätsverlag; Göttingen: Vandenhoeck and Ruprecht.

Sivan, D. 1984. *Grammatical Analysis and Glossary of the Northwest Semitic Vocables in Akkadian Texts of the 15th–13th C. BC from Canaan and Syria.* Alter Orient und Altes Testament, 214. Kevelaer: Butzon and Bercker; Neukirchen-Vluyn: Neukirchener Verlag.

Tropper, J. 1994. "Is Ugaritic a Canaanite language?" In G. Brooke, A. Curtis, and J. Healey (eds.), *Ugarit and the Bible.* Proceedings of the International Symposium on Ugarit and the Bible, Manchester, September 1992, pp. 343–353. Ugaritisch-Biblische Literatur 11. Münster: UGARIT-Verlag.

CHAPTER 6

Aramaic

STUART CREASON

1. HISTORICAL AND CULTURAL CONTEXTS

1.1 Overview

Aramaic is a member of the Semitic language family and forms one of the two main branches of the Northwest Semitic group within that family, the other being Canaanite (comprising Hebrew, Phoenician, Moabite, etc.). The language most closely related to Aramaic is Hebrew. More distantly related languages include Akkadian and Arabic. Of all the Semitic languages, Aramaic is one of the most extensively attested, in both geographic and temporal terms. Aramaic has been continuously spoken for approximately 3,500 years (*c.* 1500 BC to the present) and is attested throughout the Near East and the Mediterranean world.

Aramaic was originally spoken by Aramean tribes who settled in portions of what is now Syria, Lebanon, Jordan, Turkey, and Iraq, a region bounded roughly by Damascus and its environs on the south, Mt. Amanus on the northwest and the region between the Balikh and the Khabur rivers on the northeast. The Arameans were a Semitic people, like their neighbors the Hebrews, the Phoenicians, and the Assyrians; and unlike the Hittites, Hurrians, and Urartians. Their economy was largely agricultural and pastoral, though villages and towns as well as larger urban centers, such as Aleppo and Damascus, also existed. These urban centers were usually independent political units, ruled by a king (Aramaic *mlk*), which exerted power over the surrounding agricultural and grazing regions and the nearby towns and villages. In later times, the language itself was spoken and used as a lingua franca throughout the Near East by both Arameans and non-Arameans until it was eclipsed by Arabic beginning in the seventh century AD. Aramaic is still spoken today in communities of eastern Syria, northern Iraq, and southeastern Turkey, though these dialects have been heavily influenced by Arabic and/or Kurdish. These communities became increasingly smaller during the twentieth century and may cease to exist within the next few generations.

1.2 Historical stages and dialects of Aramaic

The division of the extant materials into distinct Aramaic dialects is problematic due in part to the nature of the writing system (see §2) and in part to the number, the kinds, and the geographic extent of the extant materials. Possible dialectal differences cannot always be detected in the extant texts, and, when differences can be detected, it is not always clear whether the differences reflect synchronic or diachronic distinctions. With these caveats in mind, the extant Aramaic texts can be divided into five historical stages to which a sixth stage may be added: *Proto-Aramaic*, a reconstructed stage of the language prior to any extant texts.

1.2.1 Old Aramaic (950–600 BC)

Though Aramaic was spoken during the second millennium BC, the first extant texts appear at the beginning of the first millennium. These texts are nearly all inscriptions on stone, usually royal inscriptions connected with various Aramean city-states. The corpus of texts is quite small, but minor dialect differences can be detected, corresponding roughly to geographic regions. So, one dialect is attested in the core Aramean territory of Aleppo and Damascus, another in the northwestern border region around the Aramean city-state of Samʾal and a third in the northeastern region around Tel Fekheriye. There are a few other Aramaic texts, found outside these regions, most of which attest Aramaic dialects mixed with features from other Semitic languages, for example, the texts found at Deir ʿAlla.

1.2.2 Imperial or Official Aramaic (600–200 BC)

This period begins with the adoption of Aramaic as a lingua franca by the Babylonian Empire. However, few texts are attested until *c.* 500 BC when the Persians established their empire in the Near East. The texts from this period show a fairly uniform dialect which is similar to the "Aleppo–Damascus" dialect of Old Aramaic. However, this uniformity is due largely to the nature of the extant texts. Nearly all of the texts are official documents of the Persian Empire or its subject kingdoms, and nearly all of the texts are from Egypt. It is likely that numerous local dialects of Aramaic existed, but rarely are these dialects reflected in the texts, one possible exception being the Hermopolis papyri (see Kutscher 1971).

1.2.3 Middle Aramaic (200 BC–AD 200)

This period is marked by the emergence of local Aramaic dialects within the textual record, most notably Palmyrene, Hatran, Nabatean, and the dialect of the Aramaic texts found in the caves near Qumran (the Dead Sea Scrolls). However, many texts still attest a dialect very similar to Imperial Aramaic, but with some notable differences (sometimes called *Standard Literary Aramaic*; see Greenfield 1978).

1.2.4 Late Aramaic (AD 200–700)

It is from this period that the overwhelming majority of Aramaic texts are attested, and, because of the abundance of texts, clear and distinct dialects can be isolated. These dialects can be divided into a western group and an eastern group. Major dialects in the west include Samaritan Aramaic, Jewish Palestinian Aramaic (also called Galilean Aramaic) and Christian Palestinian Aramaic. Major dialects in the east include Syriac, Jewish Babylonian Aramaic, and Mandaic. This period ends shortly after the Arab conquest, but literary activity in some of these dialects continues until the thirteenth century AD.

1.2.5 Modern Aramaic (AD 700 to the present)

This period is characterized by the gradual decline of Aramaic due to the increased use of Arabic in the Near East. Numerous local dialects, such asṬuroyo in southeastern Turkey and

Maʾlulan in Syria, were attested in the nineteenth century, but by the end of the twentieth century many of these dialects had ceased to exist.

2. WRITING SYSTEM

2.1 The alphabet

Aramaic is written in an alphabet which was originally borrowed from the Phoenicians (*c.* 1100 BC). This alphabet represents consonantal phonemes only, though four of the letters were also sometimes used to represent certain vowel phonemes (see §2.2.1). Also, because the Aramaic inventory of consonantal phonemes did not exactly match the Phoenician inventory, some of the letters originally represented two (or more) phonemes (see §3.2). During the long history of Aramaic, these letters underwent various changes in form including the development of alternate medial and final forms of some letters (see Naveh 1982). By the Late Aramaic period, a number of distinct, though related, scripts are attested. Below are represented two of the most common scripts from this period, the Aramaic square script (which was also used to write Hebrew) and the Syriac Estrangelo script, along with the standard transliteration of each letter. Final forms are listed to the right of medial forms. In Christian Palestinian Aramaic an additional letter was developed to represent the Greek

Table 6.1 Aramaic consonantal scripts

Square script	Estrangelo	Transliteration
א	ܐ	ʾ
ב	ܒ	b
ג	ܓ	g
ד	ܕ	d
ה	ܗ	h
ו	ܘ	w
ז	ܙ	z
ח	ܚ	ḥ
ט	ܛ	ṭ
י	ܝ	y
כ ך	ܟ ܟ	k
ל	ܠ	l
מ ם	ܡ ܡ	m
נ ן	ܢ ܢ	n
ס	ܣ	s
ע	ܥ	ʿ
פ ף	ܦ	p
צ ץ	ܨ	ṣ
ק	ܩ	q (or ḳ)
ר	ܪ	r
ש	ܫ	š
ת	ܬ	t

Table 6.2 Aramaic vowel diacritics

Tiberian	Transliteration	Jacobite	Transliteration
בִ or בִי	bi or bî	ܒܺܝ or ܒܺ	bī or bî
בֵ or בֵי	bē or bê	ܒܶ	be
בֶ	be		
בַ	ba	ܒܰ	ba
בָ	bā or bo	ܒܳ	bā
בֹ or בוֹ	bō or bô		
בֻ or בוּ	bu or bû	ܒܽ or ܒܽܘ	bū or bû

letter π in Greek loanwords. It had the same form as the letter *p* of the Estrangelo script, but was written backwards.

2.2 Vowel representation

2.2.1 Matres lectionis

Prior to the seventh or eight century AD, vowels were not fully represented in the writing of Aramaic. Instead, some vowels were represented more or less systematically by the four letters ʾ, *h*, *w*, and *y*, the *matres lectionis* ("mothers of reading"). The first two, ʾ and *h*, were only used to represent word-final vowels. The last two, *w* and *y*, were used to represent both medial and final vowels. The letter *w* was used to represent /u:/ and /o:/. The letter *y* was used to represent /e:/ and /i:/. The letter ʾ was used to represent /a:/ and /e:/, although its use for /a:/ was initially restricted to certain morphemes and its use for /e:/ did not develop until the Middle or Late Aramaic period. The letter *h* was also used to represent /a:/ and /e:/. The use of *h* to represent /e:/ was restricted to certain morphemes and eventually *h* was almost completely superseded by *y* in the texts of some dialects or by ʾ in others. The use of *h* to represent /a:/ was retained throughout all periods, but was gradually decreased, and eliminated entirely in the texts of some dialects, by the increased use of ʾ to represent /a:/. Originally, *matres lectionis* were used to represent long vowels only. In the Middle Aramaic period, *matres lectionis* began to be used to represent short vowels and this use increased during the Late Aramaic period, suggesting that vowel quantity was no longer phonemic (see §3.3.2 and §3.3.3).

2.2.2 Systems of diacritics

During the seventh to ninth centuries AD, at least four distinct systems of diacritics were developed to represent vowels. These four systems were developed independently of one another and differ with respect to the number of diacritics used, the form of the diacritics, and the placement of the diacritics relative to the consonant. Two systems were developed by Syriac Christians: the Nestorian in the east and the Jacobite in the west. Two systems were developed by Jewish communities: the Tiberian in the west and the Babylonian in the east. The symbols from two of these systems, as they would appear with the letter *b*, are represented in Table 6.2 along with their standard transliteration.

The Tiberian system also contains four additional symbols for vowels, all of which represent "half-vowels." The phonemic status of these vowels is uncertain (see §3.3.3.1) and one of the symbols can also be used to indicate the absence of a vowel:

(1)

Symbol	*Transliteration*
בְ	ə or no vowel
בֱ	ĕ
בֲ	ă
בֳ	ŏ

2.3 Other diacritics

The Tiberian system and the two Syriac systems contain a variety of other diacritics in addition to those used to indicate vowels. The Tiberian system marks two distinct pronunciations of the letter *š̌* by a dot either to the upper left or to the upper right of the letter, and it indicates that a final *h* is not a *mater lectionis* by a dot (*mappiq*) in the center of the letter. The Syriac systems indicate that a letter is not to be pronounced by a line (*linea occultans*) above that letter. Both the Tiberian and the Syriac systems also contain diacritics that indicate the alternate pronunciations of the letters *b, g, d, k, p,* and *t* (see §3.2.3). The pronunciation of these letters as stops is indicated in the Tiberian system by a dot (*daghesh*) in the center of the letter, and in the Syriac system by a dot (*quššāyā*) above the letter. The pronunciation of these letters as fricatives is indicated in the Tiberian system either by a line (*raphe*) above the letter or by the absence of any diacritic, and in the Syriac system by a dot (*rukkākā*) below the letter (see also Morag 1962 and Segal 1953).

3. PHONOLOGY

3.1 Overview

The reconstruction of the phonology of Aramaic at its various stages is complicated by the paucity of direct evidence for the phonological system and by the ambiguous nature of the evidence that does exist. The writing system itself provides little information about the vowels, and its representation of some of the consonantal phonemes is ambiguous. Transcriptions of Aramaic words in other writing systems (such as Akkadian, Greek, or Demotic) exist, but this evidence is relatively fragmentary and difficult to interpret. The phonology of the language of the transcriptions is not always fully understood and so the effect of the transcriber's phonological system on the transcription cannot be accurately determined. Furthermore, no systematic grammatical description of Aramaic exists prior to the beginning of the Modern Aramaic period. So, the presentation in this section is based upon (i) changes in the spelling of Aramaic words over the course of time; (ii) the information provided by the grammatical writings and the vocalized texts from the seventh to ninth century AD; (iii) the standard reconstruction of the phonology of Proto-Aramaic; and (iv) the generally accepted reconstruction of the changes that took place between Proto-Aramaic and the Late Aramaic dialects.

3.2 Consonants

The relationship of Aramaic consonantal phonemes to Aramaic letters is a complex one since the phonemic inventory underwent a number of changes in the history of Aramaic. Some of these changes took place after the adoption of the alphabet by the Arameans and produced systematic changes in the spelling of certain Aramaic words.

Table 6.3 Old Aramaic consonantal phonemes

Manner of articulation	Bilabial	Inter-dental	Dental/ Alveolar	Palato-alveolar	Palatal	Velar	Uvular	Pharyngeal	Glottal
	Place of articulation								
Stop									
Voiceless	p		t			k			ʔ (ʾ)
Voiced	b		d			g			
Emphatic			tʼ (ṭ)			kʼ (q)			
Fricative									
Voiceless		θ (š)	s	š				ħ (ḥ)	h
Voiced		ð (z)	z					ʕ (ʿ)	
Emphatic		θʼ (ṣ)	sʼ (ṣ)						
Trill							ʀ (r)		
Lateral cont.									
Voiceless			ɬ (š)						
Voiced			l						
Emphatic			ɬʼ (q)						
Nasal	m		n						
Glide	w				y				

3.2.1 Old Aramaic consonantal phonemes

Table 6.3 presents the consonantal phonemes of Old Aramaic with the transliteration of their corresponding symbols in the writing system (see Table 6.1). Only one symbol is listed in those cases in which the transliteration of the written symbol is identical to the symbol used to represent the phoneme. In all other cases, the transliteration of the written symbol is placed in parentheses. Phonemes listed as "Emphatic" are generally considered to be pharyngealized. Note that three letters (*z*, *ṣ* and *q*) each represented two phonemes and that one letter (*š*) represented three phonemes, although in one Old Aramaic text (Tel Fekheriye) the /θ/ phoneme was represented by *s* rather than *š* each of which, therefore, represented two phonemes. That the letter *š* has /ɬ/as one of its values and *q* has /ɬʼ/ as one of its values is likely (see Steiner 1977), but not certain. An alternative for *q* is /ðʼ/. No satisfactory alternative has been proposed for *š*.

In texts of the Samʾal dialect of Old Aramaic and in the Sefire texts found near Aleppo, the word *npš* is also spelled *nbš*. The occasional spelling of words with *b* rather than *p* also occurs in Canaanite dialects and Ugaritic and suggests that voicing may not have distinguished labial stops in some of the dialects of Northwest Semitic.

3.2.2 Imperial Aramaic consonantal phonemes

By the Imperial Aramaic period, three changes had taken place among the dental consonants: (i) /ɬ/ had become /s/; (ii) /ɬʼ/ had become /ʕ/; and (iii) /ð/, /θ/, and /θʼ/ had become /d/, /t/, and /tʼ/, respectively. These changes reduced the phonemic inventory of dentals to the following:

(2)

	Stop	*Fricative*	*Lateral continuant*	*Nasal*
Voiceless	t	s		
Voiced	d	z	l	n
Emphatic	t' (ṭ)	s' (ṣ)		

These changes in the phonemic inventory produced changes in the spelling of Aramaic words. For example, words containing the phoneme /ð/ and spelled with the letter *z* became spelled with the letter *d* because the phoneme /ð/ had become /d/. Similar spelling changes took place in words spelled with the letters *š*, *ṣ* and *q*. For some time, both spellings are attested in Aramaic texts, but the change is complete by the Late Aramaic period, except in Jewish Aramaic dialects in which the letter š is retained for the phoneme /s/ in a few words, perhaps under the influence of Hebrew which underwent the same sound change but which consistently retained the older spelling.

3.2.3 Stop allophony

At some time prior to the loss of short vowels (see §3.3.2), the six letters *b*, *g*, *d*, *k*, *p*, and *t* each came to represent a pair of sounds, one a stop, the other a fricative. For example, *b* represented [b] and [v] (or, possibly, /β/); *p* represented [p] and [f] (or, possibly, /φ/); and so forth. At this stage, the alternation between the stop and fricative articulations was entirely predictable from the phonetic environment. The stop articulation occurred when the consonant was geminated (lengthened) or was preceded by another consonant. The fricative articulation occurred when the consonant was not geminated and was also preceded by a vowel. This alternation was purely phonetic in the case of the four pairs of sounds represented by *b*, *p*, *g*, and *k*. In the case of the two pairs of sounds represented by *d* and *t* the alternation was either phonetic or morphophonemic. If the development of this alternation occurred prior to the shift of /ð/ to /d/ and /θ/ to /t/ (see §3.2.2), then the presence of these two phonemes would have made the alternation morphophonemic. If it occurred after this shift, then the alternation was phonetic. At a later stage of Aramaic, short vowels were lost in certain environments and, as a result, the environment which conditioned the alternation was eliminated in some words. The fricative articulation, however, was not eliminated and so the alternation between the two articulations became phonemic in all six cases.

3.3 Vowels

The inventory of Aramaic vowel phonemes is more difficult to specify than that of consonantal phonemes, since vowels are not fully represented in the writing system until the beginning of the Modern Aramaic period. Prior to that time, the *matres lectionis* (see §2.2.1) were the only means by which vowels were represented. In the Old and Imperial Aramaic periods, the *matres lectionis* were only used to indicate long vowels. During the Middle Aramaic period they began to be used to indicate short vowels as well, and this expansion of their use continued into the Late Aramaic period. This change in the use of the *matres lectionis* suggests that vowel quantity was not phonemic by the Middle Aramaic period and that vowel quality was the only relevant factor in their use. Given this evidence and the data provided by the four systems of vowel diacritics that were developed at the beginning of the Modern Aramaic period, three distinct stages of the phonology of Aramaic vowels can be distinguished: Proto-Aramaic, Middle Aramaic, and Late Aramaic.

3.3.1 Proto-Aramaic

The reconstructed Proto-Aramaic inventory of vowel phonemes is equivalent to the reconstructed Proto-Semitic inventory of vowel phonemes:

(3)

	Front	*Central*	*Back*
High	/i/ and /i:/		/u/ and /u:/
Low		/a/and/a:/	

In addition, when /a/ was followed by /w/ or /y/, the diphthongs /au/ and /ai/ were formed.

3.3.2 Middle Aramaic

A number of vowel changes took place between the Proto-Aramaic and the Middle Aramaic periods; providing a relative chronology, much less an absolute chronology, of these changes is problematic. Questions of chronology aside, these changes can be divided into three groups:

1. Changes which did not affect the system of vowel phonemes, such as the shift of /a/ to /i/ ("attenuation") in some closed syllables.

2. Changes which occurred in every dialect of Aramaic:

(i) Stressed /i/ and /u/ were lowered, and perhaps lengthened, to /e/ or /e:/ and /o/ or /o:/.
(ii) In all dialects, but differing from dialect to dialect as to the number and the specification of environments, /ai/ became /e:/ (or possibly /ei/) and /au/ became /o:/ (or possibly /ou/).
(iii) In the first open syllable prior to the stressed syllable and in alternating syllables prior to that, short vowels were lost. In positions where the complete loss of the vowel would have produced an unacceptable consonant cluster, the vowel reduced to the neutral mid-vowel [ə]. Because the presence of this vowel is entirely predictable from syllable structure, it is not analyzed as phonemic.
(iv) Quantity ceased to be phonemic.

3. Changes which apparently occurred in some dialects, but not others:

(i) The low vowel /a:/ was rounded and raised to /ɔ/.
(ii) Unstressed /u/ was lowered to /ɔ/ in some environments.
(iii) Unstressed /i/ was lowered to /ɛ/ in some environments.
(iv) Unstressed /a/ was raised to /ɛ/ in some environments.

A dialect in which all of these changes occurred would have the vowel system of (4), along with the diphthongs /ai/ (or /ei/) and /au/ (or /ou/), if they had been retained in any environments:

(4)

	Front	*Central*	*Back*
High	/i/		/u/
Mid	/e/		/o/
	/ɛ/		/ɔ/
Low		/a/	

A dialect in which only the first two sets of changes occurred would have the same system but without the vowels /ɛ/ and /ɔ/.

3.3.3 Late Aramaic

At the beginning of the Modern Aramaic period, four sets of diacritics were independently developed to represent Aramaic vowels fully. These sets of diacritics represent the phonemic distinctions relevant to four dialects of Late Aramaic. The distinctions indicated by these systems are qualitative, not quantitative, indicating that vowel quantity was not phonemic by this time. In all of these systems, the pronunciation of the low vowel(s) is/are uncertain and so two options are usually given. Also indicated in (5)–(8) are the standard transliteration equivalents in the writing system.

3.3.3.1 The Tiberian system

(5)

	Front	*Central*	*Back*
High	/i/ = <i> and <î>		/u/ = <u> and <û>
Mid	/e/ = <ē> and <ê>		/o/ = <ō> and <ô>
	/ɛ/ = <e>		/ɔ/ = <o> and <ā>
Low		/æ/ or /a/ = <a>	

The phonemic status of the /ɛ/ vowel is uncertain, because its alternation with other vowels in the system is nearly always predictable. If /ɛ/ is not a phoneme, then this system would be equivalent to the Babylonian system (see §3.3.3.2).

The Tiberian system also contains four additional symbols for vowels (see §2.2.2), all of which represent vowels of very brief duration: the neutral mid vowel /ə/, and very brief pronunciations of /ɛ/, /ɔ/, and /a/. Diachronically, these vowels are the remnants of short vowels which were reduced in certain syllables (see §3.3.2). They are only retained in positions where the complete loss of the vowel would produce an unacceptable consonant cluster and so they represent a context-dependent phonetic (rather than a phonemic) phenomenon.

3.3.3.2 The Babylonian system

(6)

	Front	*Central*	*Back*
High	/i/ = <i> and <î>		/u/ = <u> and <û>
Mid	/e/ = <ē> and <ê>		/o/ = <ō> and <ô>
Low	/æ/ (or /a/) = <a>		/a/ (or /ɔ/) = <ā>

This system is essentially equivalent to the Tiberian system, but without /ɛ/. It is probable that /ɛ/ is absent in this dialect because it never developed from /i/ and /a/, rather than because it first developed and then was subsequently lost. This system also contains a symbol for the neutral mid vowel /ə/ but, unlike the Tiberian system, the diacritic is not ambiguous (i.e., it does not also represent the absence of a vowel; see §2.2.2).

3.3.3.3 The Nestorian system

(7)

	Front	*Central*	*Back*
High	/i/ = <i> and <î>		/u/ = <u> and <û>
Mid	/e/ = <ē> and <ê>		/o/ = <ō> and <ô>
	/ɛ/ = <e>		/ɔ/ = <ā>
Low		/æ/ or /a/ = <a>	

This system is essentially the same as the Tiberian and the Middle Aramaic system, though the /ɛ/ vowel is much more common and is certainly a phoneme in this system.

3.3.3.4 The Jacobite system

(8)

	Front	*Central*	*Back*
High	/i/ = <ī> and <î>		/u/ = <ū> and <û>
Mid	/e/ = <e>		/o/ = <ā>
Low		/a/ = <a>	

This system has the smallest of all inventories and is a result of two changes from the Middle Aramaic (= Nestorian) system: (i) the raising of /e/ and /o/ to /i/ and /u/ respectively; and (ii) the raising of /ɛ/ and /ɔ/ to /e/ and /o/ respectively.

3.4 Syllable structure

Aramaic has both closed (CVC) and open (CV) syllables. During the time that vowel quantity was phonemic in Aramaic, a closed syllable could not contain a long vowel, whereas an open syllable could contain either a long or a short vowel. After vowel quantity was no longer phonemic, such restrictions were no longer relevant to the phonemic system, although vowels in closed and open syllables very likely differed phonetically in quantity.

The only apparent restriction on vowel quality in Aramaic syllables occurs in connection with the consonants /ʔ/, /ʕ/, /ħ/, /h/, and /ʀ/. At an early stage in Aramaic, a short high vowel preceding these consonants became /a/. A preceding long high vowel retained its quality, but, in some dialects, /a/ was inserted between the high vowel and the consonant.

3.5 Stress

There is one primary stressed syllable in each Aramaic word (with the exception of some particles; see §§4.6, 4.7.4, and 4.8.1). In Proto-Aramaic, words having a final closed syllable were stressed on that syllable; and words having a final open syllable were stressed on the penultimate syllable, regardless of the length of the word-final vowel. At a very early stage, word-final short vowels were either lost or lengthened and so the stressed, open penultimate syllable of words with a final short vowel became the final stressed, closed syllable. Stress remained on this syllable and the rules regarding stress were not altered. These rules remain unaltered throughout most of the history of Aramaic, though in some dialects of Late Aramaic, stress shifted from the final syllable to the penultimate syllable in some or all words which had a closed final syllable.

3.6 Phonological processes

3.6.1 Sibilant metathesis

In verb forms in which a /t/ is prefixed (see §4.4.1) to a root which begins with a sibilant, the sibilant and the /t/ undergo metathesis: for example, /ts/ → /st/ and /tš/ → /št/. If the sibilant is voiced /z/ or pharyngealized /s'/, /t/ also undergoes partial assimilation: /tz/ → /zd/ and /ts'/ → /s't'/.

3.6.2 Assimilation of /t/

In verb forms in which a /t/ is prefixed (see §4.4.1) to a root which begins with /d/ or /t'/, the /t/ completely assimilates to this consonant. This assimilation also takes place in a few roots whose first consonant is a labial – /b/, /p/, and /m/ – or the dental/alveolar /n/.

3.6.3 Assimilation and dissimilation of /n/

Historically, the phoneme /n/ completely assimilates to a following consonant when no vowel intervenes between the two: *nC → CC. During and after the Imperial Aramaic period, some geminated (lengthened) consonants dissimilate to /n/ plus consonant, CC → nC, even in cases in which no /n/ was present historically. This dissimilation is the result of Akkadian influence and appears more commonly in the eastern dialects.

3.6.4 Dissimilation of pharyngealized consonants

In some Aramaic texts, words which have roots that historically contain two pharyngealized consonants show dissimilation of one of the consonants to its nonpharyngealized counterpart. In a few Old Aramaic texts, progressive dissimilation is shown: for example, *qṭl* (i.e., /k'tʼl/) → *qtl*. In some Imperial Aramaic texts the dissimilation is regressive: for example, *qṭl* → *kṭl* and *qṣ'* (i.e., /k'sʼʔ/) → *kṣ'*. These dissimilations may have been the result of Akkadian influence, which attests similar dissimilations.

3.6.5 Elimination of consonant clusters

At various stages of Aramaic, phonotactically impermissible consonant clusters were eliminated in various ways.

3.6.5.1 *Anaptyxis*

In Proto-Aramaic, all singular nouns ended in a short vowel, marking case (see §4.2.2). When this final short vowel was lost, some nouns then ended in a cluster of two consonants: as in */málku/ → /málk/. In order to eliminate this cluster, a short anaptyctic vowel (usually /i/, sometimes /a/) was inserted between the two consonants: /málk/ → /málik/. Stress then shifted to this vowel from the preceding vowel: /málik/ → /malík/. At a later stage, the vowel of the initial syllable was lost and the anaptyctic vowel was lowered (see §3.3.2): /malík/ → /mlík/ → /mlék/.

3.6.5.2 *Schwa*

The loss of short vowels in some open syllables (see §3.3.2) created the possibility of consonant clusters at the beginning and in the middle of words. In positions where the complete loss of the vowel would have produced an unacceptable consonant cluster, the cluster was avoided by reducing the short vowel to the neutral mid-vowel /ə/.

3.6.5.3 *Prothetic aleph*

When a word begins with a cluster of two consonants, sometimes the syllable /ʔa/ or /ʔɛ/ is prefixed to it: for example, the word /dmɔ/ is sometimes pronounced /ʔadmɔ/.

4. MORPHOLOGY

4.1 Morphological type

Aramaic is a language of the fusional type in which morphemes are unsegmentable units which represent multiple kinds of semantic information (e.g., gender and number). On the basis of morphological criteria alone, Aramaic words can be divided into three categories:

(i) nouns, (ii) verbs, and (iii) uninflected words. The final category includes a variety of words such as adverbs (see §4.5), prepositions (see §4.6), particles (see §4.7), conjunctions (see §4.8), and interjections (see §4.9). As the name suggests, words in this category are distinguished from words in the first two categories by the absence of inflection. Words in the first two categories can be distinguished from each other by differences in the categories for which they are inflected and by the inflectional material itself.

4.2 Nominal morphology

Under this heading are included not only nouns and adjectives, but participles as well.

4.2.1 Word formation

Excluding inflectional material, all native Aramaic nouns, adjectives, and participles (as well as verbs; see §4.4.1) consist of (i) a two-, three-, or four-consonant root; (ii) a vowel pattern or ablaut; and, optionally, (iii) one or more prefixed, suffixed, or infixed consonant(s). Multiple combinations of these elements exist in the lexicon of native Aramaic words, and earlier and later patterns can be identified within the lexicon.

In Old and Imperial Aramaic, the patterns found are ones that are common to the other Semitic languages. Many patterns are characterized by differences in ablaut only: for example, *qal*, *qāl*, *qil*, *qall*, *qitl*, *qutl*, *qatal*, *qatāl*, *qatīl*, and *qātil*. Additional patterns are characterized by the gemination (lengthening) of the second root consonant: for example, *qattal*, *qittal*, *qattīl*, and *qattāl*. Still others display prefixation – for example, *maqtal*, *maqtil*, *maqtāl*, *taqtīl*, and *taqtūl*; or suffixation – for example, *qatlūt*, *qutlīt*, and *qitlāy*; or reduplication – for example, *qatlal* and *qataltāl*. The semantics of some of these patterns or of individual suffixes is clear and distinct: for example, the pattern *qattāl* indicates a profession (*nomen professionalis*), the pattern *qatīl* is that of the passive participle of the Pəʿal stem; and the suffix *-āy* (the *nisbe* suffix) indicates the name of an ethnic group.

In Late Aramaic, the use of suffixes increased, apparently as a result of two historical factors. First, the loss of short vowels in open syllables prior to the stressed syllable often eliminated the single vowel which distinguished one vowel pattern from another. So, the use of suffixes may have been increased to compensate for the loss of distinct vowel patterns. Second, the contact of Aramaic with Indo-European languages, especially Greek, may have increased the use of suffixes since the morphology of those languages largely involves suffixation rather than differences in vowel patterns.

One notable nonsuffixing pattern that developed in the Middle or Late Aramaic period is the *qātōl* pattern which indicates an agent noun (*nomen agentis*). The older agent noun pattern, *qātēl* (< *qātil*), is also the pattern of the active participle of the Pəʿal stem, and by the Middle Aramaic period the participle came to be used almost exclusively as a verbal form, and so a new, purely nominal, agent noun form was developed.

4.2.2 Inflectional categories

Nouns, adjectives, and participles are inflected for gender, number, and state. There are no case distinctions in any extant dialect of Aramaic, though such distinctions did exist in Proto-Aramaic. There are also no comparative or superlative forms of adjectives at any stage of the language. There are two genders, masculine and feminine, and nouns can be distinguished from adjectives and participles in that nouns have inherent gender whereas adjectives and participles do not. There are two numbers, singular and plural, and although a few words retain an ancient dual form, there is no productive dual in Aramaic. There are three states: absolute, construct, and emphatic. The absolute and the emphatic states of a noun are free forms and the construct state is a bound form. In earlier stages of Aramaic, the absolute state represented an indefinite noun, the emphatic state represented a definite noun and the construct state represented a noun the definiteness of which was determined by the noun to which it was bound. In Late Aramaic, the absolute state was almost entirely lost and the emphatic state became used for both definite and indefinite nouns. Definiteness was then determined contextually or by the use of the numeral "one" as a kind of indefinite article. At this stage, the construct state was retained only in frozen forms and was not productive, with the exception of a few words such as *br* "son-of." However, adjectives and participles retained the absolute state throughout all periods because of their use as predicates to form clauses (see §5.2.1).

The transliterations of the written forms of the inflectional suffixes for nouns, adjectives, and participles are presented in (9). The forms of each suffix are represented both with and without vowel diacritics (see §§2.1, 2.2.2). The symbol ø represents the absence of an inflectional suffix. The letters ʾ and *h* are *matres lectionis* (see § 2.2.1). On the phonemic values of the transliteration of vowel diacritics see §3.3.3:

(9)

	Masculine		*Feminine*	
	Singular	*Plural*	*Singular*	*Plural*
Absolute	-ø	-yn (= -în)	-h (= -ā)	-n (= -ān)
Construct	-ø	-y (= -ay or -ê)	-t (= -at)	-t (= -āt)
Emphatic	-ʾ (= -ā)	-yʾ (= -ayyā)	-tʾ (= -tā)	-tʾ (= -ātā)

Several points should be noted regarding these inflectional suffixes:

1. The masculine singular emphatic is also sometimes attested as *-h*.
2. The feminine singular absolute, in some dialects, is also rarely attested as -ʾ. In Syriac, it is consistently attested as -ʾ.
3. The *y* of the masculine plural absolute is a *mater lectionis* and so is sometimes omitted in writing, especially in early texts.
4. The *y* of the masculine plural construct is either a consonant, representing the diphthong /ai/, or a *mater lectionis* representing /e:/ which had developed from /ai/ in some dialects.
5. The Samʾal dialect of Old Aramaic attests *-t* (= *-āt*) as the feminine plural absolute form, the usual form in Canaanite dialects.
6. In eastern dialects of Middle and Late Aramaic, the masculine plural emphatic appears as -ʾ or *-y* (= -ê), perhaps under Akkadian influence.

Many Aramaic nouns, adjectives, and participles show two (or more) vowel patterns which alternate depending on the phonological form of the inflectional material. These multiple patterns are the result of the phonological changes that took place during the history of Aramaic. However, explaining these alternating patterns synchronically requires a rather complex set of rules and will not be attempted here. In two groups of nouns, adjectives, and participles (those with a final consonant which was historically /w/ or /y/), these phonological changes also produced changes in the forms of some of the inflectional suffixes. Nouns, adjectives, and participles with a final consonant /w/ developed the vowel /u/ or /o/ in both the masculine singular absolute and construct as well as in the three feminine singular forms (the /w/ remained a consonant in the other seven forms). In the feminine singular absolute and construct forms, this vowel replaced the vowel of the inflectional suffix.

Nouns, adjectives, and participles with a final consonant /y/ show even more changes. The inflectional suffixes for these words are given in (10):

(10)

	Masculine		*Feminine*	
	Singular	*Plural*	*Singular*	*Plural*
Absolute	-ʾ or -y (= -ê)	-yn (= -ayin or -ên) or -n (= -an)	-y (= -î) or -yʾ (= -yā)	-yn (= -yān)
Construct	-ʾ or -y (= -ê)	-y (= -ay or -ê)	-yt (= -ît or -yat)	-yt (= -yāt)
Emphatic	-yʾ (= -yā)	-yʾ (= -ayyā or -yê)	-ytʾ (= -îtā)	-ytʾ (= -yātā)

In the masculine singular emphatic and the feminine plural forms, /y/ remains a consonant and the inflectional suffix is standard. In the other forms, /y/ generally becomes a vowel, sometimes fusing with the inflectional ending, although in some nouns it remains a consonant and the suffix is standard.

4.3 Pronouns

4.3.1 Personal pronouns

Personal pronouns occur in both independent and bound (i.e., enclitic) forms.

4.3.1.1 Independent personal pronouns

Independent forms of the personal pronouns vary slightly from dialect to dialect and from period to period. All but the rarest of forms are listed in (11):

(11)

	Singular	*Plural*
1st common	ʾnh, ʾnʾ	ʾnḥn, ʾnḥnn, ʾnḥnʾ, ʾnḥnh, nḥnʾ, ḥnn, ʾnn
2nd masculine	ʾnt, ʾt, ʾnth, ʾth	ʾntm, ʾntwn, ʾtwn
2nd feminine	ʾnty, ʾnt, ʾt, ʾty	ʾntn, ʾntyn, ʾtyn
3rd masculine	hʾ, hwʾ, hw	hm, hwm, hmw, hmwn, ʾnwn, hnwn, ʾynwn, hynwn
3rd feminine	hʾ, hyʾ, hy	ʾnyn, hnyn, ʾynyn, hynyn

The first- and second-person pronouns all have an initial *ʾn*, and the remainder of each form generally resembles the inflectional suffix of the perfect verb (§4.4.2.1). Forms written without *n* are those which have undergone assimilation of /n/ to /t/ (see §3.6.3). The third-person singular forms have an initial *h*, and the plural forms have an initial *h* or *ʾ*. The masculine has a back vowel /o/ or /u/, and the feminine has a front vowel /i/ or /e/. Most of the spelling differences reflect the presence or absence of *matres lectionis*, though some reflect historical developments. Of particular note is the replacement of the earlier final /m/ of the second and third masculine plural forms with the later /n/ under the influence of the feminine forms.

In the Samʾal dialect of Old Aramaic the first common singular is the Canaanite *ʾnk(y)*.

4.3.1.2 Bound personal pronouns

These forms are used for the possessor of a noun, the object of a preposition, the subject or object of an infinitive, or the object of a verb and they vary depending on the type of word to which they are suffixed.

The bound forms that are suffixed to nouns, prepositions, particles, and infinitives can be divided into two sets: Set I is used with masculine singular nouns, all feminine nouns, infinitives, and some prepositions; Set II is used with masculine plural nouns, the other prepositions, and the existential particles:

(12) Bound pronouns suffixed to nouns, prepositions, particles, and infinitives

	Set I		*Set II*	
	Singular	*Plural*	*Singular*	*Plural*
1st common	-y	-nʾ, -n	-y	-yn, -ynʾ
2nd masculine	-k	-km, -kwn	-yk	-ykm, ykwn
2nd feminine	-ky, -yk	-kn, -kyn	-yky	-ykn, -ykyn
3rd masculine	-h, -yh	-hm, -hwm, -hwn	-wh, -why, -wy	-yhm, -yhwm, -yhwn
3rd feminine	-h	-hyn	-yh	-yhn, -yhyn

Note the following:

1. The first common singular suffix occurring on the infinitive is more commonly *-ny* than *-y*. In Syriac, the infinitive also occurs with alternate forms of the third masculine singular (*-ywhy*) and third feminine singular (*-yh*).
2. In Set I, the third masculine singular *-yh* and the second feminine singular *-yk* reflect the presence of an internal *mater lectionis* in Late Aramaic texts.
3. The differences in the second- and third-person plural forms of both sets are a result of the presence or absence of *matres lectionis* and the shift of final /m/ to /n/ in the masculine forms. In Samaritan Aramaic, the third plural forms of both sets are also attested without *-h-*. In Jewish Babylonian Aramaic, the second- and third-person plural forms of both sets are also attested without the final *-n*.
4. In Sets I and II, the first common plural form without ʾ reflects the absence of a *mater lectionis* in earlier texts and the absence of a final vowel in later texts.
5. In Jewish Palestinian Aramaic, the third feminine singular, second masculine singular, second feminine singular, and the first common plural forms in Set II are also attested without the initial *y*, suggesting a shift of /ai/ to /a/. The first common singular, first common plural, and third feminine singular forms in Set II are also attested as *-ʾy*, *-ynn*, and *-yhʾ* respectively, in this dialect.
6. The second feminine singular form of Sets I and II is also written without the final *y* in Jewish Palestinian Aramaic, suggesting the loss of the final vowel, and in Syriac the *y* is written but not pronounced.
7. The third masculine singular form *-wh* of Set II probably reflects the absence of a *mater lectionis* in earlier texts. The *-wy* form reflects the loss of the intervocalic /h/ in later texts. The Samʾal dialect of Old Aramaic attests *-yh*, suggesting the diphthong /ai/ rather than /au/. This diphthong is the historically earlier vowel which became /au/ in all other dialects.

The bound forms of the pronouns that are attached to verbs will vary depending on three factors: (i) the tense of the verb; (ii) the phonological form of the verb; and (iii) the dialect. Most variation is a result of the phonological form of the verb rather than verb tense, although the forms used with the imperfect frequently show an additional *-n-* (= /inn/). In some dialects of Late Aramaic, this additional *-n-* is also found in forms that are used with the perfect. Other differences in bound pronouns across dialects tend to reflect broader phonological changes in the language, such as the loss of word-final vowels or consonants.

Bound forms of the third-person plural pronouns are generally not suffixed to verbs, although there are attested forms in Old Aramaic, particularly in the Samʾal dialect, and in Jewish Babylonian Aramaic and Jewish Palestinian Aramaic. More commonly, an independent form of the pronoun is used instead. However, in some dialects, these forms are not stressed and so they are phonologically enclitic to the preceding verb form, even though they are written as separate words.

In (13)–(15), *y*, *w*, and *ʾ* are all *matres lectionis*, but *h* represents a true consonant:

(13) Bound pronouns suffixed to verbs: perfect tense

	Singular	*Plural*
1st common	-ny, -y, -n	-n, -nn, -nʾ
2nd masculine	-k	-kn, -kwn
2nd feminine	-ky	-kyn
3rd masculine	-h, -yh, -hy, -yhy	
3rd feminine	-h, -hʾ	

Note the following:

1. The first common singular form *-y* is attested in Jewish Palestinian Aramaic and Samaritan Aramaic. In Jewish Babylonian Aramaic, the form *-n* is attested and it represents the loss of the final vowel. The final vowel is also lost in Syriac, but the form is still written *-ny*.
2. Syriac also attests the third masculine singular forms *-why* and *-ywhy*.
3. The first common plural form *-n* represents the loss of the final vowel, and the form *-nn* represents the additional *-n-*. Both forms are only attested in Late Aramaic dialects.
4. Jewish Babylonian Aramaic also attests a second masculine plural form *-kw*, as well as second masculine singular (*-nk*), second masculine plural (*-nkw*), and third feminine singular (*-nh*) forms with the additional *-n-*.
5. Old Aramaic attests the third masculine plural forms *-hm* and *-hmw*.
6. Jewish Babylonian Aramaic attests the third masculine plural forms *-ynwn*, *-ynhw* and the third feminine plural forms *-nhy* and *-ynhy*. Samaritan Aramaic attests the third masculine plural form *-wn* and third feminine plural form *-yn*.

(14) Bound pronouns suffixed to verbs: imperfect tense

	Singular	*Plural*
1st common	-n, -ny, -nny	-n, -nn
2nd masculine	-k, -nk, -ynk	-kwn, -nkwn
2nd feminine	-ky, -yk	-kyn, -nkyn
3rd masculine	-h, -hy, -nh, -nhy	
3rd feminine	-h, -nh	

Note the following:

1. In Old and Imperial Aramaic, forms with and without the additional *-n-* are attested. In Jewish Palestinian Aramaic, Jewish Babylonian Aramaic, and Samaritan Aramaic, the forms with *-n-* are much more commonly attested than the forms without *-n-*. In Syriac, the forms with *-n-* are not attested at all.

2. In Old Aramaic, the first common singular form -*n* is pronounced with a final vowel but is written without a *mater lectionis.* In Jewish Babylonian Aramaic, the form -*n* represents the loss of the final vowel. In Syriac, the final vowel is also lost, but the form is still written -*ny.*
3. No second feminine singular forms with additional -*n*- happen to be attested in the extant texts. The form -*ky* is pronounced with a final vowel in Old and Imperial Aramaic, but in Jewish Babylonian Aramaic and Syriac the final vowel is lost, though in Syriac the form is still written -*ky.*
4. The third masculine singular forms -*hy* and -*nhy* are only found in Old and/or Imperial Aramaic.
5. Syriac also attests the third masculine singular forms -*yhy* and -*ywhy* and the third feminine singular form -*yh.*
6. Jewish Babylonian Aramaic attests the third masculine singular forms -*yh* and -*ynyh,* the third feminine singular form -*ynh,* and the second masculine plural form -*ynkw.*
7. In Jewish Palestinian Aramaic, the first common plural form -*nn*ʾ is also attested.
8. Old Aramaic attests the third masculine plural forms -*hm* and -*hmw.*
9. Jewish Babylonian Aramaic attests the third masculine plural forms -*ynwn,* -*ynhw* and the third feminine plural form -*ynhy.* Samaritan Aramaic and Jewish Palestinian Aramaic attest the third masculine plural form -*nwn.* Jewish Palestinian Aramaic also attests the third feminine plural form -*nyn.*

(15) **Bound pronouns suffixed to verbs: imperative**

	Singular	*Plural*
1st common	-ny, -n, -yny, -yn, -y	-n, -yn, -nʾ, -ynʾ, -nn
3rd masculine	-h, -hy, -yh, -why, -yhy	
3rd feminine	-h, -yh, -hʾ	

Note the following:

1. The first common singular form -*ny* is attested in all dialects. The first common singular form -*y* is only attested in Jewish Palestinian Aramaic and Samaritan Aramaic. In Jewish Babylonian Aramaic, the forms -*yn* and -*n* are attested in addition to -*ny* and represent the loss of the final vowel. In Syriac, the forms -*ny* and -*yny* are attested, but the *y* is not pronounced.
2. The third masculine singular form -*h* is attested in Old Aramaic, Imperial Aramaic, Jewish Babylonian Aramaic, and Samaritan Aramaic. This form is also written with a *mater lectionis* as -*yh* in Jewish Babylonian Aramaic and Jewish Palestinian Aramaic. The form -*hy* is attested in Old Aramaic, Imperial Aramaic, Jewish Palestinian Aramaic, and Syriac, although in Syriac the *h* is not pronounced. The forms -*why* and -*yhy* are only attested in Syriac and the *h* is not pronounced.
3. Only Syriac attests the third feminine singular form -*yh* and only Jewish Palestinian Aramaic attests the third feminine singular form -*h*ʾ.
4. First common plural bound pronouns are only attested in Late Aramaic. Syriac attests -*n* and -*yn.* Jewish Palestinian Aramaic attests -*n* and -*n*ʾ. Samaritan Aramaic attests -*n* and -*nn.* Jewish Babylonian Aramaic attests -*yn*ʾ.
5. Jewish Babylonian Aramaic attests the third masculine plural form -*nhw* and the third feminine plural form -*nhy.* Jewish Palestinian Aramaic attests the third masculine plural form -*nwn* and the third feminine plural form -*nyn.*

In Late Aramaic, as a result of the use of the participle as a verb form, shortened forms of the first- and second-person independent pronouns became suffixed to the participle to indicate the subject. In Syriac and Jewish Babylonian Aramaic, third-person forms developed alongside the first- and second-person forms, and all of these forms are commonly used in a variety of nonverbal clauses, not just those with participles. In these uses, the pronouns are written as separate words, but are phonologically enclitic to the preceding word (see §5.2.1).

4.3.2 Demonstrative pronouns

4.3.2.1 Near demonstratives

In Old, Imperial, and Middle Aramaic, the singular forms of the near demonstratives are characterized by an initial *z* or *d* (= historical /ð/; see §3.2.2) followed, in the masculine forms, by *n* and a final *mater lectionis* -*h* or -ʾ. The forms are as follows: masculine singular *znh*, *znʾ*, *dnh*, *dnʾ* and feminine singular *zʾ*, *zh*, *dʾ*. In Middle Aramaic, the masculine singular forms *dn* and *zn* are also attested, suggesting that the final vowel was being lost in this period. Gender is not distinguished in the plural forms of the near demonstrative. These forms are all characterized by an initial *ʾl*. They are *ʾl*, *ʾlh*, *ʾln*.

In the Late Aramaic period, the near demonstratives are often attested with an initial *h*. This *h* generally replaces the initial *d* of the singular forms and the initial ʾ of the plural form. However, some singular forms in some dialects attest both the *h* and the *d*. For example, Syriac attests masculine singular *hn* and *hnʾ*, feminine singular *hdʾ*, and plural *hlyn*. Jewish Palestinian Aramaic attests masculine singular *dyn*, *dnʾ*, *hyn* and *hn*, feminine singular *dʾ*, and plural *hlyn* and *ʾlyn*. Jewish Babylonian Aramaic attests many forms including masculine singular *dyn* and *hdyn*, feminine singular *hdʾ* and *hʾ*, and plural *ʾlyn* and *hlyn*. Samaritan Aramaic attests masculine singular *dn*, feminine singular *dh*, and plural *hlyn* and *ʾlyn*.

4.3.2.2 Far demonstratives

In Old, Imperial, and Middle Aramaic, the far demonstratives are like the near demonstratives in that the singular forms are characterized by an initial *z* or *d* and the plural forms by an initial *ʾl*, but, unlike the near demonstratives, this initial element is followed by *k*. The forms are as follows: masculine singular *znk*, *zk*, *dk*; feminine singular *zk*, *zkʾ*, *dk*, *zky*, *dky*; and plural *ʾlk*, *ʾlky*. In addition to these forms, there are sporadic attestations of the third-person independent personal pronouns being used as demonstratives. This usage is common in the Canaanite dialects, and these attestations are generally found in Aramaic dialects influenced by Canaanite such as the Samʾal dialect of Old Aramaic and some Middle Aramaic dialects influenced by Hebrew.

In the Late Aramaic period, the third-person independent personal pronouns become more commonly used as far demonstratives, although in most dialects they do not displace the earlier forms, but are simply attested alongside them. In Syriac, the earlier forms are lost entirely and the far demonstratives are distinguished from the personal pronouns by the vowel of the first syllable of the singular forms and by the presence of *h* rather than ʾ as the initial consonant of the plural forms.

4.3.3 Reflexive pronouns

The equivalent of a reflexive pronoun is expressed by suffixing a bound form of a personal pronoun to *npš* "life, soul" or *grm* "bone."

4.3.4 Possessive pronouns

Possessive pronouns are usually expressed by bound forms of the personal pronouns, but in Middle and Late Aramaic the particle *z/dyl* (= particle *z/dy* + preposition *l*) with a suffixed bound form became used as a possessive pronoun.

4.4 Verbal morphology

4.4.1 Word formation

Excluding inflectional material, all native Aramaic verbs (as well as nouns; see §4.2.1) consist of (i) a two-, three-, or four-consonant root; (ii) a vowel pattern or ablaut; and, optionally, (iii) one or more prefixed or infixed consonants. The root provides the primary semantic value of the verb form. The other two elements (ii and iii) provide semantic distinctions of voice, causation, and so forth; and variations in these two elements define a system of verbal stems or conjugations which are morpho-semantically related to each other. Of these two elements, the vowel pattern is less important than the additional consonant(s) since vowels frequently change from one inflected form to another. The distinctions between the stems are generally, but not always, maintained despite these vowel changes. Furthermore, some of these vowel patterns differ slightly from one dialect to another. For these reasons, the vowel patterns will not be treated in the following discussion.

4.4.1.1 Major verb stems

Numerous verb stems exist in Aramaic, but there are only six primary stems. They can be defined morphologically as follows, assuming in each case a three-consonant root.

1. *Pəʿal*: This stem is the most frequently attested of the six. It is also the simplest stem morphologically, characterized by the absence of any consonants other than the root consonants. For this reason, it is considered the basic stem. This stem attests multiple vowel patterns in both of the primary finite forms of the verb, and it is the only stem with multiple vowel patterns.
2. *ʾEthpəʿel* or *ʾIthpəʿel*: This stem is characterized by the presence of a prefixed *ʾt-*. Historically, this prefix is *ht-*, and forms with *ht-* are sporadically attested in all periods.
3. *Paʿʿel*: This stem is characterized by the gemination (lengthening) of the second root consonant.
4. *ʾEthpaʿʿal* or *ʾIthpaʿʿal*: This stem is characterized by the gemination (lengthening) of the second root consonant and by a prefixed *ʾt-*. Historically, this prefix is *ht-*, and forms with *ht-* are sporadically attested in all periods.
5. *Haphʿel* or *ʾAphʿel*: This stem is characterized by the prefixation of the consonant *h-* or the consonant *ʾ-*. The forms with *h-* are historically earlier than the forms with *ʾ-* and had almost entirely disappeared by the Middle Aramaic period, though a few forms with *h-* survive into the Late Aramaic period.
6. *ʾEttaphʿal* or *ʾIttaphʿal*: This stem is characterized by a prefixed *ʾtt-*. The second *t* is historically the *h-* or *ʾ-* of the *Haphʿel/ʾAphʿel* which has been assimilated to the preceding *t*.

Certain modifications of these stems occur when there are two or four root consonants rather than three. Verbs with four root consonants only have forms corresponding to the *Paʿʿel* and the *ʾEthpaʿʿal/ʾIthpaʿʿal* stems, the two middle root consonants taking the place of the geminated (lengthened) second root consonant of a verb with three root consonants. Verbs with two root consonants develop a middle root consonant *-y-* in the *Paʿʿel* and the *ʾEthpaʿʿal/ʾIthpaʿʿal*, and the distinction between the *ʾEthpəʿel/ʾIthpəʿel* and the *ʾEttaphʿal/ʾIttaphʿal* forms is completely lost, with the retention of the latter forms only.

4.4.1.2 *Voice and other semantic distinctions*

This system of stems expresses a variety of semantic distinctions, and a variety of relationships exist between the stems. One of the primary distinctions is that of voice. The *Pəʿal*, the *Paʿʿel*, and the *Haphʿel/ʾAphʿel* stems all express the active voice. The three stems with prefixed *ʾt-* all express the passive voice. Each of the passive stems is directly related only to its morphologically similar active stem, and the relationships of the passive stems to one another simply mirror the relationships of the active stems to one another. In Proto-Aramaic, it is likely that the stems with prefixed *ʾt-* were reflexive, but in the extant dialects of Aramaic, reflexive uses of these stems are only sporadically attested.

The relationships of the active stems to one another are more complex. The *Paʿʿel* and the *Haphʿel/ʾAphʿel* are directly related to the *Pəʿal*, but not to each other. The *Haphʿel/ʾAphʿel* expresses causation. A *Haphʿel/ʾAphʿel* verb of a particular root is usually the causative of the *Pəʿal* verb of that same root. For example, the *Haphʿel/ʾAphʿel* verb *hkšl/ʾkšl* "to trip someone up" is the causative of the *Pəʿal* verb *kšl* "to stumble." There are, however, a number of *Haphʿel/ʾAphʿel* verbs, some of which are denominative, for which there is no corresponding *Pəʿal* verb or which do not express causation.

The relationship of the *Paʿʿel* stem to the *Pəʿal* stem varies depending on the semantic class into which the verb in the *Pəʿal* stem falls. The verbs in the *Pəʿal* stem exhibit a number of semantic distinctions, the two most important of which are (i) the distinction between stative verbs and active verbs, and (ii) the distinction between one-place predicates (usually syntactically intransitive) and two-place predicates (usually syntactically transitive). As a general rule, to which there are exceptions, if the *Pəʿal* verb is stative and/or a one-place predicate, the *Paʿʿel* verb of that same root is "factitive" (i.e., causative). If there is a *Haphʿel/ʾAphʿel* verb of that same root, it is roughly synonymous with the *Paʿʿel* verb or there is a lexically idiosyncratic difference in meaning; for example, *Pəʿal qrb* "to come near," *Paʿʿel qrb* "to bring near, to offer up," *Haphʿel/ʾAphʿel hqrb/ʾqrb* "to bring near," or, in some dialects only, "to fight." If the *Pəʿal* verb is a two-place predicate, the *Paʿʿel* verb of that same root will be "intensive," though in some cases, the two verbs are synonymous or there is a lexically idiosyncratic difference in meaning; for example, *Pəʿal zmr* "to sing," *Paʿʿel zmr* "to sing." There are, furthermore, numerous *Paʿʿel* verbs, many of which have four root consonants and for which there is no corresponding *Pəʿal* verb.

By the Late Aramaic period, the relationships between the stems had broken down through the process of lexicalization. Although some of the relationships still held between individual verbs of the same root, in many cases they did not. This breakdown was aided by the similarity in meaning of some pairs of verbs and, in the case of the *ʾEthpəʿel/ʾIthpəʿel* and the *ʾEthpaʿʿal/ʾIthpaʿʿal*, by their increasing morphological similarity due to vowel changes in the language.

4.4.1.3 *Minor stems*

In Old Aramaic, it is possible that a set of passive stems existed, corresponding to each of the three major active stems, and differing from them in vowel pattern only. Possible attestations of such stems are quite rare and many are disputed.

In all periods of Aramaic, and especially in Late Aramaic, a number of still additional stems are attested, but these are limited, occurring in no more than a few roots. One notable pair of stems is the *Šaphʿel* and its passive, the *ʾEštaphʿal/ʾIštaphʿal.* These stems correspond in form and meaning to the *Haphʿel/ʾAphʿel* and the *ʾEttaphʿal/ʾIttaphʿal,* but with a prefixed *š-* rather than *h-* or *ʾ -*. In the *ʾEštaphʿal/ʾIštaphʿal,* metathesis of /š/ and /t/ has taken place (see §3.6.1). The forms of these stems that are attested in Aramaic are apparently loanwords from two possible sources: (i) Akkadian in the Imperial and Middle Aramaic periods, and (ii) (an)other Northwest Semitic language(s) in which the *Šaphʿel* was the standard causative stem in the Old and/or Proto-Aramaic periods. Neither of these stems is productive in any extant Aramaic dialect.

4.4.2 Inflectional categories

Verbs are inflected for three persons, two genders (not distinguished in the first person), two numbers, and two primary "tenses," the perfect and the imperfect. There is also a set of second- and third-person jussive forms (attested in Old and Imperial Aramaic only), a set of second-person imperative forms, and an infinitival form, which is not inflected. In the active stems, there are two sets of participial forms, an active set and a passive set. In the passive stems, there is one set of (passive) participial forms. Participles are inflected like adjectives (see §4.2.2). The perfect and the imperative are characterized by inflectional suffixes, and the imperfect is characterized primarily by prefixes, though some forms have both prefixes and suffixes. The vowels that are associated with the root consonants of these forms will vary depending on the stem of the verb, the phonological form of the inflectional material, and the position of stress. As with nouns, variations in these vowels are the result of the phonological changes that took place during the history of Aramaic. However, explaining these alternating patterns synchronically requires a set of rather complex rules and will not be attempted here.

The exact semantic value of the two primary tenses is uncertain. It is likely that at the earliest stages of Aramaic, the perfect and the imperfect expressed distinctions of aspect and, secondarily, distinctions of tense and modality. The perfect was used to express perfective aspect, and tended to be used to express past tense and realis mode; whereas the imperfect was used to express imperfective aspect, and tended to be used to express non-past tense and irrealis mode. However, as early as the Imperial Aramaic period, tense began to be the primary distinction between the two forms and the participle began to be used more commonly as a verbal, rather than a nominal, form. By the Late Aramaic period, the perfect had become the past tense, the participle had become the non-past tense, and the imperfect was used to express contingency, purpose, or volition and occasionally to express future action. In conjunction with this shift, the system was augmented by "composite tenses" (see §4.4.2.6) that were used to express further distinctions of aspect and modality.

4.4.2.1 Perfect tense

The perfect is characterized by inflectional suffixes. In (16), the written forms of these inflectional suffixes are represented in transliteration, both with and without vowel diacritics (see §§2.1, 2.2.2). Earlier or more broadly attested suffixes are listed above later or more narrowly attested suffixes. The symbol ø represents the absence of an inflectional suffix, either graphically and phonologically or only phonologically. In these forms, only *t* and *n* represent true consonants; all other letters are *matres lectionis* (see §2.2.1). On the phonemic values of the transliteration of the vowel diacritics, see §3.3.3. Verbs with a final root consonant that was historically /w/ or /y/ attest slightly altered forms of some of these suffixes.

(16)

	Singular	*Plural*
3rd masculine	-ø	-w (= -û or -ø) -wn (= -ûn)
3rd feminine	-t (= -at)	-ʾ or -h (= ā) -n (= -ān) or -yn (= -ên) or -y (= -ø or -î)
2nd masculine	-tʾ or -th or -t (= -tā) -t (= -t)	-tn or -twn (= -tôn or -tûn)
2nd feminine	-ty (= -tî) -t or -ty (= -t)	-tn or -tyn (= -tên or -tîn)
1st common	-t or -yt (= -et, -ēt, or -ît)	-nʾ or -n (= -nā) -n (=-n) or -nn (= -nan)

Note the following:

1. The third feminine singular suffix is also sometimes attested as *-ʾ* or *-h* (= *-ā*) in Jewish Babylonian Aramaic and in Samaritan Aramaic.
2. The second masculine singular suffix *-tʾ* or *-th* always represents *-tā* and is attested in all periods, although in Late Aramaic it is only attested in Jewish Palestinian Aramaic as a rare form. The spelling *-t* is also attested in all periods. In earlier periods, when *matres lectionis* were less frequently used, *-t* represents *-tā* written without a *mater lectionis.* In later periods, when *matres lectionis* were more frequently used, it represents *-t.*
3. The second feminine singular suffix *-ty* (= *-tî*) is an earlier form. In Late Aramaic, *-ty* is only found in Syriac and Samaritan Aramaic, where it represents *-t.*
4. The first common singular suffix is written with a *mater lectionis* only in some Late Aramaic texts. Its pronunciation varied from dialect to dialect and sometimes within individual dialects.
5. The third masculine plural suffix *-w* is attested in all periods and all dialects. It represents *-û* in all dialects except Syriac where its value is -ø. The suffix *-wn* (= *-ûn*) is a later alternate form found in Syriac and Jewish Palestinian Aramaic.
6. There are no distinct forms of the third feminine plural suffix attested in Old or Imperial Aramaic. In a few texts, third masculine plural forms are used with feminine plural subjects. The suffix *-ʾ* or *-h* (= *-ā*) is attested in most dialects of Middle and Late Aramaic. The suffix *-n* (= *-ān*) is attested in Jewish Palestinian Aramaic and in Jewish Babylonian Aramaic. The suffix *-y* (= *-î*) is attested in Samaritan Aramaic, and the suffixes *-yn* (= *-ên*) and *-y* (= *-ø*) are attested in Syriac. These last two forms may have developed by analogy to the second feminine plural suffix.
7. The second masculine plural suffix is also attested as *-tm* (= *-tūm* or *-tōm*) in Old Aramaic. The suffixes *-tn* and/or *-twn* are attested in all periods.
8. No forms with a second feminine plural suffix are attested in Old Aramaic. The suffixes *-tn* and/or *-tyn* are attested in all other periods.
9. The first common plural suffix *-nʾ* always represents *-nā* and it is attested in all periods, but not in all dialects. The suffix *-n* is also attested in all periods. In earlier periods, it represents *-nā* written without a *mater lectionis.* In later periods, it represents *-n.* The form *-nn* (= *-nan*) is an alternate form only found in some dialects of Late Aramaic.

4.4.2.2 *Imperfect tense*

The imperfect is characterized by inflectional prefixes, and, in some forms, suffixes as well. In the *ʾAphʿel* and the three stems with prefixed *ʾt-*, a prefixed consonant replaces the *ʾ* of the stem. In the earlier forms of these stems with prefixed *h-* or *ht-*, the *h-* remains and the consonant is prefixed to it. In (17), forms which are almost exclusively attested in eastern Late Aramaic are listed below forms which are attested in western Late Aramaic and all earlier dialects. All letters represent true consonants except *y* in the second feminine singular suffix, and *w* in the second and third masculine plural suffixes, which are *matres lectionis.* Verbs with a final root consonant that was historically /w/ or /y/ attest slightly altered forms of the suffixes.

(17)

	Singular	*Plural*
3rd masculine	y- . . . -ø	y- . . . -n or -wn (= -ûn)
	n- . . . -ø	n- . . . -wn (= -ûn)
	or l- . . . -ø	or l- . . . -wn (= -ûn)
3rd feminine	t- . . . -ø	y- . . . -n (= -ān)
		n- . . . -n (= -ān)
		or l- . . . -n (= -ān)
2nd masculine	t- . . . -ø	t- . . . -n or -wn (= -ûn)
2nd feminine	t- . . . -n or –yn (= -în)	t- . . . -n (= -ān)
1st common	ʾ- . . . -ø	n- . . . -ø

Note the following:

1. The vowel following the prefix of each of these forms is determined by the stem and/or the initial root consonant of the particular verb.
2. In Syriac, the third masculine singular and plural, and the third feminine plural prefix is *n-* rather than *y-*.
3. In Jewish Babylonian Aramaic, the third masculine singular and plural, and the third feminine plural prefix is *l-* rather than *y-*. This prefix also occurs sporadically in other dialects.
4. In Syriac, there is an alternate third feminine singular form with the suffix *-y* (= -ø).
5. In Samaritan Aramaic, the second feminine singular suffix is *-y* (= *-î*), and in Jewish Babylonian Aramaic this suffix is attested as an alternate form.
6. In the Samʾal dialect of Old Aramaic, the third masculine plural suffix is attested as *-w* (= *-û*).
7. In Samaritan Aramaic and Jewish Babylonian Aramaic, the second and third masculine plural suffixes each have an alternate form *-w* (= *-û*).

4.4.2.3 *Jussive*

In Old and Imperial Aramaic, quasi-imperative forms of the second and third persons, called "jussive forms," are attested. These forms can be distinguished from the imperfect by the absence of the final *-n* in the plural forms as well as in the second feminine singular form. No distinction between the imperfect and the jussive is found in the other forms. By the Middle Aramaic period, no distinct jussive forms remained, although forms without the final *-n* were retained in some dialects either as the only imperfect form or as an alternate imperfect form (see §4.4.2.2).

4.4.2.4 *Imperative*

The four imperative forms are closely related to the corresponding second-person imperfect forms. They differ from the imperfect forms in two ways: (i) they lack the prefix of the imperfect form (in the *ʾAphʿel* and the three stems with prefixed *ʾt-* the *ʾ* is present); and (ii) in most dialects, they lack the final *-n* of the imperfect forms, and what remains is a *mater lectionis* indicating the final vowel. Verbs with a final root consonant that was historically /w/ or /y/ attest slightly altered forms of these suffixes.

(18)

	Singular	*Plural*
2nd masculine	-ø	-w (= -û)
2nd feminine	-y (= -î)	-h or -ʾ (= -ā)

Note the following:

1. In Jewish Palestinian Aramaic, the final *-n* is retained in the feminine singular and the two plural forms.
2. In Samaritan Aramaic, the final *-n* is optionally retained in the feminine plural.
3. In Syriac, the feminine singular suffix *-y* represents -ø, as does the masculine plural suffix *-w*. There is also an alternate form of the masculine plural suffix with final *-n* (*-wn* = *-ûn*). Finally, the standard feminine plural suffix is not attested in this dialect. Instead the feminine plural suffixes *-y* (= -ø) and *-yn* (= *-ên*) are attested.

4.4.2.5 *Infinitive*

Each of the stems has a single infinitive form and this form is not inflected, although bound forms of the personal pronoun may be suffixed to it to indicate its subject or object (see §4.3.1.2). The infinitive is an action noun (*nomen actionis*) and, as such, it commonly occurs as the object of a preposition, especially the preposition *l* (see §5.3).

The *Pəʿal* infinitive has the historical form **maqtal* which becomes *miqtal* or *meqtal*, or remains *maqtal*, depending on the dialect and/or the first root consonant of the word. When a bound form of a personal pronoun is attached to one of these forms and the bound form begins with a vowel, the vowel preceding the final root consonant is reduced to /ə/ (e.g., *miqtəlî*). Other, less common, forms of the *Pəʿal* infinitive are attested in a number of periods and dialects. For example, in Old Aramaic, a few infinitives without the prefixed *m-* are attested, and in Old and Imperial Aramaic a few infinitives with final *-at* or *-ût* or *-ā* (written with a *mater lectionis*) are attested. The form with final *-ā* resembles one of the common forms of the infinitives in the other stems and it is also attested in Jewish Palestinian Aramaic, Jewish Babylonian Aramaic, and Samaritan Aramaic. Also noteworthy is the form *miqtôl* attested in Jewish Palestinian Aramaic and Jewish Babylonian Aramaic.

The infinitives of the other stems are all formed in the same way. In every period and nearly every dialect, the infinitive has *ā* preceding and following the final root consonant (the second *ā* being written with a *mater lectionis*). In Syriac, the forms have final *-û* (written with a *mater lectionis*) rather than *-ā*. When a pronominal suffix is attached to any of these forms, *-ā* becomes *-at* or, more commonly, *-ût*, and *-û* becomes *-ût*. Sporadically throughout all periods of Aramaic, forms with final *-at* or *-ût* also occur without a suffix attached. In Old, Imperial, and Middle Aramaic, the infinitives of these stems do not have any kind of prefix, but in most dialects of Late Aramaic the prefixed *m-* of the *Pəʿal* stem is also found on the other stems (this prefix replaces the *ʾ* of the *ʾAphʿel* and the three stems with prefixed *ʾt-*). Jewish Babylonian Aramaic is one dialect that does not attest the prefix *m-* and, furthermore, it attests an additional set of infinitive forms which are the common forms in this dialect. These forms have *ô* preceding the final root consonant and *ê* following the final root consonant (both vowels are written with a *mater lectionis*). These forms are also sporadically attested in Jewish Palestinian Aramaic.

4.4.2.6 Composite tenses

As early as the Imperial Aramaic period, "compound" or "composite" tenses are attested which consist of an active participle combined with a finite form of the verb *hwʾ/h* "to be." An active participle in combination with a perfect form of *hwʾ/h* is used to express past progressive or habitual action, and an active participle in combination with an imperfect form of *hwʾ/h* is used to express future progressive or habitual action. By the Late Aramaic period, these tenses had become much more commonly used, and additional tenses had developed in some of the dialects. For example, in Syriac, the perfect of *hwʾ/h* is used with the perfect of another verb either as a pluperfect or as a stylistic variant of the perfect verb.

4.5 Adverbs

In earlier dialects of Aramaic, there are relatively few adverbs and adverbial modification was frequently accomplished by the use of the absolute forms of nouns and adjectives: for example, *š/sgyʾ* "much, very." In some cases, the noun or adjective may have retained an old accusative suffix /-a/. One possible example is *klʾ* "completely" a form of the noun *kl* "all, every." A few examples of adverbs which are not related to nouns are: *tnh, tnn* "here"; *tmh, tmn* "there"; *kn* "thus, so"; and *ʾdn, ʾdyn* "then."

In Late Aramaic, these adverbs were retained and others were added to the lexicon through the increased use of adverbial suffixes such as *-ʾyt* in Syriac, which can be suffixed to any adjective to form an adverb.

4.6 Prepositions

All prepositions may have bound forms of the personal pronouns suffixed to them (see §4.3.1.2), and some prepositions are attested in combination with the particle *z/d(y)* (see §4.7.4), forming subordinating conjunctions (§4.8.2). Morphologically, prepositions can be divided into three categories:

1. *Inseparable prepositions*: Three prepositions, *b* "in," *l* "to," and *k* "like, as" (the last only attested in a few dialects) are phonologically and graphically proclitic to the following word. The preposition *mn* "from," in some of its forms, also falls into this category.
2. *Independent unstressed prepositions*: These prepositions are written as separate words but receive no stress and so are phonologically proclitic to the following word. Some common prepositions are *ʿl* "over, to," *ʿm* "with," and *ʿd* "up to, until." Also included in this group are the preposition *mn* "from," in some of its forms, and the marker of the direct object, *ʾyt* in Old Aramaic, *yt* in Imperial Aramaic, Middle Aramaic, and Jewish dialects of Late Aramaic (see §5.2.2).
3. *Independent stressed prepositions*: These prepositions are written as separate words and are not phonologically proclitic to the following word. Some examples are: *ngd* "opposite," *qdm* "before, in front of," and *ʾḥry* "behind, after."

4.7 Particles

4.7.1 Existential particles

The particle *ʾyt(y)* "there-is/are" expresses existence. The particle *lyt(y)* "there-is/are-not," a contraction of the negative particle *lʾ* (see §4.7.2) and the existential particle *ʾyt(y)*, expresses nonexistence. Both of these particles may have bound forms of the personal pronouns suffixed to them (see §4.3.1.2).

4.7.2 Negative particles

The particle *lʾ* "not" is used to negate verbs, clauses and, rarely, nouns. The particle *ʾl* "not" is used in prohibitions, which are expressed in Aramaic not by imperative verbs, but by jussive or imperfect verbs.

4.7.3 Interrogative particles

Numerous interrogative particles are attested in each of the Aramaic dialects, and the forms frequently vary from dialect to dialect. However, *mn*, *mʾn* "who," and *mh*, *mʾ* "what" are constant throughout nearly all dialects. In texts influenced by Hebrew (the Biblical Aramaic texts and the Targums), a particle *h* is attested which may be prefixed to the first word of a clause to indicate that it is a question. In Jewish Babylonian Aramaic, the particles *my* and *ʾtw* have this function.

4.7.4 The particle *z/d(y)*

This particle is spelled *zy*, *z*, or *dy* in earlier texts and *d* or *dy* in later texts (see §3.2.2). In some dialects and periods, it is phonologically and graphically proclitic to the following word. It is an extremely important particle which indicates that the following noun or clause stands in some subordinate relationship to what precedes it. It has five primary uses: (i) to express a "genitive" relationship between two nouns; (ii) to introduce a relative clause modifying a preceding noun; (iii) to indicate the object clause of a verb; (iv) to introduce direct or indirect speech; (v) to express purpose or result. This particle is also used in combination with prepositions to form subordinating conjunctions (see §4.8.2).

4.8 Conjunctions

4.8.1 Coordinating conjunctions

A number of coordinating conjunctions are attested. Most notable is the ubiquitous *w* "and, but, or" which is always phonologically and graphically proclitic to the following word. Also attested are the less common *ʾw* "or," *(ʾ)p* "also," and *brm* "but," which are neither phonologically nor graphically proclitic to the following word. In Syriac, the conjunction *dyn* "but, and then," equivalent to Greek δέ, is quite common.

4.8.2 Subordinating conjunctions

A number of prepositions are used with the particle *z/d(y)* to form subordinating conjunctions: for example, *mn* "after," *ʿd* "until," and *k* "when." Other widely attested subordinating conjunctions are: *dlmʾ* "lest, perhaps"; *ʾlʾ*, *ʾlw* "except that, however";

bdyl d "so that, because"; *hn, ʾn* "if"; and *kl qbl* "because, on account of, inasmuch as." In Syriac, the conjunction *gyr* "for, because," equivalent to Greek γάρ, is quite common.

4.9 Interjections

Examples of the few attested interjections are: *ʾrw, hn, hʾ* "behold," and *hy, ʾy, wy* "alas."

4.10 Numerals

4.10.1 Cardinals

The cardinal numerals 1 through 10 are not inflected for number, only for gender and state, and they rarely occur in the construct and emphatic states. The numeral 2, in both the masculine, *tryn*, and the feminine, *trtyn*, forms, retains the Proto-Aramaic dual inflectional suffix *-yn*. In (19) the most common absolute forms of the numerals 1 through 10 are listed. The forms listed as "masculine" are those which modify masculine nouns, and those listed as "feminine" modify feminine nouns, despite the fact that the masculine forms of the numerals 3 through 10 are morphologically feminine, and the feminine forms are morphologically masculine (cf. §4.2.2 and §5.1).

(19)

	Masculine	*Feminine*
1	ḥd	ḥdh, ḥdʾ
2	tryn	trtyn
3	tlth, tltʾ	tlt
4	ʾrbʿh, ʾrbʿʾ	ʾrbʿ
5	ḥmšh, ḥmšʾ	ḥmš, ḥmyš
6	šth, štʾ, ʾšth, ʾštʾ	št, šyt
7	šbʿh, šbʿʾ	šbʿ
8	tmnyh, tmnyʾ	tmnh, tmnʾ, tmny
9	tšʿh, tšʿʾ	tšʿ, tyšʿ
10	ʿšrh, ʿšrʾ, ʿsrh, ʿsrʾ	ʿšr, ʿsr

Note the following:

1. In these forms, final *-h* or *-ʾ* is a *mater lectionis*. Forms with *-h* occur in earlier dialects and forms with *-ʾ* occur in Late Aramaic, except Jewish Palestinian Aramaic and Samaritan Aramaic, which attest *-h*.
2. The final *-y* in the feminine form of 8 is a *mater lectionis* as is the medial *-y-* in the feminine forms of 5, 6, and 9, but not in the masculine form of 8. In that form, it is a consonant.
3. The medial *-y-* in both forms of the numeral 2 represents the Proto-Aramaic diphthong */ai/, which may have been retained in these forms as late as the Imperial Aramaic period. By the Middle or Late Aramaic period, this diphthong in this particular form had become /eː/ (see §3.3.2) in all dialects and so the *y* then functions only as a *mater lectionis*.
4. In some dialects, the masculine form of 6 is sometimes written with a prothetic *aleph* (see §3.6.5.3).
5. The numeral 10 is written with *š* in earlier dialects and with *s* in later ones (see §3.2.2).

The numerals 11 through 19 are inflected only for gender and consist of a combination of a form of the relevant digit (absolute, construct, or alternate) and an alternate form of the numeral 10. The forms of these numerals vary across the Aramaic dialects, and in some dialects multiple forms of some of these numerals are attested.

The numerals 20, 30, 40, 50, 60, 70, 80, and 90 are not inflected. They each have a single form which is characterized by a suffixed *-în*. These forms are essentially equivalent to the masculine plural absolute form of the corresponding digit, except for the numeral 20 which is equivalent to the masculine plural absolute form of 10: for example, *tlāt* "3," *tlātîn* "30"; and *ʿsar* "10," *ʿasrîn* "20."

The numeral 100 is a feminine noun and the numeral 1,000 is a masculine noun. They are fully inflected for number and state, their plural forms being used in combination with the digits 3 through 9 to form 300, 3,000, and so forth. The numerals 200 and 2,000 are formed using the dual inflectional suffix rather than the digit 2.

Bound forms of the personal pronouns can be suffixed to the numerals 2 through 10, though they are rarely attested.

4.10.2 Ordinals

There are distinct ordinal forms of the numerals 1 through 10. These forms have the same root consonants as the corresponding cardinals, except for the numeral 1, and, except for the numerals 1 and 2, they are characterized by the vowel *î* preceding the final root consonant and the suffix *āy* following the final root consonant: for example, *tlāt* "3," *tlîtāy* "3rd." In some dialects of Middle and Late Aramaic, the suffix is *āʾ*. These numerals are adjectives and can be fully inflected for gender, number, and state, although they are most commonly attested in the absolute state. For ordinal numerals higher than 10, the corresponding cardinal numeral is used.

In some dialects of Late Aramaic, cardinal numerals with the prefixed particle *z/d(y)* are also used as ordinals: for example, *dtryn* "who [is] 2" = "2nd."

5. SYNTAX

5.1 Noun phrase structure

Any noun or adjective can constitute a noun phrase by itself. An adjective which stands alone is interpreted as a concrete noun meaning "one who has the quality designated by the adjective."

Adjectives can be either attributive or predicative (see §5.2.1). An attributive adjective stands in an appositional relationship to a noun. The adjective nearly always follows the noun and agrees with it in gender, number and state:

(20) A. ʾnš ṭb
man good
"a good man"

B. ʾnšʾ ṭbʾ
the-man the-good
"the good man"

With the decreased use of the absolute state in Late Aramaic, the second example came to mean either "the good man" or "a good man" (see §4.2.2).

Demonstrative pronouns may be used either attributively or predicatively (see §5.2.1), but these uses cannot be distinguished by the form of the demonstrative itself, except in Jewish dialects of Late Aramaic in which an attributive demonstrative has a prefixed *h*- (this *h* is in addition to the *h* which is characteristic of some forms of the demonstrative pronouns in Late Aramaic; see §4.3.2.1). An attributive demonstrative may either precede or follow the noun it modifies, which must be in the emphatic state:

(21) A. byt᾽ dnh
the-house this
"this house"
B. dnh byt᾽
this the-house
"this house"

Though the position of the pronoun is not fixed, one position or the other tends to be preferred in each dialect and/or time period. With the increased use of the emphatic state, the demonstrative came to be used in some instances as little more than a definite article (see §4.2.2).

The modification of nouns by cardinal numerals shows a number of idiosyncrasies which differ from dialect to dialect. There are a few features that all cardinal numerals show in all dialects.

1. The numerals 1 to 19, which are the only numerals that distinguish gender, must agree in gender with the noun they modify. However, the numerals 3 to 10 show "chiastic concord" – the morphologically masculine form modifies feminine nouns and the morphologically feminine form modifies masculine nouns (see §4.10.1).
2. Numerals other than 1 may either precede or follow the noun, and the noun is plural.
3. The numeral 1 nearly always follows the noun and, of course, the noun is singular.
4. The numerals 2 to 10 can occur in either the absolute or the construct state with a following noun, but there is no difference in meaning: for example, (i) *tryn* (absolute) *᾽nšyn*; and (ii) *try* (construct) *᾽nšyn* – both meaning "two men."
5. The numerals 100 and 1,000 are nouns which may be modified by other numerals.

The ordinal numerals are adjectives and have the syntax of adjectives (see [20] above).

Modification of a noun by a prepositional phrase, an adverb, or a clause is accomplished through the use of the particle *z/d(y)* "who, which"; for example:

(22) ᾽nš᾽ dy bbyt᾽
the-man who in-the-house
"the man who [is] in the house"

The particle *z/d(y)* can be omitted in this construction, though this is extremely rare.

The relationships between two noun phrases that are expressed by the genitive case in some languages are expressed in Aramaic in two different ways.

On the one hand, genitive relationships can be expressed by a construct chain in which a noun in the absolute or emphatic state is preceded by one or more nouns in the construct state. The definiteness of all nouns in a chain is determined by the definiteness of the final noun:

(23) A. br mlk
son-of.CONSTRUCT king.ABSOLUTE
"a king's son"
B. br mlkʾ
son-of.CONSTRUCT the-king.EMPHATIC
"the king's son"

Most construct chains consist of two nouns, though construct chains of three nouns are not uncommon and chains of four nouns are attested. The use of the construct chain decreased over time, and by the Late Aramaic period the construction is only attested in chains that had been reanalyzed as compound nouns or in chains formed with a few words such as *br* "son-of" and *byt* "house-of."

On the other hand, genitive relationships can be expressed by a construction using the particle *z/d(y)* in which one noun is followed by the particle and a second noun. The second noun may be in either the absolute or emphatic state. The first noun may appear in one of three forms: (i) in the absolute state; (ii) in the emphatic state; or (iii) it may be suffixed with a bound form of the personal pronoun that agrees in gender and number with the second noun, although this form may only be used if the second noun is in the emphatic state:

(24) A. brʾ dy mlkʾ
the-son.EMPHATIC of the-king.EMPHATIC
"the king's son"
B. brh dy mlkʾ
son-his (= the king) of the-king.EMPHATIC
"the king's son"

Constructions in which one or the other or both nouns are in the absolute state are rare and occur most commonly in constructions expressing the "genitive of material":

(25) trʿn zy ʾbn
gates.ABSOLUTE of stone.ABSOLUTE
"stone gates"

5.2 Clause structure

5.2.1 Nonverbal clauses

Nonverbal clauses in Aramaic can be formed by the juxtaposition of a noun (phrase) or a pronoun used as a subject with an adjective, participle, prepositional phrase, adverb, or noun (phrase) used as a predicate. In such a clause, the predicate usually precedes the subject, except for the participle, which usually follows the subject. A predicative adjective or participle must agree with its subject in gender and number, and must also be in the absolute state, regardless of the state of its subject:

(26) ṭb khnʾ
good.ABSOLUTE the-priest
"The priest is good."

When a noun (phrase) is the predicate, an additional personal pronoun is often used, either preceding or following the subject:

(27) A. ywḥnn hw' khn'
John he the-priest
"The priest is John."

B. ywḥnn khn' hw'
John the-priest he
"John is the priest."

In Syriac and Jewish Babylonian Aramaic, the use of such pronouns was greatly expanded and they became used in all kinds of nonverbal clauses. In connection with this use, additional bound forms of the personal pronoun were developed (see §4.3.1.2).

5.2.2 Verbal clauses

In Aramaic, a finite verb form, by itself, can constitute a verbal clause. Since the verb is inflected for person as well as gender and number, no other element is necessary to constitute a clause.

A verbal clause may contain a subject noun (phrase), although the subject is commonly omitted in Aramaic if it is contextually identifiable. The verb agrees in gender and number with its subject. If a plural subject is of mixed gender, the verb is masculine. Not uncommmonly, a singular verb will occur with a plural subject or a masculine verb will occur with a feminine subject. Such disagreements between subject and verb are much more commonly attested when the subject follows the verb; when the subject precedes the verb, the verb rarely disagrees with it.

An indefinite direct object of a verb is not specially marked in Aramaic. A definite direct object of a verb is sometimes marked in Old Aramaic by the particle *'yt* (see §4.6). A later form of this particle, *yt*, is sometimes used in Imperial Aramaic, Middle Aramaic, and Jewish dialects of Late Aramaic, often in imitation of the Hebrew particle *'t*. More commonly in these periods and dialects, and exclusively in all other dialects of Late Aramaic, the preposition *l* is used to mark the definite direct object of a verb. In Late Aramaic, a definite direct object often occurs both as a bound pronoun suffixed to the verb and as a noun (phrase) marked with the preposition *l*:

(28) ktbh lktb'
he-wrote-it the-book
"He wrote the book."

Finally, the direct object of a verb may be omitted from a clause if it is identifiable from the immediate context.

The indirect object of a verb is also marked by the preposition *l* "to" which often leads to ambiguity. The indirect object may also be omitted from a clause if it is identifiable from the immediate context.

Two kinds of verbal adjuncts are particularly noteworthy. First, the agent of a passive verb is rarely indicated in most Aramaic dialects; however, in Syriac, the agent is more commonly expressed and when it is, the preposition *mn* marks it. Second, the absolute form of a noun or adjective can be used within a clause as an adverb rather than as a verbal complement. This use of nouns and adjectives is more common in earlier dialects and it decreases in later dialects as the number of true adverbs increases (see §4.5).

5.2.3 Subordinate clauses

There is no difference in the structure of a subordinate clause as compared with a main clause, except, of course, for the presence of a subordinating conjunction. However, this particle is sometimes omitted and the subordinate nature of the clause must then be inferred.

At times, a subordinate relationship exists between two formally coordinate clauses. There are two notable examples of such a relationship. The first is the conditional clause. In general, the protasis of a conditional clause begins with a conditional particle and will either precede or follow the apodosis to which it is subordinate. However, sometimes the protasis and the apodosis will be joined by the coordinating conjunction *w* (the so-called *waw* of apodosis) in which case, the protasis will always precede the apodosis; for example:

(29)	hn	kn	ʿbdw . . .	wṣdqh	yhwh	lk
	if	thus	you-do . . .	and-merit	will-be	to-you

“If you act in this way . . . (then) you will have merit.”

The second is verbal hendiadys, a construction in which two verbs are conjoined and share all verbal complements, but the first verb expresses a modification of the second rather than an independent action, as in the following:

(30)	ʾsgy	wqrʾ	lhwn
	he-increased	and-he-called	to-them

“He called to them often.”

This construction tends to occur in dialects and texts which are influenced by Hebrew, where the construction is more common.

5.2.4 Word order

The word order of the elements in a clause is not grammatically fixed in Aramaic and varies in part by the place of any given clause within the larger discourse. However, there are certain orders which can be considered “standard” and appear to have no special discourse function. In most dialects of Aramaic, this standard order is VSO (verb, subject, object, indirect object), although a pronominal object or indirect object will frequently precede a nominal subject. In Imperial Aramaic, the verb is often the final element of the clause, a result of Akkadian influence. Verbal adjuncts usually follow verbal complements within a clause.

A subordinate clause usually follows, but sometimes precedes, all of the elements of the main clause to which it is subordinated, although there are occasional examples of a subordinate clause being followed by complements or adjuncts of the main clause. These examples are most common when the elements of the main clause are particularly long and/or the subordinate clause is particularly short. In general, though, each clause is a discrete unit.

Negative particles, interrogative particles, coordinating conjunctions, and subordinating conjunctions will nearly always occur as the first element of a clause. Two regular exceptions to this tendency are the Syriac particles *gyr* “for, because” and *dyn* “but, and then” which are postpositive, like their Greek counterparts γάρ and δέ.

5.3 Infinitival syntax

The infinitive has aspects of nominal syntax and aspects of verbal syntax. As a verb, the infinitive can occur with its own complements and adjuncts. As a noun, it and its associated elements can occur as a complement or an adjunct of a verb. As a complement, it most commonly occurs as an object (usually marked with *l*), though its use as a subject, especially the subject of a nonverbal clause, is not uncommon. As an adjunct, it nearly always occurs as the object of the preposition *l*.

The functions of the infinitive as an adjunct are numerous and they parallel the functions of subordinate clauses. Frequently the same function can be expressed either by an infinitive or by a subordinate clause and there are even attestations of infinitives and subordinate clauses being conjoined with *w* "and." Two of the more common functions of the infinitive, both with the preposition *l*, are purpose/result and "epexegetic" or explanatory. There are also a few isolated examples of the temporal use of the infinitive with prepositions such as *k* "as, when" and *b* "in, when." This use of the infinitive was never common in Aramaic, and all of the examples of this use after the Old Aramaic period are in texts influenced by Hebrew, where the temporal use of the infinitive is quite common.

Because the infinitive most commonly occurs with the preposition *l* prefixed to it, this *l* became reanalyzed, apparently as early as the Imperial Aramaic period, as part of the infinitive form itself rather than as a preposition indicating the function of the infinitive within a clause. As a result, the word order of the complements of the infinitive became less rigid. In Old Aramaic, the infinitive precedes all of its complements, but in Imperial Aramaic and many dialects of Middle and Late Aramaic, the object of the infinitive commonly precedes it, even though the infinitive has *l* prefixed to it.

In dialects of Aramaic influenced by Hebrew and in the Old Aramaic Sefire texts, the infinitive is sometimes used in the same way as the Hebrew infinitive absolute, a use in which the infinitive occurs with a verb of the same root and stem to express the certainty of the action:

(31)	mbnʾ	bnʾ
	to-build	he-builds
	"He will certainly build."	

In this use, the infinitive never occurs with prefixed *l*.

5.4 Additional syntactic constructions

5.4.1 Possession

To express the notion of possession, the particle *ʾyt(y)* "there-is/are" or the verb *hwʾ/h* "to be" is used in combination with the preposition *l* "to." The thing possessed is the subject of the verb or the particle, and the possessor is the object of the preposition:

(32)	ʾyt	lʾnšʾ	ksp
	there-is	to-the-man	silver
	"The man has silver."		

5.4.2 Comparison

A comparative construction is formed by the use of a predicative adjective in combination with the preposition *mn* "from." One of the compared objects is the subject of the clause, and the other is the object of the preposition:

(33) ṭb ʿbdʾ mn mlkʾ
good the-servant from the-king
"The servant is better than the king."

5.4.3 Impersonal constructions

Two impersonal constructions are commonly attested. In the first, a masculine plural (or, less commonly, singular) active verb is used without an explicit or contextually understood subject to express the equivalent of a passive verb:

(34) lk trdyn mn ʾnšʾ
you.OBJ. they-will-drive-out from humanity
"You will be driven out from human society."

In the second, a passive participle is used in combination with the preposition *l* "to" to express the equivalent of an active finite verb:

(35) ṭwrʾ bṣyn lh
the-mountains be-searched.PASS.PART. to-him
"He searched the mountains."

This construction can even be used with an intransitive verb which normally would not have a passive participle:

(36) qym ly qdm šlyṭnʾ
be-stood.PASS.PART. to-me in-front-of powerful-men
"I have stood in front of powerful men."

This construction was borrowed from Persian where it is commonly attested.

6. LEXICON

Because of its use as a lingua franca and its contact with many other languages throughout its history, Aramaic contains numerous loanwords in addition to its core lexicon of native words. Nearly all of these loanwords are nouns. Aramaic borrowed very few verbs directly from other languages, although sometimes denominative verbs were created from loaned nouns. In the Imperial Aramaic period, Aramaic acquired words from Akkadian, Persian, and Egyptian. In the Middle Aramaic period, Greek words were added to the lexicon and these additions increased in the Late Aramaic period. Latin words were also added in the Late Aramaic period, as were a second group of Persian words in the eastern dialects. Finally, Hebrew was a constant source of loans in Jewish dialects of Aramaic.

6.1 Akkadian

Most Akkadian loanwords are administrative or architectural terms such as *sgn* (< *šaknu* "prefect"), *pḥt* (< *pîḫātu* "governor"), *ʾgrh* (< *egirtu* "letter"), and *trbṣ* (< *tarbiṣu* "courtyard"); though other terms such as *mlḥ* (< *malāḫu* "boatman") and *ʾšp* (< *āšipu* "enchanter") are also attested (see Kaufman 1974). Another notable loanword is the *Šaphʿel* verb *šyzb* (< *ušēzib* "to save"). Akkadian loanwords are completely assimilated to Aramaic, both phonologically and morphologically.

6.2 Persian

Like Akkadian, many Persian loanwords are administrative terms, reflecting the Persian rule of the Near East, and these words are all completely assimilated to the Aramaic inflectional system (despite the fact that Persian is an Indo-European language). Some examples are: *prtrk* (< *frataraka* "governor"), *hmrkry'* (< *hmārakara* "accountant"), and *'zdkr'* (< *azdākara* "messenger"). A number of Persian words for very common items or concepts became the common Aramaic terms as well, for example: *ptgm* (< *patigāma* "word"), *rz'* (< *rāza* "secret"), and *zn'* (< *zana* "kind"); see Muraoka and Porten 1998.

6.3 Egyptian

Egyptian loanwords are very rare in Aramaic and are restricted to Imperial Aramaic texts from Egypt. These words do not become part of the broader Aramaic lexicon. For whatever reason, a considerable number of these words relate to boats, though commodities and other terms are also attested. Some examples are: *tqm* (< *tgm* "castor oil"), *qntḥntr* (< *qnḥ-ntr* "divine shrine"), *ṭp* (< *dp* "part of a ship's mast"), and *šnt'* (< *šnt* "linen robe"); see Muraoka and Porten 1998.

6.4 Greek

Greek loanwords, which total over two thousand from various dialects, represent the largest group of non-native words in the Aramaic lexicon. They are not always completely assimilated to the Aramaic inflectional system. Many loanwords show multiple forms which reflect Greek rather than Aramaic inflectional suffixes. In some cases, forms with Aramaic inflectional suffixes coexist with forms that reflect Greek suffixes. Some examples are: *'rṭyqy'*, *'rṭyqws* (< αἱρετικός "heretic"), *'wsy'*, *'wsy's* (pl.) (< οὐσία "essence"), and *ṭks'*, *ṭksyn* (pl.) (< τάξις "order, row"); see Krauss 1898–1899.

6.5 Latin

Latin loanwords are relatively rare and are mostly restricted to dialects of western Late Aramaic. They are similar to Greek loanwords in that they are not always fully assimilated to the Aramaic inflectional system. Some examples of Latin loanwords are: *dwn'ṭyb'* (< *donativa* "imperial gift"), *ṭblh* (< *tabula* "board, tablet"), and *qlnds* (< *kalendas* [acc.] "first day of the month"); see Krauss 1898–1899.

6.6 Hebrew

Hebrew loanwords are only attested in Jewish dialects of Aramaic, and their status in those dialects is not always clear. This uncertainty is a result, in part, of the similarity of Hebrew and Aramaic. Frequently, words in the two languages only differed by a single vowel or by an inflectional suffix. Also, Hebrew and Aramaic coexisted for a very long time in Jewish communities, and literate members of those communities would have been well acquainted with both languages. So, when a Hebrew word appears in an Aramaic text, it may be a loanword, or it may simply be a Hebrew word which is being used because the writer of the text could assume that the readers of the text would be acquainted with it.

Bibliography

The bibliography contains all the special studies cited in the chapter as well as other bibliographies, surveys of Aramaic dialects, and at least one grammar for each of the major dialects of Aramaic.

Brock, S. 1996. *Syriac Studies: A Classified Bibliography, 1960–1990.* Kaslik, Lebanon: Université Saint-Esprit de Kaslik.
Cantineau, J. 1930. *Le nabatéen I. Notions générales – écritures, grammaire.* Paris: Ernest Leroux.
______. 1935. *Grammaire du palmyrénien épigraphique.* Cairo: L'Institut Français d'Archéologie Orientale. Reprint 1987, Osnabrück: Otto Zellar Verlag.
Crichton, W. (trans.). 1904. *Compendious Syriac Grammar.* London: Williams and Norgate.
Dalman, G. 1905. *Grammatik des jüdisch-palästinischen Aramäisch nach der Idiomen des palästinischen Talmud, des Onkelostargum und Prophetentargum und der jerusalemischen Targume* (2nd edition). Leipzig: Hinrichs. Reprint 1981, Darmstadt: Wissenschaftliche Buchgesellschaft.
Degen, R. 1969. *Altaramäische Grammatik der Inschriften des 10-8 Jh. v. Chr.* Abhandlungen für die Kunde des Morgenlandes 38/3. Wiesbaden: Steiner.
Drijvers, H. 1973. "XIII. Syriac and Aramaic." In J. Hospers (ed.), *A Basic Bibliography for the Study of the Semitic Languages*, vol. I, pp. 283–335. Leiden: Brill.
Fitzmyer, J. 1966. *The Genesis Apocryphon of Qumran Cave I.* Biblica et Orientalia 18. Rome: Pontifical Biblical Institute.
______. 1979. "The phases of the Aramaic language." In *A Wandering Aramean. Collected Aramaic Essays*, pp. 57–84. SBL Monograph Series 25. Missoula, MT: Scholars Press.
Fitzmyer, J. and S. Kaufman. 1992. *An Aramaic Bibliography, Part I: Old, Official, and Biblical Aramaic.* Baltimore and London: Johns Hopkins University Press.
Folmer, M. 1995. *The Aramaic Language in the Achaemenid Period.* Orientalia Lovaniensia Analecta 68. Louvain-La-Neuve: Peeters.
Greenfield, J. 1978. "Aramaic and its dialects." In H. Paper (ed.), *Jewish Languages. Theme and Variation*, pp. 29–43. Cambridge, MA: Association for Jewish Studies.
Grossfeld, B. 1972. *A Bibliography of Targum Literature*, vol. I. Bibliographica Judaica 3. Cincinnati: Hebrew Union College Press; New York: KTAV Publishing House.
______. 1977. *A Bibliography of Targum Literature*, vol. II. Bibliographica Judaica 8. Cincinnati: Hebrew Union College Press; New York: KTAV Publishing House.
______. 1990. *A Bibliography of Targum Literature*, vol. III. New York: Sepher-Hermon Press.
Hug, V. 1993. *Altaramäische Grammatik der Texte des 7. Und 6. Jhs. v. Chr.* Heidelberger Studien zum Alten Orient 4. Heidelberg: Heidelberger Orientverlag.
Kaufman, S. 1974. *The Akkadian Influences on Aramaic.* Assyriological Studies 19. Chicago: University of Chicago Press.
Krauss, S. 1898–1899. *Griechische und lateinische Lehnwörter in Talmud, Midrash und Targum* (2 vols.). Berlin: S. Calvary. Reprint 1987, Hildesheim: Olms.
Kutscher, E. 1970. "Aramaic." In T. A. Sebeok (ed.), *Current Trends in Linguistics*, vol. VI: *Linguistics in South West Asia and North Africa*, pp. 347–412. The Hague: Mouton.
______. 1971. "The Hermopolis papyri." *Israel Oriental Studies* 1:103–119.
Levias, C. 1900. *A Grammar of the Aramaic Idiom Contained in the Babylonian Talmud.* Cincinnati: Bloch Publishing and Printing.
Macuch, R. 1965. *Handbook of Classical and Modern Mandaic.* Berlin: Walter de Gruyter.
______. 1982. *Grammatik des samaritanischen Aramäisch.* Berlin: Walter de Gruyter.
Margolis, M. 1910. *A Manual of the Aramaic Language of the Babylonian Talmud.* Munich: Beck.
Morag, S. 1962. *The Vocalization Systems of Arabic, Hebrew, and Aramaic; Their Phonetic and Phonemic Principles.* Janua Linguarum. Series Minor 13. The Hague: Mouton.
Muraoka, T. and B. Porten. 1998. *A Grammar of Egyptian Aramaic.* Handbuch der Orientalistik 32. Leiden: Brill.
Naveh, J. 1982. *Early History of the Alphabet.* Leiden: Brill.
Nöldeke, T. 1875. *Mandäische Grammatik.* Halle: Buchhandlung des Waisenhauses. Reprint 1964, Darmstadt: Wissenschaftliche Buchgesellschaft.
______. 1898. *Kurzgefasste syrische Grammatik* (2nd edition). Leipzig: Weigel.
Rosenthal, F. 1939. *Die aramaistische Forschung seit Th. Nöldeke's Veröffentlichungen.* Leiden: Brill. Reprint 1964.
Rosenthal, F. (ed.). 1967. *An Aramaic Handbook* (4 vols.). Wiesbaden: Otto Harrassowitz.

Schulthess, F. 1924. *Grammatik des christliche-palästinischen Aramäisch.* Tübingen: Mohr. Reprint 1965, Hildesheim: Olms.

Segal, J. 1953. *The Diacritical Point and the Accents in Syriac.* Oxford: Clarendon Press.

Segert, S. 1975. *Altaramäische Grammatik mit Bibliographie, Chrestomathie und Glossar.* Leipzig: VEB Verlag Enzyklopädie.

Steiner, R. 1977. *The Case for Fricative-Laterals in Proto-Semitic.* New Haven, CT: American Oriental Society.

Stevenson, W. 1962. *Grammar of Palestinian Jewish Aramaic* (2nd edition). Oxford: Clarendon Press.

CHAPTER 7

Ancient South Arabian

NORBERT NEBES AND PETER STEIN

1. HISTORICAL AND CULTURAL CONTEXTS

Ancient (or Epigraphic) South Arabian (for terminology see Macdonald 2000:30), which is considered part of the southern branch of the Semitic language family, is divided into four main dialects, Sabaic, Minaic, Qatabanic, and Hadramitic, which are named after the most important peoples of southwest Arabia in the first millennium BC. These peoples founded their towns at the eastern edges of the central Yemeni highlands, in the wadi deltas that lead into Ramlat as-Sabʿatayn, the desert edge of the Rubʿ al-ḫālī, where favorable natural and geographical conditions prevail. Since Ramlat as-Sabʿatayn is also called Ṣayhad by the medieval Yemenite geographers, the term Ṣayhadic, coined by A. F. L. Beeston, has also been used in Sabaic scholarship recently as a generic term for the Ancient South Arabian dialects.

The dialect attested for the longest period and by the most inscriptions by far is Sabaic, the core area of which comprises the region of Mārib and Ṣirwāḥ, but which later also extended to a large part of the highland.

The first Sabaic inscriptions begin in the eighth century BC; the first Sabaic monuments of any length that can be dated reliably by a synchronism with Assyrian sources are to be placed in the early seventh century BC (Wissmann 1982:148). Sabaic is documented for a period of over 1,400 years and may be periodized into three main phases: (i) *Early Sabaic*, with mainly boustrophedon inscriptions dated from the eighth to the fourth century BC, and to which also the texts of the following two centuries from the area of Mārib and the highland are assigned; (ii) *Middle Sabaic*, from the first century BC until the end of the fourth century AD – most of the Sabaic documents, in which the dedicatory inscriptions from the Awām-temple in the oasis of Mārib comprise the largest self-contained text corpus, come from this period; (iii) *Late Sabaic*, of the monotheistic period, which ends in the sixth century AD. In the inscriptions from this period the traditional gods are no longer called upon, but only a single divinity (Raḥmānān). The last inscription dated according to the Himyarite calendar comes from the year AD 554/9.

Under Sabaic are also generally subsumed the inscriptions composed in the *Haramic* dialect, which exhibit linguistic influences from North Arabic. Another group of inscriptions in Sabaic were written by the Himyar, a people who first appeared in the southern highlands in the late second century BC; during the second and third centuries AD, they played an ever more important role in South Arabia, until from the fourth century they controlled large parts, and finally all, of Yemen from their capital Ẓafār.

The epigraphic documentation of Minaic, Qatabanic, and Hadramitic begins to increase from the middle of the first millennium BC, as the Sabaeans lose their dominance over South Arabia.

The first inscriptions written in the *Minaic* dialect appear at about the same time as the earliest Sabaic written evidence (eighth century BC) – though in smaller numbers – and come from the ancient cities along the large Wadi Maḏāb, which lies to the northwest of Mārib. Minaic trading colonies, and thus Minaic inscriptions, are also found outside South Arabia, as in the ancient oasis of Dedān (the present-day al-ʿUlā in Saudi Arabia), and even beyond the Arabian peninsula, as on the island of Delos and in Egypt, in testimony to the presence of Minaic merchants far to the north. Minaic disappears as a dialect around the end of the second century BC.

To the southeast of Mārib, in the wadis Ḥarīb and Bayḥān, lies the *Qatabanian* heartland and its main city Timnaʿ. The Qatabanic dialect area, following the area controlled by the Qatabanian kings, extends far to the southwest, to ˇGabal al-ʿAwd (not far from Ẓafār), and, according to Latin and Greek authors, to the Bāb al-Mandab on the Red Sea. Around the end of the second century AD, 150 years after the destruction of Timnaʿ, Qataban is finally crushed by Sabaʾ and Hadramawt, after which the epigraphic documentation of this dialect ceases.

Hadramitic inscriptions are concentrated in the ancient region along the large Wadi Hadramawt in the eastern part of southwest Arabia and in the royal city of Šabwa which, situated at the southwestern entrance to the wadi, plays a significant role in antiquity as the starting point of the incense route. Hadramitic inscriptions are also found a few hundred kilometers southeast of Šabwa in Samārum (modern Ḫawr Rūrī near Salāla in Oman on the coast of the Indian Ocean), which was founded by Hadramitic colonists toward the end of the first century BC. At the beginning of the fourth century AD the Himyar incorporate Hadramawt into their area of control, after which the epigraphic documentation of Hadramitic likewise ends and is replaced by Sabaic.

2. WRITING SYSTEM

The Ancient South Arabian writing system, which is also commonly called the *Ancient South Arabian monumental script* and which is used for all Ancient South Arabian dialects equally, is a segmental script of twenty-nine graphemes that primarily, but not exclusively, serve to represent consonants. A striking feature of the Ancient South Arabian script is the geometric form of the letters, which, in the early period, stand in a fixed relationship of height and width to one another and can reach a height of over 30 centimeters in monumental exemplars. In contradistinction to the later North Arabic script the individual letters are not joined to one another, each letter standing rather on its own. Words are separated from each other by a vertical dividing line. The Ancient South Arabian script has no punctuation marks. The direction of writing is horizontal, from right to left. A characteristic of the inscriptions of the Early Sabaic period from the Mārib area is boustrophedon writing, in which the direction of writing changes, and which is later given up in favor of the sinistrograde style. A peculiarity specific to the Late Sabaic inscriptions is letters carved out of the stone in relief.

Inscriptions are written primarily on well-worked stone surfaces, stone blocks, or smoothed rock faces. Inscriptions can also, however, be cast in bronze or prepared on iconographic objects of bronze or on coins or amulets, and the like.

At the beginning of the 1970s, the first instances of writing on wooden sticks, in a hitherto unknown minuscule script, were discovered in Yemen. The understanding of these sticks, which come from the Yemenite Ǧawf and of which several thousand have come to light in the

Table 7.1 The Ancient South Arabian consonantal script

Character	Transcription	Character	Transcription
𐩠	h	𐩯	s_3
𐩡	l	𐩰	f
𐩢	ḥ	𐩱	ʾ
𐩣	m	𐩲	ʿ
𐩤	q	𐩳	ḍ
𐩥	w	𐩴	g
𐩦	s_2	𐩵	d
𐩧	r	𐩶	ġ
𐩨	b	𐩷	ṭ
𐩩	t	𐩸	z
𐩪	s_1	𐩹	ḏ
𐩫	k	𐩺	y
𐩬	n	𐩻	ṯ
𐩭	ḫ	𐩼	ẓ
𐩮	ṣ		

meantime, is made especially difficult because of the script and the unknown vocabulary. Concerning the contents of the roughly thirty examples published thus far, probably dating to the second/third centuries AD, it can be said at present that they are documents partly written in the form of letters that have to do with legal and economic matters (Ryckmans, Müller, and Abdallah 1994).

Apart from a large number of graffiti, mostly of personal names, the inscriptions written in the monumental script can be assigned to quite varied text genres. The most widely attested group in all Ancient South Arabian dialects is that of the dedicatory inscriptions, which sometimes contain reports of entire military campaigns. Besides these, building inscriptions, irrigation regulations, grave inscriptions, law texts, and other types of legal documents, as well as so-called penitential and expiatory inscriptions have been found (Müller 1994: 307–312).

In view of the record of documentation, it is principally Sabaic that will be treated in the following summary, with examples from the earlier or later periods noted. The abbreviations used to identify inscriptions are those of *Sab. Dict.* (pp. xx–xxv) and Stein 2003 (pp. 274–290).

3. PHONOLOGY

3.1 Preliminary remarks

The Ancient South Arabian writing system is, like that of many other Semitic languages, primarily devised for the representation of consonants, and expresses vowels only in very restricted cases. In the absence of an oral tradition, the precise pronunciation of its graphemes is unknown, and a conventional reconstruction of the sound values is possible only by comparison with other Semitic languages.

Figure 7.1 The great inscription of Karibʾil Watar (c. 685 BC) R 3945: section of lines 11-20

3.2 Consonants

3.2.1 Consonantal inventory

The following overview gives a rough classification of the Ancient South Arabian consonants according to manner and place of articulation, modeled on the reconstructed Proto-Semitic phonological system.

3.2.2 Sibilants

The classification of the graphemes represented above by s_1, s_2, and s_3 was long debated. The usual transcription in the older literature – *s*, *š*, and *ś* – is modeled on the form of the letters and on parallels in classical Arabic, and quickly leads to confusions in etymological comparisons with other Semitic languages which likewise exhibit three distinct "s"-sounds that are, however, transcribed differently. The following shows the correlation between the older and newer transcription systems (for comparison the corresponding Arabic and Hebrew sounds are also given):

(1)

Ancient South Arabian		Classical Arabic	Hebrew
New	Old		
s_1	s	s	š
s_2	š	š	ś
s_3	ś	s	s

Table 7.2 The consonantal phonemes of Ancient South Arabian

Manner of articulation	Bilabial	Labio-dental	Inter-dental	Dental/alveolar	Palato-alveolar	Palatal	Velar/uvular	Pharyn-geal	Glottal
	Place of articulation								
Stop									
Voiceless				t			k		ʾ (/ʔ/)
Voiced	b			d			g		
Emphatic				ṭ (/t'/)			q		
Fricative									
Voiceless		f	ṯ (/θ/)	s_3	s_1		ḫ	ḥ (/ħ/)	h
Voiced			ḏ (/ð/)	z			ġ	ʿ (/ʕ/)	
Emphatic			ẓ (/θ'/)						
Affricate				ṣ (/tˢ'/)					
Nasal									
Voiced	m			n					
Lateral continuant									
Voiceless				s_2					
Voiced				l					
Emphatic				ḍ (/ɬ'/)					
Liquid				r					
Glide									
Voiced	w					y			

3.2.3 Glides

The graphemes *w* and *y* represent primarily consonants – as in other Semitic languages – but also serve as so-called *matres lectionis* (see, *inter alia*, Ch. 8, §2) to indicate vowels (cf. Nebes 1997:114f.). Thus, parallel writings (sometimes in one and the same text, e.g., J 651/12–13, 20) such as *ywm* and *ym* "day" or *byt* and *bt* "house" allow conclusions to be drawn about the occurrence of the monophthongs /o:/ and /e:/ respectively.

3.3 Vowels

The few statements that can be made about the vocalization of Ancient South Arabian are based on the use of the glides *w* and *y*. The final writings of plural forms of verbs (Sab. *hqnyw* "they dedicated"), personal pronouns (*hmw*; *-hw*), and enclitic particles (*-mw*; *-my*) are in all likelihood to be read as vocalic (presumably as long /u:/ and /i:/). The same holds for imperfect forms of verbs II-*w/y*, such as, *ykwn* "he will be", of which defective writings (*ykn*) are also attested (see also above, §3.2.3, on monophthongization). Apart from these few hints, practically nothing is known about the vocalization of the Ancient South Arabian texts preserved for us. The question of a possible differentiation of syllables according to vowel quantity, therefore, likewise cannot be answered with certainty, nor are any broad conclusions possible concerning the accentual relationships of Ancient South Arabian.

3.4 Sabaic phonological variation and change

3.4.1 Sound change

Orthographic evidence suggesting various sound changes occurs. The letters *ṣ* and *ẓ* commonly alternate (and also strongly resemble each other in the script), for example in the word for "statuette", which in the Middle Sabaic dedicatory inscriptions from the Awām temple in Mārib appears as both *ṣlm* and (rarely) *ẓlm* (e.g., J 688/3). In Late Sabaic the sibilant s_3 is increasingly replaced by s_1, for example in *m*s_1*nd* instead of *m*s_3*nd* "inscription". In some dialects, *w* and *y* alternate in verbal and nominal forms of weak roots in comparison with the Sabaic "Standard", for example in derivations of *rḍw* "(to have) pleasure", so that the root is also listed in the dictionaries under *rḍy*, or in *qwl/qyl* "tribal leader", the plural of which always appears as *ʾqwl* (cf. *ʾqwln* beside *qyln* in ʿAbadān 1/40).

3.4.2 Assimilation

As in Hebrew, *n* can assimilate to a following consonant (see Ch. 3, §3.1.2). No firm rules for this phenomenon in Sabaic have thus far been discerned, however, since unassimilated forms are attested just as often in apparently identical contexts (compare, e.g., *hkrn* "to alter, damage" [infinitive] and *hnkrn*; *ʾf*s_1 "souls" and *ʾnf*s_1). In Middle Sabaic, assimilation of *n* seems to be the rule.

3.4.3 Metathesis

In some texts, from the southern dialect area, metathesis is a common phenomenon, which nevertheless appears to be restricted to relatively few words, and particularly to the plurals *ʾywn* (instead of *ʾwyn*) from *wyn* "vineyard" and *ʾlwd* (instead of *ʾwld*) from *wld* "child".

3.4.4 Regional variation

The texts of certain regions exhibit certain peculiarities that indicate some dialectal coloring of Sabaic. Our grammatical "standard" is based on the texts from Mārib and the central Yemeni highlands.

3.5 Non-Sabaic phonological features

In Hadramitic the sounds s_3 and *ṯ* have fallen together to a large extent, a development that is expressed in the alternation of the corresponding graphemes. Thus the number "3" appears as s_2ls_3 (e.g., R 2687/5; cf. Sab. s_2*lṯ*), and the pronominal suffix of the third person feminine as -s_3 and -*ṯ*. Similarly, Minaic writes the phoneme /s/ in foreign proper names as *ṯ* (e.g., *dlṯ* "Delos" in R 3570/3), but nevertheless keeps the phoneme distinct in the language proper.

Particularly distinctive of Minaic is the insertion of an etymologically unexplained *h* in certain nominal endings, pronouns, and particles (see the forms in the relevant section).

Here too, probably, also belong the Minaic plural forms *bhn* and *bhnt* of *bn* "son" and *bnt* "daughter". The meaning of these spellings is uncertain. Perhaps they are plene-writings of a long vowel different from /u:/ and /i:/, as is suggested especially by comparison within Semitic. The same phenomenon can be observed in the hadramitic ending *–hn* marking the determinate state.

4. MORPHOLOGY

4.1 Word structure

Ancient South Arabian shares the fundamental common feature of the Semitic language family: the inflectional morphological system based on a (usually triconsonantal, or *triradical*) root. This means that from a basic scaffold of, as a rule, three consonants, a whole variety of verbal and nominal forms are built by means of the affixing and infixing of a few formative elements (as is common, the root *fʿl* "to do, make" will serve as the paradigmatic root in what follows); semantically, such forms can always be traced back in some way to the basic meaning of the root (e.g., verbal forms of various stems, such as *yfʿlnn*, *ftʿl*, s_1*tfʿl*, or nouns such as *mfʿl*, *fʿlt*, etc.). Additional types of morphological differentiation (such as by the lengthening of vowels and consonants) are not visible in the consonantal script, but should be assumed.

As in other Semitic languages, there are also a number of biradical nouns (e.g., s_1*m* "name", *yd* "hand") and a few quadriradical roots (e.g., *kwkb* "star" s_2*ʾml* Robin-al-Lūmī 1/2 "left, northern"). Verbs that go back originally to biradical roots (so-called weak verbs; see §4.4.3) have largely been brought into line with the triradical system by means of the insertion of "weak" radicals.

Ancient South Arabian distinguishes three numbers (singular, dual, and plural) and two genders (masculine and feminine).

4.2 Nominal morphology

4.2.1 Noun patterns

The system of noun patterns in Ancient South Arabian can be only incompletely reconstructed because of the inadequacy of the script; it ought for the most part, however, to have been similar to that of the other Semitic languages in its essential features.

The heavy use of *broken plurals* (see Appendix 1, §3.3.2.4) in Ancient South Arabian is noteworthy. Most of these have the pattern *ʾfʿl*: for example, *ʾbyt* from *byt* "house"; *ʾqwl* from *qwl/qyl* "tribal leader". In addition to these there are many other forms of broken plurals, such as *mfʿlt* from singular *mfʿl* (e.g., *mḥfdt* from *mḥfd* "tower"; *mqymt* from *mqm* "might") and the converse (e.g., *mṣnʿ* from *mṣnʿt* "fortress"), or *fʿl* from singular *fʿlt* (e.g., *ʾnṯ* from *ʾnṯt* "woman"), as well as the so-called *nisbe*-plural *ʾfʿl(n)* (e.g., *ʾḥbs*$_2$*n* from *ḥbs*$_2$*y* "Abessynian"). Further, several different plurals can be formed from one noun (cf. the numerous plural forms of *ḫrf* "year" in *Sab. Dict.*).

In contrast, the external "sound" plural is markedly rare and apparently restricted to a few words.

4.2.2 Noun state

As in other Semitic languages, nouns in Ancient South Arabian exhibit, in addition to number and gender, three states (for the forms in Sabaic see [**2**] below); a fourth state, the so-called "absolute", is limited to a few syntactic contexts, mainly numerals (see §4.6.1.1):

1. *Indeterminate state* (*status indeterminatus*): marked in the singular as a rule by "mimation" (*-m* occurring in final position); denotes an indefinite noun: for example, *ṣlmm ḏ-ḏhbm* "a(ny) statuette of bronze"; *kl qṭntm* Gl 1142/9 "each [type of] flock".
2. *Determinate state* (*status determinatus*): corresponds to the form of a noun marked with a definite article in other languages, for example, *ḏn ṣlmn ḏ-ḏhbn* "this statuette of bronze"; *ṣlmnhn* "the two statuettes"; *$s_2$ltn ṣlmtn* "the three statuettes [of women]"; *hgrn $s_2$bwt* "the city [of] Šabwa"; *kl ʾqwln* "all of the tribal leaders." Proper names are naturally definite (e.g., *$s_2$bwt* in the example above).
3. *Construct state* (*status constructus*): in possessive phrases, the form of the governing noun (*nomen regens*) joined to an immediately following genitive; the second (genitive) member of the construction may be a pronominal suffix, a governed noun (*nomen rectum*), or an asyndetic relative clause (see §5.4.2). The accompanying *nomen rectum* is usually definite, but may also be indefinite. As examples consider the following: *ʾwld-hw* "his children"; *ʿdy ḫlf hgrnhn ns$_2$qm w-ns$_2$n* J 643/25 "in the vicinity of the two cities [of] Našqum and Naššān"; *mlky s_1bʾ* "the two kings of Saba'"; *nḍʿ w-s_2ṣy s_2nʾm* C 407/33 "harm and malice of a[ny] enemy"; *kl s_1bʾt w-ḍbyʾ w-tqdmt s_1bʾy w-ḍbʾ w-tqdmn mrʾy-hmw* J 581/6–7 "all expeditions, battles, and attacks, which their two lords led" (the three verbs cannot be meaningfully rendered literally in the translation); compare also §5.4.2. As the last two examples show, several *nomina regentes* may appear in succession in the construct state.

In several instances a genitive relationship is expressed by means of a relative pronoun (see §4.3.3), only rarely, however, by means of apposition, as in *ṯlṯt ṣlmm ḏhbm* J 567/9 "three statuettes of bronze" (similarly in rare cases by a following asyndetic relative clause; see §5.4.2).

Because of the lack of vocalization, the Ancient South Arabian case system can only be reconstructed on the basis of the construct state of the external plural of *bn* "son", which, especially in Early Sabaic texts, appears both as *bnw* (nominative syntactically) and as *bny* (oblique; see Stein 2002a).

The inflectional endings which mark each of the states are summarized below:

(2)

	Masculine			*Feminine*		
	Constr.	*Indet.*	*Det.*	*Constr.*	*Indet.*	*Det.*
Singular	-ϕ	-m	-n	-t	-t-m	-t-n
Dual	-ϕ/-y	-n	-nhn	-t-y	-t-n	-t-nhn
External plural	-w/-y	-n	-nhn	-t	-t-m	-t-n

Note the following:

1. The feminine endings presented above are the "regular" forms. There is also a set of "natural" feminines which are formed like the masculine, that is, without the ending *-t*.
2. The masculine singular endings are likewise those of the broken plurals of masculine forms.
3. In Masculine dual constr. the first ending is attested in Early Sabaic, the second in Middle Sabaic and Late Sabaic.
4. In Masculine constr. plural the first ending is nominative, the second oblique.

4.3 Pronominal morphology

4.3.1 Personal pronouns

Forms of the first and second persons are only very sparsely attested thus far, the latter primarily in the minuscule inscriptions of the wooden sticks (see §2). Typical of a Semitic language, personal pronouns occur in both independent and suffixed (clitic) forms. A gender distinction is not attested in the first person and in the dual number (see Appendix 1, §3.3.3).

The independent personal pronouns serve as subjects of nominal clauses and, more often, of verbal clauses. In the latter case, the pronoun is placed at the beginning of the clause and the following verb is usually separated by *f-* (see §5.1). Consider the following examples: *mrʾ ʾt* Ry 508/11 (Late Sabaic) "you are lord"; *w-ʾt* s_3*ḫln* A-40-4/3 (beside *w-ʾnt f-*s_3*ḫln*; see §4.4.4); *w-hmw f-ḥmdw* C 2/7–8 "and they thanked"; *w-t ʾwlw bn-hw b-wfym hwʾ w-kl* s_2*wʿ-hmw* J 631/13–14 "and they returned from there safely, [namely] he himself and all their retinue". The personal pronouns of the third person are identical with the second group of demonstrative pronouns (see §4.3.2).

The clitic personal pronouns (pronominal suffixes) appear on both noun and verb forms: for example, *bny-hw* "his sons"; *ḫmr-hw* "he granted to him"; *l-kmw* YM 11729/3 "to you (pl.)"; *l-krbn-kmw* (< *l-ykrbn-kmw*) YM 11733/2 "may he bless you (pl.)"; and so forth.

The independent pronouns and and pronominal suffixes are summarized in (3):

(3)

	Independent pronouns	Pronominal suffixes
Singular		
1st com.	ʾn	(-n)
2nd masc.	ʾnt, ʾt	-k
2nd fem.		-k
3rd masc.	hʾ, hwʾ	-hw
3rd fem.	hʾ, [hyʾ]	-h, -hw
Dual		
2nd com.	ʾtmy	-kmy
3rd com.	hmy	hmy
Plural		
1st com.		(-n)
2nd masc.	ʾntmw	-kmw
2nd fem.		
3rd masc.	hmw	-hmw, (-hm)
3rd fem.	[hn]	-hn

Regarding the pronouns of (3), note the following:

1. The first common singular pronoun *ʾn* is attested in a few Late Sabaic texts: *sṭrw ḏn ms*$_3$*ndn ʾn ʾbrh* C 541/3–4 "I, Abraha, wrote this inscription" (the verb as *plural maiestatis*); see also §4.4.2 on VL 24/3 = J 2353/3.
2. First com. sing. *-n* (accusative) so far attested only in feminine personal names such as s_2*fnns*$_1$*r* (= s_2*f-n ns*$_1$*r*) "[the god] Nasr protected me".
3. The second feminine singular clitic *-k* occurs in the "Sun Hymn" (Robin 1991:122), and in Oost. Inst. 14/5f.
4. The third feminine clitic of the form *-hw* is attested only in Middle Sabaic.

4.3.2 Demonstrative pronouns

These may be divided into two groups according to their form and function: *Demonstrative 1* indicates the immediate situation of the speaker or reader of an inscription, whereas *Demonstrative 2* points back to something mentioned previously in the text. A demonstrative pronoun precedes the noun it modifies, which appears in the determinate state: for example, *ḏn ṣlmn ḏ-ḏhbn* J 578/4–5 "this (i.e., the present) statuette of bronze"; *h' fnwtn* R 4815/5,7 "this (i.e., the aforementioned) canal"; *hmw 'ḥmrn* J 576/10,16 "these (i.e., the aforementioned) Himyarites". The demonstratives of the second group distinguish special forms for the oblique case: for example, *b-hwt bytn* E 13 §10 "in that castle".

(4)

	Demonstrative 1	*Demonstrative 2*	
		Nominative	*Oblique*
Singular			
Masculine	ḏn	h', hw'	hwt
Feminine	ḏt, (ḏtn?)	h', hy'	hyt
Dual			
Common	ḏyn	hmy	hmt, (hmyt)
Plural			
Masculine	'ln	hmw	hmt
Feminine	'lt	hn	hnt

4.3.3 Relative pronouns

The relative pronoun, either inflected or in the frozen form *ḏ-*, appears before independent or attributive relative clauses (see §5.4.1 and §5.4.2) or before nouns in a circumlocution for a construct chain, as in *ṣlmn ḏ-ḏhbn* "the statuette of bronze" (see also the example from J 657 in §4.6.1.1), in which the nouns often agree in definiteness (thus *ṣlmn ḏ-ḏhbn* vs. *ṣlmm ḏ-ḏhbm*). The standard forms of the relative pronoun are as follows:

(5)

	Masculine	*Feminine*
Singular	ḏ-	ḏt, t-
Dual	ḏy	ḏty
Plural	'l, 'lw, 'ly, 'lht	'lt

Note the following:

1. In feminine singular, the second form is Late Sabaic.
2. In masculine plural, the first form is Early Sabaic, the second and third ones are Middle Sabaic nominative and oblique respectively, the last one is Late Sabaic.

4.3.4 Indefinite pronouns

For the indefinite pronouns *mn* "someone" and *mhn* "something" see §5.4.1 and §5.3.6.

4.4 Verbal morphology

4.4.1 Verb-stems

The following verb-stems may be distinguished graphically (on the fundamental nature of Semitic verb-stems, see Appendix 1, §3.3.5.2):

(6) 0_1(fʿl), 0_2(fʿl), H (hfʿl), T_{in}(ftʿl), T_{Pr}(tfʿl), ST($s_1$tfʿl).

For the stem 0_2 see below, §4.4.5.

These are inflected regularly throughout, retaining their formative elements even with prefixes (e.g., *yhfʿlnn*). Possible additional stems, marked by vocalic or consonantal lengthening, may also be assumed, but are not yet clearly ascertained on the basis of the script.

Likewise active and passive forms of the verb cannot be outwardly distinguished. However, a differentiation of voice can be demonstrated for many verbs on syntactic grounds (see the example from J 669 in §5.3.6), a distinction that must have been marked vocalically.

4.4.2 Verb inflection

As in other Semitic languages, two conjugation types exist in Ancient South Arabian: the suffix-conjugation, usually termed the *perfect*, and the prefix-conjugation, or *imperfect*. The latter is further divided into a simple, unaugmented "short form" and a form augmented by *-n* called the "long form" or *N-imperfect* (see Nebes 1994b). The base of the prefix-conjugation of the simple stem (for both short and long forms) has the shape *fʿVl* as in Arabic (see Nebes 1994a).

The forms of the two conjugations are presented in (7). The final *-w* or *-y* of dual and plural forms usually disappears (in the orthography) before a following suffix, as in *ln hbrrw b-ʿly ʾḥḍrn w-hs*$_1$*ḥt-hmw* E 13 §9 "when they set out against the Hadramites and defeated them". Likewise the prefix *y-* is sometimes not written after a preceding precative particle *l-*, as in *l-hṣbḥnn* beside *l-yhṣbḥnn* "may [ʿAṯtar and ʾAlmaqah] keep [you happy]" in the minuscule inscriptions YM 11729/2–3 and YM 11732/2 (cf. also Ghul Document A/1–2); the ending *-nn* clearly marks these forms as finite. Such defective imperfect forms are to be distinguished from the precative infinitives discussed in §5.6.2.

(7) Summary of finite verb forms

	Suffix-conjugation	*Prefix-conjugation*	
		Short form	*Long form*
Singular			
3rd masc.	fʿl	y-fʿl	y-fʿl-n
3rd fem.	fʿl-t	t-fʿl	t-fʿl-n
2nd masc.	fʿl-k	t-fʿl	t-fʿl-n
2nd fem.	fʿl-k		
1st com.	(fʿl-k)		
Dual			
3rd masc.	fʿl, fʿl-y	y-fʿl-y	y-fʿl-nn
3rd fem.	fʿl-ty, (fʿl-tw)	[t-fʿl-y]	t-fʿl-nn
Plural			
3rd masc.	fʿl-w	y-fʿl-w	y-fʿl-nn
3rd fem.	fʿl-y, fʿl-n (?)	t-fʿl-n (?)	t-fʿl-nn
2nd masc.	fʿl-kmw		t-fʿl-nn

Regarding these finite verb forms, note the following:

1. The forms of the second-person masculine are thus far attested almost exclusively in the minuscule inscriptions on wooden sticks (cf. Ryckmans, Müller, and Abdallah 1994 with publication of several texts and further bibliography).
2. The second-person singular *fʿl-k* is attested as feminine with certainty only in the "Sun Hymn" (Robin 1991:122).

3. The first-person singular is not certainly attested in texts published to date. Perfect forms probably occur in VL 24 = J 2353: for example, line 3, *w-brʾk-h ḥ* "and I built them (the irrigation works)".
4. Both of the third feminine plural forms, *fʿl-y* and *fʿl-n*, are attested only rarely; also perhaps *fʿl-tw* (cf. Nebes 1985:34–38).
5. In dual 3rd masc., the first form is Early Sabaic, the second one is later.

4.4.2.1 The suffix-conjugation

The suffix-conjugation, or perfect, (*fʿl*) may appear in both main and subordinate clauses and is primarily used for the past and the pluperfect. It may occur in statements that, according to their meaning, denote *duration* as well as those that describe *punctual* actions. Compare, for example, the following: (i) *w-thrgw b-ʿmhmw bn* s_2*f*s_2*rqm ʿdy mqṭt* s_2*m*s_1*n w-lyl lylm ʿdy* s_2*rq kwkbn ḏ-ṣbḥn* J 649/32–34 "And they fought with them from daybreak until sunset and (from) the falling (?) of night until the rising of the morning-star"; (ii) *w-wdqy hmy btnhn ḏ-hmdn w-btʿ bn hwt ḏnmn* J 651/20–21 "And both these houses of Hamdān and of Bataʿ collapsed because of this rain".

The basic time reference for the perfect is anteriority to a given "relative moment". In the past, as in both of the preceding examples, the relative moment lies in the temporal sphere of the author; in the pluperfect, it lies in the syntactically superordinate clause, as in *w-ḥmdw mqm ʾlmqh k-ḫlhmw bn qblm ḏ-wdq ʿl-hmw* YM 440/6–8 "And they expressed their gratitude for the power of Almaqah, that he had saved them from a misfortune that had come upon them".

In the protasis of conditional sentences and in relative clauses with conditional connotation, the suffix-conjugation has a present meaning. This is explained, as in Arabic, by the specific relationship of anteriority of the apodosis and protasis; see the examples in §5.3.6.

4.4.2.2 The prefix-conjugation

Concerning the distribution of the short (*yfʿl*) and long (*yfʿln*) forms of this imperfect, it should be noted that *yfʿln* forms constitute over three-quarters of the attestations. A rigorously consistent differentiation of functions between the two types cannot be established. A historical consideration of the uses reveals, however, that in Early Sabaic *yfʿl* is attested considerably more often than *yfʿln*. To be noted as well is that in the Middle Sabaic period *yfʿl* appears considerably more often than *yfʿln* in narrative contexts, where both long and short types are used to describe a "progression of action" as, for example, in the following: *w-bnhw f-ygbʾw ʿdy hgrn nʿḍ w-bnhw f-yhṣrn mlkn ʾls*$_2$*rḥ yḥḍb w-ḏ-bn ḫms*$_1$*hw w-ʾfrs*$_1$*hw ʿdy ʾrḍ mhʾnfm w-yqmʿw w-hbʿln hgrnhn* J 576/7–8 "From there they went to the city of Naʿḍ. From there King ʾIlšaraḥ Yaḥḍib, along with part of his main army and his riders, set out for the region of Muhaʾnifum. [Then] they destroyed and seized the both cities".

As a common denominator to which the overwhelming majority of examples may be reduced, the terms that suggest themselves for the relative time reference of the imperfect are *simultaneity* and *posteriority*. The "relative moment" is either the present moment of the writer/speaker or to be found in the immediate syntactic context (e.g., a superordinate clause).

The long form of the imperfect (*yfʿln*), seldom the short form (*yfʿl*), occurs in statements with the present and future reference: for example, *mḏbḥt b-h yḏbḥn mlkn ṯwrm b-ywm ts*$_1$*ʿm ḏ-ṯwr* C 671/1–4 = R 3104/1–4 "altar on which the king on the 9th day [of the month of] ḏū Ṯawr offers a bull".

In subordinate clauses introduced by conjunctions and in relative clauses which have a syntactically superordinate clause situated in the past, *yfʿln* and, less often, *yfʿl* may have modal nuances: for example, *bkn wqhhw… l-*s_1*bʾ w-qtdmn… w-l-*s_2*ym l-hw mḍrfn* s_1*wn ṭmḥnyn ḏ-yḥmynhw bn ḏʿbn* J 651/28–33 "When [their lord] … commanded him to carry out and direct [the work] … [and] to erect the dam-works for it [i.e., the city of Mārib] further up the wadi, which would protect it from flooding" (potentiality or intentionality).

The prefix-conjugation also forms the basis for the production of other modal verb forms: (i) *l-yfʿln* denotes the *precative* (used to express wishes); (ii) *l-yfʿl* serves as the *jussive* (expressing indirect commands; for the imperative, see §4.4.4); and (iii) *ʾl yfʿl* functions as the *vetitive* (used to express negative wishes). These can be respectively illustrated by the following: (i) *w-l-yḫmrnhw ʾlmqhw ḥẓy w-rḍw mrʾhmw* J 667/14–15 "And may Almaqahū grant him the goodwill and the pleasure of their lord"; (ii) *w-l yḏbḥw bn ms*$_2$*mnhn ʿṯtr w-*s_2*ms*$_1$*m w-ḏbḥm b-hrn* C 74/11–13 "And let them offer [an animal sacrifice] to ʿAṯtar and to Šamsum and an animal sacrifice [to Almaqah] in Hirrān from [the yield of] both cultivated areas"; and (iii) *w-ʾl yhwfd b-h ʿmd w-ʿlbm* C 610/3 (Early Sabaic) "And neither vines nor ʿilb-trees may be planted there".

4.4.3 Weak verbs

Both tri- and biradical spellings of verbs II-*w/y* occur, the latter being the more common, as in *ykwnn* and *yknn* "he will be"; *hqwḥ* and *hqḥ* "he completed" (on triradical roots, see §4.1). Since no semantic distinction is generally discernible between the bi- and triradical forms of the verbs in question, it may be assumed in principle that these are purely graphic variants of one and the same verb form, and not forms of different verbal stems (such as *kwn* as a stem with doubling of the second radical beside *kn* as the simple stem). This does not preclude in any way the existence of derived verbal stems, but the identification of the latter can only be made on the basis of comparative contexts (many verbs are attested only in one or the other written form).

Verbs II-*geminatae* (i.e., with the second consonant doubled) are written either tri- or biradically, as in *hbrr* "to come forth", versus *ḥg* "to make a pilgrimage"; alternative spellings of individual roots are only rarely attested thus far (see the entries under *ḍrr* and *kll* in *Sab. Dict.*), which suggests the existence of different verbal stems.

Verbs III-*w/y* exhibit sound forms for the most part, as in *hwfy-hw* "he granted to him"; *yhrḍwn* "he will satisfy"; shortened forms are rare: compare *w-hrḍ-hw* C 365/5 "and [because] he satisfied him"; *l-yʾt* (< *l-yʾty*) R 4176/10,11 (Early Sabaic) "may it come". Noteworthy is the alternation of *w* and *y* in a few roots; with *yhrḍwn* above compare *yhrḍyn* and, in general, §3.4.1.

Verbs I-*w* lose their first radical in the prefix-conjugation (thus *l-yzʾn* "may he continue [… to do]", etc.). The few instances of verbs I-*y* exhibit both spellings (*yyfʿn* or *yfʿn* "it will be proclaimed"). The *hfʿl* and s_1*tfʿl* stems are as a rule regularly formed (e.g., *hwfy* "he fulfilled", rarely *hfy*; s_1*twfy* "he was protected"). In the *ftʿl* stem the first radical is missing in the orthography, as in *tqhw* "they complied/completed" (cf. in contrast the sound form of the *tfʿl* stem, as in *tws*$_3$*ʿw* "they attacked"). Since verbs I-*n* exhibit a similar appearance (e.g., *tḍʿn* "to harm", infinitive), an assimilation of the first radical to the infix, as in Arabic, suggests itself.

As a rule, the first consonant of verbs I-*n* is assimilated to a following consonant, as in *hkl* beside *hnkl* "he carried out". (see also §3.4.2).

4.4.4 Imperative

The imperative is attested in the minuscule script of the wooden sticks. It has the form *fʿl(-n)*: for example, *w-ʾnt f-*s_3*ḫln* YM 11742/2 "and you (sg.), look after … !"

4.4.5 Infinitive and participle

From the Middle Sabaic period onwards, the infinitive is morphologically divided into two forms: a non-augmented form (*fʿl*) of the basic stem 0_1, and a form augmented by *-n* for all derived stems (e.g., *hfʿln, tfʿln*, etc.). This rule, restricted to the region of Mārib and the central Yemeni highlands, also allows a morphological distinction between the basic stem 0_1 (infinitive *fʿl*) and a derived stem 0_2 (infinitive *fʿln*). See Stein 2002b. This *-n* is to be distinguished from that of the determinate state (see §4.2.2), which, like other formative elements (mimation, etc.), may not appear on the infinitive.

Characteristic of the usage of the individual Ancient South Arabian dialects, and in particular of Sabaic, are the various functions of the infinitive. Two basic uses underlie these: (i) the infinitive stands as the predicate, in which position it is interchangeable with a finite verb form; and (ii) the infinitive assumes the role of a part of the clause dependent on the predicate (in this position it is no longer interchangeable with a finite verb form; see Nebes 1988). On infinitival syntax, see §5.6.

The (active) participle of the basic stem has the form *fʿl*, as in *wḍʾm ʾw bhʾm* C 548/2 "going out or in"; *bn nkrm w-mhbʾ*s_1*m* C 29/5 "[they placed their house under the protection of ʿAṯtar], against anyone who would alter or harm it". The inscription Ṣilwī-aš-Šuẓayf 1, written in the Haramic dialect, exhibits a participle without mimation (lines 3–5): *b-hn gwz bṯḥtn w-hwʾ ʿbr* "because he passed through [the region of?] Baṯḥatān, crossing [a border]". A passive participle of the basic stem of the form *mfʿl* is difficult to confirm. The participles of the derived stems have a prefix *m-*, as in *mhbʾ*s_1 "who harms" (cf. the example from C 29 above); active and passive forms cannot be distinguished outwardly, and in general it is difficult to distinguish between participles and other nominal forms.

4.5 Particles

In addition to the conjunctions (see §§5.2–5.3) and object clause marker (see §5.3.1), the particles of Ancient South Arabian include prepositions, particles of negation, and enclitics.

4.5.1 Prepositions

The most important prepositions, with their primary meanings, are as follows:

1. *b-* "in, at" (local); "in, on, during" (temporal); "with, by" (instrumental/sociative).
2. *l-* "to(ward)" (local and temporal); expression of the dative. Sometimes there is overlap with the semantic range of *b-*, as in *l-ṯlṯm ywmm* J 631/28 "on the third day"; versus *b-ṯlṯm ywmm* J 577/12.
3. *bn* "(away) from" (local and temporal); also partitive and explanatory (e.g., *kl* s_2*ʾmt* . . . *bn ʾns*$_1$*m w-ʾblm w-ṯwrm w-bʿrm* R 3910/2–3 "every purchase of person, camel, bull, or [other] cattle"). In texts in the Haramic dialect *bn* is replaced by *mn*, otherwise unknown in Ancient South Arabian.
4. *ʿbr* "in the direction of". This preposition has a wide range of meaning and often occurs with other prepositions (e.g., *b-ḏr hs*$_2$*tʿw b-ʿbr mrʾ-hmw* E 13 §2 "In the war that [that people] had fomented against their lord").
5. *ʿd(y)* "up to" (local); "until" (temporal). In addition to expressing direction, this preposition also expresses the goal of an action and sometimes also stands simply

for local "in" (e.g., *ʾṯmr w-ʾfql ṣdqm ʿdy kl ʾ*s_1*rr-hmw* E 18/21 "[May the deity grant] proper crops in all their valleys").

6. *ʿl(y)* "(up)on", frequently combined with *b-*. This preposition often serves to express enmity (e.g., s_1*bʾt* s_1*bʾy w-ḍbʾ b-ʿly ḥbs*$_2$*t* E 19/6–7 "the campaign that they undertook and carried out against Abessynia".

Other common prepositions are *(b-)ʿm* "(together) with"; *bʿd(n)* "after" (local and temporal); *b(y)n* "between"; *ḥg(n), b-ḥg* "like, corresponding to"; *(l-/b-)qbl* "before" (local and temporal).

4.5.2 Negative particles

The negative in all applications is *ʾl*. In addition to verbal clauses it also appears in nominal clauses, particularly in the negation of existence, often with jussive force, as in *ʾl ʾ*$s_1 s_1$*ʾl* G/1379/3,7 "let there be no one who lays claim". In Late Sabaic the negation is *dʾ*, in the Haramic dialect, however, it is *lm* (followed by the short form of the prefix-conjugation like in Arabic).

4.5.3 Enclitics

Occasionally the particle *-m* or *-mw* (less often *-my*) is appended to an individual word, particularly on prepositions and on certain (for the most part lexically determined) conjunctions, yet hardly ever on verbs (see Nebes 1991). The function of the particle is probably emphasis; compare, for example, *w-b-mw hwt ḫrfn* E 69/20 "and in the very same year" and *b-hwt ḫrfn* J 751/8–9 "in that year". A second enclitic, *-n*, is mainly attached to a preposition or conjunction and causes an inversion of the original meaning, e.g., *ln* "from" opposite *l-* "to(wards)", *ʿmn* "from" opposite *(b)ʿm* "(together) with".

4.6 Numerals

In the written record preserved for Ancient South Arabian, numbers are usually written out; only rarely are they expressed with special numeric characters.

4.6.1 Cardinals

The numbers from 1 to 9 each have a masculine and a feminine form, the latter augmented with *-t*:

(8)

	Masculine	Feminine
1	ʾḥd	ʾḥt
2	ṯny	ṯty
3	s_2lṯ, ṯlṯ	s_2lṯt, ṯlṯt
4	ʾrbʿ	ʾrbʿt
5	ḫms$_1$	ḫms$_1$t
6	s_1dṯ, s_1ṯ	s_1dṯt, s_1ṯt
7	s_1bʿ	s_1bʿt
8	ṯmny, ṯmn	ṯmnyt, ṯmnt
9	ts_1ʿ	ts_1ʿt
10	ʿs_2r	ʿ$s_2$rt

Regarding the above cardinal numbers, note the following:

1. In addition to the common forms of 2 there also occurs *klʾy* (Early Sabaic; Middle Sabaic *kly*), feminine *klʾty*, for "both", which is always definite: for example, *klʾy mḥfdnhn yʾzl w-drʿ* J 557 (Early Sabaic) "both of the towers Yaʾzil and Daraʿ".
2. The first cited form of the numbers 3, 6, and 8 is attested in Early Sabaic, the second in the Middle Sabaic and Late Sabaic periods.
3. A number *ʾḥdy* "1" and *s*$_1$*t* "6" are attested in some late inscriptions from south-eastern regions, e.g., in ʿAbadān 1/23 (cf. also *s*$_1$*ty* "60" in R 5085/11 [Late Sabaic]).

The numbers from 11 to 19 are composed of the relevant unit (masculine or feminine) and *ʿs*$_2$*r* (unchangeable). The numbers 11 and 12 are thus far only attested in their masculine forms (*ʾḥd ʿs*$_2$*r* and *ṯny ʿs*$_2$*r*), the other numbers, conversely, almost exclusively in the feminine form (e.g., *ṯlṯt ʿs*$_2$*r* "13"; *s*$_1$*dṯt ʿs*$_2$*r* [Early Sabaic] "16").

The number 20 has the form *ʿs*$_2$*ry*, while the other tens up to 90 have the form of the unit with a suffixed *-y*: for example, *s*$_2$*lṯy* or *ṯlṯy* "30".

The number 100 in the singular is *mʾt*, in the dual ("200") *mʾtn*, in the plural *mʾ* (Early Sabaic), *mʾn*, or *mʾt* (e.g., *s*$_1$*bʿ mʾt* "700"). The word for 1,000, *ʾlf*, has a broken plural, *ʾʾlf*.

In compound numbers the elements (units, tens, etc.) go from smallest to largest, connected by *w-*.

4.6.1.1 *Construction of the cardinals*

The gender polarity of the numbers 3 to 10 that is common throughout the Semitic languages is also found in Ancient South Arabian. That is, a counted masculine noun takes the feminine form of the relevant number, a feminine noun the masculine form of the number.

The numeral appears before the thing counted, and agrees with it in definiteness. With an indefinite noun the number appears in the absolute state (see §4.2.2; exceptions are *mʾt* and *ʾlf*, which regularly exhibit mimation); with definite nouns the number is likewise definite. The thing counted is usually in the dual with 2, in the plural with higher numbers. A few examples will illustrate the construction: *ḫms*$_1$ *w-ʿs*$_2$*ry w-mʾt ʾfrs*$_1$*m* J 665/30–31 "125 riders"; *ḫms*$_1$ *mʾnm w-ʾlfm ʾs*$_1$*dm* J 576/15 "1,500 soldiers"; *ṯlṯt ʿs*$_2$*r ywmtm* E 13 §10 "for 13 days"; *ṯlṯtn ʾṣlmn ʾly ḏhbn* J 657/3 "the 3 statuettes of bronze" (definite).

4.6.2 Ordinals

A special form is *qdm* "first". The other ordinal numbers up to 10 differ outwardly from the cardinals only in that the masculine forms always have three consonants, thus *rbʿ* "fourth"; *s*$_1$*dṯ* "sixth". Feminine forms have the ending *-t*, as in *ṯnyt* (also *ṯnt*) "second".

Attributive ordinals are placed after the thing counted and agree with it in state and gender, as in *drm ṯntm* Ja 576/11 "a second time"; *ḫrf wddʾl... rbʿn* J 618/9–10 "the fourth year of the [eponym] Wadadʾil" (definite). Several temporal expressions are constructed differently, such as *b-ywm ts*$_1$*ʿm* "on the ninth day" (for reference see §4.4.2.2; construct state); *b-ṯlṯm ywmm* J 577/12 "on the third day".

4.6.3 Other numerals

Fractions have the same outward form as the ordinals: thus *s*$_2$*lṯ* (Early Sabaic) "a third", *rbʿ* "a fourth", and so on (e.g., *kl ṯmn qbrn ygr* DAI FH Awām 1997-2/2 (Early Sabaic) "the entire eighth of the grave Yagur"). In compounds the fraction looks like the singular, as in *s*$_2$*lṯ rbʿ kl qbrn ygr* DAI FH Awām 1997-5/2 (Early Sabaic) "three-fourths of the entire grave Yagur". For "half" there is a specific word, *fqḥ*: for example, *w-kwn fqḥm l-ṣbḥm w-ḥmym w-fqḥm l-bʿṯtr* DAI FH Awām 1997-5/4 (Early Sabaic) "and one half [of the grave] belongs to Ṣubḥum and Ḥamyum and one half to Biʿaṯtar". In addition, fractions can also be expressed periphrastically, as in *ʾṣbʿm bn ṯmny ʾṣbʿ* C 640/2 "a finger out of eight fingers" (= "one-eighth").

Multiplicatives are only rarely attested; they are formed by the addition of *ʾḏ* ("time(s)") to the numeral, as in s_2*lṯtʾḏ* C 366 (Early Sabaic) "three times" or "for the third time"; s_1*dṯ ʾḏ* Schm/Mārib 19/A4 (Early Sabaic; fragmentary context).

4.7 Non-Sabaic morphological features

In contrast to Sabaic as an "H-language", all other Ancient South Arabian dialects are so-called "S-languages"; in other words, they form the causative stem and the pronouns with s_1, thus s_1*fʿl* (Sab. *hfʿl*), -s_1*w* (Sab. *-hw*), and so forth.

4.7.1 Nominal morphology

Outside of Sabaic, external plurals are met with more commonly, especially in Minaic. In particular, an *h* often appears word-finally in construct state forms – in Minaic even in the singular (see §3.5).

An *h* can also be inserted in the external plural ending of the feminine, as in Minaic *ʾnṯhtn* R 3306A/3 = as-Sawdāʾ 37/3 "the women"; *w-ʾrḍhty* M 275/3 "and the lands of…".

(9) Summary of non-Sabaic nominal endings

		Construct	*Indeterminate*	*Determinate*
Singular/Broken plural	Minaic	-h, -ϕ	(-m)	-n
	Qatabanic	-ϕ	-m	-n
	Hadramitic	-ϕ	-m	-hn, -n
Dual	Minaic	-y, -hy	-ny	-nhn, -nyhn
	Qatabanic	-y, -w, -h(y)	-myw	-nyhn
	Hadramitic	-y, -hy	-nyw	-yhn, -yn
External plural	Minaic	-hw, -hy	-hn	
	Qatabanic	-w, -y, (-h)		
	Hadramitic	(-hy)		(-yhn)

Many of the forms given are attested only rarely on account of the limited extent of what has been preserved. Note that the interpretation of the endings *-hy* and *-yhn* as plural is not completely certain; for discussion of the attestations see Beeston 1984: §H 13:2, 3.

4.7.2 Pronominal morphology

4.7.2.1 *Personal pronouns*

With a few exceptions in Qatabanic inscriptions (e.g., *ʿbd-k* J 367 "your (sg.) servant"), only third-person forms are attested. The distinctive long forms of the third-person masculine singular pronominal suffix in Qatabanic and Hadramitic (-s_1*ww*) are attached to external plurals and duals of nouns, but not to verbal forms (so Beeston 1984: §Q 23:2, H 23:2). The forms of the suffixed personal pronouns are as follows:

(10)

	Minaic	Qatabanic	Hadramitic
Singular			
3rd masc.	$-s_1$, $-s_1w$	$-s_1$, $-s_1ww$	$-s_1$, $-s_1ww$
3rd fem.	$-s_1$	$-s_1$, $-s_1yw$	-ṯ,-ṯyw, $-s_3$, $-s_3yw$
Dual			
3rd com.	$-s_1mn$	$-s_1my$	$-s_1my$
3rd masc.			$-s_1mn$, $-s_1myn$
Plural			
3rd masc.	$-s_1m$	$-s_1m$	$-s_1m$
3rd fem.	$-s_1n$	$-s_1n$	

4.7.2.2 *Demonstrative pronouns*

Whereas the forms in Qatabanic for the most part correspond to those of Sabaic (thus *ḏn*, *ḏt*, *s_1mt*, *$-s_1myt$*, etc.; exceptions are the masculine plural of the first group, *ḏtn*, and the nominative masculine of the second group, sg. *s_1w*, pl. *s_1m*), in Minaic the demonstrative pronouns of the second group are essentially not attested at all, and those of the first group only very rarely (one of the few plural forms is *ʾhlt mḥfdtn* R 3015/2 = M 239/2 "these towers"; cf. R 2965/2 = M 185/2).

4.7.2.3 *Relative pronouns*

Qatabanic exhibits *ḏ-* as a frozen relative particle as well as the form *ḏn*, as in *s_2nʾ ḏn qnyw w-bqnyn* Ry 367/9 = NAM 483/9 "[may ḏū Samāwī take revenge . . .] on every enemy of that which they have acquired and will acquire". In the following summary, uncertain and markedly rare forms are not listed:

(11)

	Minaic		Qatabanic		Hadramitic	
	Masc.	*Fem.*	*Masc.*	*Fem.*	*Masc.*	*Fem.*
Singular	ḏ-	ḏt	ḏ-, ḏw	ḏt	ḏ-	ḏt
Dual	ḏy	ḏtyn	ḏw			
Plural	ʾhl, hl		ḏtw			

4.7.2.4 *Indefinite pronouns*

Qatabanic exhibits in addition to *mn* also *ʾy* "who(ever)".

4.7.3 Verbal morphology

4.7.3.1 *Verb-stems*

In Minaic a few verbs exhibit a spelling *fʿʿl* (such as *ʿlly* "raise," e.g., M 203/2). Since consonantal length in Ancient South Arabian is not expressed in the script, such forms are probably to be understood as another verbal stem with reduplicated second radical, to be distinguished from a possible stem *fʿl* with doubling.

4.7.3.2 *Suffix-conjugation*

The dual and plural ending is not usually written in Minaic; the forms are thus identical in appearance with the singular (e.g., *s_3lʾ* both "he dedicated" and "they dedicated"). The plural of the third-person feminine is attested in Qatabanic and Hadramitic as *fʿln* (see Robin 1983:181–184; Nebes 1985:34).

4.7.3.3 *Prefix-conjugation*

The indicative forms in Qatabanic, in contrast to the other dialects, are formed with a prefix *b-*, as in *kl mngw byktrbwn* AM 757/11 "all things that they will request" (vs. jussive *w-l-yqny* R 3688/4 "and may he acquire"). Here too the prefix *y* can be lost in writing; see the example in §4.7.2.3. The form of the third-person masculine plural of the prefix-conjugation in Qatabanic is *y-fʿl-wn* (see the example above).

Qatabanic *b-yfʿl* for the most part corresponds to Sabaic *yfʿln*, in being used for indicative statements of the present and the future: *w-kl* s_1*hmm w-qnym bykn w-yks*$_3$*ʾ ws*$_1$*ṭ d̲tn ʾbytn* Folkard 1/5–6 "And all of the servants and flocks that are present and live in these houses"; *w-l yftḫ d̲n ftḫn w-mḥrtn b-ʿḍm ʾw ʾbnm kn-m byḥrg mlkn* R 3566/21 "And this decree and decision is to be published on wood or stone, as the king will command". The use of the prefix-conjugation for the past in a narrative context is only very rarely attested, with a few certain examples thus far only in Minaic: *w-yfqr zydʾl b-wrḫh ḥtḫr w-yfnnw kb bn kl ʾbytth ʾlʾlt mṣr* R 3427/2 = M 338/2 "And Zaydʾil died in the month of Hathor, and they sent linen from all the temples of the gods of Egypt".

Occasionally, prefixed verbal forms augmented with *b-* are also found in Minaic. Imperfects of the form *yfʿln* ("long form") are rarely attested in Minaic and are often of uncertain number; the other dialects exhibit no such forms at all.

4.7.3.4 *Infinitive*

The infinitive is regularly formed without an *n*-augment; in Qatabanic, however, mimation may appear in certain cases (cf. Nebes 1988:70f., 73, and §5.8.3 below).

4.7.4 Non-Sabaic particles

The prepositions exhibit a number of distinctive features in comparison with those in Sabaic. Thus, for Sabaic *l-* Minaic usually has the preposition *k-*, Hadramitic *h-* (for further specifics on Hadramitic see Beeston 1984: §H 33:3). The forms that end in *-y* in Sabaic end in *-w* in Qatabanic, thus *ʿdw*, *ʿlw*, and so forth.

In Minaic the particle *k* in its various functions has a preposed s_2, as in *bn* s_2*-kd̲* R 2980/13 = Shaqab 19/13 "from (the possibility) that". In contrast to Sabaic the other dialects have a temporal conjunction *mty* (Hadramitic *mt*) "when".

The negative in Minaic (only sparsely attested) is the particle *lhm*.

Enclitic *-m(w)* is common to all dialects; in addition, Minaic and Qatabanic also exhibit a particle *-ʾy* (Minaic also *-m-ʾy*), while Hadramitic has *-hy* (see Nebes 1991). In Hadramitic the particle *-m* also occurs on verb forms, as in *b-ʿbr d̲t ynṣf-m* Rb I/84 no. 196/2–3 "because he will perform a ritual(?)".

4.7.5 Numerals

Different forms for the number 1 are found in Qatabanic (*ṭd*, fem. *ṭt*; also *ʿ*s_1*tn*) and Minaic (*ʿ*s_1*t*). The words for 3 and 6 correspond in these dialects to the Early Sabaic forms (thus s_2*lt̲(t)*, s_1*dt̲(t)*). Hadramitic exhibits both s_2*lt̲(t)* and the spelling s_2*ls*$_3$*(t)*.

The tens in Minaic and Hadramitic may exhibit an *h* in the ending: for example, *ʾrbʿhy* (Minaic, also *ʾrbʿy*) "40"; *t̲mnhy* "80".

Distributives are expressed in Qatabanic by repetition of the numeral: *b-ʿ*s_2*r ʿ*s_2*r ḫbṣtm mṣʿm l-ṭt ṭt ywmm* R 3854/6–7 "ten full Ḫabṣat-coins each for each day".

5. SYNTAX

5.1 Word order

The first clause of an inscription begins with the subject, less commonly (though often in legal documents) with an adverb such as *kn*, *ḥgn*, among others, "thus". In all other main clauses, which are usually introduced by the conjunction *w-* (see §5.2), as well as in subordinate clauses introduced by a conjunction, the verbal predicate normally precedes (VS).

In main clauses introduced by *w-*, the subject, object, or a locative or temporal prepositional phrase may appear at the beginning:

(12) A. w-ʾws$_1$ʾl f-ḥmd mqm ʾlmqh
and==Awsʾil and==he-thanked power-of Almaqah
"And Awsʾil expressed his gratitude for the power of Almaqah" (J 644/7)
B. w-bythmw nʿmn f-ʿḏbw
and==house=their Nuʿmān and==they-repaired
"And their house Nuʿmān they repaired" (C 648/4)
C. w-bn hgrn nʿḍ f-ytʾwlw
and==from city=DET. Naʿḍ and==they-returned
"And from the city of Naʿḍ they returned" (J 576/10)

The predicate, as the examples show, is introduced by *f-*, although there are also many cases without *f-* (e.g., *w-ʾlmqh l-yḫmrnhw* J 692/4–5 "and may Almaqah grant to him"). It is rare, when a nominal element is preposed, that the predicate is introduced by *w-* (e.g., *w-frs$_1$hw ndf w-zḫn* J 649/20–21 "and his horse Nadīf was wounded"; Nebes 1995:22–45; 218–219; 221–231).

The preposing of nominal elements is less common in verbal subordinate clauses, except for resumptive pronouns in relative clauses (see §5.4.2):

(13) k-hʾ mtʿhw
that==he he-saved=him
"That he [i.e., Almaqah] had saved him" (J 619/10–11)

Resumptive constructions, in which a preposed nominal or prepositional element is resumed by a pronoun elsewhere in the sentence, are uncommon:

(14) w-ʾdmhw frʿm . . . w-ʾs$_1$d b-ʿmhw
and==servants=his Fāriʿum . . . and==soldiers-of in==with=him
wkb b-wfym blthmw
it-found in==success=INDET. mission=their
"And as for his servants, [namely] Fāriʿum . . . and the soldiers with him, their mission had a successful conclusion" (E 13 §11)

The predicate of a nominal clause may consist of a noun or a prepositional phrase; nominal clauses may be main or subordinate clauses. The subject normally stands first, as in (15A); when the predicate consists of a prepositional phrase, it often stands before an indefinite subject, as in (15B):

(15) A. w-ḏn-m wtfn mṣdqm
and==this==ENCL. document-of-transfer=DET. binding=INDET.
"And this document of transfer is binding" (Gl 1572/7)

B. w-ʾl l-hmw b-hw kl mwm
and==not to==them in==it any water=INDET.
"while they had no water in it [i.e., the castle Šaqīr]" (E 13 §10)

5.2 Coordination

The coordinating conjunction is the particle *w-* "and"; in addition, there is a disjunctive particle *(f-)ʾw* "or". Main clauses and syntagms of equal syntactic status are connected by *w-*. The use of *f-* between clauses of equal rank is rare in Sabaic; it is found primarily in inscriptions in the Haramic dialect:

(16) f-ḫṭʾt w-tḫlʾn f-hḏrʿt w-ʿnw
and==she expiated and==will-pay-fine and==she-submitted and== be-humbled.INF.
"Then she expiated and will pay a fine. Then she submitted and humbled herself" (C 568/5–7)

5.3 Subordination

A subordinate clause introduced by a conjunction follows its main clause. Exceptions are conditional sentences and complex sentences with a conditional connotation. In the latter sentence types, as well as in other occasional instances of preposed hypotactic clauses introduced with a conjunction, the following main clause is often introduced by *f-*, though also with *w-* or *ϕ* (Nebes 1995:46–53; 219–221; 231–234).

5.3.1 Object clauses

Object clauses are introduced by the particle *k-*. Depending on the temporal relationship, they may contain the conjugational form *fʿl* (perfect tense) for anteriority and *yfʿln* (imperfect tense; see §4.4.2) for posteriority:

(17) A. w-ys_1mʿw k-nblw hmw ʾgrn b-ʿbr ʾḥzb ḥbs_2t
and==they-heard that==sent those Nagranites in==direction-of bands-of Abessynians
"And they heard that the aforesaid Nagranites had sent [a delegation] to the Abessynian bands" (J 577/10)

B. w-tb$s_2$rw b-ʿm ʾlmqh
and==they-received-good-news in==with Almaqah
k-yḫmrnhmw $s_1$qym mlym
that==he-would-grant=them irrigation=INDET. winter(?)=INDET.
"And they received from Almaqah the good news that he would grant them irrigation in the winter(?)" (J 653/7–8)

5.3.2 Temporal clauses

For the temporal notion "when," the conjunctions *ywm* (properly: "on the day when"; Early Sabaic/Middle Sabaic), *bkn* (Middle Sabaic), and *k-* (Late Sabaic) are used, followed invariably by *fʿl* (perfect) as predicate:

(18) A. ydʿʾl ḏrḥ bn $s_1$mhʿly mkrb s_1bʾ gnʾ ʾwm
Yadaʿʾil Ḏarīḥ son-of Sumuhūʿalī *mukarrib*-of Sabaʾ he-walled Awām

byt ʾlmqh ywm d̲bḥ ʿt̲tr
temple-of Almaqah day-of he-sacrificed ʿAt̲tar

"Yadaʿʾil D̲arīḥ, son of Sumuhūʿalī, *mukarrib* of Sabaʾ, surrounded Awām, the temple of Almaqah, with a wall [on the day] when he offered an animal sacrifice to ʿAt̲tar" (C 957; Early Sabaic)

B. b-d̲t hws$_2$ʿhmw ʾlmqh b-wḏʿ s$_2$ʿbn
in==REL. he-granted=them Almaqah in==subjugate.INF. tribe=DET.
ngrn bkn qs$_1$dw w-nzʿ ydm
Nagrān when they-rose-up and==withdraw.INF. hand=INDET.
bn ʾmrʾhmw ʾmlk s$_1$bʾ b-ʿbr ʾḥbs$_2$n
from lords=their kings-of Sabaʾ in==direction-of Abessynians=DET.

"Considering that Almaqah granted them [i.e., both kings of the Sabeans] the subjugation of the tribe of Nagrān, when they [i.e., the Nagrānites] rose up and withdrew from their lords, the kings of Sabaʾ, their support against the Abessynians" (J 577/8)

C. w-ts$_1$ṭrw d̲n ms$_1$ndn qyln s$_2$rḥʾl yqbl d̲-yzʾn
and==he(!)-put-up this inscription=DET. *qayl*=DET. Šaraḥʾil Yaqbal REL.== Yazʾan
k-qrn b-ʿly ngrn
when==he-took-up-position in==against Nagrān

"The *qayl* Šaraḥʾil Yaqbal of the clan Yazʾan put up this inscription when he had taken up a position against Nagrān" (J 1028/6; Late Sabaic)

Other temporal relationships are expressed by the conjunctions *bʿd(n) d̲-* (and the like) "after"; *ln, ln d̲-* "from the time that, since"; *ʿd(y) d̲-/d̲t, t̲w* "until"; *brt̲n* "when"; and *ʾd̲* "when" (Haramic only):

(19) A. f-yṣnʿw b-hwt bytn s$_2$qr ḫms$_1$t
and==they-took-up-a-defensive-position in==that castle=DET. Šaqīr five
ʿs$_2$r ymtm . . . ʿdy d̲t nfṣ mrʾhmw s$_2$ʿrm ʾwtr
ten days=INDET. until REL. he-arrived lord=their Šāʿirum Awtar
w-mṣrhw bʿd d̲t s$_1$bṭw mṣr ḥḍrmwt
and==troops=his after REL. they-defeated troops-of Hadramawt
b-ḫlf d̲t ġylm
in==district-of d̲āt Ġaylim

"They took up a defensive position in the aforementioned castle Šaqīr for 15 days . . . until finally their lord Šāʿirum Awtar and his troops arrived, after they had defeated the troops of Hadramawt in the district of d̲āt Ġaylim" (E 13 §10)

B. w-l-h[ʿ]nnhw bn ḫlẓ ḫlẓ ln
and==for==save.INF.=him from illness-of he-suffered-illness since
d̲-ʾtw bn mqmn d̲-lḥgm
REL.==he-returned from observation-post=DET. REL.==Laḥgum

"And so that he [i.e., Almaqah] would save him from the illness from which he suffered since the time that he had returned from the observation post of Laḥgum" (J 633/4–6)

C. b-d̲t ḫmrhw ṣdqhw b-ms$_1$ʾlhw brt̲n blthw
in==REL. he-granted=him right=his in==oracle=his when he-sent=him

mrʾhw $s_2$mr yhrʿs_2
lord=his Šammar Yuharʿiš
"Considering that he [i.e., Almaqah] granted him [i.e., the author] what was fitting, in his oracle, when his lord Šammar Yuharʿiš despatched him" (BR M.Bayḥān 5/3–4)

D. ġ$s_2$nm bn gnyt ġlwnyn ʾḏ bny
Ġašnum son-of Gāniyat Ġulwānite=DET. when he-built
w-qyḥ bʾry ʾlhhw ḏ-s_1m[wy ḏ-]yġ[rw]
and==he-plastered wells.DUAL-of god=his ḏū-Samāwī REL.=Yaġruw
"Ġašnum, the son of Gāniyat, the Ġulwānite, [wrote this] when he built and plastered the two wells of his god ḏū Samāwī of Yaġruw" (Ko 4/1–6)

5.3.3 Circumstantial clauses

Circumstantial clauses expressing simultaneity with the verbal predicate, analogous to the Arabic type *wa-huwa yafʿalu*, cannot be identified in Old South Arabian with certainty. With a nominal predicate, however, such syntagms are attested in Middle and Late Sabaic and in the inscriptions in the Haramic dialect (Nebes 1990):

(20) A. w-$s_3$mkw bn ḥyrthmw mh$s_1$knm
and==they-went-up from encampment=their Muhaskanum
w-ʾfr$s_1$hmw b-ʾnḥrm
and==riders=their on==fast-horses=INDET.
w-ṭrydm
and==well-conditioned-horses=INDET.
"And they went up from their encampment Muhaskanum, their riders on fast, well-conditioned horses" (J 576/15-16)

B. bhn qrbh mrʾ ywm ṯlṯ ḥgtn
because he-approached=her man day-of third pilgrimage=DET.
w-hʾ ḥyḍ
and==she menstruating
"Because on the third day of the pilgrimage a man had approached her, when she was menstruating" (C 533/2–4; Haramic)

The nominal clause that is simultaneous with what precedes may also be introduced by the temporal conjunction *bkn* or *k-*

(21) A. w-[b-ḏ]t $s_2$fthw rmn b-mqmtm bkn
and==in==REL. he-promised=him Rummān in==power=INDET. when
ʾbhw ḏn[m y]ẓfr ws_1ṭ ḍr ḥmyrm
father=his Ḏanam Yaẓfur in war-of Himyar.
"And considering that Rummān promised him with power, when his father Ḏanam Yaẓfur found himself at war with Himyar" (C 140/10–12)

B. w-qds_1w bʿt mrb k-b-hw
and==they-consecrated church-of Mārib while==in==it
qs_1s_1m
priest=INDET.
"And they consecrated the church of Mārib, while a priest was there" (C 541/66–67; Late Sabaic)

5.3.4 Causal clauses

Causal relationships are formed with the conjunctions *(l-)qbl(y) d̲-/d̲t*; less often *ʿln*, *ʿln d̲-/d̲t*; in the inscriptions in the Haramic dialect with *bhn*:

(22) A. hqny ʾlmqh d̲-hrn d̲n ms$_3$ndn l-qbl d̲t
he-dedicated Almaqah REL.==Hirrān this tablet=DET. because
s$_1$ʾlhw ʾlmqh b-ms$_1$ʾlhw
he-asked=him Almaqah in==oracle=his
"He dedicated this (bronze) tablet to Almaqah of Hirrān, because Almaqah had asked him in his oracle" (C 79/1–4)

B. w-ʾl ḥrb b-hwt wrḫn ʿln d̲-ʾl
and==not he-undertook in==this month=DET. on-account-of REL.==not
tqrʿ s$_1$lṭm
he-drew lots=INDET.
"And in this month he did not undertake this procedure [to obtain an oracle in the temple], because he had not drawn [appropriate] lots" (NNAG 12/7–8)

C. tnḫy w-tnd̲rn l-d̲-s$_1$mwy
he-publicly-confessed and==do-penance.INF. to==d̲ū-Samāwī
bhn qrb mrʾtm
because he-approached woman=INDET.
"He publicly confessed and did penance before d̲ū Samāwī, because he had approached a woman" (C 523/1–3; Haramic)

5.3.5 Comparative clauses

Comparative clauses are introduced by *ḥgn*, *ḥngn*, *ḥg(n) d̲t*, or *ḥg(n) k-*:

(23) w-ḥmdw b-d̲t s$_1$tkml ʾḫ[wnhm]w b-ʿm
and==they-thanked in==REL. it-was-accomplished alliance=their in==with
mlk ḥbs$_2$tn ḥgn s$_1$tkml ʾḫwnhmw b-ʿm
king-of Abessynia=DET. just-as it-was-accomplished alliance=their in==with
ydʿʾb ġyl[n ml]k ḥḍrmwt b-qdmy d̲t hqnytn
Yadaʿʾab Ġaylān king-of Hadramawt in==before this dedication=DET.
"And they thanked [Almaqah] that their alliance with the king of Abessynia came into being, just as their alliance with Yadaʿʾab Ġaylān, the king of Hadramawt, had come into being before this dedication" (C 308/14–16)

5.3.6 Conditional sentences

The conditional particles of the protasis are *hm* and *hmy*; the apodosis is introduced by *f-*, *w-*, or *ϕ*:

(24) A. w-hm ʾl tʾḫd̲ f-ḫlt nfs$_1$hw
and==if not he-is-seized and==it-is-at-the-mercy-of life=his
l-d̲-yhrgnhw
to==REL.==he-kills-him
"And if he is not seized, then his life is at the mercy of him who kills him" (R 4088/4–8)

B. w-hmy hfnk f-tʿlmn b-hmy
and==if you-sent and==sign.IMPERATIVE in==them
"And if you send [the two copies of the contract], then sign them" (YM 11749/2)

The temporal *bkn* has a conditional nuance when the predicate is *yfʿln* (imperfect; see Nebes 1994b: 49):

(25) w-bkn ymtn bʿrm b-ʿm d̲-ys_2ʾmnhw
and==when it-dies head-of-cattle=INDET. in==with REL.==he-buys=it
w-ygzn s_1bʿm ywmm f-brʾm
and==it-passes seven=INDET. day=INDET. and==free-of-responsibility=INDET.
mhs_2ʾmn bn mwthw w-bṯlthw
buyer=DET. from death=its and==loss=its
"And if a head of cattle dies on the one who buys it, and seven days have already passed, then the seller is not responsible for its death and loss" (R 3910/5–6)

In an inscription in the Haramic dialect, *hn* appears as a conditional particle:

(26) hn l-yngs_1n s_1lḥhw . . . l-yẓlʿn l-ʾlt
if it-defiles weapons=his JUSS.==he-pays to==these of
ʿṯtr w-ʾr$s_2$wwn ʿs_2r ḥyʾlym
ʿAṯtar and==priests=DET. ten Ḥayyʾil-coins=INDET.
"If his weapons are defiled . . . then he should pay ten Ḥayyʾil-coins to the congregation of ʿAṯtar and to the priests as penance" (C 548/2–5)

In addition, a conditional connotation is expressed by sentences introduced by *mʿn-mw* and *mhn-mw* when the predicate has *yfʿln* (imperfect):

(27) A. ḥgn $s_2$ftthw ʾmthw mb$s_2$mt k-mʿn-mw
as she-promised=him maidservant=his Mubaššimat that==as-soon-as
yḫmrnhw ḥyw lhw wldm thqnynhw
he-will-grant=her live=INF. to==her child=INDET. she-will-dedicate=him
"As his maidservant Mubaššimat promised him [i.e., Almaqah] that, as soon as he would grant her that a child would survive for her, she would dedicate to him" (J 717/4–7)

B. w-$s_2$ftw ʾlmqhw k-mhn-mw yldn l-hmw
and==they-promised Almaqahū that==as-soon-as it-is-born to==them
bnm w-yḥywn f-yhqnynn ṣlmm
son=INDET. and=he-survives and==they-will-dedicate statuette=INDET.
"And they promised Almaqahū that, as soon as a son were born to them and he survived, they would dedicate a statuette" (J 669/9–12)

Iterative expressions are introduced by *ʾhnn (-mw)*, *(b-)ʾhn (-mw)*, and *hn-mw*. The subordinate clause may precede the main clause, as in the "publication-clause" found in legal contexts:

(28) ʾhnn ʿkr w-l-yyfʿn bn
whenever it-is-contested and==JUSS.==it-will-be-made-known among
byt d̲-ḥbb w-ʾqyn ṣrwḥ
house-of REL.==Ḥubāb and==administrators-of Ṣirwāḥ

w-nkrm
and==foreigner=INDET.
"Whenever objection is raised, it [i.e., this document] will be made known among the members of the clan d̲ū Ḥubāb, and the administrators of Ṣirwāḥ, and every other [person]" (Gl 1533/10–11)

It may also follow the main clause, however:

(29) w-l-wzʾ ʾlmqh ḫ̮mr ʿbdhw ʾbkrb
and==for==continue.INF. Almaqah grant.INF. servant=his Abkarib
mhrgm w-ġnmm ʾhn-mw ys$_1$bʾnn
killings=INDET. and==flocks=INDET. whenever they-campaign
w-s$_2$wʿn mrʾhmw mlkn
and==follow.INF. lord=their king=DET.
"And may Almaqah continue to grant his servant Abkarib killings and flocks, whenever they go on a campaign and follow their lord the king" (C 407/27–29)

5.4 Relative clause constructions

Ancient South Arabian distinguishes independent and nonindependent, i.e. attributive relative clauses. Of the latter type, Ancient South Arabian exhibits both syndetic constructions, introduced with *d̲*-, and asyndetic constructions (i.e., with the conjunction omitted).

5.4.1 Independent relative clauses

Independent relative clauses are formed with the relative pronoun *d̲*- and its inflectional derivatives, and with the indeclinable *mn* and its compounds:

(30) A. w-ʿtb bn ns$_2$n ʾl wḍʾt s$_2$fthmw ns$_1$rn
and==he-destined from Naššān REL. it-came-forth saying=their toward
ʾlʾltn
gods=DET.
"And he [i.e., Karibʾil] destined from Naššān those concerning whom the saying had come forth from [the direction of] the gods" (R 3945/16; Early Sabaic)

B. w-b-d̲t hwfyhmw w-yhwfyn ʾlmqh d̲t
and==in==REL. he-granted=them and==he-will-grant Almaqah REL.
tnbʾhw
he-promised=him
"And considering that Almaqah granted and might [in the future] grant them what he [i.e., Almaqah] promised him [i.e., the author]" (J 558/5)

C. t̲w yqhn mlkn d̲-yrḍyn
until he-commands king=DET. REL.==it-pleases
"Until the king would command what would please [him]" (Ry 507/9; Late Sabaic)

Independent relative clauses introduced by *mn*, *mn-mw*, *mn-m*, *d̲*-, and related compounds may have a conditional connotation (serving as protases):

(31) A. mn-mw ḏ-ys$_2$ʾmn ʿbdm f-ʾw
whoever==ENCL. REL.==he-buys male-servant=INDET. and==or
ʾmtm w-bʿrm w-s$_2$ʾmtm
female-servant=INDET. and==cattle=INDET. and==purchase=INDET.
f-l-yknn mʿdhw ʾḥd wrḫm
and==JUSS.==it-will-be period=its one month=INDET.
"Whoever buys a male or female servant or cattle, or makes any purchase [at all], its period of time [i.e., in which the purchase price must be paid and in which complaints may be registered] is to be [at most] one month" (R 3910/3–4)

B. w-ḏ-yrḥḏn b-hw l-ys$_1$bṭn hms$_1$y
and==REL.==he-washes in==it JUSS.==he-receives fifty
s$_1$bṭm b-mqmn
blows=INDET. in==place=DET.
"And whoever washes in it [i.e., in the cistern reserved for the goddess Nawšam] is to receive fifty blows on the spot" (Rob Maš 1/11–12)

5.4.2 Attributive relative clauses

These may be syndetic or asyndetic. Regarding the former, the rule in Sabaic is that relative clauses must be introduced by the relative pronoun if the antecedent is marked by the definite (*-n*) or indefinite (*-m*) article:

(32) A. hqny ʾlmqh . . . ṣlmn ḏ-s$_2$fthw
he-dedicated Almaqah statuette=DET. REL.==he-promised=him
"He dedicated to Almaqah . . . the statuette that he had promised him" (C 409/2–4)

B. w-ḫmrhw mrʾhw ʾlmqh ḫyw l-hw ġlmm
and==he-granted=him lord=his Almaqah live.INF. to==him boy=INDET.
ḏ-ys$_1$tmyn mrs$_1$ʿm
REL.==he-is-named Marsūʿum
"And his lord Almaqah granted him that a son, who is named Marsūʿum, survived for him" (J 655/7–10)

In Sabaic, asyndetic relative clauses normally require the construct state of the antecedent:

(33) w-hṯb ʾbḍʿ whbhw mlk
and==he-gave-back districts-of.CONSTR. he-gave=him king-of.CONSTR.
s$_1$bʾ l-ʾlmqh w-l-s$_1$bʾ
Sabaʾ to==Almaqah and==to==Sabaʾ
"And he [i.e., Karibʾil] gave back to Almaqah and Sabaʾ the districts that the king of Sabaʾ had given to him [i.e., Sumuhūyafaʿ]" (R 3945/14–15; Early Sabaic)

These constructions, which are very common in Sabaic, and also known from Akkadian, frequently occur in connection with paronomastic expressions:

(34) A. s$_1$bʾt s$_1$bʾ
campaign-of.CONSTR. he-undertook
"The campaign that he undertook"

B. mrḍ mrḍ
illness-of.CONSTR. he-became-ill
"The illness with which he became ill"

C. ʾmlʾ s^1tmlʾ
requests-of.CONSTR. he-requested-fulfillment
"The requests whose fulfillment he requested"

It rarely happens that the relative pronoun is missing with a definite or indefinite antecedent:

(35) w-kwn hʾ mtʿtn mtʿ bn hwt ṯyln
and==it-was this saving-event=DET. he-saved from this lava-flow
b-wrḫ . . .
in==month-of
"And this saving event by means of which he [i.e., Taʾlab] protected [them] from this lava-flow, took place in the month . . . " (C 323/8–9)

It is also exceptional that the relative pronoun is used with a preceding antecedent in the construct state:

(36) bkn mtʿhmw bn ʿws₁ ḏ-kwn b-ʾrḍn
when he-saved=them from plague-of.CONSTR. REL.==it-was in==land=DET.
"When he [i.e., Almaqah] saved them from the plague that raged in the land" (C 81/3–4)

The resumptive personal pronoun, which indicates the syntactic integration of the antecedent into the relative clause, is obligatory in genitive constructions, and sometimes also appears in the case of adverbial constructions in which the collocation *preposition* + *pronoun* stands before the verb of the relative clause:

(37) A. ṣlmn ḏ-ṣrfn ḏ-mdlthw ʾrbʿ mʾnm
statuette=DET. REL.==silver=DET. REL.==value=its four hundred=INDET.
w-ʾḥd ʾlfm rḍym
and==one thousand=INDET. coins-of-good-quality=INDET.
"The silver statuette, whose value corresponds to 1,400 coins of good quality" (J 609/4–6)

B. ṣlmn ḏ-ḏ[h]bn ḏ-b-hw ḥmd ḫyl
statuette=DET. REL.==bronze=DET. REL.==in==it he-thanked power-of
w-mqm ʾlmqh
and==might-of Almaqah
"The bronze statuette, with which he expressed his gratitude for the power and might of Almaqah" (J 739/4–5)

5.5 Asyndetic constructions

It should be noted that apart from asyndetic relative clauses, verbal asyndeton is markedly rare in Sabaic, confined to a few uncertain cases:

(38) bkn rkby bn $s_1$rn bryn yrtʿnn ʿdy
when they.DUAL-were-ridden from wadi=DET. Bāriyān they-will-graze until
ḫbtn
Ḫabtān
"When they [the two horses] were ridden from Wadi Bāriyān to Ḫabtān, in order (?) to graze there" (J 745/9–11)

5.6 Infinitival syntax

As noted above (see §4.4.5), the infinitive appears in two basic constructions.

5.6.1 Replaceable by a finite verb

If the infinitive can be replaced by a finite verb, it continues a preceding verb paratactically with *w-*. The statement denoted by the infinitive corresponds to the preceding verb in person, tense, and mode. As a rule, the infinitive follows the verb immediately, and several infinitives may join together in an "infinitive chain":

(39) w-y'ttmw w-tqdmn w-rtḏḥn b-ʿm
and==they-regrouped and==confront.INF. and==join-battle.INF. in==with
hmt 'ḥbs_2n
those Habashites
"And they [i.e., the Sabaeans] regrouped, came to confrontation, and joined battle with those Abessynians" (J 575/5)

5.6.2 Not replaceable by a finite verb

In the positions in which the infinitive cannot be replaced by a finite verb, it occurs primarily as the object. In this function it is found especially after verbs with certain meanings: for example, after verbs of granting (e.g., *ḫmr, hwfy, hws_2ʿ*); of promising (e.g., *$s_2$ft*) and of commanding (e.g., *wqh*); of preventing and hindering (e.g., *mnʿ*). In these cases the infinitive may or may not be introduced by a preposition (*ḫmr φ-fʿl(n), hwfy φ-fʿl(n), hws_2ʿ b-fʿl(n); $s_2$ft l-fʿl(n); wqh l-fʿl(n); mnʿ bn fʿl(n)*), according to what the individual verb governs:

(40) A. b-ḏt hws_2ʿ 'lmqh mr'yhmw b-$s_2$kr
in==REL. he-granted Almaqah lords.DUAL.=their in==defeat.INF.
w-nqm w-qtl w-hṯlʿn
and==take revenge.INF. and==kill.INF. and==subjugate.INF.
w-hs_1ḥtn ḏ-rydn w-mṣrhw
and==rout.INF. ḏū-Raydān and==troops=its
"Considering that Almaqah granted to their two lords to defeat, take revenge on, kill, subjugate, and rout ḏū Raydān and his troops" (J 2107/8–9=NAM 429/8–9)

B. f-'l ymnʿw bny gdnm ... bn hyʿ l-hmw
and==not they-may-prevent Banū Gadanim from perform.INF to==them
[h]' fnwtn ms_1b' mwn
this canal=DET. watercourse-of water=DET.
"They may not prevent the Banū Gadanim from having this canal serve them as a watercourse" (C 611/7–8)

Less often *fʿl(n)* functions as subject, as for example in conjunction with the legal formula *'l s_3n:*

(41) f-'l s_3n q$s_2$bn mḥmyn
and==not it-is-permitted reconstruct.INF. field-irrigated-by-a-dam-canal=DET.
"Therefore it is not permitted to reconstruct a field irrigated by a dam-canal" (C 380/4)

Infinitives with *l-* are common for purpose and result:

(42) bkn blthmw mrʾhmw ʾls$_2$rḫ yḥḍb ... l-gzmn
when he-sent=them lord=their Ilšaraḥ Yaḥḍib to=extirpate.INF.
hmt ʾḥbs$_2$n
those Habashites
"When their lord Ilšaraḥ Yaḥḍib ... sent them to extirpate those Abessynians" (J 575/2)

Likewise the request formulas of the form *w-l-fʿl(n)* that appear in the closing clauses of votive inscriptions (as in *w-l-ḫmr, w-l-hwfyn, w-l-hws$_2$ʿn* "and may [the deity] grant"; *w-l-mtʿn* "and may [the deity] save"; *w-l-hʿnn* "and may [the deity] help", etc.) must be considered as infinitives expressing purpose in relation to the introductory *hqny*, albeit, in many cases, the syntactic construction of the whole inscription can only be understood if these syntagms are taken as independent clauses.

The complements of a dependent infinitive are not construed "nominally", in the form of a construct chain, but rather "verbally" – in other words, by the use of case endings, the logical subject or object of the infinitive would be put in the nominative or accusative (Nebes 1987). This is apparently so, for instance, in the cases in which the infinitive is followed by an independent personal pronoun that distinguishes between nominative and genitive/accusative forms:

(43) b-ḏt ḫmrhmw tʾwln hmw w-ʾfrs$_1$hmw
in=REL. he-granted=them return.INF. they and==cavalry=their
w-gys$_2$hmw b-wfym
and==army-their in==safety=INDET.
"Considering that he [i.e., Almaqah] granted them that they, their cavalry, and their army returned safely" (J 616/28–29)

5.7 Agreement

As a rule, the predicate agrees with a preceding subject in gender and number:

(44) ʾḫtʾmhw w-s$_2$fnrm ... s$_2$mty wṯnn
Uḫtʾummuhū and==Šāfnīrām they-set-up boundary-stone=DET.
l-ʾlmqh
for==Almaqah
"Uḫtʾummuhū and Šāfnīrām ... set up the boundary stone for Almaqah" (C 389/1–5)

In the Middle Sabaic period especially, the verb often appears in the plural for an expected dual:

(45) ʾs$_1$dm ʾṣḥḥ w-ʾḫyhw rbʾwm bnw ḏ-ʿs$_2$rm
Asadum Aṣḥaḥ and==brother=his Rabbʾawām sons-of REL.==ʿĀširum
hqnyw
they-dedicated
"Asadum Aṣḥaḥ and his brother Rabbʾawām, members of the clan ʿĀširum, dedicated" (NAM 2659/1–2)

When the verb *kwn* "to be" forms the predicate, the rules of agreement are frequently not adhered to:

(46) ḫwm w-ʿws$_1$ w-mwtt kwn b-ʾrḍn
epidemic-of and==plague-of and==death-of it-was in==land=DET.
"Epidemic, plague, and death, which prevailed in the land" (J 645/13–14)

5.8 Non-Sabaic syntactic features

While in the areas of phonology and morphology the other Ancient South Arabian dialects exhibit significant differences from Sabaic and can also be clearly distinguished from one another, specific observations in the area of syntax are possible only to a very limited extent. This is connected with the fact that, in comparison with Sabaic, the textual basis for the other dialects is extremely meager, and elaborate narrative contexts on the basis of which syntactic relationships could be described are lacking. Moreover, many longer Qatabanic and Minaic inscriptions, especially in the case of legal documents, offer serious difficulties of interpretation at present because of their vocabulary. Specific differences from Sabaic and from the other dialects can be noted primarily for Qatabanic.

5.8.1 Attributive relative clauses

Like Sabaic, Qatabanic distinguishes three constructions: syndetic relative clauses with *ḏ-* when the antecedent is marked as definite, and asyndetic relative clauses when the antecedent is in the construct state (especially in paronomastic constructions). If, however – as the third possibility – the antecedent is indefinite, with mimation, then as in Arabic the relative pronoun is not used:

(47) b-kl mngwm b-yktrbw[n] ʿmn tḥrgs$_1$
in==all-of matters they-will-ask from authority=his
"In all matters which they will ask from his [i.e., Warafū's] authority" (AM 177+208/10–11)

5.8.2 Asyndetic constructions

Qatabanic exhibits asyndetic coordination to a larger extent than Sabaic, both in nominal phrases, as in the titulature of Qatabanic rulers, *qẓr qyn ršw* "treasurer, administrator, and priest", and with finite verbs, as in:

(48) ʿs$_1$yw ẓrbw bnyw qbrs$_1$m nfs$_1$m
they-bought they-acquired they-built tomb=their Nafīsum
"They have bought, acquired, and built their tomb Nafīsum" (J 343/2)

5.8.3 Infinitival constructions

Dependent infinitives may exhibit an *-m* in Qatabanic:

(49) w-hmw ys$_1$s$_1$lb kbrn bn lṣq
and==if he-neglects Kabīr=DET. from prosecute.INF.
w-qrw w-ʿthdm w-s$_1$ʿḏbm
and==accuse.INF. and==look-after.INF. and==punish.INF.
ḥg-ḏn ḏ-mḥrn
according-to==this REL==ordinance=DET.
"And if the Kabīr neglects to prosecute, to accuse, to look after, and to punish according to this ordinance" (R 3854/8–9)

6. LEXICON

In addition to the normal common Semitic words such as kinship terms, parts of the body, numbers, and so forth, Ancient South Arabian possesses a very independent vocabulary, which seems to be relatively isolated within the Semitic lexicon. In many cases a semantic comparison with other Semitic languages, even when the root and the corresponding derivative are attested in them, is scarcely helpful, and rarely leads to a satisfactory solution in a specific epigraphic context. As an example may be mentioned the wooden sticks, the interpretation of which is made extremely difficult not only because of the minuscule script, but primarily because of the partly unknown vocabulary.

Nevertheless, because of their geographical and chronological proximity there exist a number of lexical connections not only with North Arabian, as shown by the inscriptions in the Haramic dialect, but also with classical Ethiopic (see Müller 1983). Yet Ancient South Arabian is clearly distinct from its neighboring sister languages in vocabulary as well as in grammar. It can practically be stated that an Ancient South Arabian inscription with the (extensive) lexicon of classical Arabic or Ethiopic cannot be translated and understood properly.

Nor does Ancient South Arabian have close lexical connections with the Modern South Arabian languages, a fact that confirms the discovery, already made on the basis of morphology and syntax, that the Modern South Arabian languages in no way represent the linguistic continuation of Ancient South Arabian.

Many words, especially terms from agriculture and irrigation technology, are found in the works of Yemenite writers of the Arabic Middle Ages, and continue in part to survive today in Yemenite Arabic dialects (see al-Selwi 1987).

In the monotheistic period, the vocabulary of the Sabaic inscriptions is augmented by some Greek and Jewish Aramaic expressions, especially in the religious sphere (see Beeston 1994).

7. READING LIST

An informative cultural and historical survey of the present state of research into Ancient South Arabia is presented in the catalog of the Vienna Yemen-Exhibition (Seipel 1998), in which additional literature is also cited. A tightly packed, informative summary of the individual dialects is given in Beeston 1984; the detailed review of Müller 1986 should be consulted for corrections. The grammars of Höfner 1943 and Bauer 1966 contain much useful information, particularly as far as the older material is concerned, but for recently published texts, the number of which has increased sharply in the last two decades, they are no longer up to date. Recently, a detailed analysis of Sabaic phonology and morphology based on the entire epigraphic material has been prepared by Stein 2003. The relevant dictionary is *Sab. Dict.*, in which the epigraphic material published up to 1981 is critically reviewed in very succinct form. The other dictionaries are helpful only for the advanced student. Still lacking are detailed monographic presentations of the phonology, morphology, or syntax, as well as a concordance that would systematically make the vocabulary of the Ancient South Arabian dialects accessible.

Since 1973, W.W. Müller has produced an annual annotated bibliography on Ancient South Arabia in the journal *Archiv für Orientforschung* (Vienna), now available as Müller 2001, and since 1985, in *Bibliographie linguistique*, a bibliography on the South Arabian languages, in which the Ancient South Arabian dialects are also covered. A comprehensive bibliography for the ancient source material has been published recently by Kitchen 2000.

Acknowledgments

Sections 1, 2, 4.4.2.1, 4.4.2.2, 5, 6, and 7 were written by Norbert Nebes, sections 3 and 4 by Peter Stein. The authors thank Prof. Dr. Walter W. Müller of Marburg for checking the manuscript and for valuable suggestions and proposals.

Selected Bibliography

Grammar of Ancient South Arabian

Avanzini, A. 1992. "H-forms in Qatabanian inscriptions". In *Yemen. Studi archeologici, storici e filologici sull'Arabia meridionale*, vol. 1, pp. 13–17. Rome: Istituto Italiano per il Medio ed Estremo Oriente.

Bauer, G. M. 1966. *Jazyk južnoaravijskoj pis'mennosti.* Moscow: Nauka.

Beeston, A. F. L. 1984. *Sabaic Grammar.* Journal of Semitic Studies Monograph 6. Manchester: University of Manchester.

Gruntfest, Y. B. 1965. "Konsekutivnye konstrukcii v južnoarabskom yazyke". In *Kratkie Soobščenija Instituta Narodov Azii, 86, Istorija i Filologija Bližnego Vostoka, Semitologija*, pp. 129–147. Moscow: Institut narodov Azii.

Höfner, M. 1943. *Altsüdarabische Grammatik.* Porta Linguarum Orientalium XXIV. Leipzig: Otto Harrassowitz. Reprint 1976, Osnabrück: Zeller.

Kogan, L. E., and A. V. Korotayev. 1997. "Sayhadic (Epigraphic South Arabian)". In R. Hetzron (ed.), *The Semitic Languages*, pp. 220–241. London: Routledge.

Müller, W. W. 1986. "Rez. von A. F. L. Beeston, Sabaic Grammar". *Journal of Semitic Studies* 31:270–275.

Nebes, N. 1985. "Zwei Miszellen zur sabäischen Verbalmorphologie". *Bibliotheca Orientalis* 42: 27–39.

———. 1987. "Zur Konstruktion von Subjekt und Objekt abhängiger Infinitive im Sabäischen". In C. Robin and M. Bâfaqîh (eds.), *Ṣayhadica – Recherches sur les inscriptions de l'Arabie préislamique offertes par ses collègues au Professeur A.F.L. Beeston* (*L'Arabie préislamique 1*), pp. 75–98. Paris: Paul Geuthner.

———. 1988. "The infinitive in Sabaean and Qatabanian inscriptions". *PSAS* 18:63–78.

———. 1990. "Gibt es im Sabäischen 'Zustandssätze' analog dem arabischen Schema *wa-huwa yaf'alu* und *wa-huwa fī l-bayti*?". In W. Diem and A. Falaturi (eds.), *XXIV. Deutscher Orientalistentag vom 26. bis 30. September 1988 in Köln*, pp. 61–69. ZDMG Supplement VIII. Stuttgart: Steiner.

———. 1991. "Die enklitischen Partikeln des Altsüdarabischen". In *Études sud-arabes. Recueil offert à Jacques Ryckmans*, pp. 133–151. Publications de l'Institut Orientaliste de Louvain T. 39. Louvain-la-Neuve.

———. 1994a. "Zur Form der Imperfektbasis des unvermehrten Grundstammes im Altsüdarabischen". In W. Heinrichs and G. Schoeler (eds.), *Festschrift Ewald Wagner zum 65. Geburtstag*, vol. I, pp. 59–81 (BTS 54). Beirut/Stuttgart: Steiner.

———. 1994b. "Verwendung und Funktion der Präfixkonjugation im Sabäischen". In N. Nebes (ed.), *Arabia Felix. Beiträge zur Sprache und Kultur des vorislamischen Arabien. Festschrift Walter W. Müller zum sechzigsten Geburtstag, unter Mitarbeit von R. Richter, I. Kottsieper und M. Maraqten*, pp. 191–211. Wiesbaden: Otto Harrassowitz.

———. 1995. *Die Konstruktionen mit /FA-/ im Altsüdarabischen. Syntaktische und epigraphische Untersuchungen.* Veröffentlichungen der Orientalischen Kommission der Akademie der Wissenschaften und der Literatur. Mainz 40. Wiesbaden: Otto Harrassowitz.

———. 1997. "Stand und Aufgaben einer Grammatik des Altsüdarabischen". In R. Stiegner (ed.), *Aktualisierte Beiträge zum 1. Internationalen Symposion Südarabien, interdisziplinär an der Universität Graz, mit kurzen Einführungen zu Sprach- und Kulturgeschichte*, pp. 111–131. Graz: Leykam.

Robin, C. 1983. "Compléments à la morphologie du verbe en sudarabique épigraphique". In *Matériaux arabes et sudarabiques*, pp. 163–185. Paris: Groupe d'Études de Linguistique et de Littératures Arabes et Sudarabiques.

Sima, A. 2001. "Altsüdarabische Konditionalsätze". *Orientalia*, 70:283–312. Rome: Pontifical Biblical Institute.

Stein, P. 2002a. "Gibt es Kasus im Sabäischen?". In N. Nebes (ed.), *Neue Beiträge zur Semitistik. Erstes Arbeitstreffen der Arbeitsgemeinschaft Semitistik in der Deutschen Morgenländischen Gesellschaft vom 11. bis 13. September 2000 an der Friedrich-Schiller-Universität Jena*, pp. 201–222. Wiesbaden: Otto Harrassowitz.

———. 2002b. "Zur Morphologie des sabäischen Infinitivs". *Orientalia*, 71:393–414. Rome: Pontifical Biblical Institute.

———. 2003. *Untersuchungen zur Phonologie und Morphologie des Sabäischen*, Rahden/Westf.: Marie Leidorf.

Dictionaries

Arbach, M. 1993. "Lexique madhābien, comparé aux lexiques sabéen, qatabanite et ḥaḍramawtique". Dissertation, Aix-en-Provence.

Avanzini, A. 1980. *Glossaire des inscriptions de l'Arabie du Sud 1950–1973. II (ʾ-h)*. Quaderni di Semitistica 3. Florence: Istituto di Linguistica e di Lingue Orientali, Università di Firenze.

Biella, J. C. 1982. *Dictionary of Old South Arabic. Sabaean Dialect.* Harvard Semitic Studies No. 25. Chico, CA: Scholars Press.

Ricks, S. D. 1989. *Lexicon of Inscriptional Qatabanian.* Studia Pohl 14. Rome: Pontifical Biblical Institute.

Sab. Dict.: A. F. L. Beeston, M. A. Ghul, W. W. Müller, J. Ryckmans. 1982. *Sabaic Dictionary.* Louvain-la-Neuve: Peeters/Beyrouth: Librairie du Liban.

Other literature cited

Al-Selwi, I. 1987. *Jemenitische Wörter in den Werken von al-Hamdānī und Našwān und ihre Parallelen in den semitischen Sprachen.* Berlin: Reimer.

Beeston, A. F. L. 1994. "Foreign loanwords in Sabaic". In N. Nebes (ed.), *Arabia Felix. Beiträge zur Sprache und Kultur des vorislamischen Arabien. Festschrift Walter W. Müller zum 60. Geburtstag*, pp. 39–45. Wiesbaden: Otto Harrassowitz.

Kitchen, K. A. 2000. *Documentation for Ancient Arabia. Part II. Bibliographical Catalogue of Texts.* Liverpool: University Press.

Macdonald, M. C. A. 2000. "Reflections on the linguistic map of pre-Islamic Arabia". *Arabian archaeology and epigraphy* 11:28–79.

Müller, W. W. 1983. "Äthiopische Marginalglossen zum sabäischen Wörterbuch". In S. Segert and A. Bodrogligeti (eds.), *Ethiopian Studies. Dedicated to Wolf Leslau on the Occasion of his Seventy-Fifth Birthday*, pp. 275–285. Wiesbaden: Otto Harrassowitz.

———. 1994. "Die altsüdarabische Schrift". In H. Günther and O. Ludwig (eds.), *Schrift und Schriftlichkeit. Ein interdisziplinäres Handbuch internationaler Forschung*, pp. 307–312. Berlin: de Gruyter.

———. 2001. *Südarabien im Altertum. Kommentierte Bibliographie der Jahre 1973 bis 1996 unter Mitarbeit von E.-M. Wagner hrsg. von N. Nebes.* Rahden/Westf.: Marie Leidorf.

Robin, C. (ed.). 1991. *L'Arabie antique de Karibʾîl à Mahomet. Nouvelles données sur l'histoire des Arabes grâce aux inscriptions.* Revue du Monde Musulman et de la Méditerranée 61. Aix-en-Provence: Edisud.

Ryckmans, J., W. W. Müller and Y. M. Abdallah. 1994. *Textes du Yémen antique inscrits sur bois.* Publications de l'Institut Orientaliste de Louvain, 43. Louvain-la-Neuve.

Seipel, W. (ed). 1998. *Jemen, Kunst und Archäologie im Land der Königin von Sabaʾ.* Vienna: Kunsthistorisches Museum.

Wissmann, H. von. 1982. *Die Geschichte von Sabaʾ* II. *Das Großreich der Sabäer bis zu seinem Ende im frühen 4. Jh.v.Chr. Hrsg. von W. W. Müller.* Vienna: Österreichische Akademie der Wissenschaften.

CHAPTER 8

Ancient North Arabian

M. C. A. MACDONALD

1. HISTORICAL AND CULTURAL CONTEXTS

In the western two-thirds of the Arabian Peninsula, from southern Syria to Yemen, inscriptions testify to the use of a number of different ancient languages and scripts. In the southwest, these inscriptions may date from as early as the thirteenth century BC and continue up to the seventh century AD, while in central and north Arabia they seem to be concentrated in the period between the eighth century BC and the fourth century AD. Some languages, like Aramaic and, later, Greek, came to the region from outside, but the rest were indigenous tongues expressed in scripts developed locally.

Literacy seems to have been extraordinarily widespread, not only among the settled populations but also among the nomads. Indeed, the scores of thousands of graffiti on the rocks of the Syro-Arabian desert suggest that it must have been almost universal among the latter (see Macdonald 1993:382–388). By the Roman period, it is probable that a higher proportion of the population in this region was functionally literate than in any other area of the ancient world.

1.1 North Arabian

The ancient languages in the southwest of the Peninsula are known as Ancient (or Old) South Arabian (see Ch. 7), while those in central and northern Arabia and in the desert of southern Syria are classed as North Arabian. This latter category is divided into two subgroups. The first of these is *Arabic*, which is subdivided into (i) Old Arabic (that is Arabic attested in pre-Islamic texts which have survived independently of the early Arab grammarians, thus the Namārah inscription but not the "Pre-Islamic poetry," see Macdonald, forthcoming); (ii) Classical and Middle Arabic; and (iii) the vernacular dialects. The second subgroup is called *Ancient North Arabian*. The most striking difference between the two subgroups lies in the definite article, which is *ʾal-* in Arabic, but is *h-* or zero in Ancient North Arabian (see §4.3.1). Until recently, this division was largely unrecognized by linguists working outside the field, and Ancient North Arabian (which was sometimes misleadingly called "Proto-Arabic") was usually treated as a collection of early dialects of Arabic. However, it is now clear that Ancient North Arabian represents a linguistic strain which, while closely related to Arabic, was distinct from it (Macdonald 2000:29–30).

1.1.1 Arabic

Arabic, and thus by implication the North Arabian group as a whole, has traditionally been classified, along with the Ancient South Arabian, Modern South Arabian and Ethiopic

Figure 8.1 Pre-Islamic Arabia

languages, as *South West Semitic* (e.g., Brockelmann 1908–1913: i, 6). However, more recently, it has been grouped instead with Canaanite and Aramaic, under the rubric Central Semitic (e.g., Faber 1997; see Appendix 1, §2.3), and this classification is certainly more appropriate for Ancient North Arabian.

Old Arabic seems to have coexisted with Ancient North Arabian throughout north and central Arabia but, in contrast to Ancient North Arabian, it remained a purely spoken language. The earliest Old Arabic inscriptions in what we think of as the Arabic script (in fact the latest development of the Nabataean Aramaic alphabet) date from the early sixth century AD. Before that, Old Arabic was written only on very rare occasions and then, necessarily, in a "borrowed" script (Ancient South Arabian, Dadanitic, Nabataean, or Greek). At present, seven such documents in Old Arabic have been identified, and in a number of others, Old Arabic features occur in texts which are otherwise in Sabaic (an Ancient South Arabian language), Dadanitic, Safaitic, Nabataean, and possibly East Arabian Aramaic (see Macdonald 2000:50–54 and forthcoming).

1.1.2 Ancient North Arabian

Ancient North Arabian is made up of a number of interrelated dialects, attested only in inscriptions. These are dated roughly between the eighth century BC and fourth century AD, after which the language disappears from the record. Well over forty thousand of these texts have been discovered so far and it is known that scores of thousands remain to be recorded. However, approximately 98 percent of these are graffiti, informal inscriptions the majority of which consist only of names. The amount of linguistic evidence they can provide is therefore relatively meager and our knowledge of the structure of these dialects is extremely fragmentary – a situation exacerbated by the nature of the writing systems used (see §2). Despite this, a surprising amount of information is to be found in these inscriptions, and more is being identified every year.

Ancient North Arabian was used by the settled peoples and nomads of central and north Arabia and by the nomads in what is now southern Syria and eastern and southern Jordan. It is attested in the following dialects (see Macdonald 2000:29–30, 32–36, 40–46): (i) Oasis North Arabian (ONA), consisting of Taymanitic, Dadanitic, Dumaitic, and Dispersed Oasis North Arabian; (ii) Safaitic; (iii) Hismaic; (iv) Thamudic B, C, D, and "Southern Thamudic"; and, possibly, (v) Hasaitic.

1.1.2.1 Oasis North Arabian

Of these dialects, the earliest attested are those belonging to the group known as *Oasis North Arabian.* From at least the middle of the first millennium BC, local dialects of Ancient North Arabian were spoken in the major oases of northwest Arabia: Taymā', Dadan (modern al-ʿUlā; for the spelling Dadan, see Sima 2000 and Macdonald 2000, n. 1) and probably Dūmā (modern al-Ǧawf); see Figure 8.1. The populations of these settlements were heavily involved in the trade in frankincense and other aromatics which were brought from South Arabia to Egypt, the Mediterranean coast, Syria, and Mesopotamia where there seems already to have been a considerable Arab presence. It is therefore not surprising that brief texts in scripts similar to those used in these oases have been found outside Arabia, principally in Mesopotamia. In the past they have been known by such misnomers as "Chaldaean" and "Old Arabic," but I have recently suggested that a better term would be *Dispersed Oasis North Arabian* (Macdonald 2000:33), a label which I hope emphasizes the fact that they are a heterogeneous collection of texts which have in common only the fact that they are written in varieties of the Oasis North Arabian alphabet and that they were found outside Arabia.

Dumaitic is so far represented by only three brief texts found near Sakākā in northern Saudi Arabia (Winnett and Reed 1970:73, 80–81 [WTI 21–23], 207, 216, where they are called "Jawfian"). They are in a distinctive variety of the Oasis North Arabian script (see Fig. 8.3) which differs in certain important respects from Taymanitic and Dadanitic. At present they are undatable, but they may be from the middle of the first millennium BC.

Taymanitic refers to the dialect and script used in the oasis of Taymā' and its surroundings, probably in the sixth and fifth centuries BC. It is represented by short inscriptions with very distinctive linguistic and orthographic features. The number of known Taymanitic texts has recently been doubled (from *c.* 200 to *c.* 400) by Kh. M. Eskoubi's edition of new texts, including two which mention *nbnd mlk bbl* "Nabonidus king of Babylon," who spent ten years of his reign 552–543 BC, in Taymā' (Eskoubi 1999: nos. 169 and 177; Müller and Said 2001).

Dadanitic is a new term which covers the inscriptions in the local language and script of the oasis of Dadan. These were formerly divided into "Dedanite" and "Lihyanite," following

Figure 8.2 Examples of the Ancient North Arabian scripts

the nomenclature of successive kingdoms in the oasis, but, needless to say, linguistic and paleographical developments did not necessarily parallel political changes, and this particular subdivision has proved misleading. Dadanitic is the only Ancient North Arabian dialect and script in which large numbers of monumental inscriptions were written. These are concentrated in and around the oasis, with only occasional examples found elsewhere. In addition, there are hundreds of Dadanitic graffiti in and around the settlement. There is no firm dating evidence for the inscriptions of Dadan, though dates ranging from the sixth century BC through the first century AD have been proposed. Dadan was also the site of a South Arabian (Minaean) trading station and there are numerous monumental inscriptions and graffiti in Ma<u>dh</u>ābic, the South Arabian language used by the Minaeans (see Ch. 7). The prosperity of Dadan may have been eclipsed in the first century AD by the neighboring oasis of Ḥegrā (modern Madāʾin Ṣāliḥ), some twenty kilometers to the north, which became an important city of the Nabataean kingdom.

1.1.2.2 Safaitic

This is the language of most of the graffiti found in the deserts of black, broken-up lava in southern Syria, northeastern Jordan, and northern Saudi Arabia. The vast majority were written by the nomads who lived in this area between roughly the first century BC and the fourth century AD. So far, some twenty thousand Safaitic inscriptions have been recorded, and there are many times this number still awaiting study, as can be seen by any visitor to these desert areas.

1.1.2.3 Hismaic

Hismaic was the language of the nomads of the Ḥismā sand-desert of southern Jordan and northwest Saudi Arabia, and some of the inhabitants of central and northern Jordan. They were contemporaries and close neighbors of the Nabataeans, whose capital, Petra, was not far away from the northern end of the Ḥismā in Wādī Ramm, southern Jordan. Thus, they probably date to the first centuries BC/AD and possibly a little later. In the past, Hismaic has been called "Thamudic E" (see below), and misleadingly "Tabuki Thamudic" and "South Safaitic." The last-mentioned is a complete misnomer since the dialect and script are quite distinct from those of Safaitic.

1.1.2.4 Thamudic

Thamudic is not the name of a dialect or script but of a sort of "pending" category into which are placed all texts which appear to be Ancient North Arabian but which are not Oasis North Arabian, Safaitic, or Hismaic. Both Taymanitic (formerly "Thamudic A") and Hismaic (formerly "Thamudic E") were originally included in this category until the advent of properly recorded texts and intensive studies made it possible to define them as distinct dialects with their own scripts (see Macdonald and King 1999). The rubrics "B," "C," "D," and "Southern Thamudic" represent relatively crude subdivisions of those texts still in this "pending" category. There is no way of dating most of these inscriptions, though one Thamudic B inscription (Ph 279 aw) appears to mention a "king of Babylon" and so presumably dates to a time before the fall of the Babylonian Empire in 539 BC. By contrast, a Thamudic D inscription (JSTham 1) at Madāʾin Ṣāliḥ (ancient Ḥegrā) gives a summary of an adjacent Nabataean tomb inscription which is dated to AD 267. The vast majority of the Southern Thamudic texts remains unpublished, but for an excellent summary presentation see Ryckmans 1956.

1.1.2.5 Hasaitic

This term refers to the language of a number of inscriptions, almost all gravestones, most of which have been found in northeastern Arabia. They consist almost entirely of genealogies and exhibit very few linguistic features. The language is regarded (provisionally) as Ancient North Arabian because of certain characteristic expressions such as *ḏ'l* "of the lineage of" (see §3.1.1). They are written in the Sabaic (Ancient South Arabian) script, with certain minor adaptations.

1.2 Sources of Ancient North Arabian

A large number of the Safaitic, and the vast majority of the Thamudic, inscriptions published so far, were recorded in the nineteenth and early twentieth centuries and are known only from hand copies, often by copyists who could not read the script. Many of these copies are inaccurate, and, in the case of the texts classed as Thamudic, this has proved a major obstacle to their successful interpretation. It is only since large numbers of texts have been photographed that the study of Taymanitic, Safaitic, and Hismaic has been placed on a secure footing.

The dialects of Ancient North Arabian on which we have most information are Dadanitic and Safaitic. The discussion below will therefore concentrate mainly on these, with details from the others where they are available.

The principal resource in the interpretation of the Ancient North Arabian inscriptions has always been the grammar and vocabulary of Classical Arabic and this has been both a blessing and a curse. On the credit side, Classical Arabic has provided a model against which the linguistic phenomena attested in Ancient North Arabian can be evaluated, though there is always a temptation to interpret the, often enigmatic, data in such a way as to make them fit this model, thus obscuring real differences (as is the case in Caskel 1954). Moreover, it should never be forgotten that, unlike most languages, Classical Arabic represents a conscious choice and amalgam of dialects and, to a greater or lesser extent, a systematization of grammatical structures by Arab scholars of the eighth and ninth centuries AD.

Similarly, it should be remembered that the concept of a descriptive dictionary of a living language is no older than the nineteenth century. Prior to that, the purpose of a dictionary was prescriptive, fixing the language in what was considered to be its most "correct" form. Thus, even the immensely rich vocabulary of Classical Arabic represents a choice by the grammarians and lexicographers of what was available to them, and much that might have helped in the reconstruction of Ancient North Arabian was no doubt excluded. Arabic dictionaries can anyway be a trap to the unwary, since they contain meanings which have developed over a wide geographical area and many centuries of intense literary activity, but with little or no indication of when and where a particular sense is first attested. Moreover, as in all languages, words can have meanings which are restricted to certain contexts, and, unless these are quoted (as they are in the great Arabic-Arabic lexica, but not in shorter European compendia), a completely false interpretation can be given. The widespread misapprehension that Ancient North Arabian texts can be read simply by using an Arabic dictionary has led many astray and has resulted in a far greater degree of uncertainty in the interpretation of Ancient North Arabian than in most other ancient languages.

One further point should be noted. In the past, some discussions of Ancient North Arabian grammar have sought to identify linguistic features in the personal names found in Ancient North Arabian inscriptions and have then treated these as if they represented the language of the texts (e.g., Littmann 1943:xii–xxiv; Caskel 1954:68–71; and even sporadically in Müller 1982). Not surprisingly, this has led to confusion, with marked differences appearing between the apparent linguistic features of the names and those of the language used by their bearers. It is important to remember that a name does not "mean" anything except the person, group, place, and so forth to which it refers. It is usually only in exceptional circumstances that parents invent one (e.g., the seventeenth-century English Puritan called "Praise-God Barebones"). Names often continue in use over a very long period and can travel extensively, so the vast majority of names available to parents in any particular society at any particular time have been inherited, often from a linguistic environment very different from their own. The etymology of a name, while interesting in itself, is therefore linguistically irrelevant to the text in which it appears.

In this chapter, the following conventions will be used: /d/ = the etymological phoneme; [d] = the sound; *d* = the letter in a particular script. Letters between { } are doubtful readings. Many Ancient North Arabian texts have been reread or reinterpreted since their original publication, so in some cases the readings and interpretations quoted here will differ from those in the original editions. All examples quoted have been checked on photographs whenever these are available.

2. WRITING SYSTEMS

It is generally held that the Semitic consonantal alphabet was invented in the first half of the second millennium BC (see Ch. 5, §2.2). Later in the same millennium, two separate traditions developed out of the proto-alphabet, each with its own letter-forms, letter-order and (possibly) letter-names. One was the Phoenico-Aramaic (or Northwest Semitic), from which are ultimately derived almost all traditional alphabetic scripts in use today. The other was the Arabian (or South Semitic) alphabetic tradition, which was used almost exclusively in Arabia in the pre-Islamic period and which was the basis of the Ethiopic syllabary (see *WAL* Ch. 14, §2), the only form in which it survives today (Macdonald 2000:32).

The Arabian alphabetic tradition is subdivided into two families: (i) the Ancient South Arabian, of which Sabaic is the most famous and from which the Ethiopic syllabary was developed; and (ii) the Ancient North Arabian. While the Ancient North Arabian scripts are clearly related to each other and to the Ancient South Arabian, the exact relationship has not yet been established. One problem is the lack of securely dated texts from both North and South Arabia; a second has already been touched on – the fact that so many Ancient North Arabian inscriptions are known only from unreliable hand copies. However, the major obstacle to a paleographical analysis of the Ancient North Arabian inscriptions is the fact that the vast majority of them are informal texts written by innumerable individuals who learned to write, not in schools, but casually from a companion, and whose letter-forms were not therefore part of a slowly evolving tradition, but represent a multiplicity of individual choices (Macdonald 1993:382–388; 2004a).

An indication of this is provided by the four Safaitic abecedaries which have been discovered so far. Each is in a different letter-order and none of them bears any relation to the inherited orders of the Northwest and South Semitic alphabets. The letters have simply been arranged according to the writers' differing perceptions of similarity in their shapes (see Macdonald 1993:386 and Macdonald *et al.* 1996:439–443). By contrast, the only known Dadanitic abecedary is in the South Semitic letter-order, while the unique Hismaic example more or less follows the Northwest Semitic order, but with significant differences which suggest that it was unfamiliar to the writer (Macdonald 1986:105–112).

The alphabets of Dadanitic, Hismaic, and Safaitic are each made up of twenty-eight letters. This is probably also true of Thamudic B, C, and D and Hasaitic, though some signs have yet to be identified in these scripts. Taymanitic seems to have had a slightly different phonemic repertoire from the other Ancient North Arabian dialects (see §3.1.2), and only twenty-six or twenty-seven letters have been identified with certainty.

Figure 8.3 shows the most common letter-forms in the different Ancient North Arabian scripts. With the exception of the sign for *ġ* and the leftmost sign for *f*, the forms in the Hasaitic row are those of the South Arabian alphabet. It will be noted that the forms of some letters are remarkably stable throughout all the scripts: for example, ,ʿ *t*, *w*, and *y*. On the other hand, in some cases the same, or very similar, shapes are used in different alphabets to represent quite different phonemes. Thus, the sign used for *g* in Hismaic is identical to that for *ṯ* in Thamudic B, Safaitic, and South Arabian/Hasaitic; while the sign for *ḏ* in South Arabian (and Hasaitic) is used for *ḍ* in Thamudic B, C, and D and in Safaitic, but for *ṯ* in Hismaic. The reasons for this are not yet understood.

In the scripts used by the inhabitants of the great oases, namely, Dumaitic, Taymanitic, and Dadanitic, the direction of writing is almost always right-to-left. In Taymanitic, texts of more than one line were often, but by no means always, written boustrophedon (i.e., continuously, with the lines running in alternate directions). However, the practice of breaking at the end of the line and placing the beginning of the next line under that of the one before is also quite common in Taymanitic and is the norm in Dadanitic. Texts were written without spaces between the words, but word-dividers are the norm in Dadanitic monumental texts and are commonly, though not consistently, used in Dadanitic graffiti and in Taymanitic and Dumaitic. Hasaitic is written either in separate lines or boustrophedon and, since it uses the South Arabian script, employs word-dividers.

By contrast, the scripts used primarily by nomads (Thamudic B, Hismaic, and Safaitic) can be written in any direction (left to right, right to left, downwards, upwards, in a circle or coil, etc.). They meander across the uneven surfaces of the rocks on which they are carved, over the edge onto an adjacent face and occasionally onto an adjacent rock. They are written continuously without word-dividers (Macdonald 2004c). This absence of word-dividers applies equally to Thamudic C and D, which were probably also written by nomads, though these show a marked preference for writing in vertical columns.

In common with all Semitic alphabets, the letters of the North Arabian scripts represent consonants only. However, in contrast to most of the Northwest Semitic scripts, none of the South Semitic alphabets, with the exception of Dadanitic, developed *matres lectionis*, letters which, in addition to their consonantal values, can in certain contexts represent a long vowel. It has been suggested that in Safaitic the letters ,ʾ *w*, and *y* were occasionally used to represent long vowels (Winnett and Harding 1978:12; Robin 2001:553), but this is incorrect and the handful of examples quoted can all be more convincingly explained in other ways.

However, in Dadanitic, final /a:/ was usually represented by *-h* (as in Hebrew) and final /u:/ by *-w*, though the evidence for other *matres lectionis* is less convincing (Drewes 1985). In contrast to the Northwest Semitic scripts, the letter *ʾalif* does not seem to have been used to mark a vowel in Ancient North Arabian.

The diphthong /ai/ is represented in final position in Dadanitic (*pace* Drewes 1985:170–171), though the representation of final /au/ is much less certain. However, diphthongs (if they existed) are rarely if ever represented in the other Ancient North Arabian scripts. Thus, in Safaitic the word for "death" appears as *mt* (cf. Arabic *mawt*), that for "raiding party" as gs^2 (cf. Arabic *ǧayš*), and so forth. Littmann claimed that Greek transliterations of names apparently similar to those found in the Safaitic inscriptions showed that the diphthongs /ai/ and /au/ had been monophthongized to [e:] and [o:] respectively (1943:xiii). However, by the Roman period, there were no appropriate diphthongs left in Koine Greek with which to transliterate any which may have existed in Safaitic, so the question must remain open.

As in all Semitic alphabets, doubled consonants are written singly in the Ancient North Arabian scripts (e.g. **ʾumm* "mother" appears as *ʾm*). However, it has been suggested

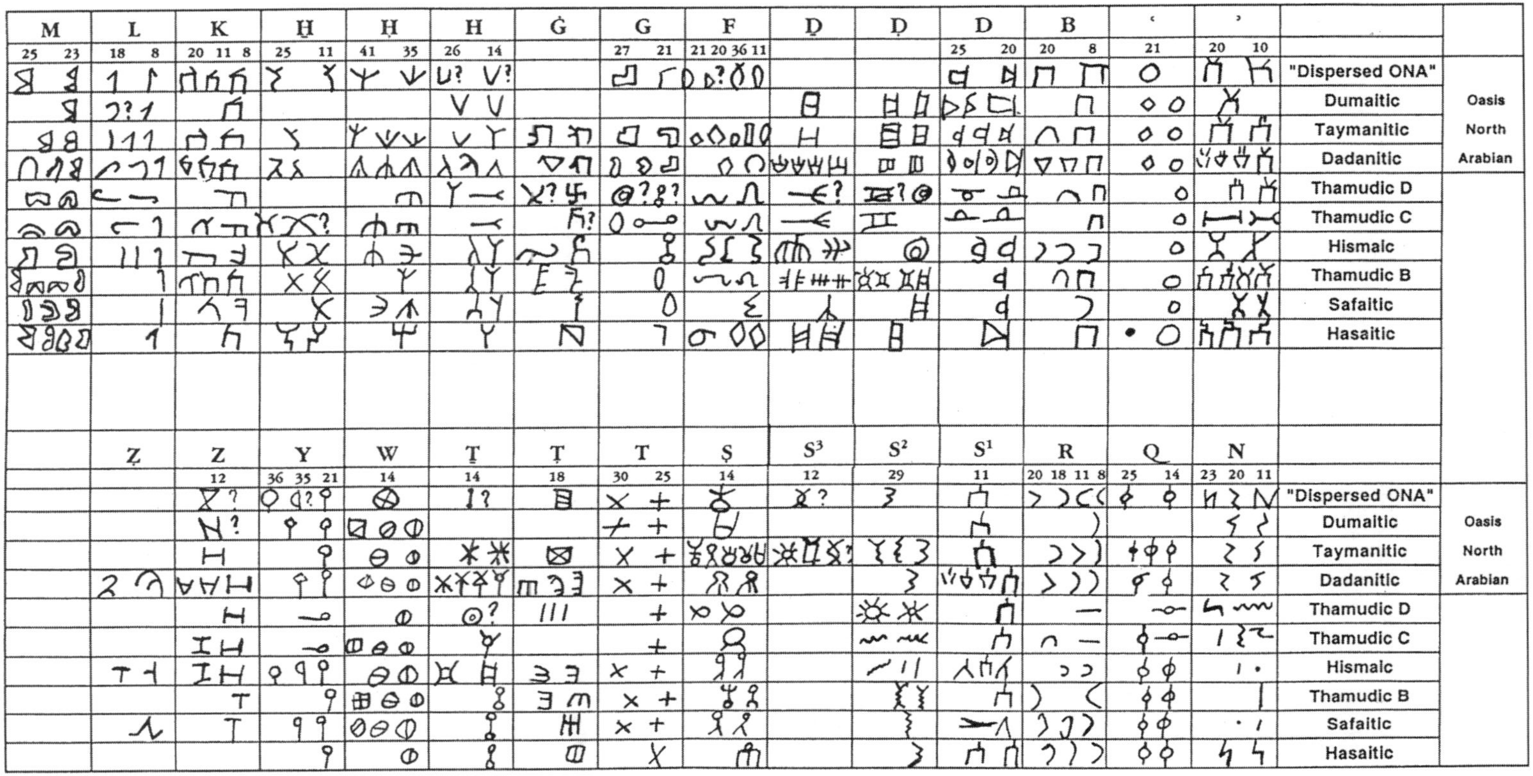

Figure 8.3 *Letter-forms in the Ancient North Arabian scripts*

N.B. There are no chronological implications in the order in which the scripts are arranged. The numbers above the letter-forms in the "Dispersed ONA" row refer to the photographs of the inscriptions in which they occur, published in Sass 1991.

that doubled /l/ and /n/ are occasionally expressed in writing. This is based mainly on the spelling *kll* "all" (cf. Classical Arabic *kull*) which is found in Dadanitic, Hismaic, and Safaitic (Littmann 1943:xiii). But it is perfectly possible that the word was pronounced with a short vowel between the two *l*'s (e.g., **kulil*). The other supposed examples of this feature are also capable of alternative explanations (see §4.2.1) and at present the hypothesis must be regarded as not proven.

3. PHONOLOGY

3.1 Consonants

Given the nature of the sources, our knowledge of the phonology of the dialects of Ancient North Arabian is necessarily fragmentary. Most dialects appear to have had a consonantal phonemic repertoire of roughly twenty-eight sounds. Unless there is evidence to the contrary, these are usually assumed to have been similar, though not always identical, to their equivalents in Classical Arabic. They are presented in Table 8.1 using the Roman letters with which Ancient North Arabian texts are conventionally transliterated, rather than phonetic symbols, to emphasize that this is a purely hypothetical schema based partly on the traditional pronunciation of the cognate phonemes in Classical Arabic, as described by the early Arab grammarians (eighth century AD), and partly on reconstructions (see below).

The phonemes /b, /d/, /ḏ/, /h/, /k/, /l/, /m/, /n/, /t/, /ṯ/, /w/, /y/, /z/ were probably pronounced more or less like their equivalents in Classical Arabic. There is no way of telling whether certain phonemes had aspirated allophones (the so-called "bghadhkphath"), as, for example, in Masoretic Hebrew and Aramaic of the Christian era. The phoneme shown here as /f/, could have been pronounced [p] in some or all positions (as in Ugaritic, Hebrew, Aramaic, Akkadian, etc.) or as [f] throughout, as in Arabic. It is worth noting that in Safaitic (as also in early Arabic) the letter *f* is used to transliterate both Greek φ and π (e.g., *flfṣ*

Table 8.1 The consonantal phonemes of Ancient North Arabian

	Place of articulation									
Manner of articulation	Bilabial	Labio-dental	Inter-dental	Dental/ Alveolar	Palato-alveolar	Palatal	Velar	Uvular	Pharyn-geal	Glottal
Stop										
Voiceless				t			k	q		ʾ
Emphatic				ṭ						
Voiced	b			d			g (?)			
Fricative										
Voiceless		f	ṯ	s³	s¹	y		ẖ	ḥ	h
Emphatic			ẓ	ṣ						
Voiced	w		ḏ	z			ġ		ʿ	
Emphatic			ḍ							
Trill				r						
Lateral cont.										
Voiceless				s²						
Voiced				l						
Nasal	m			n						

for Φίλιππος), the well-known confusion of [b] and [p] in Arabic being a much later phenomenon.

3.1.1 Stops

In Hismaic, there is a small amount of evidence for the occasional confusion of /d/ and /ḏ/, probably under the influence of the Aramaic used by the neighboring Nabataeans: for example, *d-s²ry* for the divine name *ḏ-s²ry*; *dkrt* for *ḏkrt*; and *d ʾl* "he of the lineage of" for *ḏ ʾl* (Macdonald 2004d). However, there is no evidence for the supposed alternation of /t/ and /ṯ/ in this dialect. On both these, see King 1990:69–70. However, in Dadanitic the numerial "three" is found as *ṯlṯt*, *ṯlt*, and *tlt* (see §4.4.1 and Table 8.2) which might suggest a weakening of the distinction between these two sounds in this dialect, though it may equally have been confined to the phonetic conditions of this particular word.

It is impossible to tell whether /g/ was pronounced [g], as in some Arabic dialects, or [ǰ] as in Classical Arabic, or even [ž] as in some dialects of Syria and Southern Iraq. It is also impossible to determine whether /k/ had an allophone [č] in certain positions, as in many dialects in Syria, Iraq, Arabia and the Gulf Coast.

The phonemes /ḫ/ and /ġ/ were probably realised as [x] and [γ] respectively as in Arabic. The consonant transcribed /q/ in Table 8.1 may have been a uvular stop as in Classical Arabic, or, alternatively, an "emphatic" correlate of /k/ (i.e., /k'/), as in Hebrew and Aramaic. Whatever its exact pronunciation it appears generally to have remained distinct since only one instance has so far been identified in which it is confused with another phoneme. This is in an unpublished Safaitic text in which the author spells the word *qyẓ* "he spent the dry season" as *ʾyḍ* in an unequivocal context. This is the earliest attestation of a pronunciation in which the etymological phonemes /q/ and /ẓ/ had fallen under /ʾ/ and /ḍ/ respectively, a feature of modern urban Arabic in such cities as Damascus, Jerusalem, and Cairo.

In the orthography of the Ancient North Arabian scripts, the letter ʾ represents a phonemic consonant in all contexts and never the equivalent of Classical Arabic *hamzat al-waṣl*, that is, a prosthetic glottal stop, the sole function of which is to carry an initial vowel and which disappears when the latter is assimilated to a preceding vowel. Thus *bn* ("son," in all positions) as against Classical Arabic *(ʾ)ibn*. This contrasts with Old Arabic personal names found in Nabataean orthography (for instance in the Nabataean inscriptions of Sinai), where ʾ is regularly written in *ʾbn* (e.g., the name *ʾbn-ʾl-qyny*). For a discussion of this phenomenon see Macdonald, forthcoming. There are a few personal names in Safaitic texts written with two successive ʾs, e.g., ʾʾs¹d (cf. Classical Arabic *āsud* < **ʾaʾsud*; see Littmann 1943:xii–xiii), but as yet no examples in words have been identified, so we do not know whether this was a living feature of the language or merely a fossil inherited in particular names.

Very occasionally, ʾ is found unexpectedly in medial position and it has been suggested that this may represent a medial /a:/ (Winnett and Harding 1978:12). However, this is highly unlikely and the few examples cited are all capable of other explanations.

The ending which in Arabic appears as *-ah* in pause but *-at* before a vowel (i.e., *tāʾ marbūṭah*), is always written as *-t* in Ancient North Arabian, implying that it was pronounced **-at* in all contexts.

3.1.2 Fricatives

The voiceless nonemphatic sibilants in Ancient North Arabian, Ancient South Arabian, Old Arabic, and Classical Arabic up to the ninth century AD, present a complex problem (see

Beeston 1962). Proto-Semitic had a voiceless dental fricative */s/, a voiceless palato-alveolar fricative */š/, and a third sibilant, conventionally written */ś/, the exact nature of which is uncertain but which may have been a lateral dental fricative [ɬ]. While the Ancient (and Modern) South Arabian languages (in common with Hebrew and early Aramaic) retained all three, in Arabic and, with one possible exception, the Ancient North Arabian dialects they were reduced to two:

(1) The voiceless nonemphatic sibilants in Ancient North Arabian

Proto-Semitic		Ancient North Arabian (except Taymanitic)	Proto-Semitic		Taymanitic
*/š/ ⎫			*/š/	→	[š] (written s¹)
*/s/ ⎬	→	[š] (written s¹)	*/s/	→	[s] (written s³)
*/ś/	→	[ɬ] ? (written s²)	*/ś/	→	[ɬ] ? (written s²)

We know from the phonetic descriptions by the early Arab grammarian Sibawaihi (died c. AD 796) that in early Classical Arabic, س the reflex of Proto-Semitic */s/ + */š/, was pronounced something approaching [š], and that ش the reflex of Proto-Semitic */ś/, was pronounced something approaching [ɬ]. It was only subsequently that the pronunciation of س shifted to the [s] (sīn), and that of ش to the [š] (šīn) of later Arabic. This can be tabulated as follows:

(2) The voiceless nonemphatic sibilants in Arabic

Proto-Semitic		Arabic before the 9th century AD		Arabic after the 9th century AD
*/š/ ⎫				
*/s/ ⎬	→	[š] (written س)	→	[s] (written س)
*/ś/	→	[ɬ] (written ش)	→	[š] (written ش)

This means that Ancient North Arabian /s¹/ (which is cognate with later Arabic س sīn) was actually pronounced like something approaching [š], while Ancient North Arabian /s²/ (which is cognate with later Arabic ش šīn) was probably pronounced something like Welsh -ll- [ɬ]. These findings are confirmed by the treatments of loans from Aramaic. Thus, for example, the Aramaic name of the great Syrian sky-god, Baʿal-Šamīn "lord of heaven," was borrowed into Dadanitic and Safaitic as bʿls¹mn, that is, with Aramaic /š/ represented by Ancient North Arabian s¹, not s².

It follows from this that Ancient North Arabian (and Arabic before the ninth century AD) had no [s]. However, there is one possible exception. Taymanitic appears to have had a letter, graphically related to South Arabian s³ (= [s]), which seems to represent [s] in transliterations of the name of the Egyptian god Osiris occurring in two personal names. Rather different forms of what is probably the same letter have been identified in two other Taymanitic texts (see Müller and Said 2001:114–116) and there is one further example on a seal of Babylonian design, but in a context which raises considerable difficulties. Since, at present, only a little over four hundred Taymanitic inscriptions are known, and few of them are more than twenty letters long, no firm conclusions can be drawn from this until more evidence appears. However, it seems unlikely that the Taymanitic alphabet would have employed a letter to represent a sound which did not exist in the Taymanitic dialect, and so there is certainly a possibility that, at some stage in its history, Taymanitic used all three voiceless nonemphatic sibilants (see Macdonald 1991).

In Taymanitic, Thamudic D, and possibly Thamudic C, it seems that /ḏ/ had probably merged with /z/ (as in Hebrew), since the *z* sign is used for both phonemes.

3.1.3 Emphatics

The etymological phonemes /ṣ/, /ṭ/, /ḍ/, and /ẓ/ are emphatics. In most Semitic languages /ṣ/ is the emphatic correlate of [s]. However, since there was no [s] in Safaitic and Hismaic, *ṣ* is often used in these dialects to transliterate Greek *sigma* (e.g., *qṣr* for καῖσαρ ["Caesar"]; *flfṣ* for Φίλιππος ["Philip"]; etc.) and in the Hismaic abecedary *ṣ* is put in the position of Phoenico-Aramaic *samek* (= [s]). It is not certain whether this implies a weakening of the "emphatic" quality or whether it was simply felt to be the nearest equivalent to the foreign sound. The fact that in other transliterations the letter s^1 (approximately[š]) was used for Latin *s* (e.g., *tts*^{1} for *Titus*) and Greek *sigma* (e.g., *grgs*^{1} for Γεωργός [George]), points perhaps to the latter (see Macdonald 1992b).

The phoneme /ṭ/ was almost certainly the emphatic correlate of /t/, and /ḍ/ was, at least in origin, that of /d/. However, the Akkadian transliteration of the Ancient North Arabian divine name *rḍw* as *Ruldaiu* points to a strongly lateralized pronunciation of /ḍ/, at least in North Arabia in the seventh century BC. It has also been suggested that the god 'Οροτάλτ, who Herodotus says was worshiped by the Arabs in eastern Egypt in the fifth century BC, represents a garbled transliteration of a similar pronunciation of the divine name *rḍw*, though this is more speculative. On the other hand, in the Roman period, Greek transcriptions of names which include /ḍ/ always represented it by *sigma* (e.g., Σαιφηνος for *h-ḍfy*, "the Ḍayfite", Macdonald 1993:306). In Nabataean, native Aramaic words show the cognate of North Arabian /ḍ/ as /ʿ/ ([ʕ]) (e.g., Nabataean *ʾrʿʾ* against Safaitic *ʾrḍ* "earth, land"), as is normal from Imperial Aramaic onwards. However, in loanwords and transcriptions of names which are linguistically North Arabian, /ḍ/ is consistently represented by *ṣ* (e.g., Nabataean *ṣryḥʾ* from Arabic *ḍarīḥ* "trench, cist," or the name *rṣwt* as against Safaitic *rḍwt*). Kofler quotes examples of the confusion of /ḍ/ and /ṣ/ in early Arabic dialects and suggests that /ḍ/ may have been pronounced more as a fricative than a stop (1940–1942:95–97). There is no example in Safaitic and Hismaic of a confusion of /ḍ/ and /ṣ/, so the two sounds seem to have remained distinct in these dialects. However, if /ḍ/ was pronounced as the emphatic correlate of /ḏ/ (rather than of /d/), i.e., as an emphatic interdental fricative, as it is in all modern Bedouin dialects, it would have shared its place of articulation, emphatization, and fricative release with /ṣ/, and the two sounds would have been sufficiently similar for /ḍ/ to be transcribed by /ṣ/ in scripts such as Nabataean Aramaic which had no letter for /ḍ/ (I owe this interesting observation to Professor Clive Holes).

The conventional symbol ẓ (originally taken over from the Cairene pronunciation of Classical and Modern Standard Arabic) is unfortunate since the phoneme it is intended to represent was probably the emphatic correlate of an interdental (/ṯ/, or perhaps /ḏ/), and not a dental sibilant. The former would be more likely, at least in Hismaic and Safaitic, if, as suggested above, /ḍ/ was pronounced as the emphatic correlate of /ḏ/. In Dadanitic, Hismaic, and Safaitic, /ẓ/ is clearly distinguished from other phonemes except in the one example of *ʾ yḍ* for *qyẓ* mentioned above. It has been suggested that, in Dadanitic, /ẓ/ might have fallen under /ṭ/ (as in Aramaic), but no conclusive evidence has yet been presented for this shift and the two phonemes appear to be represented by distinct letter-forms. A sign for *ẓ* has not yet been identified in Dumaitic, Taymanitic, Thamudic B, C, and D, or in Hasaitic, but since it is a relatively rare phoneme, it is, at present, impossible to determine whether this is significant.

3.1.4 The sounds /w/ and /y/

In Safaitic, there is considerable alternation of /w/ and /y/, which when represented in the Ancient North Arabian scripts are always consonants, not vowels (Robin 2001: 553 is incorrect on this point). This variation is found in all positions, e.g., *wrẖ/yrẖ* "month"; *ts²wq/ts²yq* (unpublished) "he longed for"; *s²ty/s²tw* (CSNS 324) "to winter." In each case, the first item in these pairs is the common form and the second a much less frequent variant. Given the difficulty of dating most of the texts, it is impossible to say at present whether these variations represent chronological developments or synchronic dialectal differences.

However, forms with *-w* and *-y* are almost equally common in the divine name *rḍw/rḍy* in Safaitic inscriptions. This deity is also found in Dumaitic and Thamudic B texts, but there only as *rḍw*. The Dumaitic, and at least some of the Thamudic B inscriptions, are considerably earlier than the Safaitic, and this might seem to suggest that the form *rḍw* is the older and that the advent of *rḍy* marks a change of pronunciation. However, the Akkadian transliteration *Ruldaiu*, which is securely dated to the early seventh century BC, implies a pronunciation **ruḍayu* (i.e., *rḍy*), and it therefore seems more likely that the two spellings represent dialectal (?) differences. It is not yet possible to tell whether the same is true of the other cases of *w/y* variation.

In a number of other cases, Safaitic and Hismaic have /-y/ where Classical Arabic has /-a:/ or /-a:ʔ/, thus Safaitic *s¹my* "sky, clouds," as against Arabic *samāʾ*, or Safaitic and Hismaic *bny* "he built" and *byt* "he spent the night," as against Arabic *banā* and *bāta*. In some of these cases, there is evidence that Dumaitic and Thamudic B agreed with Arabic. Thus, the divine name *ʿtr-s¹m*, which occurs in Dumaitic and Thamudic B texts and in which *s¹m* is the word for "heaven," implies a pronunciation *s¹amā (in which the /-a:/ would not appear in the consonantal script), as opposed to Safaitic *s¹my* (*s¹umiyy ?), see Macdonald *et al.* 1996:479–480.

Conversely, there are some words in which final /-a:/ is written with a *-y* in Arabic, but which in Ancient North Arabian did not end in consonantal /y/. These are most notably the prepositions which in Safaitic, Hismaic, and Thamudic B appear as *ʾl* (cf. Arabic *ʾilā*) "towards, for," and *ʿl* (cf. Arabic *ʿalā*) "on, over, against." In Dadanitic, both *ʿl* and *ʿly* are found, though the former is more common. This implies that the final sound may have been a diphthong *-ay* (/-ai/), which would have been left unwritten in all the Ancient North Arabian scripts, except Dadanitic (see §2), where it would appear as *-y* (*pace* Drewes 1985, who believes diphthongs had been monophthongized in Dadanitic and that final *-y* represented [e:]). The forms without *-y* in Dadanitic may then represent either an uncertainty about writing diphthongs or a pronunciation with a final short vowel, as in some modern Arabic dialects (i.e., *ai > *ā (as in Classical Arabic) > *a).

3.1.5 Nasal assimilation

As in Hebrew and Aramaic, but in contrast to Arabic, vowelless /n/ is frequently assimilated in most Ancient North Arabian dialects. This is particularly common in Safaitic and Hismaic where, for example, *mn* (cf. Arabic *min*) "from" and *mn* (cf. Arabic *man*) "whoever" are sporadically reduced to *m* (though curiously not in *mn ngd* "from high ground," CSNS 381). Thus, the plural of *nfs¹t* ("funerary monument") sometimes appears as *ʾfs¹* (< *ʾanfus¹), and the verb *intaẓar ("to wait for") always appears as *tẓr* (= *ittaẓar ?). Similarly, in Taymanitic, Thamudic B, Hismaic, and Safaitic (though rarely in Dadanitic), *bnt* ("daughter") is occasionally spelled *bt*. However, this feature has not yet been identified in Hasaitic, where we find *bnt* (*passim*) and *ʾnṯt*, "wife" (CIH 984a) compare Dadanitic and Thamudic B *ʾṯt*, though the corpus of Hasaitic texts is as yet so small that no firm conclusions can be drawn from this.

Assimilation of vowelless /n/ would also account for a feature characteristic of Taymanitic, that is the reduction of *bn* to *b* ("son of") in genealogies, which contrasts with *bn* (= *banī, lit. "the sons of") where the /*n*/ is followed by a vowel (Macdonald 1992a:31).

3.2 Vowels

Little of substance can be said about the vowels of Ancient North Arabian. The vowel inventory is assumed to have consisted of both short and long /a/, /i/, and /u/, but there is no evidence for or against this, except for final /a:/ and /u:/ in Dadanitic (see §2). Attempts to show that the diphthongs /au/ and /ai/ had been monophthongized to /o:/ and /e:/ respectively (as in many spoken Arabic dialects) are not convincing, though they cannot entirely be refuted either (see, again, §2).

4. MORPHOLOGY

Since Safaitic and Dadanitic are by far the best attested of the Ancient North Arabian dialects, the morphological descriptions below will concentrate on them, with information from the others when it is available.

It should be noted that several unusual forms have been attributed to Dadanitic on the basis of their apparent occurrence in JSLih 71 (= CLL 91). However, it is now recognized that, with the exception of the article *hn-* in the tribal name, the language of this text is Old Arabic, not Dadanitic. See Beeston *et al.* 1973:69–70 and Macdonald 2000:52–53 and forthcoming.

As in all Semitic languages, the morphology of the Ancient North Arabian dialects is based on the triliteral root, found in its simplest form in the third singular masculine of the suffix-conjugation (often known as the "perfect").

The fact that, in most dialects of Ancient North Arabian, final *-y* is written in words such as *bny* "he built," *s*^{1}*my* "sky, clouds" and the gentilic ending (e.g., Safaitic *h-nbṭy* "the Nabataean" which in Arabic would be *al-nabaṭī*) suggests the presence of final short vowels, since without them the /-y/ would have become a long vowel [i:] or a diphthong [ai], and would not then have been represented in the orthography of any of the scripts, except in the case of the diphthong, that of Dadanitic. By contrast, the tiny amount of evidence available suggests that final short vowels may not have been present in the forms of Old Arabic represented in the documents so far identified (see Macdonald, forthcoming).

4.1 Nominal morphology

Nouns, adjectives, and pronouns will be discussed in this section. The purely consonantal Ancient North Arabian scripts must often conceal distinctions of number and possibly of case which would have been marked by changes in vowels. As in Arabic, the endings of nouns and adjectives can vary according to whether they stand alone ("in pause," "pausal forms") or are annexed to another noun or to an enclitic pronoun ("in construct"), see §5.1.3 below and Appendix 1, §3.3.2.1.

4.1.1 Gender

The normal feminine singular ending in all Ancient North Arabian dialects is *-t* (even in pause; see §3.1.1): for example, *mrʾt* "woman," Dadanitic (JSLih 64/2); *frs*^{1}*t* "mare,"

Thamudic B (e.g., HU 494); *bkrt* "young she-camel," Safaitic (e.g., WH 344). Participles (see §4.2.6) are also marked for gender, and the feminine singular takes the *-t* ending of the nominals, as in *rġmt* (**raġīmat*) "humbled" (fem.), Safaitic (NST 2).

The word **ym* "day" (attested only in the dual *ymn* and the plural *ʾym*) appears to have been treated as feminine in Dadanitic and Safaitic, as it is in Jibbālī and Mehrī, though it is masculine in most other Semitic languages (see §4.4.1).

4.1.2 Number

Nominals in Ancient North Arabian have three numbers, singular (unmarked), dual and plural. On "external" (§4.1.2.2) and "internal" (§4.1.2.3) plurals in Semitic, see Appendix 1, §3.3.2.4.

4.1.2.1 Dual

Clear evidence of the dual is found only in Dadanitic, Thamudic B, and Safaitic.

"In pause" (see §4.1), the normal ending of the dual is *-n* (cf. Classical Arabic *-āni*): for example, Dadanitic *h-mṯbr-n* "the two tomb-chambers" (JSLih 45/3); Thamudic B, *h-gml-n* "the two camels" (HU 296/2); Safaitic, *h-bkrt-n* "the two young she-camels" (e.g., WH 402, beside a drawing of them), *ym-n* "two days" (CSNS 796 and see p. iii).

A curious, and as yet unexplained, form of the dual in pause is found in one Safaitic text (LP 305), where *ḍll-y* "lost" (i.e., "dead") refers to two people and is contrasted with *ḍll-n*, referring to three, in the same text (see §4.1.2.2). *Ḍll-y* is similar to the form of the dual which, in Classical Arabic, would be used in the oblique case "in construct" (see §4.1), namely *ḍalīlay*. However, in LP 305, while it would be in the oblique case (if this existed in Safaitic), it is clearly in pause and one would anyway not expect *y* to be used to represent a diphthong in the Safaitic script.

In Classical Arabic the *-n* of the dual is dropped in construct, leaving a long vowel (*-ā*), in the nominative, or a diphthong (*-ay*) in the oblique case. In Dadanitic, the only dialect with an orthography that represents some *final* long vowels and diphthongs, the ending seems to be a diphthong, represented by *-y*, regardless of case (if, indeed, this existed); thus, "nominative" *kbry* s^2*ʿt h-n{ṣ}*, "the two kabirs of the company of H-NṢ" (JSLih 72/3–4; cf. Arabic *kabīrā*); "oblique" *b-ḥqwy kfr*, "on two sides of a tomb" (JSLih 77/7; cf. Arabic *ḥaqway*). As yet, there are not enough examples to assess the significance of this. Compare the situation in the modern spoken Arabic dialects where the dual ending in nouns is always -ē(n) (presumably <*ay(n)) regardless of whether the noun is grammatically in the "nominative" or "oblique" case. Again, this is a feature found in the early Arabic papyri (see Hopkins 1984:98–104).

When the second element of the construct was a pronominal suffix, the diphthong (*-ay) was considered to be *medial* and was therefore not represented in the Dadanitic script. The result is that the form *ʾḫw-hm* (JSLih 79/3) could represent either the dual "their two brothers" (*ʾaḫaway-hum, cf. Classical Arabic *ʾaḫawā-hum*, since the context requires it to be in the nominative) or the plural "their brothers" (cf. Classical Arabic *ʾuḫuwwuhum*).

A similar problem is found in Safaitic, where one of the few examples of the dual in construct yet identified is *ʾḫw-h* "his two brothers" (see LP 386, where the two persons are named). However, in C 657 *ʾḫw-h* is followed by the names of three persons, and in the other examples the numbers are not specified. It therefore appears that the form *ʾḫw* in Safaitic probably represents both the dual (*ʾaḫaway) and the plural (*ʾuḫuww) as in Dadanitic. The supposed plural *ʾḫwn* (in C 2534, 2779, 2955, cf. Arabic *ʾiḫwān*) should almost certainly be read *ʾḫwl* (plural of *ḫl* "maternal uncle").

The form *bny-h* in Safaitic has also been regarded as a possible dual (e.g., in C 3365, WH 1249, 3838, cf. Arabic *ibnay-hi* "his two sons," oblique case). However, since Safaitic orthography does not show diphthongs, it is more likely that *bny-h* represents a diminutive (cf. Arabic *bunayyi-hi*, "his little son"), as it must do in C 4076, where it refers to only one person.

4.1.2.2 *External masculine plural*

In pause this is formed by adding *-n* to the singular and is thus indistinguishable in the purely consonantal script from the regular form of the dual in pause. In construct the *-n* is dropped:

(3) A. Dadanitic
In pause — *ʾṣdqn* "rightful heirs[?]" (CLL 65/2)
In construct — *bnw s¹ʿdʾl* "the sons of S¹ʿdʾl" (AH 1/2–3, see Sima 1999:35–36)
B. Safaitic
In pause — *ẓbyn* "male gazelles" (CSNS 550 beside a drawing of six, cf. Ar. *ẓabyān*)

Participles (see §4.2.6) are similarly marked: thus, *ḍll-n* "lost" (i.e., "dead" in LP 305, referring to three people, cf. Arabic, oblique case, *ḍalīlīn*).

4.1.2.3 *Internal masculine plural*

In Arabic, this type of plural is often marked by changes in vowels within the word, and such changes would be invisible in the Ancient North Arabian consonantal scripts. Still, a few types have forms which show up even in the Ancient North Arabian orthographies, such as the following:

(4)

Pattern	Dadanitic
ʾafʿāl	*ʾym* (sg. **ym*, "day," e.g., JSLih 68/4, 349, cf. Ar. *ʾayyām*)
	ʾẓll (sg. *ẓll*, "ẓll-ceremony", U 43, 115, etc. see Sima 1999: 95–96)
	ʾẓl (sg. *ẓll*, "ẓll-ceremony", U 50/3)
ʾafʿilat	*ʾẓlt* (sg. *ẓll*, "ẓll-ceremony", U 32/3–4 and see Wright 1896–1898: i, 212)
fiʿlat	*ẓlt* (sg. *ẓll*, "ẓll-ceremony", U 13/3, and see Stiehl 1971:6 and cf. Wright 1896–1898: i, 209, XII/4 for the form)
fuʿʿāl	*ḥgg* (sg. **ḥg*, "pilgrim", JSLih 6/4, cf. Ar. *ḥuǧǧāǧ*)

Note also Dadanitic *ʾẖw-hm* ("their brothers," JSLih 79/3, *ʾuẖuww as in Safaitic, see §4.1.2.1).

Pattern	Safaitic
ʾafʿāl	*ʾs²yʿ* (sg. **s²ʿ*, "companion," cf. Ar. *ʾašyāʿ*)
	ʾẖwl (sg. *ẖl*, "maternal uncle," e.g., HCH 71, cf. Ar. *ʾaẖwāl*)
fuʿūl	*ẖṭṭ* (sg. **ẖṭ*, "line, carving," cf. Ar. *ẖuṭūṭ*)

Note also Safaitic *ʾẖw-h*, see §4.1.2.1.

4.1.2.4 *External feminine plural*

This is *-t*, and so is identical in appearance to the singular (see §4.1.1), the change presumably lying in the vowel of the ending (cf. Arabic sg. *-ah/at*; pl. *-āt*); thus Safaitic *ẓbyt* "female gazelles" (WH 3373, the plural confirmed by the accompanying drawing); and Hismaic *nʿrt* "girls" (unpublished).

4.1.2.5 Collective nouns

These are represented in Safaitic by *ʾbl* ("camels," cf. Arabic *ʾibil*), and *mʿzy* ("goats," cf. Arabic *miʿzan*). It is not clear whether they are grammatically feminine, as in Classical Arabic.

4.1.3 Case

Since the Safaitic script shows no vowels, it is impossible to be certain whether case endings existed. However, by the same token, the spelling of such nouns as *mʿzy*, *ẓby*, and the gentilic (see §4.1.6) – for example, *h-yhdy*, "the Jew" (which in Arabic would be *al-yahūdī*) – imply that the final *-y* was pronounced with a short vowel, since, if it were not, it would itself become a long vowel and so would not be shown. Beyond this, little can be said with certainty at present. The same applies to Dadanitic.

4.1.4 State

Caskel argued that the expression *h-{ṣ}lmn* (CLL 19/3–4 = JSLih 62/3–4) indicates that, at an early period, a *determinate state*, marked by a suffixed *-n*, existed in Dadanitic, as in the Ancient South Arabian languages (1954:68). However, such an explanation would mean that the word was doubly defined (with a prefixed article *h-* and the suffixed *-n*), and Caskel's attempt to explain the former as a demonstrative is unconvincing in view of the fact that elsewhere in Dadanitic the demonstrative adjective always follows the defined noun, thus *h-{ṣ}lmn hḏh* (JSLih 82/1). It is much more likely that *ṣlmn* is a dual or an external plural, or perhaps a diminutive (see Brockelmann 1908–1913: i, 394), with a specialized meaning such as "statuette" as opposed to "statue" (cf. Aramaic *ṣlmnytʾ* which seems to mean "small female idols" in *Israel Exploration Journal* 29 (1979), p. 119).

4.1.5 Determination

There is no visible mark of indetermination (comparable to *tanwīn* in Arabic), and had *tanwīn* been present it would have been represented in the Ancient North Arabian scripts. Determination is marked by the definite article (see §4.3.1) or annexation either to another noun or to a pronominal suffix.

4.1.6 Diminutives

If diminutives were formed in Ancient North Arabian in the same way as in Arabic, by use of the fuʿayl form, they would be invisible in the Ancient North Arabian orthographies. Only exceptional forms such as *ʾḫyt* (cf. Arabic *ʾuḫayyat* "little sister", C 893) and *bny* (cf. Arabic *bunayy* "little son", WH1249) can be identified.

4.1.7 Adjectives

These follow the noun and agree with it in gender, number, and determination: for example, in Safaitic *h-gs*^{2} *h-rdf* (*ha-gays^{2} h-radīf) "the rear guard" (LP 146); or *kll ʿs*^{2}*r ṣdq* "every true kinsman" in Safaitic (HCH 191) and Hismaic (MNM 6).

As in Arabic, an adjective referring to a noun in the plural signifying nonsentient beings is put in the feminine singular, thus *rtg {q}ds*^{1}*t* (cf. Arabic *rutuǧ qadīsah*) "sacred portals" (CLL 85/3).

A gentilic adjective (Arabic *nisbah*) is formed with *-y*: for example, *h-rmy*, "the Roman." For demonstrative adjectives, see §4.1.8.4.

4.1.8 Pronouns

Independent and enclitic personal pronouns are attested in Ancient North Arabian, as are relative and demonstrative pronouns.

4.1.8.1 Independent personal pronouns

Only three independent personal pronouns are so far securely attested in Ancient North Arabian:

1. First singular *ʾn*: There is only one certain example in each of Safaitic (WH 1403b) and Dadanitic (JSLih 347/2). It is found occasionally in Hismaic (unpublished) and Thamudic D (e.g., JSTham 637), and is frequent in Thamudic B and C. It has not yet been found in Hasaitic.
2. Second singular *ʾt*: two possible examples are known so far, both in Thamudic B (HU 796 and 627?).
3. Third plural masculine *hm*: known from only one example in Dadanitic (JSLih 79/3).

4.1.8.2 Enclitic personal pronouns

Enclitic personal pronouns can be attached to verbs representing the object (e.g., *qtl-h* "he killed him") or to nouns indicating possession (e.g., *ʾb-h* "his father") or to prepositions which govern them (e.g., *l-h* "for him"). Those so far attested on verbs in Ancient North Arabian are shown in **1** through **4**.

1. First singular or plural *-n*: If the enclitic pronouns of the first persons singular and plural on verbs were similar to those in Classical Arabic (i.e., *-nī* = "me," *-nā* = "us") they would be indistinguishable in all Ancient North Arabian scripts except Dadanitic, where no certain example of either has yet been found. Thus, in Safaitic *ʿwḏ-n* "protect me/us" (unpublished); in Hismaic *dkrt-n lt* "may Lt be mindful of me/us" (unpublished); and in Thamudic B, where it is best attested, as in *flṭ-n* "deliver me/us" (LP 495).
2. Third singular masculine or feminine *-h*: This occurs in Dadanitic: for example, *rḍ-h w-s¹ʿd-h* "favor him and help him" (e.g., U 4/4); *rḍ-h w-ʾḫrt-h w s¹ʿd-h* "favor her and her descendants and help her" (U 6/4–5). It is surprisingly rare in Taymanitic and Thamudic B, C, and D, but is found in both Safaitic – thus *yʿwr-h* "he will scratch it out" (e.g., LP 329), *qtl-h* "he killed him" (LP 385, etc.); and in Hismaic: for example, *ḫṭṭ-h* "he inscribed it" (JSTham 665).
3. Third dual *-hmy*: Several examples are found in Dadanitic, such as *s¹ʿd-hmy* "help both of them" (U 69/5–6). This presumably represents a diphthong *-humay in contrast to Classical Arabic *-humā*.
4. Third plural *-hm*: This is found in Dadanitic *rḍ-hm* "favor them" (of four persons, AH 1/5 [see Sima 1999:35–36]).

On nouns and prepositions, the following enclitic personal pronouns are found:

5. First singular: If the enclitic pronoun of the first person singular was *-*ī* on nouns and prepositions, as in Arabic and most Semitic languages, one would not expect it to show up in any of the Ancient North Arabian orthographies. However, there are a

handful of possible examples in Thamudic B: for example, *wdd-y* "my beloved" (HU 736), *s¹mʿ l-y* "listen to me" (HU 713). Since, the orthography of Thamudic B does not represent vowels in other cases, as far as we can tell, it would seem that the enclitic pronoun may have been pronounced *īya or *ayya, as when in Classical Arabic it is attached to a word ending in a long vowel, a diphthong, or *ʾalif maqṣūrah.*

6. Second singular *-k*: Safaitic *ʿwḏ-k* "your protection" (referring to one deity, unpublished) and Thamudic B *b-k* "in you" (e.g., HU 207, WTI 25, etc.) are attested. It is not yet identified in Dadanitic, Thamudic C and D, Hismaic, or Hasaitic.
7. Third singular masculine and feminine *-h*: This is common in Safaitic *ʾb-h* "his father" (e.g., WH 1275), *l-h* "for him" (e.g., WH 3420), "for her" (e.g., CSNS 412). The frequent omission of the definite article *h-* immediately after the third singular enclitic personal pronoun (e.g., *l-h rgm* "the cairn is his/hers," as in the examples above) suggests that the suffix may have been pronounced *-uh (masc.) / *-āh (fem.), as in many Arabic dialects, rather than *-hu (masc.) / *-hā (fem.), as in Classical Arabic. The /h/ of the article may have been assimilated to that of the enclitic pronoun, leaving only its vowel and the possible reinforcement of the initial consonant of the following word (see §4.3.1), thus *l-uh ha-(r)rugm > *l-uh-a-(r)rugm "the cairn is his." See also *s¹ʿd-h-rḍw* for *s¹ ʿd-h h rḍw "help him O Rḍw" (CSNS 2), though this could also represent an optative perfect *s¹ʿd-h rḍw* "may Rḍw help him." In Hismaic we find *kll-h* "all of it" (unpublished), *b-h* "in it" (unpublished); and in Dadanitic *ml-h* "his winter crop" (e.g., U 35/5), "her winter crop" (U 6/3). In Hasaitic there is *ʾḫt-h* "her sister" (Ja 1046). The nature of the texts in Taymanitic and Thamudic B, C, and D means that no certain examples of this suffix have yet been identified.
8. Second dual *-km*: In Safaitic there is *ʿwḏ-km*, "your protection" (referring to two deities, unpublished); compare Classical Arabic *-kumā.*
9. Third dual *-hmy*: This is found only in Dadanitic: *ṯmrt-hmy* "their fruit-trees" (U 69/4); compare Classical Arabic *-humā.*
10. Third dual *-hm*: In Dadanitic there are also examples of *-hm* being used to refer to two people. This could represent a difference in orthography or in pronunciation, or could simply be the use of the plural instead of the dual (see §5.2). Thus *ml-hm* "their winter crop" (referring to a man and a woman, following a verb in the dual U 19/5); *ml-hm* (referring to two men but following a verb in the 3rd pl. masc., U 36/4). In contrast to Dadanitic (cf. **9**), this is the form which would be expected in the Thamudic B and Safaitic orthographies which show neither vowels nor diphthongs. There is one possible example in Thamudic B, *{h-}gml-n kl-hm* "both the camels" (HU 160) and one in Safaitic, *ʿl-hm* "on account of both of them" (HCH 34, referring to two persons).
11. First plural *-n*: Safaitic provides *ʾlh-n* "our god" (C 2526), *l-n* "for us" (C 2840). Hismaic has *ʾs²yʿ-n* "our companions" (unpublished); *wqʿ-n* "our inscription" (MNM 6).
12. Third plural masculine *-hm*: Examples include Dadanitic *ʾḫrt-hm* "their descendants" (referring to three persons, U 90/5); Thamudic B: *kl-hm* (?) "all of them" (HU 160); Safaitic *ʾḫ-hm* "their brother" (LP 413); Hismaic *kll-hm*, "all of them" (unpublished).
13. Third plural feminine: At present there is no certain evidence for this, though Caskel sought unconvincingly to restore one, *-[h]n*, in CLL 69/1, 2.

4.1.8.3 Relative pronouns

1. *mn/m* "who, whoever": Compare Arabic *man.* In Safaitic this relative pronoun occurs in the very common curse *ʿwr m(n) yʿwr* "blind whoever scratches out [the writing],"

and in Hismaic in the expression *kll mn yqry* "anyone who may read" (MNM 6). No certain example of *mn* has yet been found in the other dialects. There is no example in Ancient North Arabian of *mn* or *m* used as an interrogative pronoun, but this is probably due to the nature of the texts.

2. *mh* "which, that which": So far this has been found only in Dadanitic: for example, *m{h} ʾẖḏ* "that which has been taken" (CLL 82/2–3); and *m-l-hm* "that which [belongs] to them" (U 19/5, where the three elements are treated as one unit and the *ā of *mh* is not shown by a *mater lectionis* since it is no longer in final position).

3. *ḏ* "who, whoever, which, that which": Compare the relative pronoun *ḏū* which was particularly characteristic of the early Arabic dialect of the tribe of Ṭayyiʾ (Wright 1896–1898:i, 272–273; Kofler 1940–1942:259–260; Rabin 1951:203–205). In Safaitic, this relative pronoun has so far been found only with reference to people, thus in the very common *ʿwr ḏ yʿwr h-*s^1*fr* "blind whoever scratches out the writing," or *ʿyr m-ḏ qtl-h* "recompense from him who killed him" (LP 385). In Dadanitic, however, *ḏ-* is found referring to both people and things. Thus, *ḏ-kn l-hm b-bdr* "that which [belongs] to them at Bdr" (U 73/4–5) which parallels *m-kn l-h b-ḏṯʿl* "that which [belongs] to him at Ḏ-ṯʿl" (U 59/3–4). There are as yet no certain occurrences in the other dialects.

4. *ḏ* followed by the name of a social group is the normal way of expressing group affiliation in Dadanitic (cf. **5**), as in South Arabian (e.g., AH 1/1–3 [see Sima 1999: 35–36]: N *w*-N *w*-N *w*-N *bnw* N *ḏ*-N.Trib., see also JSLih 197/2, 216/2).

5. *ḏ ʾl:* This phrase is used as one of three ways of expressing affiliation to a social group in Safaitic and is the only method used in Hismaic and Hasaitic. There is no certain example of *ḏ ʾl* in Dadanitic, where *ḏ-* plus the ethnicon is the norm (cf. **4**, the apparant example in AH 19/2 [= U 47/2] has been reread from the photograph as *ḏ ʾlh* and interpreted as an error for *ḏ ʾhl* (?) in Sima 1999:19, 84–85). It is not found at all in Taymanitic, where *ʾl* is simply placed after the last name in the genealogy (see Macdonald 1992a:31, 40, n. 74). There is also no certain example in any of the types of Thamudic. The phrase *ḏ ʾl* is made up of a particle *ḏ* + *ʾl*, a noun meaning any social group from immediate family to nation (cf. Arabic *ʾāl*). It is placed before the name of the group, thus *ḏ ʾl ḥẓy* "of the lineage of Ḥẓy." The masculine *ḏ* seems to have been considered an inseparable particle, since in texts employing word-dividers it is always attached to *ʾl*, in contrast to the feminine *ḏʾt*, which is always separated from *ʾl*. The feminine, *ḏʾt ʾl*, is found in Safaitic (e.g., CSNS 412), Hismaic (unpublished), and Hasaitic (e.g., *Atlal* 6, 1982:139, lines 6–7). Here the ʾ is consonantal, in contrast to Classical Arabic *ḏāt* (perhaps < **ḏaʾt* [?]; cf. the Hebrew feminine demonstrative *zōʾt* < **zāʾt*?). A possible plural is found in Safaitic *ḏw ʾl yẓr* "members of the *ʾl Yẓr*" (C 2156); compare Classical Arabic *ḏawū*. Littmann (1943:xvi) compared this particle *ḏ* to Classical Arabic *ḏū* "possessor of" (< "he of… "?). This is probably also the case with *ḏ* (without *ʾl*) in Dadanitic (see **4**). The exact relationship of this particle to the relative and demonstrative pronouns (§4.1.8.4) is not yet clear.

4.1.8.4 Demonstrative pronouns

A demonstrative pronoun, *zn* (or perhaps *ḏn*) is found in Thamudic D (*zn N*, "this is N") and is used for both masculine and feminine: thus *zn ġnm bn ʿbdmnt* "this is Ġnm son of ʿbdmnt" (JSTham 584); and *zn rqs*^{2} *bnt ʿbdmnt* "this is Rqs^2 daughter of ʿbdmnt" (JSTham 1, and another example in 219). It has been suggested that another demonstrative pronoun, *zt*, is attested in Thamudic C, but this is highly questionable. No demonstratives have yet been identified in Taymanitic or Thamudic B.

The only evidence at present for a demonstrative pronoun in Dadanitic is the adverb *b-ḏh* "here", literally "in this", (Jshih 279). Caskel (1954:64) suggested that some Dadanitic inscriptions begin with a demonstrative pronoun *ḏ*, "this": for example, *ḏ* / *ms¹lmh* "this is Ms¹lmh" (CLL 102); *ḏ ʿlm ʾfkl lt* "this is ʿlm priest of Lt" (CLL 104). However, the *ḏ*-sign at the beginning of these graffiti is almost certainly an apotropaic sign (perhaps *ḏ* for the deity *ḏ-ġbt*); see JSLih 284, where it occurs at the beginning and the end of the text and 297, where these signs are excluded from the cartouche around the name.

4.2 Verbal morphology

The different dialects of Ancient North Arabian contribute fragmentary evidence on verbal inflection for three persons (first, second, and third), three numbers (singular, dual, and plural) and two genders (masculine and feminine), at least in the third-person singular in which the vast majority of these inscriptions are couched. The various verb-stems (see §4.2.2) are inflected in two conjugations – one suffixed, the other prefixed (see §4.2.3). The verb appears in active and passive voice, though the morphology of the latter is difficult to identify, as discussed in §4.2.4. In a similar fashion, modal distinctions are obscured by the orthography; see §4.2.5.

A notable difference between Arabic and Ancient North Arabian lies in the treatment of verbs in which the third radical is /w/ or /y/. In Arabic, even in the pre-Islamic period, verbs of the form *šatawa ("to pass the winter") and *banaya ("to build") appear to have been contracted to *šatā and *banā respectively, since in purely consonantal scripts (e.g., Sabaic) they appear with no final radical (e.g., *bn* for *banā in the ʿIgl bn Hfʿm inscription from Qaryat al-Faw, see Beeston 1979b:1–2) and in those which use *matres lectionis* (e.g., Nabataean) they appear with final -ʾ (= -ā). However, in Ancient North Arabian the third radical is always retained, thus *s²tw* (more commonly *s²ty*, see above) and *bny* (see Macdonald, forthcoming).

This feature is also found in verbs which have a middle radical /w/ or /y/. In Classical Arabic, this is commonly reduced to -ā- when between two short vowels: for example, *ḥawara > *ḥāra*, and *bayata > *bāta*. But in Safaitic, these verbs are written with the middle radical intact, both in the base stem (cf. Arabic Form I), for example *ḥwr* "he returned," *byt* "he spent the night," etc.; and in the ʾ-prefix stem (cf. Arabic Form IV), for example, *ʾʿwr* "he blinded in one eye" (MSTJ 11, cf. Arabic *ʾaʿāra* but also *ʾaʿwara*). It has been suggested that verbs of this type are sometimes found in a contracted form in the base stem (e.g., Safaitic *ṣf* [supposedly representing *ṣāfa] for *ṣyf* "he spent the early summer"), and that the forms with medial *w* or *y* represent the equivalent of the Arabic Forms II (faʿʿala) or III (fāʿala), where the middle radical has a consonantal value (for Dadanitic, Caskel 1954:67; for Safaitic, Littmann 1943:xvii–xviii). However, the only plausible case of such contraction yet identified in an Ancient North Arabian text is *kn* (cf. Arabic *kāna* "he/it exists") in the Dadanitic phrase *ḏ kn-l-h* "that which is to him" (i.e., "is his," e.g., in U 85/3). In most cases, the sense requires the verb written with medial *w/y* to be the equivalent of Classical Arabic Form I rather than Forms II or III, though it should be noted that in most modern Arabic dialects forms I and II of many verbs are used interchangeably with little discernible difference in meaning (I am most grateful to Professor Clive Holes for this information).

There appears to be an interesting difference between Safaitic and Hismaic as regards verbs which (in Arabic) have ʾas their third radical. Thus, *yqrʾ* "he may read" (C 4803) in Safaitic (and Classical Arabic) as against *yqry* in Hismaic (MNM 6). On this root's significance for the etymology of Classical Arabic *qara'a* (meaning "to read") in Ancient North Arabian, see Macdonald, forthcoming. See also Safaitic *ks¹'* "a track" (C 523, cf. Arabic *kus'* "rear, behind") as against Hismaic *ks¹y*, "pursuing" (unpublished, cf. Arabic *kas'*). It is also possible that this '/y contrast is sometimes found in medial position. In one Hismaic text (CTSS 3) we find *d̲yl* for *d̲ 'l*, the normal marker of affiliation to an ethnic or social group. However, this example is so far unique, and elsewhere in Hismaic we find *d̲ 'l*, as in Safaitic. All in all, there are at present too few examples of this apparent '/y contrast to be sure that it is really a dialectal feature.

In certain cases, Safaitic has a geminate verb where the equivalent in Classical Arabic has w or y as the third radical. Thus Safaitic *ġzz* "to raid" as against Arabic *ġazā* (root ġ-z-w, see Beeston 1979a:134).

4.2.1 Verb patterns

Arabic grammar knows fifteen possible *forms* or *patterns* of the verb (conventionally illustrated by the verb *fa'ala*), of which only the first ten are common. Several of these are distinguished by vowel lengthening or by doubling of the second or third radical. Since vowels and doubled consonants are not expressed in the Ancient North Arabian scripts (apart from some final long vowels in Dadanitic which are irrelevant in this case), it would be impossible to distinguish between the equivalents of Arabic Forms I (fa'ala), II (fa''ala), and III (fā'ala), all of which would appear simply as **f'l*, except possibly in the case of geminate verbs (see below). Similarly, V (tafa''ala) and VI (tafā'ala) would both appear as **tf'l*. This means that there is no way of telling whether Ancient North Arabian had a structure of verbal Forms similar to that of Classical Arabic. It therefore seems more prudent to describe the stems simply by the ways in which they appear in the texts.

It might be thought that the geminate verbs would be an exception to the above, since one would expect the equivalent of the Arabic Form I to appear as *ḥl* (*ḥalla), and the equivalent of the Arabic Form II to appear as *ḥll* (*ḥallala). However, the *ḥl* form is rare in Safaitic and is always found in exactly the same contexts as *ḥll* with no apparent difference in sense between the two. Similarly, the verb *wdd* "he loved," which is very common in Thamudic B, is rarely, if ever, found as *wd*. In Dadanitic, there is no clear example of the *ḥl* form in the base stem, though there is considerable variation in the '-prefix stem, namely: *'ẓll* (U 14/2, etc.) as against *'ẓl* (U 18/2, etc.); *'ẓllt* (U 68/4, etc.) as against *'ẓlt* (U 6/2, etc.); *'ẓllw* (U 119/5, etc.) as against *'ẓlw* (U 90/3, etc.) – where Arabic would have *'aẓalla*, *'aẓallat*, *'aẓallū*, respectively. Similarly, in Dadanitic, the active participle *'rr* (HE 1) implies a pronunciation such as *'ārir, in contrast to Arabic *'ārr*. This suggests that in most contexts the second and third radicals of geminate verbs were separated by a vowel in Ancient North Arabian (at least in the pronunciation of some speakers), thus *ḥalal, *'ārir, * 'aẓlal, and so forth, in contrast to Classical Arabic where they were not, thus *ḥalla, 'ārr, 'aẓall*. These verbs cannot therefore be used as evidence of a fa''ala (Form II) in Ancient North Arabian.

4.2.2 Verb-stems

Before presenting the Ancient North Arabian verb-stems, three things must be noted. First, because in Arabic, verbs which contain one or more of the phonemes /'/, /w/, or /y/ behave somewhat differently from those which do not, examples of such verbs in Ancient North Arabian are listed below with the form of the cognate verb in Classical Arabic given for comparison. Second, reconstructions of the vocalized and unassimilated forms of Ancient

North Arabian verbs are purely hypothetical and are based on the equivalent forms in Classical Arabic. They represent only one of several possible realizations of the forms found in the texts, and should not be taken as anything more than a working hypothesis. Finally, references to texts are usually given only for unique or unusual occurrences.

4.2.2.1 Safaitic verb-stems

(5) Base Stem fʿl (cf. Arabic Forms I, II, and III)

Radicals	Safaitic	cf. Arabic
	ḏbḥ "he sacrificed"	*ḏabaḥa*
I = ʾ	*ʾḫḏ* "he took possession of"	*ʾaḫaḏa*
I = ʾ, III = *y*	*ʾty* "he came"	*ʾatā*
I = *w*	*wǧm* "he grieved"	*waǧama*
I = *y*, II = ʾ	*yʾs¹* "he despaired" (SIJ 118)	*yaʾisa*
II = *w*	*ḥwr* "he returned"	*ḥāra*
II = *w*, III = *y*	*nwy* "he migrated with the whole tribe"	*nawā*
II = *y*	*byt* "he spent the night"	*bāta*
III = ʾ	*dṯʾ* "he spent the season of the later rains"	
III = *w*	*s²tw* "he spent the winter"	*šatā*
III = *y*	*bny* "he built"	*banā*
II = III	*ḥll* "he camped"	*ḥalla*

Three derived stems can be identified in Safaitic: (i) the ʾ-prefix (ʾfʿl) stem (cf. Arabic Form IV *ʾafʿala*); (ii) the *t*-prefix (tfʿl) stem (cf. Arabic Forms V *tafaʿʿala* and VI *tafāʿala*); and (iii) the *t*-infix (ftʿl) stem (cf. Arabic Form VIII *iftaʿala*). These are illustrated below.

(6) ʾ-prefix stem ʾfʿl (cf. Arabic Form IV)

Radical	Safaitic	cf. Arabic
	ʾs²rq "he migrated to the inner desert"	*ʾašraqa*
I = *y*, II = ʾ	*ʾyʾs¹* "it drove to despair" (root y-ʾ-s¹, WH 1022)	*ʾayʾasa*
II = *w*	*ʾʿwr* "he blinded in one eye" (root ʿ-w-r, MSTJ 11)	*ʾaʿāra* / *ʾaʿwara*
III = *y*	*ʾʿly* "he raised up" (root ʿ-l-y, WH 1696)	*ʾaʿlā*

Note that *ʾyʾs¹* presents a rare occasion when a diphthong may have been expressed in Safaitic (*ʾayʾasa), unless a short vowel or, more likely, a *shewā* was inserted to ease the transition to the second ʾ.

Safaitic *t*-prefix stems are illustrated by the following:

(7) *t*-prefix stem tfʿl (cf. Arabic Forms V and VI)

Radical	Safaitic	cf. Arabic
I = *n*	*tnẓr* "he looked out for" (root n-ẓ-r, WH 3294)	*tanaẓẓara*
II = *w*	*ts²wq* "he longed for" (root *s²-w-q)	*tašawwaqa*

(8) *t*-infix stem ftʿl (cf. Arabic Forms VIII)

Radical	Safaitic	cf. Arabic
	qttl "he died mad" (root q-t-l, MHES p. 286)	*iqtatala*
I = *n*	*tẓr* "he waited" (root n-ẓ-r)	*intaẓara*
I = *y*, II = ʾ	*tʾs¹* "he despaired" (root y-ʾ-s¹, LP 679)	*ittaʾasa*

On the assimilation of **ntẓr* to *tẓr*, see §3.1.5.

4.2.2.2 *Dadanitic verb-stems*

The Dadanitic base stem can be illustrated by *nḏr* "he vowed" (U 10/2). Examples of base stems with ʾ, w and y radicals and with geminate radicals are presented in (9):

(9) Base stem fʿl (cf. Arabic Forms I, II and III)

Radical	Dadanitic	cf. Arabic
	nḏr "he vowed" (U 10/2)	*naḏara*
I = ʾ	*ʾḫḏ* "he took possession of" (JSLih 45/3)	*ʾaḫaḏa*
I = ʾ, III = *w*	*ʾgw* "he made provision for, attended to" (?) (U 71/2), see Müller in Stiehl 1971:566	
I = *w*, III = *y*	*wdy* "he erected" (?) (JSLih 40/5)	
II = *w*	*kn* "it is" (e.g., U 73/4)	*kāna*
III = *y*	*bny* "he built" (CLL 74/1)	*banā*
II = III	*ʿrr* "he dishonored" (HE 1/4–6)	*ʿarra*

Regarding *ʾgw*, note, however, that Sima (1999: 93–94) takes this as an ʾ-stem of a verb **ngw* which he interprets as "to clear out [an underground water channel]."

Dadanitic is the only Ancient North Arabian dialect in which there is clear evidence of a *h*-prefix stem (10) and even here it coexists with the ʾ-prefix (11) which is the norm in Safaitic. There are insufficient clear examples of verbs in the other dialects to draw any conclusions:

(10) *h*-prefix stem hfʿl

Radical	Dadanitic
	hmtʿ meaning uncertain (*hamtaʿa, root *m-t-ʿ, JSLih 7/3)
I = *w*	*hdqt* "she offered" (*hawdaqat, root *w-d-q, JSLih 62/3)
	hwdqw "they offered" (*hawdaqū, 3rd pl., JSLih 49/5–6)

The retention of the initial *w* of the root in *hwdqw* may reflect uncertainty about representing diphthongs in the Dadanitic script.

(11) ʾ-prefix stem ʾfʿl (cf. Arabic Form IV)

Radical	Dadanitic	cf. Arabic
I = *w*	*ʾdq* "he offered" (root *w-d-q, CLL 62/3)	*ʾawdaqa*
I = *w*, III = *y*	*ʾfy* "he accomplished" (root *w-f-y, U 4/2)	*ʾawfā*
II = III	*ʾẓll* "he performed the *ẓll*-ceremony" (root *ẓ-l-l, e.g., U14/2)	*ʾaẓalla*
	ʾẓl "he performed the *ẓll*-ceremony" (root *ẓ-l-l, e.g., U 18/2)	

It is possible that *tqṭ* (e.g., in JSLih103) represents a ***t*-infix stem (ftʿl)** in Dadanitic. Caskel interpreted this as a metathesized *t*-infix stem of *qṭṭ*, thus *iqtaṭṭa > *itqaṭṭa (CLL

p. 64). However, this is improbable. More likely it represents the *t*-infix stem of a root *wqṭ (*ittaqaṭa), or of a root *nqṭ (*intaqaṭa which, with the expected nasal assimilation (§3.1.5), would become *ittaqaṭa).

Caskel sought to identify one verb with an *n*-prefix (equivalent to the Arabic Form VII) and another with a *st*-prefix (equivalent to the Arabic Form X), but in both cases the interpretations are very uncertain (Caskel 1954:64–65).

4.2.3 Verb conjugations

Two conjugations are identifiable in Ancient North Arabian, one in which person, number and gender are indicated by suffixes and one in which these are indicated by prefixes (and in some persons suffixes as well). If two prefix-conjugations existed, as in some Semitic and Hamitic languages, the Ancient North Arabian writing system, which shows neither vowels nor doubled consonants, has rendered them indistinguishable. On the uses of the suffix- and prefix-conjugations see §§5.3.1 and 5.3.2.

4.2.3.1 Safaitic verb conjugations

Examples of those forms which are attested for the suffix-conjugation in Safaitic are listed in (12).

(12) The suffix-conjugation in Safaitic

Base stem			
Person	Radical	Safaitic	cf. Arabic
3rd sg. masc.		*ḏbḥ* "he sacrificed"	*ḏabaḥa*
	I = ʾIII = *y*	*ʾty* "he came" (e.g., NST 3)	*ʾatā*
	II = *y*	*myt* "he died" (e.g., WH 387)	*māta*
	III = *y*	*rʿy* "he pastured"	*raʿā*
	II = III	*ḥl* "he camped" (Form I)	*ḥalla*
		ḥll "he camped" (Form II)	*ḥallala*
3rd sg. fem.		*gls*^{1}*t* "she stopped briefly" (SIAM i 30)	*ǧalasat*
	II = y	*mtt* "she died" (NST 2)	*mātat*
2nd sg. fem.		*whbt* "may you give" (C 4037, optative §5.3.1)	*wahabti*
ʾ-prefix stem			
Person	Radical	Safaitic	cf. Arabic
3rd sg. masc.		*ʾs*^{2}*rq* "he migrated to the inner desert"	*ʾašraqa*
***t*-prefix stem**			
Person	Radical	Safaitic	cf. Arabic
3rd sg. masc.	II = *w*	*ts*^{2}*wq* "he longed for"	*tašawwaqa*
3rd sg fem.		*ts*^{2}*wqt* "she longed for"	*tašawwaqat*
***t*-infix stem**			
Person	Radical	Safaitic	cf. Arabic
3rd sg. masc.	I = *n*	*tẓr* "he waited"	*intaẓara*

The terminations of the dual, if it existed (cf. Dadanitic and Classical Arabic -*ā*) and the plural (cf. Dadanitic and Classical Arabic -*ū*) of the suffix conjugation are not visible in Safaitic orthography.

Examples of those forms which are attested for the prefix-conjugation in Safaitic are listed in (13).

(13) The prefix-conjugation in Safaitic

Base stem

Person	Radical	Safaitic	cf. Arabic
3rd sg. masc.		*yḫbl* "he may damage"	*yaḫbalu*
	I = *w*	*yʿwr* "he may scratch out"	*yaʿūru*
			yuʿawwiru
	III = ʾ	*yqrʾ* "he may read" (C 4803)	*yaqraʾu*
	III = *y*	*yqry* "he may read" (Hismaic, MNM 6)	
	II = III	*yrbb* "he is training" (C 1186)	*yurabbibu*
3rd pl. masc.	II = *w*	*yʿwrn* "they may scratch out" (WH 2112)	*yaʿūrūna*
			yuʿawwirūna
1st pl.	III = *y*	*nngy* "may we escape" (WH 135)	*nanǧū*
	II = III = *y*	*nḥyy* "may we live prosperously" (Thamudic B, LP 495)	*naḥyā*

ʾ-prefix stem

Person	Radical	Safaitic	cf. Arabic
3rd sg. masc.		*ys²rq* (in *l-ys²rq* "in order to go into the inner desert", LP 180)	*yušriq* (Jussive)

***t*-prefix stem**

Person	Radical	Safaitic	cf. Arabic
3rd sg. masc.	II = *n*	*ytẓr* "he will wait for" (?) (WH 3929)	*yantaẓiru*

4.2.3.2 Dadanitic verb conjugations

(14) The suffix-conjugation in Dadanitic

Base stem

Person	Radical	Dadanitic	cf. Arabic
3rd sg. masc.	I = ʾ	*ʾḫd* "he took possession of" (e.g., JSLih 45/3)	*ʾaḫaḏa*
	I = ʾ, III = *w*	*ʾgw* "he made provision for" (?) (U 71/2) (see Müller in Stiehl 1971:566)	
	III = *y*	*bny* "he built" (CLL 74/1)	*banā*
	II = III	*ʿrr* "may he dishonor" (HE 1/4, see §5.3.1)	*ʿarra*
3rd sg. fem.		*nḏrt* "she vowed" (JSLih 73/4–5)	*naḏarat*
	III = *y*	*bnt* "she built" (root b-n-y, CLL 90/3)	*banat*
3rd pl. masc.	I = ʾ	*ʾḫdw* "they took possession of" (JSLih 79/2)	*ʾaḫaḏū*
	III = *y*	*bnyw* "they built" (CLL 26/2)	*banaw*

On this last, *bnyw*, compare the form binyaw (instead of Classical Arabic *banaw*) in some "old sedentary dialects" of eastern Arabia and many others in Saudi Arabia [Clive Holes].

ʾ-prefix stem

Person	Radical	Dadanitic	cf. Arabic
3rd sg. masc.	I = *w*	*ʾdq* "he offered" (?) (root w-d-q, CLL 62/3)	*ʾawdaqa*
3rd sg. fem.	I = *w*, III = *y*	*ʾft* "she accomplished" (root w-f-y, U 5/2)	*ʾawfat*
	II = III	*ʾẓllt* "she performed the ẓll-ceremony" (U 68/4)	
		ʾẓlt "she performed the ẓll-ceremony" (U 6/2)	*ʾaẓallat*
3rd du. masc.	II = III	*ʾẓlh* "they two performed the ẓll-ceremony" (U 19/3, but see §5.2)	*ʾaẓallā*
3rd pl. masc.	II = III	*ʾẓllw* "they performed the ẓll-ceremony" of four persons (AH 1/3-4, see Sima 1999:35–36)	*ʾaẓallū*

***h*-prefix stem**

Person	Radical	Dadanitic
3rd sg. masc.		*hmtʿ* meaning uncertain (*hamtaʿa, root m-t-ʿ, CLL 39/3)
3rd sg. fem.	I = *w*	*hdqt* "she offered" (?) (*hawdaqat, root w-d-q, JSLih 62/3)
3rd pl. masc.	I = *w*	*hwdqw* "they offered" (?) (*hawdaqū, JSLih 49/5-6)

***t*-infix stem**

Person	Radical	Dadanitic
3rd sg. masc.	I = *n* or *w*	*tqṭ* (*ittaqaṭa ? root n-q-ṭ or w-q-ṭ, e.g., CLL 6, JSLih 103)

(15) The prefix-conjugation in Dadanitic

Base stem

Person	Radical	Dadanitic	cf. Arabic
3rd sg. masc.		*yqʿd* "it will remain" (?) (JSLih 40/4)	*yaqʿudu*

4.2.4 Voice

Since no short vowels are expressed in the Arabian consonantal scripts, it is impossible to tell whether the Ancient North Arabian verbal system had a fully operational passive voice, indicated by changes of internal short vowels, as in Arabic. Thus, *s^1 nt qtl mʿn* (LP 297) presumably means "the year Mʿn was killed," but it is not clear whether *qtl* here is a verb in the passive of the suffix-conjugation (equivalent to Arabic *qutila*), or a *maṣdar*, or verbal noun (equivalent to Arabic *qutl*, i.e., "the year of Mʿn's being killed"), or even a passive participle (cf. Arabic and Aramaic *qatīl*) acting as a verb to produce a virtual relative (i.e. "the year [in which] Mʿn [was] killed"), as, for example, in Nabataean (Cantineau 1930–1932:i, 108); see §5.4.

In Dadanitic, a verb in the passive can occasionally be identified. Thus, for instance, the context in CLL 82/3 requires *ʾh̲d* to be a third singular masculine passive of the suffix-conjugation in *m{h} ʾh̲d ʿl-hmy* "that which has been acquired on behalf of both of them." A possible example of the passive of the prefix-conjugation is *lh yʿd* "he will not be threatened" (root *w-ʿ-d, CLL 31/6, cf. Arabic *lā yūʿadu*).

4.2.5 Mood

Similarly, the fact that no short vowels are indicated in the scripts makes it impossible to tell whether there were indicative, subjunctive, and jussive moods in the prefix-conjugation, distinguished by final short vowels (or lack of them) as in Classical Arabic.

The absence of short vowels in the scripts also means that the imperative can only be identified from context, and there is no visible distinction between the masculine and feminine forms. Thus, in Safaitic, for example, *flṭ* "deliver!" occurs in some contexts where it must be masculine (cf. Arabic *ifliṭ* [masc.]) and others where it must be feminine (cf. Arabic *ifliṭī* [fem.]); similarly with *ʿwr* "blind!" (masc. and fem.; cf. Arabic *ʿawwir* [masc.], *ʿawwirī* [fem.]).

In Dadanitic, many inscriptions end with invocatory formulas consisting of a series of verbs in the imperative or in the suffix-conjugation with an optative sense (see §5.3.1). The most common of these formulas is *f-rḍ-h w-s*^{1}*ʿd-h w-ʾẖrt-h* "and so favour him and help him and his descendants" (see JSLih 8, where the deity is mentioned, and U 14/5–6, etc., where it is not; see Sima 1999:105 for the variants of this formula at al-ʿUḏayb). Here *rḍ* is the masculine imperative of *rḍy* "to favor" (equivalent to Arabic *irḍa*) whereas *s*^{1}*ʿd* can be compared with the Arabic Form III imperative *sāʿid*.

In the case of verbs whose first radical is *w* there seems to be a distinction between Safaitic and Thamudic B, though the small number of examples is restricted to the verb *whb*, which in Classical Arabic is exceptional in this respect (see Wright 1896–1898:i, 78–79). We cannot therefore be certain how widespread a phenomenon this was. In Safaitic (in all but two examples), the initial *w* of *whb* is retained in the imperative, whereas in Thamudic B it seems to be dropped (as in Classical Arabic). Thus, in Safaitic we find *w-whb l-h nqmt* "and give to him booty" (C 1808, cf. Classical Arabic *hab*); and *h rḍw whb l-h*... "O Rḍw give to him..." (WH 190). On the other hand, there are two Safaitic texts in which the imperative appears as *hb*: *h rḍw hb l-ʿbdʾl nqmt* "O Rḍw give to ʿbdʾl booty" (LP 460) and *h ʾlt flṭ l-bgʿ w-hb l-h nʿm* "O ʾlt [grant] deliverance to Bgʿ and give to him prosperity" (LP 504), though in both cases this could be due to haplography, as it could be in the Thamudic B text *h rḍw hb s*^{2}*km* "O Rḍw give a gift" (unpublished).

4.2.6 Participles

As a verbal noun, the participle in Ancient North Arabian was inflected according to gender, number, and voice. On the uses of the participle see §5.4.

4.2.6.1 Active participle

Base stem

	sg. masc.	*qtl* (cf. Ar. "*qātil*): Safaitic, in *ṯʾr mn qtl-h* "revenge on his killer" (CSNS 1004);
	pl.	*qbrn* (cf. Ar. *qābirūna*): Safaitic, in *qbrn ḏw ʾl yẓr* "members of the ʾl Yẓr having performed the burial" (C 2156), see §5.4;
II = *w*	sg. masc.	*mʿwr* (cf. Ar. *muʿawwir*): Safaitic, in *ʿwr l-m ʿwr* "blindness to a scratcher-out" (WH 408, etc.)
II = *w*, III = *y*	sg. masc.	*nwy* (cf. Ar. *nāwin*): Safaitic, in *rʿy h-nẖl nwy* "he pastured this valley while on migration" (C 3181)
III = *y*	sg. masc.	*rʿy* (cf. Ar. *rāʿin*): Safaitic, in *ṣyr rʿy ḥrt* "he was on his way to permanent water pasturing the *ḥarra* [basalt desert]" (C 3131)
II = III	sg. masc.	*ʿrr* (**ʿārir*, cf. Ar. *ʿārr*): Dadanitic, in *ʿrr ḏġbt ʿrr h-s*^{1}*fr ḏh* "may Ḏġbt [the chief deity of Liḥyān] dishonor him who dishonors [lit. 'the dishonorer of] this inscription" (HE 1)

4.2.6.2 Passive participle

There appear to be two morphological types of passive participle in the base stem – the *faʿīl*-type and the *mafʿūl*-type. Safaitic singular and plural examples of each follow:

1. *The faʿīl-type*: Singular masculine *qtl* "killed" (e.g., LP 658; see §4.2.4); singular feminine (i.e., of the form *faʿīlat*) *trḥt* "untimely dead" (e.g., NST 2); plural masculine *ḥrbn* "plundered and left destitute"(C 657, *pace* ed.; cf. Arabic *ḥarībīn*, oblique case).
2. *The mafʿūl-type*: Singular masculine *mqtl* "killed, murdered" (e.g., HCH 76; cf. Arabic *maqtūl*); plural masculine *mḥrbn* "plundered and left destitute" (HCH 71; cf. Arabic *maḥrūbīn*, oblique case).

In Dadanitic, the only clear participial form, *h-mqtl* (JSLih 40/9), is in a damaged context and could represent either an active participle (cf. Arabic *muqattil* "mass killer") or a passive (cf. Arabic *maqtūl* "killed, murder victim"). There are no certain cases in the other dialects.

The feminine, dual, and external masculine plural forms of participles are similar to those of other nouns; see §4.1.2.

4.3 Particles

4.3.1 The definite article

The most obvious difference between the two branches of North Arabian lies in the form of the definite article. In Old and Classical Arabic and the majority of the vernaculars, it is *ʾal-*, while in Ancient North Arabian it is either *h-* (*hn-*) or in some dialects possibly zero. The earliest evidence for both comes from the fifth century BC in the epithet of a goddess which Herodotus (3.8) quotes in its Old Arabic form, Ἀλιλάτ (*ʾal-ʾilat), and which occurs in its Ancient North Arabian form, *hn-ʾlt*, in a number of Aramaic inscriptions on silver bowls found at Tell al-Maskhūṭah in northeastern Egypt (Rabinowitz 1956). In both cases, it means literally "*the* goddess."

A definite article has not yet been identified in Hasaitic (except in names) or in Thamudic C and D, and there are doubts whether Hismaic employed one at all (see below). In Taymanitic, Thamudic B, and Safaitic, it is *h-* in all contexts. Since the script shows neither vowels nor the doubling of consonants, it is impossible to tell how this *h-* was vocalized and whether it was followed by systematic strengthening or doubling of the following consonant (as, for instance, in Hebrew, but in contrast to Arabic; see Macdonald, forthcoming, *contra* Ullendorff 1965). In Dadanitic (and in some names spread over a wide geographical and chronological range) it has the form *hn-* before ʾ and ʿ. In an inscription in the Safaitic script, the gentilic *hn-ḥwly* (a tribe apparently from the region of Dadan) attests to the use of this form before *ḥ* (Macdonald 1993:308). There are as yet no examples of the article before a word beginning with *h*, but it is possible that it was *hn-* here as well.

Traditionally, it has been assumed that this *hn-* in Dadanitic was the survivor of the original form of the article before all phonemes, in all Ancient North Arabian dialects. However, had this been so, we would expect to find scattered examples of this form in other dialects (which so far we have not) and in front of other phonemes in Dadanitic (see Macdonald 2000:41–42). At present, therefore, it seems more likely that this was a development peculiar to Dadanitic and that, even there, it was simply a euphonic or dissimilatory phenomenon before glottal and pharyngal consonants.

It was once thought that a definite article *hl-* existed in Dadanitic. However, the only examples were in two texts, one of which has now been identified as being an abecedary in the South Semitic order (JSLih 158, see Müller 1982:22); while the other is not in the

Dadanitic language but in Old Arabic written in the Dadanitic script, where *h-l-* represents a preposed demonstrative, *h-*, plus the Old Arabic definite article (ʾ)l- (JSLih 71/8, see Beeston *et al.* 1973:69–70 and Macdonald 2000:70, n. 90 and forthcoming). Compare the situation in many modern Arabic dialects, where an invariant demonstrative *ha-* with a relatively weak demonstrative force is placed before the article (e.g., ha-l-bēt "this house," ha-s-sana "this year"; Holes 1995:152–153).

In Safaitic, the distinction between the definite article and the nearer demonstrative ("this") is not always clear and it is possible that the article had a mild demonstrative implication (e.g., *h-dr* "the/this place," *h-s¹nt* "this year"), as it can have in Arabic (e.g., *ʾal-yawm* "the/this day," i.e., "today"). This, of course, is different from the case in JSLih 71/8 and the modern Arabic dialects mentioned in the previous paragraph, where the demonstratives *h-* and ha- respectively are prefixed to the article. In Hismaic, on the other hand, *h-* is relatively rare in contexts where it would appear to represent the definite article. Thus, for instance, there is, as yet, no example in Hismaic of affiliation to a social group being expressed by the *nisbah* (see §4.1.6), in contrast to Safaitic where it is common (e.g., *h-g̲dly* "the G̲dlite"), while in "signatures" to rock drawings *l*N *bkrt* alternates with *l*N *h-bkrt*, "by N is the young she-camel," where in Safaitic only the latter is found. The few possible examples of *h-* as definite article in Hismaic could equally well represent the nearer demonstrative "this" and there is, as yet, no case where it could not. It is therefore an open question whether Hismaic employed a form of determination which does not show up in the script (e.g., a final vowel, as in the Aramaic "determined state"), or had no definite article (as, in effect, in Syriac).

4.3.2 Demonstrative adjectives

In Dadanitic and Hismaic demonstrative adjectives are formed with *d̲* and follow a noun defined by the article or a pronominal suffix.

In Dadanitic the masculine demonstrative adjective is *d̲h* (probably *d̲ā), for example *h-s¹fr d̲h* "this writing" (HE 1) and the feminine is *d̲t* (probably *d̲āt), for example *h-ṣfḥt d̲t* "this section of cliff" (JSLih 66/2). The demonstrative adjective *hd̲h* (probably *hād̲ā) is found in *h-{ṣ}lmn hd̲h* "this statuette (?)" (JSLih 82/1, cf. Arabic *hād̲ā*).

In Hismaic, a demonstrative adjective *d̲ʾ* is attested only once, in *wqʿ-n d̲ʾ* "this our inscription" (MNM 6, *pace* ed. who reads *d̲h*, though ʾ is clear on the photograph). This is a curious form since it would be highly unusual for the ʾ to represent a vowel in Hismaic. If the ʾ represents a consonant, perhaps compare *d̲ʾt* in §4.1.8.3, **5**. It seems possible that in the relatively rare cases in Hismaic where *h-* is prefixed to a noun with no other visible form of definition, that this represents a demonstrative adjective rather than the definite article. See the discussion in §4.3.1.

In Safaitic, the prefixed *h-* is the only form of demonstrative so far clearly attested (see §4.3.1).

4.3.3 Introductory particles

Most of the Ancient North Arabian graffiti and the majority of the Dadanitic monumental inscriptions begin with the name of the "author" (see §5.1.1). In the Taymanitic, Thamudic B, C, and D, Safaitic, and some Hismaic graffiti, the name is usually introduced by a particle. In Taymanitic, this is often *l* (known as the *lām auctoris*), which is probably the preposition "for, of" (see §4.3.4) which in this context means "by" in the sense of authorship, as it can in Arabic. However, a particle *lm* is also used, apparently with the same meaning (perhaps cf. Hebrew *lᵉmô*, found only in the Book of Job, the language of which is thought to exhibit many

North Arabian features). This particle is characteristic of Taymanitic (Winnett 1980:135–136). What is possibly a dialectal variant of this, *nm*, is found as an introductory particle in Thamudic B, while Thamudic D texts often begin *zn* "this is . . . ." In Safaitic, all but a handful of texts begin with the *lām auctoris*, while in Hismaic the author's name can be introduced by the *lām auctoris*, or by the conjunctions *w* or *f* (see §4.3.6). In Dadanitic, no introductory particle is used (except possibly in JSLih 128). Since most of the Hasaitic inscriptions are gravestones they begin *wgr w-qbr* "tomb-chamber and grave" (see Livingstone 1984:102) or *nfs^1 w-qbr* "memorial and grave."

4.3.4 Vocative particles

The vocative particle is *h* in Dumaitic, Dadanitic (JSLih 8), Thamudic B, Safaitic, Hismaic, and Hasaitic (sole example unpublished). None has yet been identified in Taymanitic and Thamudic C and D. Given the nature of these texts it is not surprising that it has been found only in prayers (e.g., *h rḍw s^1 ʿd* N, "O Rḍw help N"; *h lt s^{1}lm*, "O Lt [grant] security"). In origin, it was probably a sound used to attract attention (*hā), and can be paralleled in Arabic by the *hā* which forms the initial part of a number of interjections and of the demonstrative *hāḏā* "this" (Wright 1896–1898:i, 268, Brockelmann 1908–1913:i, 503).

It has been suggested that in Safaitic the forms *hylt* "O Lt" (or "O Ylt") and so forth represent a variant vocative particle, *hy*, equivalent to Arabic *hayā* (Winnett and Harding 1978:47) or *ʾayyuhā* (Littmann 1943:21), though other explanations for this are possible. In fact, the particle *ʾyh* (*ʾayyuhā) occurs in the invocation *w-ʾyh lt* "and O Lt" in a Safaitic inscription (unpublished) recently found in southern Syria.

In some Hismaic texts an *-m* is suffixed to the divine names *Lh* and *Lt* in invocations, thus *h lh-m*, *h lt-m* (King 1990:80). This is probably an asseverative particle which may be compared with the *-mma* in Arabic *allāhumma* (sometimes *yā allāhumma*), and possibly the *-m-* in such names as *ʾabîmāʾēl* (Genesis 10:28), and *ʾbmʿṯtr*, and others from Haram and its environs on the northern borders of Yemen, where the local form of Sabaic may have have included a number of North Arabian features (Müller 1992:20).

4.3.5 Prepositions

1. *ʾl* "towards" (cf. Arabic *ʾilā*), "for" (after the verb *ts^{2}wq* "to yearn"): Safaitic and Hismaic.

2. *ʿdky* "up to": Dadanitic (JSLih 72/6, see Müller 1982:33 and Beeston 1979a:4).

3. *ʿl* "over, on, for, against" (cf. Arabic *ʿalā*): Safaitic and Hismaic; in Dadanitic it is usually found as *ʿly* with nouns (e.g., JSLih 81/4, 5) but as *ʿl* with pronominal suffixes (e.g., JSLih 77/3). This suggests that the final sound was a diphthong, which would not be represented in the Safaitic and Hismaic scripts. Since Dadanitic orthography only shows diphthongs in final position, the *-y* was not written when followed by a pronominal suffix. However, there are also a few examples in Dadanitic of the form *ʿl* without a pronominal suffix (e.g., U 73/4) which may indicate a pronunciation with final *-ī* or simply an uncertainty about the representation of diphthongs.

4. *ʿn pace* Caskel (1954:72), there is no clear evidence in Ancient North Arabian for a preposition *ʿn* "from" (cf. Arabic *ʿan*).

5. *b* "in, at, with, by" (cf. Arabic *bi-*): Taymanitic, Dadanitic, Thamudic B, Safaitic, and Hismaic.

6. *bʿd* "after" (cf. Arabic *baʿda*): Safaitic (e.g., SIJ 787).

The preposition occurs in Dadanitic with the meaning "for the sake of" (e.g., U 5/4, etc.). Compare Hebrew *baʿad* which is used in this sense and in a very similar context in Ezekiel

45:22 and Job 42:8 (see Stiehl 1971:9). Clive Holes informs me that in eastern Arabia a woman will plead with a loved one *yā baʿad rūḥ-ī! yā baʿad ʿēn-ī! yā baʿad čibd-ī!,* which is usually explained as "O you who are [the dearest thing to me] *after* my spirit/eyes/liver," but may in fact mean "please, O X, for the sake of my spirit/eyes/liver" (personal communication) Note that Sima (1999:99–105) interprets *bʿd* as "in the direction of" in the same Dadanitic texts.

7. *bn* "between" (cf. Arabic *bayna*): Safaitic, in *h lt whbt* s^2*nʾ-h bn yd-h* "O Lt may you give his enemy into his hands" (C 4037). In Arabic, the expression *bayna yaday-hi,* "between his hands," has come to mean "in front of," but in Safaitic it seems to retain its literal sense. In the phrase s^1*nt ws*^{1}*q bn rm nbṭ,* which appears to mean "the year of the conflict between the Romans and the Nabataeans" (C 4866), either the connective *w* (see §4.3.5) was not considered necessary between the two nouns (as it would be in Arabic), or it was accidentally omitted by the author or the copyist.

8. *dn* "without" (cf. Arabic *dūna*): Hismaic (unpublished).

9. *f pace* Winnett and Harding (1978:643) and Caskel (1954:72), there is no clear evidence in Ancient North Arabian for a preposition *f* "in" (cf. Arabic *fī*).

10. *ẖlf* "after, behind" (cf. Arabic *ẖalfa*): Dadanitic (JSLih 70/4).

11. *l* "to, for, on behalf of" (cf. Arabic *li-*): Taymanitic (*nṣr l-ṣlm,* "he gave help to Ṣlm," e.g., WTay 15), Dadanitic, Thamudic B, Safaitic, Hismaic. The preposition is attested in several additional uses:

A. *Indicating possession:* Safaitic (e.g., *l*-N *bn* N *h-rgm* "the cairn is N son of N's", WH 329); Dadanitic (e.g., *l*-N *bn* N *h-qbr ḏh* "this grave is N son of N's", JSLih 312).

B. *In dating formulas:* Dadanitic (e.g., s^1*nt ẖms*^{1} **l**-*hnʾs*^{1} *bn tlmy mlk lḥyn* "year five **of** Hnʾs^1 son of Tlmy, king of Lḥyn", JSLih 75/5–7).

C. *Indicating motion:* Safaitic (e.g., *l-mdbr* "to the inner desert", LP 180).

D. *Indicating purpose:* Safaitic, used with verbs in the prefix-conjugation (e.g., *l-ys*^{2}*rq* "in order to migrate to the inner desert", LP 180).

12. *ldy* "to, up to" (cf. Arabic *ladā*): Dadanitic (JSLih 77/3).

13. *mʿ* "in company with" (cf. Arabic *maʿa / maʿ*): Safaitic (e.g., LP 325); Dadanitic (JSLih 52/3).

14. *mn/m* "from" (cf. Arabic *min*): Thamudic B, Dadanitic, Safaitic, Hismaic *passim.* In Safaitic also with the sense "on account of" (e.g. SIAM:34).

15. *qbl* "before" (temporal, cf. Arabic *qabla*): Dadanitic (CLL 80/4).

16. *tḥt* "below" (cf. Arabic *taḥta*): Dadanitic (JSLih 50/4).

4.3.6 Conjunctions

Two conjunctions, *w* "and" and *f-* "and (so)" "and (then)", are attested in Ancient North Arabian. The former is found in all dialects, the latter so for only in Dadanitic, Safaitic, and Hismaic (see the discussion in Sima 1999:110–114).

4.3.7 Other particles

1. *ʾḏh* "when" (cf. Arabic *ʾiḏā*): Dadanitic (JSLih 55/2).
2. *ʾn* "that" (cf. Arabic *ʾan*): Safaitic, in s^1*mʿ ʾn myt flfṣ* "he heard that Philip had died" (MHES p. 286).
3. *ʾn* "if" (cf. Arabic *ʾin*)?: Dadanitic (JSLih 40/6, in a very damaged context).
4. *ʾn* "verily" (cf. Arabic *ʾinna*)?: Dadanitic (JSLih 40/7, in a very damaged context).

5. *lh* negative particle (cf. Arabic *lā*): Dadanitic, *f-lh yʿd*, "and so he will not be threatened" (?) in a very damaged context (JSLih 40/6).
6. *lm* negative particle followed by the prefix-conjugation (cf. *lam* plus the jussive in Classical Arabic): Safaitic (unpublished). This particle, which is characteristic of North Arabian, is also found in some of the texts from Haram on the northern borders of Yemen which are in Sabaic with some North Arabian features (see Macdonald 2000:49–50, 55–56).

4.4 Numerals

4.4.1 Cardinal numbers

These are attested in Dadanitic, Safaitic, and Hasaitic.

4.4.1.1 Cardinal numbers in Dadanitic

The Dadanitic cardinal numbers are presented in Table 8.2.

The final entry in the table is so read by Sima, though the first and last words are more or less invisible on the published photograph and these lines were not copied by Abū al-Ḥasan.

It will be seen from Table 8.2 that there are some interesting similarities and differences between the treatments of numerals in Dadanitic and in Classical Arabic.

1. As far as we can tell on present evidence, numerals precede the nouns to which they refer; nouns following the numbers three to ten are in the plural, while those following eleven and upwards are in the singular, as in Classical Arabic. However, the situation is obscured by the fact that, in Dadanitic, the vast majority of the examples of numerals are in dates, where the noun (*s*^{1}*nt*) precedes the number and is, by definition, singular.

2. The principles of agreement in gender with the preceding or following noun appear to be roughly the same as in Classical Arabic, namely that numerals of a feminine form refer to nouns which (in the singular) are masculine and vice versa. Since *ʾym* "days" follows the forms of numerals referring to a feminine noun in both Dadanitic (*ʿs*^{2}*r ʾym*) and Safaitic (*s*^{1}*t ʾym*), it seems probable that the word **ym* "day" must have been regarded as feminine in these dialects (see §4.1.1).

3. If this is correct, it is probable that the final *t* in *ṯlt* (*ṯlt ʾym*) is part of the root (*ṯlt* < *ṯlṯ) rather than the equivalent of Arabic *tāʾ marbūṭah* (see §3.1.1). Unfortunately, the word *mʿn* in *tlt mʿn* has not yet been satisfactorily interpreted and so we cannot be certain whether or not it is the plural of a feminine noun and therefore whether the second *t* in *tlt* should be explained in the same way. However, it should be noted that the development */ṯ/ > /t/ is not typical of Dadanitic and so far appears to be peculiar to this word. The Dadanitic form, *ṯlṯt*, used with masculine nouns and Safaitic *ṯlṯt*/*ṯlṯ* are identical to the Classical Arabic forms.

4. In compound numbers, the units continue to take the opposite gender to the noun, but from twenty upwards the tens are (probably) of common gender, again as in Classical Arabic. However, an interesting difference is observable in the numbers thirteen through nineteen, where in Classical Arabic (and Safaitic, see §4.4.1.2) the ten takes the same gender as the noun and the unit the opposite. In the only Dadanitic example available so far, *s*^{1}*nt ʿ{s*^{2}*}r w-s*^{1}*bʿ* (where Classical Arabic would have *sanat sabʿa ʿašrata*), either the ten was regarded as of common gender (like twenty, etc.) or it behaved in the same way as the units, taking the opposite gender to the noun.

5. In the compound numerals, the larger unit is generally placed before the smaller, contrary to the practice in Classical Arabic. This occurs both in the numbers from thirteen through nineteen (e.g., *ʿs*^{2}*r w-s*^{1}*bʿ* "seventeen," cf. Classical Arabic *sabʿa ʿašrata* and Safaitic

Table 8.2 The cardinal numerals in Dadanitic

	Masculine	Common	Feminine
1			*s^1nt ʾḥdy* "year one" (CLL 26/4)
2			*s^1nt ṯtn* "year two" (JSLih 45/3)
3	*ṯlṯt ʾẓlt* "three ẓll ceremonies" (U 32/3–4) *ṯlṯt ʾẓl* "three ẓll ceremonies" (U 50/2–3)		*ṯlt ʾym* "three days" (JSLih 68/4) notes 2,3 *tlt mʿn* "three . . . " (?, JSLih 47/2) note 3
5			*s^1nt ḫms^1* "year five" (JSLih 75/5; Scagliarini 1996:96–97)
10	*ʿs^2rt mnh{l}* "ten canals" (JSLih 177/1)		*ʿs^2r ʾym* "ten days" (CLL 86/3) note 2
17			*s^1nt ʿ{s^2}r w-s^1bʿ* "year seventeen" (U 8/4–5)
20		*s^1nt ʿs^2rn* "year twenty" (JSLih 68/2–3; AH 63/5, 64/7–8? see Sima 1999:38)	
22			*s^1nt ʿs^2rn {w}-ṯtn* "year twenty-two" (JSLih 77/11)
29			*s^1nt ʿs^2rn w-ts^{1}ʿ* "year twenty-nine" (CLL 86/2–3; JSLih 83/6)
35			*s^1nt ṯlṯn w ḫms^1* "year thirty-five" (JSLih 82/3–4)
40		*ʾrbʿn s^1lʿt* "forty drachmas" (JSLih 177/2)	
120		*mʾt w-ʿs^2rn . . .* (JSLih 77/5)	
140		*mʾt w-ʾrbʿn . . .* (CLL 33/2)	
145		*mʾt w-ʾrbʿn w-ḫms^1 nḫl?* "one hundred and forty-five palm trees" (U 23/4–5 = AH 41)	

ṯmn ʿs^2rt, see §4.4.1.2), and from twenty onwards (e.g., *ṯlṯn w-ḫms^1*, cf. Classical Arabic *ḫamsun wa-ṯalāṯūna*). Note also that, in the teens, unit and ten are connected by *w-* in Dadanitic but not in Arabic. See the discussion in Sima 1999:119, but note that the supposed examples of *s^1tt ʿs^2r* and *s^1t ʿs^2r* are very doubtful and that the restoration *ʿs^2r w-t[s^1]{ʿ}* in AH 81/6 (n. 28) looks unlikely on the published copy.

6. The form *ṯtn* may have resulted from an original *ṯintān (i.e., without a prosthetic initial vowel, cf. Classical Arabic *ṯintāni* beside *iṯnatāni*, also ṯintēn in modern dialects of central and eastern Arabia) with the assimilation of vowelless /n/ characteristic of Dadanitic and other Ancient North Arabian dialects (see §3.1.5).

4.4.1.2 Cardinal numbers in Safaitic

In Safaitic no example of the numeral "one" has yet been found, though a verb *wḥd* "he was alone" is well attested. The dual is used for "two". The other Cardinal numbers attested in Safaitic are as follows:

(16)	*Masculine*	*Common*	*Feminine*
3	*ṯlṯt ʾs^2hr* "three months" (WH 3792a)		*ṯlṯ s^1nn* "three years" (AZNG)
4			*ʾrbʿ s^1nn* "four years" (WH 3094)
5	*ḫms^1t ʾmny* "five minas" [a coin] (C 3916)		*ḫms^1 ws^1q* "five herds of camels" (C 2088)
6			*s^1t ʾym* "six days" (unpublished)
18			*s^1nt ṯmn ʿs^2rt* "year eighteen" (LP 1064)
100		*mʾt frs^1* "a hundred horsemen" (WH 1849)	

In contrast to Dadanitic, the rules of agreement in gender and number between a numeral and the noun to which it refers appear to be the same in Safaitic as in Classical Arabic, except in the case of *s^1t ʾym* (see note 2 above). Similarly, the form of the single example of a compound number in *s^1nt ṯmn ʿs^2rt* is paralleled almost exactly by Classical Arabic *sanat ṯamāniya ʿašrata.*

4.4.1.3 *Cardinal numbers in Hasaitic*

The following cardinal numbers, all feminine, are attested in Hasaitic:

(17) 6	*s^1nt s^1t*	(unpublished)
27	*s^1nt ʿs^2{rn} w s^1b{ʿ}*	(Robin-Mulayḥa 1, *contra* ed.)
34	*ʾrbʿ w-ṯlṯn s^1nt*	giving a person's age (Livingstone 1984:100)

4.4.2 Ordinal numbers

No ordinal numbers have yet been identified.

4.4.3 Totality

The notion of totality is expressed in Safaitic, Hismaic, and Dadanitic by *kll* (*kulil (?), cf. Arabic *kull*). As in Arabic, when *kll* is followed by an undefined entity it means "each, every": for example, *kll ʿs^2r ṣdq* "every true kinsman" (HCH 191, Safaitic; MNM 6, Hismaic). When it is followed by a defined entity (so far only pronominal suffixes are attested), it means "all" or "the whole": for example, in Dadanitic *h-mqʿd kll-h* "the whole sitting-place" (HE 1); Safaitic *ʾs^2yʿ-h kll-hm* "all his companions" (LP 243).

5. SYNTAX

Given the fragmentary and formulaic nature of the available documents, no coherent description of Ancient North Arabian syntax can yet be attempted. The following notes represent some miscellaneous features which can be gleaned from the Dadanitic and Safaitic texts.

5.1 Word order

5.1.1 Word order in verbal sentences

5.1.1.1 Dadanitic

The majority of Dadanitic inscriptions begin with the subject followed by the verb followed by the object (i.e., they are SVO) and then adverbial or prepositional phrases:

(18) 1. N *bn* NN *qrb h-ṣlm l-d̲ġbt*
"N son of NN offered the statue to D̲ġbt" (JSLih 41/1–3)
2. N *ktb-h b-d̲h*
"N wrote it here" (JSLih 279)
3. N_1 *w*-N_2 [SUBJECTS] *ʾẓlh* [verb] *h-ẓll* [OBJECT] ***l**-d̲ġbt* ***b**-khl* ***bʿd*** *ml-hm* ***b**-bdr* [PREPOSITIONAL PHRASES]
"N1 and N2 have performed the ẓll ceremony **for** D̲ġbt **in** Khl **for the sake of** their winter crops **in** Bdr" (U 19/1–6)

This order may not reflect normal practice but rather the nature of the texts, which are mainly dedications, records of the performance of religious rites, and graffiti, in which the name of the "author" was inevitably given prominence.

By contrast, the VSO (or VOS) order, which is the norm in Classical Arabic, is very rarely attested in the Dadanitic inscriptions:

(19) *h̲ls[1]* N_1 *bn* N_2
died N_1 son of N_2
"N_1 son of N_2 died" (literally "was carried off," CLL 78, 79, 80)

5.1.1.2 Safaitic

Unlike the Dadanitic inscriptions, the Safaitic graffiti usually begin with the *lām auctoris* (see §4.3.2) followed by the author's name and part of his genealogy. Any statement is then linked to the genealogy by the connective *w* "and." This permits a natural word order within the statement, in contrast to the Dadanitic texts where it may have been distorted by the need to begin the first sentence with the author's name for the sake of emphasis.

The usual word order in Safaitic is VSO or VOS, as in Classical Arabic. Even if they existed, case endings, being short vowels, would not show up in Safaitic orthography and it is therefore sometimes impossible to decide which is the subject and which the object in a sentence. Thus:

(20) 1. *s[1]nt ḥrbt ʾl ʿwd̲ ʾl ṣbḥ,*
"the year the ʾl ʿwd̲ made war on [or "plundered"] the ʾl Ṣbḥ," or *vice versa* (SIJ 59, see also C 2577)
2. *s[1]nt s[1]lm ʾl bʿd ʾl ʿwd̲,*
"the year the ʿl Bʿd made peace with the ʾl ʿwd̲," or *vice versa* (C 4394, wrongly transliterated in C)

The indirect object can also precede the direct object:

(21) 1. *ngy* *b-h-bqr* *h-nh̲l,*
he fled with-the-cows the-valley
"and he fled the valley with the cows" (LP 90)

2. *bny* *l-*s^1*ʿd* *h-rgm,*
he built for-S^1ʿd the-cairn
"he built the cairn for S^1ʿd" (WH 421)

Verbs in Safaitic can take multiple direct objects: for example, *rʿy h-ʾbl h-nẖl bql,* "he pastured the camels (*h-ʾbl*) [in] the valley (*h-nẖl*) [on] spring herbage (*bql*)" (C 2670). Compare *rʿy h-nẖl bql nʿm-hm,* "he pastured their small cattle (*nʿm-hm*) [in] the valley [on] spring-herbage" (C 1534).

5.1.2 Word order in nominal sentences

In common with Arabic and other Semitic languages, the Ancient North Arabian dialects used nominal sentences instead of employing the verb "to be" as a copula.
Thus in Dadanitic: *w-ʾn* N *bn* N, "and I [am] N son of N" (CLL 57/2; also in Thamudic D e.g., JSTham 637, and Hismaic e.g., King 1990: KCJ 646)

l-N *h-mṯbr* (literally "to/for N [is] the grave-chamber"), i.e., "the grave-chamber belongs to N" (JSLih 366/1)

There are numerous examples in Safaitic. Thus

l-N *h-ẖṭṭ,* "By N [are] the carvings" (e.g., WH 368)

l-N *w-h-ẖṭṭ,* 'By N and the carving [is by him?]' (WH 353)

l-N *w-h-rgm,* "For N and the cairn [is his]" (HCH 1, 2), where we know from other texts that this person was the occupant of the grave under the cairn.

l-N *w-l-h h-bkrt,* "By N and the young she-camel [is] his [or "is by him"]" (WH 2833b)

l-N *w-l-h-rgm,* "For N and for him/her [is the] cairn" (WH 3420, etc.); for the assimilation of the article to the preceding enclitic personal pronoun, see §4.1.8.2, **7**.

w-bʾs^1 *l-h,* literally "and distress [was] to him", i.e. "he was in distress" (CSNS 779)

l N *h-dr,* literally " by/for N the place". This ia a very common expression in the Safaitic inscriptions. It is unlikely to be a claim to personal real estate, something which is impractical in the nomadic life. Instead, it almost certainly means simply "N was here".

Note also the word order in the nominal phrase

l-N *b-m*s^1*rt ʾl ʿmrt fr*s^1, "by N, a horseman (*fr*s^1) in the unit (*m*s^1*rt*) of the ʾl ʿmrt" (Macdonald 1993: 374).

5.1.3 Annexation

Annexation (the *iḍāfa* of the Arab grammarians) is a fundamental feature of Semitic grammar (see Ch. 2) in which two or more elements are bound together to form a grammatical and semantic unit. Nothing is allowed to intervene between the elements (except in certain very specific circumstances of which we have no examples in Ancient North Arabian) and thus items such as adjectives (including demonstrative adjectives) follow the final element even if they refer to the first. The unit as a whole is defined or undefined according to the nature of the final element even if one of the preceding elements would otherwise normally take the definite article (see under Safaitic, below).
Examples of annexation in Dadanitic are:
Undefined *b-ḥqwy kfr* (*ḥaqway) 'on two sides of a tomb' (JSLih 75/3)
Defined 3-element annexation *kbry* s^{2c}*t h-nṣ* "the two kabīrs of the association of H-NṢ" (CLL 77/3-4)
Defined + a demonstrative *ʿrr h-*s^1*fr ḏh* "the dishonorer of this inscription" (HE 1/5-6).
Examples of annexation in Safaitic are:

Undefined + adjective *kll ʿs²r ṣdq* "every true friend" (HCH 191, also in Hismaic MNM 6)
Defined by the article (1) *mʿwr h-s¹fr* "the scratcher-out of the writing" (e.g., WH 1679),
(2) *nmrt h-s¹lṭn* "Namārah of the government" (LP 540). When not annexed, the place-name is *h-nmrt* (e.g., LP 330, cf. the modern name, *al-Namārah*)
Defined by a name *ḥrb nbṭ* "the war of the Nabataeans" (C 3680).

5.1.4 Demonstrative Adjectives

When the modified noun is part of a noun phrase, two constructions are possible: (i) *h-ẓll ḏh l-ḏġbt* (U 33/2-3) or (ii) *h-ẓll l-ḏġbt ḏh* (U 4/3), both of which mean "this ẓll-ceremony for Ḏġbt." The second construction is bizarre and may be an error on the part of the engraver.

5.2 Agreement

In Ancient North Arabian verbs agree with their subjects in gender and number, regardless of their position in the sentence (in contrast to Classical Arabic, Wright 1896–1898: ii, 289–290).

In Dadanitic, the only dialect in which it is identifiable, the use of the dual in verbal agreement is erratic. Thus, it is used after two subjects in some texts:

(22) N_1 *w*-N_2 *ʾẓlh h-ẓll*
"N_1 and N_2 have performed the ẓll-ceremony" (U 19/1–4)

whereas in others the plural verb is used:

(23) A. N_1 *w*-N_2 *wdyw*
"N_1 and N_2 have erected (?)" (JSLih 77/2)
B. *kbry s²ʿt h-nṣ ʾḫdw*
"The two kabīrs of the association of H-NṢ have taken possession" (CLL 77/3–4)

The same variation can be seen in the use of enclitic personal pronouns (§4.1.8.2). Thus, in U 19 the two subjects are followed by a verb in the dual (*ʾẓlh*), but are later referred to by the plural enclitic personal pronoun *-hm* (lines 5–7). By contrast, in U 69, the two subjects are followed by a verb in the plural (*ʾẓllw*), but are referred to later by the dual pronominal suffix *-hmy*. See Sima 1999:117–118 for tables showing the variations in agreement in the inscriptions from al-ʿUḏayb. Compare the situation in the modern spoken Arabic dialects, where the dual is in general use on nouns, but requires plural concord in the verb, adjectives, and pronouns (Clive Holes). This is a very old feature in the dialects which can already be seen in the earliest Arabic papyri (see Hopkins 1984:94–98).

5.3 Verb conjugations

The suffix- and prefix-conjugations are each associated with particular usages.

5.3.1 The suffix-conjugation

In Dadanitic, the suffix-conjugation is used of completed acts, e.g., N *ʾḫd h-mqbr*, "N has taken possession of the tomb" (JSLih 306), and for the optative: *ʿrr ḏġbt*, "may Ḏġbt dishonor" (HE 1/4–5); or *rḍy-h*, "may he [the deity] favor him" (U 18/4–5) in contrast to the imperative, *rḍ-h*, "favor him," which is more common in this formula.

In Safaitic, the suffix-conjugation has four distinct functions. First, it is used for completed acts and, in particular, acts which preceded the author's present state or actions (where Classical Arabic would have the perfect, or *kāna* + the perfect, or *qad* + the perfect): for example, *nfr mn rm* "he had fled from Roman territory" (e.g., C 3721); *wgd ʾṯr ʿm-h f-ngʿ*, "he had found the inscription of his grandfather and so he was grieving" (e.g., C 793); *wgm ʿl* N *mqtl qtl-h ʾl ḥwlt*, "he was mourning for N, a murder-victim, whom the ʾl Ḥwlt had killed" (lit. "... killed the ʾl Ḥwlt killed him," HCH 126); *s¹mʿ ʾn myt flfṣ* "he heard that Philip had died" (MHES p. 286).

Second, the suffix-conjugation is used for descriptions of the author's state, or acts which were not complete, at the time of writing: *dṯʾ* "he is spending the season of later rains"; *rʿy* "he is pasturing"; *wgm* "he is grieving"; *ẖrṣ* "he is keeping watch" (where Arabic would use the imperfect).

Third, in Safaitic, as in Classical Arabic, it is used for the optative: *f-h lt whbt s²nʾ-h bn yd-h* "and so, O Lt, may you give his enemy into (lit. between) his hands" (C 4037). This construction is also frequent in Hismaic: for example, in *ḏkrt lt*, "may Lt be mindful of" (e.g., TIJ 58, etc.).

Fourth, the suffix-conjugation can be used as a virtual subjunctive: *s¹lm l-ḏ s¹ʾr w- ʿwr l-ḏ ʿwr h-s¹fr*, "security to whoever leaves (i.e., "may leave") intact and blindness to whoever scratches out (i.e., "may scratch out") the inscription" (e.g., LP 361). Compare the same formula using the prefix-conjugation in §5.3.2.

5.3.2 The prefix-conjugation

The handful of Dadanitic examples of the prefix-conjugation are all in damaged or doubtful contexts.

However, four distinct uses of the prefix-conjugation can be identified for Safaitic. First, it is used in clauses expressing purpose: *l-ys²rq* "in order to migrate to the inner desert" (LP 180).

Second, the Safaitic prefix-conjugation occurs with a jussive implication: *nngy* "may we escape" (WH 135). Note also *nḥyy* "may we live prosperously" in Thamudic B (LP 495).

Third, after the negative particle *lm* the prefix-conjugation has a perfect implication as in Classical Arabic (in an unpublished text).

Finally, the prefix-conjugation is used with a subjunctive implication: *s¹lm l-ḏ s¹ʾr w-ʿwr l-ḏ yʿwr*, "security to whoever leaves (i.e., "may leave") intact and blindness [cf. Arabic *ʿawar*] to whoever scratches out (i.e., 'may scratch out')" (e.g., LP 391). There seems to be no difference in meaning between invocations which use the suffix-conjugation (see §5.3.1) and those which use the prefix-conjugation.

5.4 Participles

Several different uses of participles are attested in Safaitic. An active participle can function as a finite verb with a perfective sense: for example, *w-wgd ʾṯr gs²-h qbrn ḏw ʾl yẓr* "he found the traces of his raiding party, members of the ʾl Yẓr having performed the burial" (C 2156); *wlh ʿl ʾs²yʿ-h ḥrbn ʾl ṭ{y}* "he grieved for his companions [who were] raiding [*ḥāribīn] the tribe of Ṭy'" (C 2795). In addition, active participles often form a circumstance clause (in Arabic grammar, a *ḥāl*): for example, *w-wḥd ġzz* "and he was alone on a raid" (WH 128), where *ġzz* is an active participle (*ġāziz); *ḥll h-dr ṣyr m-mdbr* "he camped at this place while returning to permanent water [*ṣyr*] from the inner desert" (C 2590), where *ṣyr* is an active participle (*ṣāyir).

Participles can be used as virtual relative clauses (see §5.5). The active participle can take a direct object, as in C 2795 above, while a passive participle can be used either on its own (e.g., *wgm ʿl s¹yd mqtl* "he mourned for S¹yd who had been killed"; CSNS 1004), or in construct with another word (e.g., N *mqtl ṭyʾ* "N victim of [i.e., who had been killed by] Ṭy"; CSNS 1011). This is probably the explanation of the passive participles which often follow the names of those for whom an author mourns: thus N *trḥ* (*tarīḥ) "N who is untimely dead"; N *rġm mny* (*raġīm manāyā) "N who has been humbled by (lit. "of") the Fates."

5.5 Relative clauses

In Safaitic, relative clauses can be formed with the relative pronoun *ḏ* (see §4.1.8.3, **3**).

(24) *h* *lt* *ʿyr* *m-ḏ* *qtl-h*
O Lt recompense from-who killed-him
"O Lt [grant] recompense from [him] who killed him" (LP 385)

and with the relative *mn* (**man*; see §4.1.8.3, **1**):

(25) *ʿwr* *l-mn* *yʿwr* *h-s¹fr*
blindness to-whoever scratches out the writing
"And blindness to whoever scratches out the writing" (SIJ 284)

Relative clauses can also be formed without a relative ponoun simply by using the prefix-conjugation with an implied or explicit reference back to the antecedant. This type of relative clause can be used in Safaitic even after a defined antecedent, contrary to the practice in Classical Arabic, though it is found at earlier stages of the language (cf. Beeston 1970:50, n.1):

(26) *l-h* *h-mhrt* *yrbb-h*
to-him [is] the-filly he is training-it
"His is the filly which he is training" (C 1186)

Such a relative clause can also be constructed using the suffix-conjugation, and again can be employed even after a defined antecedent:

(27) *wgm…* *ʿl ʾnʿm* *qtl-h* *ʾl* *ṣbḥ*
he mourned… for-ʾnʿm killed-him ʾl Ṣbḥ
"He mourned… for ʾnʿm whom the ʾl Ṣbḥ had killed" (C 4443)

5.6 Invocations

In Safaitic, invocations can be expressed in three different ways: (i) by the vocative particle *h* + divine name + imperative + predicate (e.g., *h lt ʿwr ḏ yʿwr h-s¹fr* "O Lt blind whoever scratches out the writing"); (ii) by the vocative particle *h* + divine name + an understood verb + noun (e.g., *h lt ġnmt* "O Lt [grant] booty"; cf. Arabic *ḥanānayka yā rabbi* "O Lord have mercy on me" for *taḥannan ʿalayya ḥanānan*, Wright 1896–1898:ii, 73); and (iii) by a verb in the suffix-conjugation with an optative implication + divine name + predicate. This is particularly common in Hismaic: for example, *ḏkrt lt* N., "may Lt be mindful of N."

6. LEXICON

Since Ancient North Arabian is known only from inscriptions, 98 percent of which are graffiti, there is a vast disproportion between the size of the recorded onomasticon and the surviving lexicon. The former is huge, perhaps the largest collection of personal names in any group of Ancient Near Eastern texts. Indeed, in reality it is even larger than it appears, since no vowels or doubled letters are shown and in many cases the same group of consonants must have covered several different names distinguished only by their vocalizations or by consonant doubling (e.g., *S^1lm* could represent *S^1alm, *S^1ālim, *S^1alīm, etc.).

By contrast, the lexicon that has survived is tiny and is severely limited in range by the subject matter of the texts. This is particularly true of Dadanitic, where the vast majority of the monumental inscriptions are dedications, or record the performance of religious duties, whereas the graffiti consist almost entirely of names. Similarly, since the Hasaitic inscriptions found so far are virtually all gravestones, they have yielded a very limited vocabulary. On the other hand, the Safaitic (and, to a lesser extent, the Hismaic) graffiti deal with a wide range of subjects, albeit very laconically.

In the past, the main resource for interpreting the Ancient North Arabian lexicon has been Classical Arabic. However, Modern Arabic dialects are being used increasingly to help explain features in Ancient North Arabian (particularly Safaitic) which do not occur in the Classical language. For instance, the word *ʾs^2rq* (found in Safaitic) has traditionally been translated "he went east," based on Classical Arabic *šarraqa.* However, it is clear from the texts that their authors used *ʾs^2rq* in the same way as the modern bedouins of the same area use *šarraq*, in the sense of "he migrated to the inner desert," regardless of whether that meant traveling north, south, east, or west. There are also a number of words where the meaning has not been preserved in Arabic, but can be found in the cognate in another Semitic language, for example the word *nẖl* in Safaitic which means "a valley" (cf. Hebrew and Aramaic *naḥal*), as opposed to Arabic *naẖl* "a palm tree." Similarly, the word *$ś^1$* in Taymanitic and possibly Lihyanite is probably to be interpreted as "leader" on the basis of Sabaic (see Macdonald 1992a:30–31).

However, there are also a number of words for which etymology does not seem to provide an appropriate meaning and which therefore, at present, have to be explained from their context: for example, *ẖrṣ* in Safaitic which appears to mean "he kept watch," or *wgm*, which seems to be one of the numerous words for "to mourn" in that dialect. Sima argues that the key words in the Dadanitic vocabulary of the inscriptions from al-ʿUḏayb (a side-valley near al-ʿUlā) relate to the maintenance of the irrigation system (1999:90–105), but this is often difficult to justify philologically, and the context usually seems to point to the performance of a religious ceremony.

Given the nature of the material, a complete description of Ancient North Arabian will never be possible. However, large numbers of new, well-recorded texts are becoming available (particularly in Safaitic) and much careful analysis is being undertaken. It may therefore not be too long before it will be possible to present a rather more detailed description than that offered here.

7. READING LIST

In Macdonald 2000, I have discussed the languages of pre-Islamic Arabia (i.e., not just Ancient North Arabian) at a more general level and explained the terminology. For a masterly brief discussion of Ancient North Arabian (with some different views from those expressed here) see Müller 1982. Sass 1991 presents a detailed analysis of the dispersed ONA texts though for a brief critique of his use of paleography see Macdonald 2004a. Caskel 1954 is still the most recent published overall description of Dadanitic (Lihyanite), though a number of unpublished doctoral theses have been devoted to the subject. Caskel's work is marred by many strained interpretations of the texts and an attempt to force the language into the mold of Classical Arabic. However, Sima 1999 presents an excellent edition and analysis of an important group of Dadanitic texts and, although some of his conclusions are disputed, this marks a significant advance in our knowledge of the language. For a brief general outline of the present state of Thamudic studies (plus Taymanitic and Hismaic), see Macdonald and King 1999 and references there. For a similarly brief outline of Safaitic, see Müller 1980 and Macdonald 1995. Readings of the full corpus of the Hasaitic inscriptions (though regrettably without photographs) together with an excellent study can be found in Sima 2002. Finally, it should be noted that readings and interpretations of Ancient North Arabian texts published by A. Jamme and A. van den Branden should be treated with great caution.

Abbreviations

AH	Dadanitic inscriptions originally published in Abū al-Ḥasan 1997 and republished in Sima 1999
AZNG	Safaitic inscription in Abbadi and Zayadine 1996
C	Safaitic inscriptions in *Corpus Inscriptionum Semiticarum. Pars V.* Paris, 1950–1951
CIH	South Arabian and Hasaitic inscriptions in *Corpus Inscriptionum Semiticarum. Pars IV.* Paris, 1889–1932
CLL	Dadanitic inscriptions in Caskel 1954
CSNS	Safaitic inscriptions in Clark 1979
CTSS	Hismaic inscriptions in Clark 1980
HCH	Safaitic inscriptions in Harding 1953
HE	Dadanitic and Taymanitic inscriptions in Harding 1971b
HU	Taymanitic, Hismaic, and Thamudic B, C, and D inscriptions copied by C. Huber and renumbered in van den Branden 1950
Ja 1046	Hasaitic inscription in Jamme 1966:72–73
JSLih	Dadanitic inscriptions in Jaussen and Savignac 1909–1922
JSTham	Taymanitic, Hismaic, and Thamudic B, C, and D inscriptions in Jaussen and Savignac 1909–1922
LP	Safaitic and Thamudic B inscriptions in Littmann 1943
MHES	Safaitic inscriptions in Macdonald 1995b
MNM	Hismaic inscriptions in Milik 1958–1959
MSTJ	Safaitic inscriptions in Macdonald and Harding 1976
NST	Safaitic inscriptions in Harding 1951
Ph	Taymanitic, Hismaic, and Thamudic B, C, and D inscriptions copied by H. St.J. B. Philby and published in van den Branden 1956
Robin-Mulayḥa 1	Hasaitic inscription in Robin 1994:80–81
SIAM i	Safaitic inscriptions in Macdonald 1979
SIJ	Safaitic inscriptions in Winnett 1957
TIJ	Hismaic inscriptions in Harding and Littmann 1952
U	Dadanitic inscriptions from al-ʿU<u>d</u>ayb published (and republished) in Sima 1999
WH	Safaitic inscriptions in Winnett and Harding 1978
WTay	Taymanitic inscriptions in Winnett and Reed 1970
WTI	Dumaitic, Hismaic, and Thamudic B, C, and D inscriptions in Winnett and Reed 1970

Bibliography

In the bibliography, works are listed alphabetically by author, but each one is marked with one or more of the following letters which give an indication of the subject matter:

D Dadanitic
G General
H Hismaic
Ha Hasaitic
OA Old Arabic
ONA Oasis North Arabian
S Safaitic
T Taymanitic
Th Thamudic B, C, D, Southern Thamudic

Abbadi, S. and F. Zayadine. 1996. "Nepos the governor of the Provincia Arabia in a Safaitic inscription?" *Semitica* 46:155–164. **S**

Abū al-Ḥasan, H. 1997. *Qirāʾa li-kitābāt liḥyāniyya min ǧabal ʿakma bi-minṭaqat al-ʿulā.* Al-Riyāḍ: Maktabat al-malik fahd al-waṭaniyya. [Note that the inscriptions in this work were published in facsimile without any photographs and the author's readings must therefore be regarded as unverified. However, most of these texts, together with photographs of almost eighty of them, have now been republished in Sima 1999. References to "AH [= Abū al-Ḥasan] + number" are therefore to Sima's edition not to the *editio princeps.*] **D**

______. 2002. *Nuqūš liḥyānīyah min minṭaqat al-ʿulā. (Dirāsah taḥlīlīyah muqāranah).* Riyadh: Wizārat al-maʿārif wakālat al-wizārah li-l-āṯār wa-ʾl-matāḥif. **D**

Beeston, A. 1962. "Arabian sibilants." *Journal of Semitic Studies* 7:222–233. **G**

______. 1970. *The Arabic Language Today.* London: Hutchinson. **G**

______. 1979a. "Nemara and Faw." *Bulletin of the School of Oriental and African Studies* 42:1–6. **OA**

______. 1979b. Review of Winnett and Harding 1978. *Antiquaries Journal* 59:133–134. **S**

Beeston, A. *et al.* 1973. "The inscription Jaussen-Savignac 71." *Proceedings of the Seminar for Arabian Studies* 3:69–72. **OA**

Brockelmann, C. 1908–1913. *Grundriß der vergleichenden Grammatik der semitischen Sprachen.* Berlin. Reprint 1966, Hildesheim: Olms. **G**

Cantineau, J. 1930–1932. *Le Nabatéen.* (2 vols.). Paris: Ernest Leroux. **G**

Caskel, W. 1954. *Lihyan und Lihyanisch.* Arbeitsgemeinschaft für Forschung des Landes Nordrhein-Westfalen, Geisteswissenschaften 4. Cologne: Westdeutscher Verlag. **D**

Clark, V. 1979. *A Study of New Safaitic Inscriptions from Jordan.* Ph.D. thesis, University of Melbourne. Ann Arbor, MI: University Microfilms (1983). **S**

______. 1980. "Three Safaitic stones from Jordan." *Annual of the Department of Antiquities of Jordan* 24:125–128. **H**

Drewes, A. 1985. "The phonemes of Lihyanite." In C. Robin (ed.), *Mélanges linguistiques offerts à Maxime Rodinson par ses élèves, ses collègues et ses amis*, pp. 165–173. GLECS Supplément 12. Paris: Paul Geuthner. **D**

Eskoubi, Kh. 1999. *An Analytical and Comparative Study of Inscriptions from "Rum" Region, South West of Tayma* (in Arabic). Riyadh: Ministry of Education, Deputy Ministry of Antiquities and Museums. [This book reached me too late to permit the data from these new inscriptions to be included in this survey. While the photographs of each inscription make this an important publication, it should be remembered that it is an M.A. thesis and that the author's interpretations of many of these difficult texts are disputed.] **T, Th**

Faber, A. 1997. "Genetic subgrouping of the Semitic languages." In R. Hetzron (ed.), *The Semitic Languages*, pp. 3–15. London: Routledge. **G**

Harding, G. 1951. "New Safaitic texts." *Annual of the Department of Antiquities of Jordan* 1:25–29. **S**

______. 1953. "The cairn of Haniʾ". *Annual of the Department of Antiquities of Jordan* 2:8–56. **S**

______. 1971a. *An Index and Concordance of Pre-Islamic Arabian Names and Inscriptions.* Near and Middle East Series 8. Toronto: University of Toronto Press. **G**

______. 1971b. "The Thamudic and Liḥyanite texts." In P. Parr, G. Harding, and J. Dayton (eds.), "Preliminary Survey in NW Arabia, 1968. Part II: Epigraphy," pp. 36–52, 61. *Bulletin of the Institute of Archaeology, University of London* 10:36–61. **D, T, Th**

Harding, G. and E. Littmann. 1952. *Some Thamudic Inscriptions from the Hashemite Kingdom of Jordan*. Leiden: Brill. **H**
Holes, C. 1995. *Modern Arabic. Structures, Functions and Varieties*. London: Longman. **G**
Hopkins S. 1984. *Studies in the Grammar of Early Arabic. Based upon Papyri Datable to before AH 300 / AD 912*. London Oriental Series 37. Oxford: Oxford University Press. **OA**
Jamme, A. 1966. *Sabaean and Ḥasaean Inscriptions from Saudi Arabia*. Studi semitici 23. Rome: Università di Roma. **Ha**
Jaussen, A. and M. Savignac. 1909–1922. *Mission archéologique en Arabie* (6 vols.). Paris: Leroux/ Ernest Paul Geuthner. Reprint 1997, Cairo: Institut Français d'Archéologie Orientale. **D, T, Th**
King, G. 1990. "Early North Arabian Thamudic E. A Preliminary Description Based on a New Corpus of Inscriptions from the Ḥismā desert of Southern Jordan and Published Material." Ph.D. thesis, University of London [unpublished]. **H**
Kofler, H. 1940–1942. "Reste altarabischer Dialekte." *Wiener Zeitschrift für die Kunde des Morgenlandes* 47 (1940):61–130, 232–262; 48 (1941):52–88, 247–274; and 49 (1942):15–30, 234–256. **OA**
Littmann, E. 1943. *Safaïtic Inscriptions*. Syria. Publications of the Princeton University Archaeological Expeditions to Syria in 1904–1905 and 1909. Division IV, Section C. Leiden: Brill. **S**
Livingstone, A. 1984. "A linguistic, tribal and onomastical study of the Hasaean inscriptions." In M. Gazdar, D. Potts, and A. Livingstone, "Excavations at Thaj," pp. 86–108. *Atlal* 8:55–108. **Ha**
Macdonald, M. 1979. "Safaitic inscriptions in the Amman Museum and other collections I." *Annual of the Department of Antiquities of Jordan* 23:101–119. **S**
______. 1986. "ABCs and letter order in Ancient North Arabian." *Proceedings of the Seminar for Arabian Studies* 16:101–168. **D, H, S**
______. 1991. "HU 501 and the use of s^3 in Taymanite." *Journal of Semitic Studies* 36:11–36. **T**
______. 1992a. "North Arabian epigraphic notes I." *Arabian Archaeology and Epigraphy* 3:23–43. **S, T**
______. 1992b. "On the placing of *ṣ* in the Maghribi *abjad* and the Khirbet al-Samrāʾ ABC." *Journal of Semitic Studies* 37:155–166. **H, S**
______. 1993. "Nomads and the Ḥawrān in the late Hellenistic and Roman periods: a reassessment of the epigraphic evidence." *Syria* 70:303–413. **S**
______. 1995a. "Safaitic." In *Encyclopaedia of Islam* (revised edition), vol. VIII, pp. 760–762. Leiden: Brill. **S**
______. 1995b. "Herodian echoes in the Syrian desert." In S. Bourke and J. P. Descoeudres (eds.), *Trade, Contact, and the Movement of Peoples in the Eastern Mediterranean. Studies in Honour of J. Basil Hennessy*, pp. 285–290. Supplement to *Mediterranean Archaeology* 3. Sydney. **S**
______. 2000. "Reflections on the linguistic map of Pre-Islamic Arabia." *Arabian Archaeology and Epigraphy* 11:28–79. **D, H, Ha, OA, ONA, S, T, Th**
______. 2004a. "On the uses of writing in ancient Arabia and the role of palaeography in Studying them." *Arabian Archaeology and Epigraphy* 15. **D,G,H,S,Th**
______. 2004b. "A preliminary re-assessment of the scripts used in pre-Islamic Dedan." In S. Weninger (ed.), *Epigraphik und Archäologie des antiken Südarabien*. Wiesbaden: Otto Harrassowitz. **D**
______. 2004c. "Literacy in an Oral Environment." In P. Bienkowski, C. B. Mee and E. A. Slater (eds.), *Writing and Ancient Near Eastern Society*. British Academy Monographs in Archaeology. Oxford: Oxford University Press. **D, G, H, OA, S, Th**
______. 2004d. "From Dedān to Iran in four Ancient North Arabian inscriptions." In D. F. Graf and S. G. Schmidt (eds.), *Fawzi Zayadine Festschrift*. Amman: Department of Antiquities of Jordan. **D, H**
______. Forthcoming. *Old Arabic and its Rivals in the Age of Ignorance. Six Studies on the Emergence of Arabic as a Written Language*. **OA**
Macdonald, M. and G. Harding. 1976. "More Safaitic texts from Jordan." *Annual of the Department of Antiquities of Jordan* 21:119–133. **S**
Macdonald, M. and G. King. 1999. "Thamudic." In *Encyclopaedia of Islam* (revised edition), vol. X, pp. 436–438. Leiden: Brill. **H, T, Th**
Macdonald, M., M. Al Mu'azzin, and L. Nehmé. 1996. "Les inscriptions safaïtiques de Syrie, cent quarante ans après leur découverte." *Comptes rendus de l'Académie des Inscriptions et Belles-Lettres*, pp. 435–494. **S, Th**

Milik, J. 1958–1959. "Nouvelles inscriptions sémitiques et grecques du pays de Moab." *Liber Annuus* 9:330–358. **H**

Müller, W. 1980. "Some remarks on the Safaitic inscriptions." *Proceedings of the Seminar for Arabian Studies* 10:67–74. **S**

______. 1982. "Das Altarabische und das klassische Arabisch." In W. Fischer (ed.), *Grundriß der Arabischen Philologie,* vol. I. *Sprachwissenschaft,* pp. 17–36. Wiesbaden: Dr. Ludwig Reichert. **D, H, Ha, OA, ONA, S, T, Th**

______. 1992. "Abimael." In *Anchor Bible Dictionary,* vol. I, p. 20. New York: Doubleday.

Müller, W. and S. Said. (2001). "Der babylonische König Nabonid in taymanischen Inschriften." *Biblische Notizen* 107/108:109–119. **T**

Rabin, C. 1951. *Ancient West-Arabian.* London: Taylor's. **OA**

Rabinowitz, I. 1956. "Aramaic inscriptions of the fifth century BCE from a North-Arab shrine in Egypt." *Journal of Near Eastern Studies* 15:1–9. **G**

Robin, C. 1974. "Monnaies provenant de l'Arabie du nord-est." *Semitica* 24:83–125 (esp. pp. 112–118). **Ha**

______. 1994. "Documents de l'Arabie antique III." *Raydān* 6:69–90. **Ha**

______. 2001. "Les inscriptions de l'Arabie antique et les études arabes". *Arabica* 48: 509–577. **G, OA**

Ryckmans, G. (ed.). 1950–1951. *Corpus Inscriptionum Semiticarum. Pars V.* Paris: Imprimerie Nationale. **S**

Ryckmans, J. 1956. "Aspects nouveaux du problème thamoudéen." *Studia Islamica* 5:5–17. **Th**

Sass, B. 1991. *Studia Alphabetica. On the Origin and Early History of the Northwest Semitic, South Semitic, and Greek Alphabets.* Orbis Biblicus et Orientalis 102. Freiburg Schweiz: Universitätsverlag. **ONA**

Scagliarini, F. 1996. "Šahr figlio di Han-Aws: il nome di un nuovo sovrano in un testo Liḥyanitico inedito." *Studi epigrafici e linguistici sul vicino oriente antico* 13:91–97. **D**

______. 1999. "The Dadanitic inscriptions from Ğabal ʿIkma in north-western Hejaz." *Proceedings of the Seminar for Arabian Studies* 29:143–150. **D**

Sima, A. 1999. *Die lihyanischen Inschriften von al-ʿU<u>d</u>ayb (Saudi-Arabien).* Epigraphische Forschungen auf der Arabischen Halbinsel 1. Rahden/Westf.: Leidorf. [Note, I am not convinced by Sima's interpretation of these inscriptions as referring to the maintenance of the underground water system of al-ʿUlā, hence my translations of the vocabulary of these texts frequently differ from his.] **D**

______. 2000. "Zum antiken Namen Dedan". *Biblische Notizen* 104:42–47. **D**

______. 2002. "Die hasaitischen Inschriften." In N. Nebes (ed.), *Neue Beiträge zur Semitistik,* pp. 167–200. Jenaer Beiträge zum Vorderen Orient 5. Wiesbaden: Harrassowitz. **Ha**

Stiehl, R. 1971. "Neue liḥyānische Inschriften aus al-ʿU<u>d</u>aib I," mit einem Nachtrag M. Höfners. In F. Altheim and R. Stiehl (eds.), *Christentum am Roten Meer,* vol. I, pp. 3–40, 565–566, 569–594. Berlin: de Gruyter. **D**

Ullendorff, E. 1965. "The form of the definite article in Arabic and other Semitic languages." In G. Makdisi (ed.), *Arabic and Islamic Studies in Honor of H. A. R. Gibb,* pp. 631–637. Leiden: Brill. **G**

Van den Branden, A. 1950. *Les inscriptions thamoudéennes.* Bibliothèque du Muséon 25. Louvain: Institut Orientaliste. **H, T, Th**

______. 1956. *Les textes thamoudéens de Philby.* Bibliothèque du Muséon 39 and 41. Louvain: Institut Orientaliste. **H, T, Th**

Winnett, F. 1957. *Safaitic Inscriptions from Jordan.* Near and Middle East Series 2. Toronto: University of Toronto Press. **S**

______. 1980. "A reconsideration of some inscriptions from the Tayma area." *Proceedings of the Seminar for Arabian Studies* 10:133–140. **T**

Winnett, F. and G. Harding. 1978. *Inscriptions from Fifty Safaitic Cairns.* Near and Middle East Series 9. Toronto: University of Toronto Press. **S**

Winnett, F. and W. Reed. 1970. *Ancient Records from North Arabia.* Near and Middle East Series 6. Toronto: University of Toronto Press. **D, H, T, Th S**

______. 1973. "An archaeological-epigraphical survey of the Ḥāʾil area of northern Saʿudi Arabia." *Berytus* 22:53–113. **H, S, Th**

Wright, W. 1896–1898. *A Grammar of the Arabic Language* (3rd edition, revised by W. Robertson Smith and M. J. de Goeje). Cambridge: Cambridge University Press [constantly reprinted]. **G**

APPENDIX 1

Afro-Asiatic

JOHN HUEHNERGARD

1. THE AFRO-ASIATIC FAMILY

1.1 Introduction

In the following paragraphs only a brief overview of the Afro-Asiatic family can be given, with some of the shared features that have prompted recognition of the family. Work on Afro-Asiatic is still in its infancy, and work on the reconstruction of Proto-Afro-Asiatic has barely begun. The remainder of this chapter will be concerned with one of the two well-known ancient branches of Afro-Asiatic, the Semitic branch (the other ancient branch is Egyptian, for which see *WAL* Ch. 7; for a probable ancient form of Berber, see below, §1.1.3).

The original homeland of Afro-Asiatic has been the subject of some discussion. Most scholars would place it somewhere in the vicinity of the center of the family's current geographical range, or rather further to the east, in far southern Egypt or northern Sudan. A few scholars, however, have argued for an original location in southwest Asia (see Militarev 1994; Diakonoff 1998).

Older names of the Afro-Asiatic family, still used by some scholars, include *Hamito-Semitic* and *Semito-Hamitic*, names that have generally been abandoned because they imply a subgroup of "Hamitic" languages (i.e., of all languages in the family apart from the Semitic languages) that is not indicated by any isoglosses.

The Afro-Asiatic family comprises at least five and as many as eight branches.

1.1.1 Egyptian

See *WAL* Chapter 7.

1.1.2 Semitic

See §§2–3 below.

1.1.3 Berber

Berber was formerly spoken across much of Africa north of the Sahara, but with the spread of Islam, it has been reduced to a series of linguistic islands in a sea of Arabic. Even so, Berber languages are still spoken by 10–15 million people. Berber languages in Morocco include Tashelhit in the High Atlas mountains, Tamazight in the Middle Atlas mountains, and Tarifit in the Rif mountains. In Algeria the main Berber language is Kabyle, though several other forms of Berber also occur. Tuareg is also spoken in Algeria, as well as in Mali and Niger. Smaller Berber dialects are spoken in Tunisia, Libya, Egypt (oasis of Siwa), and Mauritania. The Guanche language of the Canary Islands, extinct since the sixteenth century AD, was probably also a Berber language.

A Berber dialect (or dialects) is probably represented in the corpus of over a thousand Numidian (or Lybian, or Lybico-Berber) inscriptions in a consonantal alphabet that have been found in Tunisia, Algeria, and Morocco. Most of the inscriptions date to the second century BC (only one is actually dated, however, a Numidian–Punic bilingual from 139 BC). The texts are difficult to interpret, and thus of limited use for the earlier history of Berber. The script resembles the Tifinigh (or Tifinagh, "Punic [letters]") alphabet that is now used among the Tuareg (see O'Connor 1996).

1.1.4 Cushitic

Some forty Cushitic languages are spoken by about 15–20 million people in Ethiopia, Somalia, and surrounding countries. The earliest records of Cushitic languages date to the eighteenth century AD. Cushitic is divided into four branches:

1. *North Cushitic*: the Beja language (claimed by some scholars to be a separate branch of Afro-Asiatic; see below, §1.1.6).
2. *Central Cushitic or Agaw*: formerly the major Cushitic language in Ethiopia, which had significant influence on the later Semitic languages there, today represented by a number of languages with small numbers of speakers (Awngi, Bilin, Kemant, Xamir).
3. *East Cushitic*: numerically by far the largest branch of Cushitic, and itself further subdivided into *Lowland East Cushitic* (including Oromo, formerly called Galla, a pejorative term, with 8–10 million speakers in central Ethiopia; Afar-Saho, along the Red Sea coast of Eritrea; and Somali, the official language of Somalia), *Highland East Cushitic* (or Rift Valley Cushitic, including especially the Sidamo language), and smaller subbranches.
4. *South Cushitic*: includes languages spoken in Kenya and Tanzania (such as Alagwa, Burunge, and Iraqw).

1.1.5 Chadic

Chadic is a very large family of some 140 languages spoken by perhaps 30–40 million people in Cameroon, Central African Republic, Chad, Niger, and Nigeria. One Chadic language, Hausa, also serves as a lingua franca in much of western Africa. There are no records of Chadic languages before the modern period. The Chadic languages are divided into three large branches, each of which is further subdivided:

1. *West Chadic*: including Hausa, the Ron languages, and the Bauchi subbranch.
2. *Central Chadic*: languages such as Bura, Margi, Kotoko-Logone, Masa.
3. *Eastern Chadic*: languages such as Kera, Migama, Mubi.

1.1.6 Other possible branches

The Omotic languages, about forty in number, are spoken by about 3 million people, mostly along the Omo River in southwestern Ethiopia. The most prominent language is Wolaytta, with about 2 million speakers. Omotic was formerly considered a western branch of Cushitic, but is now considered by many scholars to be an independent branch of Afro-Asiatic, although there continues to be discussion about its status.

The Beja language, spoken by about a million people along the Red Sea coast of Sudan and southeastern Egypt, is usually considered to be North Cushitic, but it has sometimes been proposed as a separate branch of Afro-Asiatic (Hetzron 1980). It has a number of intriguing archaic features.

A language spoken by fewer than twenty individuals along the Woito River in southwestern Ethiopia, called by themselves Ongota and by their neighbors Birale or Birelle, has recently been described (Fleming *et al.* 1992) and claimed to be the remnant of another distinct branch of Afro-Asiatic (Fleming 1999).

1.2 Subgrouping of Afro-Asiatic

A number of morphological features indicate that Berber, Egyptian, and Semitic may constitute a *North Afro-Asiatic* subgroup. A connection between Berber and Chadic has also been suggested. Various other, more comprehensive subgroupings of the Afro-Asiatic branches have been proposed, but none has gained a consensus.

Macro-comparisons of Afro-Asiatic with other language phyla, such as Indo-European (the so-called Nostratic hypothesis), have not met with general acceptance.

1.3 Features of Afro-Asiatic

Most of the features enumerated here are attested in several, but usually not all, of the branches of the family.

1.3.1 Phonology

Phonological commonalities include the pharyngeal fricatives [ʕ] and [ħ], and a third series of consonants (in addition to the usual voiced and the voiceless), often called "emphatic," which in most of the branches have a glottalized realization (but are pharyngealized in Berber and in Arabic).

1.3.2 Morphology

In the morphology, the personal pronouns exhibit a number of common features across Afro-Asiatic. Most branches, for example, have both independent and suffixed forms, the latter used both for objects when attached to verbs and for possession when attached to nouns. Common forms include **ʔan(V)* and **ʔana(:)k(V)* for the first-person singular, and **k* as marker of the second person. Demonstrative pronouns also show a number of common elements across the branches.

The "root and pattern" system of noun and verb bases that is well known among the Semitic languages (see §3.3.1) seems to be a common Afro-Asiatic feature, as does the existence of a preponderance of triconsonantal roots (but also a significant number of biconsonantal roots).

Among inflectional features of the noun may be noted (i) the presence of **-t* as marker of feminine; (ii) a case system similar to that of Proto-Semitic (Sasse 1984); (iii) pluralization by means of the insertion of **a* before the final root consonant (Greenberg 1955a), as well as other "broken" plurals (see below, §3.3.2.4); (iv) a prefix **ma-* to form nouns of place, instrument, and agent; and (v) a denominative adjectival ending **-i:(y)*.

In verbal morphology, it is likely that the following may be reconstructed for Proto-Afro-Asiatic: (i) a prefix-conjugation, which marked person much as in Semitic, with

*ʔ- for first-person singular, *t- for second-person (and perhaps for third-person fem.), and *y- for third-person (masc.); (ii) the presence of *a to mark the imperfective form of the verb; and (iii) a set of derivational consonant affixes, *s for causative, *t for reflexive or middle, and *n for passive.

On the cusp bridging nominal and verbal morphology is the predicate adjective or suffix-conjugation, a predication composed of a verbal adjective and an enclitic subject pronoun (found in Semitic [see §3.3.2.1], Egyptian, and, probably, Cushitic).

1.4 Afro-Asiatic vocabulary

One of the greatest hindrances to the reconstruction of Proto-Afro-Asiatic has been the difficulty of establishing clear cognate sets across the vocabularies of the several branches (this has also, of course, impeded efforts to establish sound correspondences across the branches and to reconstruct Proto-Afro-Asiatic phonology). Essentially, this must await the working out of reconstructed proto-vocabularies for the individual branches, which is still in its beginning stages, except for Semitic. Nevertheless, a few lexical items common to at least several of the branches may be mentioned, such as **lis* "tongue," **m-w-t/mut* "to die," **s(i)m* "name," and **sin(n)* "tooth."

2. THE SEMITIC LANGUAGES

2.1 Introduction

Semitic is a close-knit family of languages first attested inAkkadian names and loanwords occurring in Sumerian cuneiform texts of the first half of the third millennium BC. Akkadian texts proper begin to appear about 2500 BC, and Eblaite shortly thereafter. Many Semitic languages continue to be spoken to this day, including (i) Arabic in many countries of Asia and Africa; (ii) Amharic, Tigrinya, and other related languages in Eritrea and Ethiopia; (iii) Hebrew in Israel; (iv) South Arabian languages such as Mehri, Jibbāli, and Soqoṭri in Yemen and Oman; and (v) many varieties of Aramaic, now scattered around the globe.

2.2 The prehistory of Semitic

It is not known when Semitic hived off from the common Afro-Asiatic stock, other than that the separation must antedate the third millennium BC; nor can anything be said with confidence about the original homeland or early movements of the ancestral Semitic speakers beyond what has been observed above in §1.1. As noted in §1.2, the closest relatives of Semitic within Afro-Asiatic seem to be Egyptian and Berber.

2.3 The subgrouping of the Semitic languages

The earliest partition within the Semitic family separated *West Semitic* from Akkadian and Eblaite (see *WAL* Ch. 8), which together are termed *East Semitic*. West Semitic languages are characterized by an innovative perfective form of the verb, a suffix-conjugation, exemplified by Arabic *katabtu* "I wrote." The West Semitic group in turn is comprised of three branches:

1. *Central Semitic*: includes (i) the Northwest Semitic languages Ugaritic; Hebrew, Phoenician, and other Canaanite dialects; and Aramaic (see Chs. 2–6); (ii) the Ṣayhadic (Old or Epigraphic South Arabian) languages (see Ch. 7); and (iii) the various forms of Arabic (see Ch. 8).

2. *Ethiopian Semitic*: attested in the ancient period in classical Ethiopic, or Gəʿəz (see Ch. 14).
3. *Mahrian Semitic or Modern South Arabian*: not attested until the modern period (unless the Old South Arabian language Ḥaḍramitic reflects an ancient member of this group).

3. DESCRIPTION OF PROTO-SEMITIC

3.1 Introduction

What follows summarizes some of the reconstructable features of Proto-Semitic as a linguistic system. It is based, of course, on the work of many scholars, not all of whose studies could be mentioned in such a brief overview; nor has it always been possible to allot space for a detailed defense of some of the reconstructions offered here.

3.2 Phonology

3.2.1 Consonants

Common Semitic is uncontroversially reconstructed with twenty-nine consonantal phonemes. The original pronunciation of the consonants is disputed, but a likely set of phonetic values is given in Table A.1:

Table A.1 The consonantal phonemes of Common Semitic

	Place of articulation						
Manner of articulation	Bilabial	Inter-dental	Dental/Alveolar	Palatal	Velar	Pharyngeal	Glottal
Stop							
Voiceless	p		t		k		ʔ
Emphatic			tʼ		kʼ		
Voiced	b		d		g		
Affricate							
Voiceless			ᵗs				
Emphatic			ᵗsʼ				
Voiced			ᵈz				
Fricative							
Voiceless		θ	s		x	ħ	h
Emphatic		θʼ					
Voiced		ð			γ	ʕ	
Lateral continuant							
Voiceless			ɬ				
Emphatic			ɬʼ				
Voiced			l				
Tap/Trill			r				
Nasal	m		n				
Glide	w			y			

As Table A.1 indicates, Proto-Semitic was characterized by a number of consonant triads consisting of a voiceless, an ejective (i.e., a so-called emphatic), and a voiced member. For two of the obstruent sets that are lacking an ejective member, namely the bilabial stop and the velar fricative sets, that member has been posited for Proto-Afro-Asiatic – *_p'_ and *_x'_. The consonantal repertoire of Proto-Afro-Asiatic is in general assumed to have been significantly larger than that of Proto-Semitic.

All of the consonants could be geminated.

In the traditional Semitological literature, the consonants here characterized as ejective are normally transcribed with an underdot, for example, _ṭ_ for /t'/, _θ̣_ for /θ'/, and so forth, as is the voiceless pharyngeal fricative, in other words, _ḥ_ for /ħ/. The velar fricatives /x/ and /ɣ/ are usually written by Semitists as _ḫ_ and either _ġ_ or _ǵ_, respectively, while the voiceless and emphatic lateral fricatives /ɬ/ and /ɬ'/ are usually written as _ś_ and either _ṣ́_ or _ð̣_, respectively. Further, the consonants here characterized as alveolar affricates are traditionally represented as simple fricatives, _s_, _s'_ or _ṣ_, and _z_, while the sibilant given above as /s/ is traditionally represented as _š_.

At least one assimilation process may be ascribed to Common Semitic, namely, the assimilation of _w_ to a following dental or alveolar, as in Akkadian _ittarad_ < *_yawtarad_ "he has descended"; Arabic _yattaħidu_ < *_yawtaħidu_ "it will be united"; Hebrew _yis's'or_ < *_yaw_^{t}_s'ur-_ "he fashions." Attested in only part of the Semitic area, perhaps reflecting an areal development, is the assimilation of *_n_ to a following consonant, which occurs regularly in Akkadian and the Northwest Semitic languages; compare Common Semitic *_yanθ'ur_ "he guarded" > Arabic _yanzˤur_, but Akkadian _is's'ur_, Hebrew _yis's'or_, Aramaic _yit't'ar_. In Ṣayhadic inscriptions the same assimilation is frequently, but not consistently, reflected.

The consonants *_w_ and *_y_ were regularly lost in the environment C_V̆, with compensatory lengthening of the following vowel, as in *_maka:n-_ < *_makwan-_ "place"; *_madi:nat-_ < *_madyinat-_ "administrative region."

The existence of syllabic allophones of the sonorants *_l_, *_m_, and *_n_ in certain environments has been suggested to account for a number of phenomena attested in the descendant languages (Testen 1998). Examples include the ancient substantives *_bn̩-_ "son" and *_sm̩-_ "name," the pronominal forms *_sm̩_ "they (masc.)" and *_sn̩_ "they (fem.)," and the proclitic asseverative particle *_l̩-_.

3.2.1.1 Major developments in the descendant languages

In most of the West Semitic languages, the common Semitic alveolar fricative *_s_ underwent a change to *_h_ when prevocalic (i.e., _s_ > _h_ / _V) as in Common Semitic *_suʔa_ > West Semitic *_huʔa_ "he"; Common Semitic *_yusaʕbir_ > West Semitic *_yuhaʕbir_ "he sent across"; Common Semitic *_baytisa_ > West Semitic *_baytiha_ (eventually to Hebrew _bayθɔh_) "to the house." In an interesting development resulting from the morphological patterning of Semitic (see §3.3.1), this sound change was blocked in most nominal and verbal forms because the conditioning environment – namely, the following vowel – did not appear in all forms; for instance, although *_sarik'-_ "stolen" would have developed into **_harik'-_ by the sound rule, no change would have occurred in the verbal form *_yasrik'_ "he stole," where *_s_ was not followed by a vowel; a principle of root integrity (essentially an overriding avoidance of root allomorphism) then blocked the change *_sarik'-_ > **_harik'-_ as well. Thus, *_s_ generally remains in West Semitic nominal and verbal roots, but is otherwise missing. In a number of languages, including Aramaic, Hebrew, Jibbāli (Mahrian branch), and the Babylonian form of Akkadian, *_s_ became a palato-alveolar _š_; note, for example, Arabic and Ethiopic _sala:m_ "well-being," but Babylonian _šala:mum_, Aramaic _šəla:m_, Hebrew _šɔlom_.

The early dental/alveolar affricates $^{*t}s$, $^{*t}s'$, $^{*d}z$ were deaffricated in most of the attested languages, becoming *s, *s', and *z, respectively. In Arabic and Ethiopic, the new voiceless *s < $^{*t}s$ merged with Common Semitic *s. In the Assyrian form of Akkadian, however, $^{*t}s$ became *š*.

The Common Semitic voiceless and ejective lateral fricatives, *ɬ and *ɬ', underwent changes in most of the attested languages, although the nonejective *ɬ is still preserved as such in the Mahrian languages, and was probably also pronounced as such in early Akkadian, Hebrew, and Arabic. The ejective *ɬ' merged with $^{*t}s'$ in Hebrew, in Akkadian, and in Ethiopian Semitic (although it is preserved as a distinct phoneme in the earliest classical Ethiopic, pronunciation unknown). In Aramaic, however, it became first *γ* and finally *ʕ*; compare Hebrew *ʔɛ́rɛs'*, Akkadian *ers'etum*, but Aramaic *ʔarʕa:*, from Common Semitic **ʔarɬ'-* "earth."

In Arabic and perhaps in some other Central Semitic languages, most of the common Semitic ejective or glottalic consonants became pharyngealized, for example, *t' > *tˤ*, $^{*t}s'$ > *s' > *sˤ*. The velar ejective *k', however, became a nonejective uvular stop *q*. The Arabic reflexes of *θ' and *ɬ' vary according to dialect, but for the classical language are usually said to be a voiced interdental or dental/alveolar fricative, *ðˤ* or *zˤ*, and a voiced dental/alveolar stop, *dˤ*, respectively.

As the result of an areal spread, the bilabial stop *p* became a labiodental fricative *f* in several branches of Semitic, namely, Mahrian, Ethiopian, and the Ṣayhadic and Arabic subbranches of Central Semitic.

A characteristic of the Northwest Semitic languages is the change of initial **w* to **y*, as in Hebrew *yɛ́lɛð*, Aramaic *yalda:* "child" < Common and Central Semitic **wald-*.

3.2.2 Vowels

Proto-Semitic (and probably Proto-Afro-Asiatic) may be reconstructed with three vowels, high front **i*, high back **u*, and low central **a*, each of which could occur short or long.

On diphthongs and triphthongs see §3.2.3.

The presence of **i(:)* in the base of a Proto-Semitic word seems to have precluded the presence of another high vowel elsewhere in the base. In other words, bases with the vowel melodies *i...i*, *i...u*, and *u...i* do not seem to have occurred, though bases with two *u* vowels, *CuC(C)u(:)C-*, can be reconstructed.

Internal reconstruction indicates the existence of a Proto-Semitic rule of vowel syncope: $a > \phi \,/\, aC_1 \_\_ C_1 V$, as in **k'alalum* > **k'allum* "light, small."

3.2.3 Syllable structure

It is likely that only three syllable shapes are to be reconstructed for Proto-Semitic – two open, CV and CV:, and one closed, CVC. These syllable-types may also be classified quantitatively, as either light, CV, or heavy, CV: and CVC. Thus, all syllables contain a single vowel, begin with a single consonant, and end either in a single consonant or in a vowel. The following conditions are not permitted: (i) sequences of two or more consonants word-finally; (ii) sequences of three or more consonants within words; (iii) sequences of two or more vowels; (iv) long vowels in closed syllables.

Since only one vowel quality was permitted in each syllable, true *phonemic* diphthongs did not occur in Proto-Semitic (nor are they attested in most of the descendant languages). Semitists, however, often speak of the phonetic sequences [V + glide] (i.e., *Vw* and *Vy*) as "diphthongs," even though Semitic syllable structure dictates that the glide functions as a consonant in such cases. The sequences **aw* and **ay* were common in Proto-Semitic, as in **mawt-* "death" and **bayt-* "house." These were frequently monophthongized, usually to [o:] and [e:], respectively, in many of the languages.

Already in Proto-Semitic the sequences **iy* and **uw* were realized as [i:] and [u:], respectively; thus the noun **di:n-* "judgment," from the root *d-y-n*, may be said to be equivalent to **diyn-* (i.e., a noun of the pattern *CiCC*), and so comparable in form to the noun **ðibħ-* "sacrifice" from the root *ð-b-ħ*. Similarly, **k'u:m-* "height," from the root *k'-w-m*, is equivalent to **k'uwm-* (i.e., of the pattern *CuCC*) and comparable to **ʕumk'-* "depth," from the root *ʕ-m-k'*.

The sequences *VwV* and *VyV*, sometimes called "triphthongs" in Semitic studies, tended to be unstable and to be reduced to "diphthongs" or to simple vowels, as in **mawit-/mayt-(< mait-)/mi:t-/mit-* "dead." For the sequences *CwV* and *CyV* see §3.2.1.

The implications of reconstructing a set of syllabic allophones of certain consonants (see §3.2.1) require further investigation. Clearly, however, the generalizations just enunciated would need to be modified if forms such as **bn-* + case ending – that is, *[bn̩um] "son" (CCVC?, CVVC?) – are to be considered valid in Proto-Semitic.

3.2.4 Stress

The evidence suggests that Proto-Semitic word stress was not phonemic, but assigned automatically (i) to the rightmost nonfinal heavy syllable (*CV:* or *CVC*), or (ii) in words having only nonfinal light syllables, to the initial syllable: **'salima*, **'salimu:*, **sa'limta(:)*, **'yislam*, **'yislamu:*, **yisla'mu:na*. This is essentially the pattern assumed to operate in both classical Arabic and Akkadian, which are widely separated within the Semitic family.

There are instances in which stress is phonemic in some of the descendant languages, but these are undoubtedly the result of internal developments: for example, classical Ethiopic *'səħtat* "she erred," but *səħ'tat* "error"; *ra'kaba:* "they (fem.) found," but *raka'ba:* "he found her"; Hebrew *'k'ɔmɔ* "she stood" versus *k'ɔ'mɔ* "standing" (fem. sg.), *'rɔs'u* "they ran" versus *rɔ's'u* "they were pleased."

3.3 Morphology

3.3.1 Morphological type and word structure

Common Semitic, like its descendants, may be characterized as a fusional language.

Certain pronouns and a small but important number of isolated substantives, that is, substantives not associated with a verbal root, may be reconstructed for Proto-Semitic as discrete, and complete, lexical items with no formal restrictions other than those imposed by the constraints of syllable structure: for example, **ʔanti(:)* "you (fem. sg.)," **suʔa* "he," **yadum* "hand," **ʕiɬ'um* "tree," **kalbum* "dog," **ʔu^{d}znum* "ear," **ħima:rum* "(male) donkey," **ʔarnabum* "hare" (see Fox 1998).

But a remarkable characteristic of Semitic morphology is that the majority of words – all verbal forms and most nouns – reflect the interdigitation of a root, consisting of an invariable sequence of consonantal radicals (usually three in number), and a pattern of vowels and other features, which include gemination of one of the root consonants (other than the first) and affixation of a small subset of the consonantal repertoire (especially *ʔ*, *m*, *n*, *s*, *t*, *y*; these also appear commonly in the pronominal systems). As examples the following forms of the root **s-l-m* "(to be) whole, sound, well" may be cited, with R_1 and so forth representing the root consonants:

(1) pattern $R_1aR_2iR_3$ (a common adjectival form): **salim-* "whole, sound, well";
pattern $R_1aR_2a{:}R_3$ (a common verbal noun form): **sala:m-* "wholeness, well-being";
pattern $muR_1aR_2R_2iR_3$ (participle of a derived verbal form): **musallim-* "(one) who makes whole."

It is possible that verbal roots consisting of fewer than three consonantal radicals were not unusual in Common Afro-Asiatic. By the Proto-Semitic period, however, the triradical root was the norm, roots that earlier may have had fewer radicals having been conformed to that norm by various analogical developments. Original biradical bases may perhaps be detected in some roots with first radical *w*, such as **w-θ-b* "dwell," that lack the *w* in certain forms, such as the verbal noun **θib-t-* "dwelling," across the descendant languages and even occasionally in cognates in Egyptian; and in some biform root pairs of the type R_1-R_2-R_2 ~ R_1-R_2-*w*/R_1-R_2-*y*, that must also be reconstructed to the proto-language. Common Semitic also probably had a small number of quadriradical roots, most of them with a sonorant in second position.

Certain constraints on the composition of the Semitic verbal root have been noted (Greenberg 1950): roots with identical first and second radicals are unattested, and roots with identical first and third radicals are extremely rare. In addition, homorganic consonants tend to be avoided within a root, except for the common root type known as the geminate, in which the second and third radicals are identical.

3.3.2 Nominal morphology

Reconstruction indicates that Proto-Semitic nouns occurred in two states, bound and free (adjectives also in a third, predicative); two genders, masculine and feminine; three cases, nominative, genitive, and accusative (and perhaps a fourth, directive); and three numbers, singular, dual, and plural. Proto-Semitic did not have a definite or an indefinite article. A definite article first evolved in the Central Semitic branch, while an indefinite article failed to develop in most of the descendant languages (apart from the occasional use of the numeral "one" for "a certain").

3.3.2.1 State

Proto-Semitic nouns occurred in two syntactic states, either (i) bound to a following qualifier or (ii) not thus bound, in other words, free. Free forms were marked with an ending that exhibited two allomorphs, **-m* after short vowels, **-na* after long vowels and diphthongs: for example, nominative singular **wa:θibum* "inhabitant," plural **wa:θibu:na* "inhabitants" (see further below). Bound forms (also called *construct forms*), which lacked this ending, governed an immediately following constituent, which was either a noun in the genitive case (2A–B), a (genitive) pronominal suffix (2C–D), or a nominalized (relative) clause (2E–F):

(2) A. *wa:θibu baytim "inhabitant of the house"
B. *wa:θibu: baytim "inhabitants of the house"
C. *wa:θibu-su(:) "its inhabitant"
D. *wa:θibu:-su(:) "its inhabitants"
E. *wa:θibu yamu:tu "the inhabitant who died"
F. *wa:θibu: yamu:tu:na "the inhabitants who died"

Nothing was permitted to intervene between a bound form and the constituent governed by it; an attributive adjective (in the free form), for example, followed the construction:

**wa:θibu baytim salimum* "the sound inhabitant of the house" (vs. **wa:θibu baytim salimim* "the inhabitant of the sound house").

In addition to occurring in the bound and free forms, adjectives of verbal roots, when functioning as the predicate of their clause, entered into a special morphological construction which was comprised of the simple base of the adjective (unmarked for case, gender, or number) followed by an enclitic subject pronoun, as in **salim-ti(:)* "you (fem. sg.) are well"; **salim-at baʕlatum* "the lady (she) is well."

The comparative degree was expressed syntactically rather than morphologically; that is, there was no special comparative form of the adjective, a comparison such as "their army is larger than our army" being expressed as "their army is large from/against our army." For the superlative, Akkadian and Arabic attest a form of the adjective augmented by a prefix resembling the causative marker of the verbal system, but it is unclear whether this reflects a Proto-Semitic feature (Speiser 1952). It is likely that the superlative could be expressed by a bound-form adjective governing a plural noun, as in "the great one of the gods" = "the greatest god."

3.3.2.2 Gender

The evidence of the descendant languages suggests that in Common Semitic any given substantive was construed either as masculine or as feminine. Of the two genders, the masculine was generally unmarked formally, whereas most feminine nouns were marked with an ending. Each of the languages, however, attests a number of unmarked words that are construed as grammatically feminine, including: (i) the words for "mother" (**ʔimm-*), "ewe" (**laxir-*), "female donkey" (**ʔata:n-*); (ii) words for the parts of the body that occur in pairs – for example, **ʕayn-* "eye," **birk-* "knee," a curious phenomenon that undoubtedly arose because the ending of the dual on nouns (nominative) and verbs and the ending of the feminine plural on some verbal and adjectival forms were formally identical, namely, **-a:*; and (iii) a semantically disparate group of other words for inanimate objects that varies from language to language and is thus difficult to reconstruct in the proto-language with any certainty. A few unmarked nouns in each language – again the set varies – are construed as both masculine and feminine.

The marker of the feminine is **-t* or **-at*, which appears after the base but before a case ending; examples are **baʕl-* "lord," **baʕl-at-* "lady"; **wa:θib-* "inhabitant (masc.)," **wa:θib-t-* (fem.). The original distribution of **-t* versus **-at* is difficult to recover with certainty. In all of the languages, for reasons of syllable structure, the ending **-at* appears after bases ending in two consonants (a sequence of three consonants being prohibited), as in **baʕl-at-*. In some of the descendant languages, such as Akkadian and Aramaic, **-at* appears only on such bases, **-t* occurring on all other forms. In Arabic, **-at* has been generalized (with a few exceptions, such as *bin-t-* "daughter"). Classical Ethiopic patterns for the most part like Akkadian and Aramaic, in other words, with **-t* unless **-at* is phonologically necessary; but there are a number of exceptions, such as *ʕəlat* "day," *xat'iʔat* "sin." In Hebrew, **-at* (> Hebrew *-ɔ*, bound-form *-aθ*) predominates on verbal adjectives (as in *kβeðɔ* < **kabidat-* "heavy"); but otherwise the occurrence of the two endings suggests a certain free variation at an earlier period: for example, *déleθ* < **dal-t-* "door," versus *ʔɔmɔ* < **ʔam-at-* "female slave."

The endings **-at/-t* have a number of semantic functions: (i) to mark the feminine singular of adjectives; (ii) to denote the female member of various pairs of words, such as **baʕl(-at)-*, "lord/lady" and **kalb(-at)-* "dog/bitch"; (iii) to denote the single member of the class represented by a collective noun (termed in traditional Semitic grammar the *nomen unitatis*), as in **bak'ar-* "cattle," **bak'ar-at-* "a cow" and **ɬiʕar-* "hair," **ɬiʕar-at-* "a hair"; and finally (iv) as a suffix on many substantives with no obvious feminine or other common semantic connotations.

The various descendant languages preserve vestiges (less rare in Arabic) of other markers of the feminine that must be reconstructed to Proto-Semitic, including **-ay* and **-a:ʔ.*

3.3.2.3 Case

Traditional Semitic grammar recognizes three cases of the noun, each of which is marked, in singular forms, by one of the short vowels. These cases are given labels borrowed from the classical Indo-European languages: nominative, marked by **-u*; genitive, marked by **-i*; and accusative, marked by **-a*.

The *nominative* is used for the subject of a clause, for the predicate of a verbless equational clause (as in "my brother is the king"), and as a citation form and for extraposition ("as for the king" = nom.). The ending *-u* also functions in a locative sense (**libbum* "in the heart") in Akkadian and vestigially in other languages; it is unclear whether the nominative and locative functions are to be considered reflexes of a single case at an earlier stage.

The *genitive* is an adnominal case, used after all bound forms and all prepositions (many of which originate as bound-form nouns). The ending that marks the genitive, **-i*, is undoubtedly connected to the morpheme **-i:y* that is suffixed to substantives to form denominative adjectives (see §3.3.2.6 below).

The so-called *accusative* is indeed used to mark the object, usually the direct object, of the verb, but also in a host of other adverbial functions, such as to indicate manner, means, location, and "time when." If, as has been suggested, Proto-Semitic at an early stage had an ergative verbal system, **-a* may have marked the absolutive case (see, e.g., Diakonoff 1988:59,101).

In dual and plural forms, the genitive and accusative are invariably marked by a common set of endings, and the two cases are sometimes jointly termed the *oblique.*

Another common Semitic noun ending that may perhaps be considered a case marker is **-isa*, the reflexes of which, in Akkadian, Ugaritic, and Hebrew, have a directional nuance, as in **baytisa* "houseward." In Akkadian, further, and more commonly, it is attached to adjectives to create adverbs: *t'a:bum* "pleasant (nom. sg.)," *t'a:biš* "pleasantly." This ending occurs only on singular forms.

3.3.2.4 Number

The dual was marked by a set of endings attached to the singular base of the noun, following the feminine marker if one was present. The evidence of Old Akkadian, Ugaritic, Ṣayhadic, and Arabic indicates that the dual was regularly used to indicate "two" of anything. In later Akkadian, in Hebrew, and in early Aramaic the use of the dual came to be restricted to words for naturally occurring pairs of objects and certain time words. In later Aramaic, in Ethiopian, and in some of the Mahrian languages the use of the dual has become obsolescent or has been lost entirely.

The plural in a northern group of the Semitic languages – namely, Akkadian and the Northwest Semitic subbranch – is indicated by a set of endings attached to the singular base of the noun, replacing the case endings of the singular; the feminine ending is altered from **-(a)t* to **-a:t* in the plural. These plural endings may to a certain extent be seen to involve the feature [+ length] vis-à-vis their singular counterparts. In the rest of the languages – Ethiopian, Mahrian, Ṣayhadic, and Arabic – pluralization is normally expressed by means of pattern replacement (called "broken plurals" or "internal plurals"), of the type **kalb-*

"dog," plural **kila:b-*. Such forms take the same case endings as singular forms. Since there is evidence for both types of pluralization in both groups of languages, in other words, vestigial use of pattern replacement in the northern group, and the use of external plural endings for certain noun types in the other languages, it is clear that both types are to be reconstructed for Proto-Semitic. It seems plausible that the external plurals were at first restricted to verbal adjectives (the endings are clearly related formally to the endings on predicate adjectives with third-person subjects), and that most other nouns either had plurals formed by pattern replacement or were collectives that had no special plural forms (or, perhaps, were simply unmarked for number). Certain features of the pattern-replacement plurals, such as *a*-insertion between the second and third root radicals, can be traced back to Common Afro-Asiatic (Greenberg 1955a; Ratcliffe 1998).

3.3.2.5 Declension

Below is presented a sample Proto-Semitic nominal paradigm, that of the active participle of the root **w-θ-b* "to sit, dwell," including feminine and external plural forms. The elements *-m* and *-na* are present only in the free (unbound) forms of the noun, but missing in bound forms (see §3.3.2.1).

(3) **The Proto-Semitic nominal paradigm**

	Masculine	*Feminine*
Singular		
Nominative	wa:θibu-m	wa:θib(a)tu-m
Genitive	wa:θibi-m	wa:θib(a)ti-m
Accusative	wa:θiba-m	wa:θib(a)ta-m
Dual		
Nominative	wa:θiba:-na	wa:θib(a)ta:-na
Genitive-accusative	wa:θibay-na	wa:θib(a)tay-na
Plural		
Nominative	wa:θibu:-na	wa:θiba:tu-m
Genitive-accusative	wa:θibi:-na	wa:θiba:ti-m

3.3.2.6 Noun derivation

A number of specific nominal patterns, when applied to verbal roots, may be identified with certain semantic classes (see Barth 1894, Fox 2003). Thus, for example, the pattern R_1*a:*R_2*i*R_3 is reconstructable as the active participle of nonstative verbal roots. Nouns of the monosyllabic patterns R_1*V*R_2R_3 are normally substantives rather than adjectives, whereas nouns of the patterns R_1*a*R_2*V*R_3 tend to be (but need not be) adjectives. Of the monosyllabic patterns just mentioned, R_1*i*R_2R_3 substantives are frequently passive: **θik'l-* "weight, what is weighed," **simʕ-* "report, what is heard," **ðibħ* "sacrifice, what is sacrificed." The pattern R_1*u*R_2R_3 is often used for abstracts of stative roots: **ʔurk-* "length," **murr-* "bitterness," **t'u:b-* (< **t'uyb-*) "goodness." In general, however, it is only the patterns of such deverbal forms that are reconstructable for the proto-language, not individual lexemes, much reshuffling having occurred in the various branches and individual languages.

Derivational endings include the following: (i) **-a:n*, an individualizing morpheme, as in Akkadian *šarra:k'a:num* "the thief in question," from *šarra:k'um* "thief"; (ii) **-i:y*, which forms denominative adjectives (including gentilics), such as **sapli:y-* "low," from

**sapl-* "bottom, under part"; and (iii) **-u:t*, which forms abstracts, as in **baʕlu:t-* "lordship," from **baʕl-* "lord."

3.3.3 Personal pronouns

The personal pronouns, like nouns, have three numbers, singular, dual, and plural. First-person forms are of common gender, while both the second and the third persons exhibit distinct masculine and feminine forms in the singular and the plural. Duals are of common gender. First-person dual forms are only rarely attested in the descendant languages, and where attested may be later innovations rather than vestiges of Proto-Semitic forms. The enclitic forms of the pronouns distinguish a nominative set, used as the subjects of predicate adjectives, as in **salim-nu(:)* "we are well" (see §3.3.5.1), and a genitive/accusative set, used as possessive pronouns on nouns, as in * *baytu-ka(:)* "your (masc. sg.) house," and as objects on verbs, as in **yanθ'ur-ka(:)* "he guarded you (masc. sg.)." For the first person, distinct genitive and accusative forms existed.

In Table A.2, the vowels occurring at the ends of many of the forms are marked as optionally long; they are short when word-final, long otherwise. The second- and third-person plural forms must be reconstructed with optional extensions, namely, **-u:* on masculine forms (e.g., **sumu:* in addition to **sum*), and **-na(:)* or **-a:* on feminine forms (e.g., **sinna(:)* or **sina:* in addition to **sin*). If Proto-Semitic is to be reconstructed with syllabic sonorants (see §3.2.1), then the second- and third-person dual and plural pronouns may be reconstructed as, for example, second masculine plural **-tm̩/*, second feminine plural **-tn̩/*, and so forth, rather than with the sequence [homorganic vowel + sonorant] as given in Table 6.2.

Possessive adjectives are attested in several of the Semitic languages, but their divergent construction makes it difficult to reconstruct such forms for the proto-language.

The Semitic languages do not attest a true reflexive pronoun, and it is unlikely that one existed in the proto-language. The reflexive was expressed by a set of derived verbal forms

Table A.2 Proto-Semitic personal pronouns

	Independent	Enclitic	
	Nominative	Nominative	Genitive-accusative
Singular			
1st com.	ʔana(:), ʔana:ku(:)	-ku(:)	-i:/-ya (gen.), -ni: (acc.)
2nd masc.	ʔanta(:)	-ta(:)	-ka(:)
2nd fem.	ʔanti(:)	-ti(:)	-ki(:)
3rd masc.	suʔa	-a	-su(:)
3rd fem.	siʔa	-at	-sa(:)/-si(:)
Dual			
1st com.	?	-nuya:?	-niya:? (gen.), -naya:? (acc.)
2nd com.	ʔantuma:	-tuma:	-kuma:/-kumay
3rd com.	suma:	-a:	-suma:/sumay
Plural			
1st com.	niħnu(:)	-nu(:)	-ni(:) (gen.), -na(:) (acc.)
2nd masc.	ʔantum	-tum	-kum
2nd fem.	ʔantin	-tin	-kin
3rd masc.	sum	-u:	-sum
3rd fem.	sin	-a:	-sin

(see §3.3.5.2) and by means of a substantive meaning "person" or "body": for example, **yanθ'ur napsa-su(:)* "he guarded his person" = "he guarded himself."

3.3.4 Demonstrative and interrogative pronouns

Proto-Semitic had a determinative-relative pronoun, **ðu:* or **θu:* (the initial consonant is voiced in West Semitic, unvoiced in Akkadian), declinable for gender, number, and case (e.g., fem. sg. nom. **ða:tu*), always used as a bound form, with the meaning "the one of, that of, he/she of," as in **θu: baytim* "the one of the house, he of the house"; *θu: ʔanθ'uru* "the one whom I guarded." It was commonly used in apposition to (and agreeing in case with) an antecedent: **baʕlum θu: baytim* "the lord(, the one) of the house," **baytu baʕlim θi: ʔanθ'uru* "the house of the lord(, the one) whom I guarded."

In West Semitic, the determinative-relative pronoun entered into the formation of a set of demonstrative pronouns, such as masculine singular **ðin*, feminine singular **ða:* "this." Another demonstrative base was **ʔV l(l)*, which appears in the plural of near demonstratives in West Semitic and as a far demonstrative (sg. and pl.) in Akkadian.

The third person pronouns were used as anaphoric or far demonstratives, as in **baytum suʔa* "that house," "the aforementioned house."

The evidence of the descendant languages for the interrogative pronouns is inconsistent. For "what?," Akkadian and Ethiopic suggest a form **min-*, while Central Semitic has **ma:-/mah-*; for "who?" most languages have **man-*, while in Ugaritic and Canaanite the form is **mi:y-*. A common Semitic interrogative adjective is **ʔayy-* "which?"

3.3.5 Verbal morphology

Proto-Semitic had two basic indicative forms, which differed primarily in aspect. The forms were conjugated for person, gender, and number by means of prefixes and, in some instances, suffixes. Essentially, a *perfective*, punctive form prefix+$R_1R_2V_1R_3$ contrasted with an *imperfective* form with gemination of the middle radical, prefix+$R_1aR_2R_2V_2R_3$, as in **yanθ'ur* "he guarded" versus **yanaθ'θ'ar* "he guards."

It seems likely that the bases of these forms were originally verbal adjectives, perfective (and passive) **naθ'ur-* "guarded" (note, for example, Akkadian *nas'ir* and Hebrew *nɔs'ur* with that meaning) and imperfective (and active) **naθ'θ'ar-* "guarding" (note the Common Semitic adjectival pattern $R_1 aR_2R_2V_2(:)R_3$ for nouns expressing durative or habitual activity, as in **dayya(:)n-* "judge"). The pattern of the imperfective base, at least, was probably an inheritance from Common Afro-Asiatic (Greenberg 1952).

The perfective paradigm of the root *nθ'r* "to guard" is presented in (4):

(4)

	Singular	*Dual*	*Plural*
1st com.	ʔanθ'ur		nanθ'ur
2nd masc.	tanθ'ur		tanθ'uru:
2nd fem.	tanθ'uri:		tanθ'urna(:)
2nd com.		tanθ'ura:	
3rd masc.	yanθ'ur		yanθ'uru:
3rd fem.	tanθ'ur		yanθ'urna(:)
3rd com.		yanθ'ura:	

Akkadian attests a third inflected indicative verbal form, called the *Perfect*, of the structure prefix+R_1 *ta*R_2 V_2R_3, as in **yantaθ'ar*, which functions as a present perfect, "he has guarded."

The existence of similar forms in other Afro-Asiatic branches, especially Berber and Cushitic, has been noted, and the suggestion offered that the Akkadian Perfect reflects a Proto-Semitic form that has been lost in West Semitic. But the Akkadian Perfect is formally identical with the perfective form of a Common Semitic – and ultimately also Common Afro-Asiatic – derived, mediopassive verbal class, and it seems likely that the former arose from the latter in an internal Akkadian development, perhaps under Sumerian influence.

In addition to these indicative forms, a number of modal forms may be posited. The imperative was confined to second-person forms, and had the shape of the perfective form without its prefixes, the initial consonant cluster being resolved by either prothesis or anaptyxis:

(5)

	Singular	*Dual*	*Plural*
2nd masc.	nuθ'ur / ʔunθ'ur		nuθ'uru: / ʔunθ'uru:
2nd fem.	nuθ'uri: / ʔunθ'uri:		nuθ'urna(:) / ʔunθ'urna(:)
2nd com.		nuθ'ura: / ʔunθ'ura:	

By itself or with a prefixed asseverative particle **l(a)-*, the perfective form could be used injunctively, as a jussive, "let him guard." Other modal forms, likewise related to or based on the perfective **yanθ'ur*, probably also occurred, but are difficult to reconstruct for Proto-Semitic with certainty, since they appear only in one or two of the branches of the family (e.g., **yanθ'ura*, with final *-a*; one or more "energic" forms, such as **yanθ'uran(na)*).

Akkadian verbs in subordinate clauses are obligatorily (and usually redundantly) marked with an ending *-u* or *-ni* (probably < **-na*). It is likely that this mark of nominalization is of Proto-Semitic origin. In Central Semitic, the perfective verb with this ending came to be used as an imperfective form, replacing the inherited Proto-Semitic form **yanaθ'θ'ar.*

3.3.5.1 Verbal nouns

Two verbal adjectives may be reconstructed for Proto-Semitic: (i) an *active participle* of the form R_1*a:*R_2*i*R_3, as in **na:θ'ir-* "guarding, who guards" (probably only for verbal roots expressing actions); and (ii) a *perfective adjective* of the form R_1*a*R_2*V*R_3, the meaning of which depended on the lexical meaning of the root: passive for transitive verbs (6A), resultative for intransitive active verbs (6B), and descriptive for stative verbs (6C):

(6) A. **naθ'ur-* "guarded" (*n-θ'-r* "to guard")
B. **waθib-* "having sat, seated" (*w-θ-b* "to sit, dwell")
C. **ħadaθ-* "new" (*ħ-d-θ* "to be(come) new")

The uninflected base of the verbal adjective could be combined with an enclitic nominative form of the person pronouns (see §3.3.3) to create a verbless (and thus tenseless) predication:

(7) **naθ'ur-ta(:)* "you (masc. sg.) are/were guarded"
**waθib-nu(:)* "we are/were seated"
**ħadaθ-at* "it (fem.) is/was new"

This construction is also attested in the oldest dialects of ancient Egyptian. In West Semitic the construction evolved in nonstative roots into an active, perfective verb, which began to replace the inherited form **ya*R_1R_2*V*R_3; the development entailed a change of vocalism between the second and third radicals, to **a*: **naθ'arta(:)* "you (have) guarded," **waθabnu(:)* "we (have) sat."

It is likely that more than one pattern was used for the *infinitive*, including R_1*a*R_2*a:*R_3 and R_1*i*R_2R_3, as in **naθ'a:r-* and **niθ'r-* "to guard, the guarding."

3.3.5.2 *Derived verbs*

The examples of verbs that have been cited thus far in this chapter reflect the basic stem of the verbal root, which Semitists usually call the *G stem*, after German *Grundstamm*. From this basic stem are derived other stems, each with a fairly predictable semantic range vis-à-vis the basic stem; derivation is by means of one of a set of prefixed consonants or by means of the doubling of the second or third root consonant:

1. *The N stem*: With prefixed *n*, the perfective form of which was based on the basic verbal adjective of the root, turning the latter into a fientic verb; for most roots the semantic result is a passive: for example, G stem perfective **yapk'id* "he sought"; adjective **pak'id-* "sought," N stem perfective **ya-n-pak'id* "it became/was sought."
2. *The C (causative) stem*: With prefixed *s* (originally, in all likelihood, a third-person pronoun serving as an agent), with causative force: **yusapk'id* "he caused (someone) to seek"; especially common with verbs of motion: G stem **yaʕliy* "he went up," C stem **yusaʕliy* "he caused (something) to go up" = "he sent/took/brought/led up."
3. *The D (doubled) stem*: Marked by gemination of the second radical, the effect of which was to increase the transitivity of the basic stem (Kouwenberg 1997); for stative verbal roots, the result is a factitive: G stem **yiħlal* "it was/became pure," D stem **yuħallil* "he purified"; for transitive verbal roots, the D stem is most often pluralic.

The G, C, and D stems could all be augmented by a prefixed *t*, associated with the notions of reciprocity, reflexivity, and the mediopassive; perfective forms of these may be illustrated by tG **yatpak'id*; tD **yutħallVl*; Ct (with *t* following the causative prefix *s*) **yustaʕliy*.

4. *The R stem*: With reduplication of the third radical (perfective $*yVR_1aR_2R_3iR_3$, imperfective $*yVR_1aR_2aR_3R_3aR_3$, verbal adjective $*R_1aR_2VR_3R_3$ or $*R_1aR_2R_3VR_3$). This stem is likely also to be reconstructed for Proto-Semitic; further investigation is required to elucidate the semantics of the stem, which is only vestigially preserved in most of the languages (apart from Arabic). It tends to involve description of physical qualities or states.

As noted above, most of these derived verbal stems have analogues elsewhere in Afro-Asiatic (Lieberman 1986).

3.3.6 Compounds

The Semitic languages, and presumably Proto-Semitic as well, exhibit remarkably few instances of compounding in either the nominal or the verbal morphology.

3.3.7 Numerals

The Proto-Semitic cardinals 1 through 10 were declined like singular nouns, except for 2 which was declined as a dual. They occurred in both masculine and feminine forms. In an unusual – and still unexplained – syntactic phenomenon reflected in nearly all the descendant languages, for the numbers from 3 to 10 the masculine form of the cardinal was used when the counted item was a feminine noun, and the feminine form of the cardinal with masculine nouns. The basic forms of the cardinals were as follows; feminine forms were marked with the addition of **-(a)t*.

(8)
1 *ʔaħad-
2 *θin-/*θn̩-
3 *θala:θ-
4 *ʔarbaʕ
5 *xamis-
6 *sidθ-
7 *sabʕ-
8 *θama:niy-
9 *tisʕ-
10 *ʕaɬr-

The cardinal 20 is the dual of 10, **ʕaɬra:-*; the other tens have the appearance of being duals (plurals in Central Semitic) of the corresponding units: for example, **θala:θa:-* 30. "Hundred" is **miʔ(a)t-*; higher numbers are difficult to reconstruct with certainty ("thousand" is West Semitic **ʔalp-*, East Semitic **liʔm-*; for "10,000; myriad" West Semitic has forms derived from the root *r-b-b* "to be(come) much, many").

Unlike the cardinals, the ordinals are generally constructed on a single pattern; the pattern, however, varies from language to language (e.g., the pattern R_1*a:*R_2*i*R_3 in classical Arabic and classical Ethiopic, as in *θa:liθ-* "third," *ra:biʕ* "fourth," *xa:mis-* "fifth"), and so cannot be reconstructed to the proto-language.

3.4 Syntax

3.4.1 Word order

Proto-Semitic was probably a VSO (Verb–Subject–Object) language. This is true of the earliest forms of most West Semitic languages. Most dialects of Akkadian were rigidly SOV, but word order in poetic texts is much freer; further, early Akkadian personal names composed of a subject and a verb are frequently VS, as in *Iddin-Si:n* "[the god] Sin has given [a child]." The normal SOV order of Akkadian is undoubtedly due to Sumerian influence.

Modifiers, including adjectives, genitives, and relative clauses, follow their head noun.

3.4.2 Clitics

Semitic is characterized by a number of prefixed monosyllabic relational particles, including the coordinating conjunction **wa-* "and," the asseverative particle **l(a)-*, and, in West Semitic, the prepositions **ba-* "in," **la-* "to, for," and **ka-* "like" (in early Akkadian dialects, too, proclitic forms of certain prepositions are attested: *an-*, *in-*, and *el-* for *ana* "to, for," *ina* "in," *eli* "on," respectively).

Much of the personal pronoun system consists of suffixed morphemes, as in **la-su(:)* "to him" **baytu-su(:)* "his house," **ʔanθ'ur-su:* "I guarded him"; two of these suffixes, denoting indirect and direct objects in sequence, could appear on finite verbs: **yantinu:-ni:-su(:)* "they (masc.) gave me it (masc.)" (Gensler 1998).

The enclitic particle **-ma(:)* served to topicalize the word to which it was attached; in Akkadian and in several modern Ethiopian languages it also developed into a coordinating conjunction. The Proto-Semitic status of other enclitic forms attested in the various languages remains to be investigated, as, for example, **-mi(:)*, an emphasizing particle in Northwest Semitic, but a marker of direct speech in Akkadian.

3.4.3 Coordination

The essential Proto-Semitic coordinating conjunction was the proclitic particle **wa-*, which was used to connect words, clauses (including connecting main clauses to preceding subordinate clauses), and sentences. Unclear as yet are the Proto-Semitic status and functions of the Central Semitic proclitic clause connector **pa-*, meaning, *inter alia*, "and then, and so" (for the very common Akkadian enclitic clause connector *-ma*, see §3.4.2).

3.4.4 Subordination

Subordinate clauses are less common in Semitic than in some languages, simple coordination usually being preferred. Nevertheless a few subordinating conjunctions may be reconstructed. A general subordinating conjunction was **ki:* (also **ki(:)ma(:)*), attested in a number of the descendant languages with the meanings "when, because, that." Several words functioned both as prepositions and as conjunctions: for example **ʕad(ay)* "up to, until." Certain bound-form nouns could also function as the equivalent of conjunctions, as in **yawma ʔanθ'uru* "the day (= when) I guarded" (with the accusative of **yawm-* "day" used adverbially; also with a preposition: **ba-yawmi ʔanθ'uru* "on the day I guarded").

Subordination was also expressed by means of infinitives, especially with the preposition "in" for circumstance and the preposition "to, for" for purpose and result: **ba-naθ'a:ri-su(:)* "in his guarding" = "while he guards/guarded" (or "while guarding him"); **la-naθ'a:risu(:)* "for his guarding" = "(in order) that he guard" (or "(in order) to guard him").

3.4.5 Verbless clauses

While a verb "to be, become" can be reconstructed for Proto-Semitic, namely, **hawaya*, the notion "to be" was not normally expressed and verbless clauses were a common feature. With a nominal or pronominal subject, the predicate could be (i) adverbial (adverb or prepositional phrase: "he [is] in the house"; "my sister [is] here"); (ii) adjectival, in which case the construction described in §3.3.5.1 was used; or (iii) nominal, with both subject and predicate in the nominative case (**ʔimmu-su(:) baʕlatu-nu(:)* "his mother is our mistress"). A third-person pronoun in apposition to the subject could be included in the clause, probably either before or after the predicate (**ʔimmu-su(:) siʔa baʕlatu-nu(:)* or **ʔimmu-su(:) baʕlatu-nu(:) siʔa* "his mother [she] is our mistress"; the pronoun is traditionally said to function as a copula in such instances).

For existential sentences, the phrase "in it," **ba-su(:)*, with the meaning "there is" may perhaps be reconstructed to Proto-Semitic, since "in it" is so used in classical Ethiopic (*bo* < **ba-hu:, botu*), various Arabic dialects (*fi:* < *fi:-hi*), and Akkadian (in which by the time of the earliest dialect the construction had developed into a finite verb, **basa:ʔum* "to be present, on hand"). A particle **yiθ-* "there is/are" can be reconstructed for Central Semitic; it is cognate with an Eblaite infinitive, *i-ša-wu* = /yVθa:wu(m)/, known from a lexical text, where it is equated with Sumerian A/AN.GÁL "be."

For "to have" Akkadian attests the irregular verb *išûm*, of uncertain etymology (connected by some scholars with **yiθ-*, etc., cited in the preceding paragraph, but the few Old Akkadian writings of *išûm* suggest that the middle radical was not **θ*). In West Semitic, however, possession is expressed with the dative preposition either as the predicate of a verbless clause or governed by the verb "to be" (e.g., "the lord has a house" by "[a] house [is] to [the] lord").

3.5 Lexicon

Additional research is needed before the percentage of Proto-Semitic vocabulary inherited from common Afro-Asiatic can be estimated.

A few Common Semitic words resemble Indo-European words or roots: **θawr-* beside PIE **tauro-* "bull"; **k'arn-* beside PIE **kr̥-n-* "horn"; and **ʕaθtar-* "morning/evening star" beside PIE **$h_2$ste:r-* "star"; the significance of these similarities is unclear. Other words show by their divergent reflexes in the descendant languages, as well as by their unusual patterns, that they were not native to Common Semitic, such as **b/par^{d}zil-* "iron," **ʔan(n)a(:)k-* "lead," **ʔuk'niy-* "lapis lazuli" (with the last compare Hittite *ku(wa)nna-*, Greek *küános*).

4. READING LIST

Surveys of the Afro-Asiatic languages and of common Afro-Asiatic features are given in Greenberg 1955b, 1970; Hodge 1971; Sasse *et al.* 1981; Hetzron 1987; D. Cohen 1988; Diakonoff 1988; Petráček 1988; and Hayward 2000. Important works dealing with specific features include Rössler 1950; Greenberg 1952, 1955a; Lieberman 1986; Voigt 1987a; Zaborski 1995. A pioneering treatment of common Afro-Asiatic vocabulary is M. Cohen 1947; the recent dictionary of Orel and Stolbova 1995 has been widely criticized in scholarly reviews.

A recent compendium in which all of the major Semitic languages are covered is Hetzron 1997. The fundamental reference work on Semitic grammar is Brockelmann 1908–1913; other general works on Semitic are Nöldeke 1904, 1910; Bergsträsser 1928; Gray 1934; Kuryłowicz 1973; Moscati 1964; Garbini and Durand 1994; Lipiński 1997; Bennett 1998; Stempel 1999; Kienast 2001.

The internal classification or subgrouping of the Semitic languages has been a subject of much discussion, and a consensus has not been reached. The subgrouping presented here is that proposed by Hetzron 1974, 1976; as modified in Huehnergard 1991, 2002; Nebes 1994; and Porkhomovsky 1997.

The current understanding of the consonantal phonology of Proto-Semitic is the result of the work of several scholars, but especially Steiner 1977, 1982; Faber 1984, 1985, 1989; and Voigt 1987b.

The Semitic root and pattern system is discussed recently in McCarthy 1979; Goldenberg 1994; and Fox 2003. The pronominal systems are considered in Barth 1913; Rundgren 1955; Castellino 1962; Pennacchietti 1968; nominal inflection, *inter alia*, in Diem 1975; Voigt 1987a; Ratcliffe 1998. Of the many important studies of the Semitic verbal system only a very small selection may be noted here: Rundgren 1959; Retsö 1989; Tropper 1990.

Works on comparative and historical Semitic syntax continue to be few, but mention should be made of D. Cohen 1984; Khan 1988; and Gensler 1998.

The Common Semitic lexicon was considered in an important series of articles in Fronzaroli 1964–1971. A complete Semitic etymological dictionary does not exist; the fascicles of the *Dictionnaire des racines sémitiques* (Cohen 1970–) that have thus far appeared cover about one-third of the Semitic roots.

Bibliography

Barth, J. 1894. *Die Nominalbildung in den semitischen Sprachen* (2nd edition). Leipzig: Hinrichs.
———. 1913. *Die Pronominalbildung in den semitischen Sprachen.* Leipzig: Hinrichs.
Bennett, P. 1998. *Comparative Semitic Linguistics: A Manual.* Winona Lake, IN: Eisenbrauns.

Bergsträsser, G. 1928. *Einführung in die semitischen Sprachen: Sprachproben und grammatische Skizzen.* Munich: Max Hueber. Translated (with notes, bibliography and an appendix on the scripts) by P. Daniels as *Introduction to the Semitic Languages. Text Specimens and Grammatical Sketches.* Winona Lake, IN: Eisenbrauns, 1983.

Brockelmann, C. 1908–1913. *Grundriss der vergleichenden Grammatik der semitischen Sprachen* (2 vols.). Berlin: von Reuther.

Castellino, G. 1962. *The Akkadian Personal Pronouns and Verbal System in the Light of Semitic and Hamitic.* Leiden: Brill.

Cohen, D. 1970–. *Dictionnaire des racines sémitiques ou attestées dans les langues sémitiques.* Paris/The Hague: Mouton; Louvain-la-Neuve: Peeters.

______. 1984. *La phrase nominale et l'évolution du système verbal en sémitique: études de syntaxe historique.* Collection Linguistique 72. Paris: Société de Linguistique de Paris.

______. (ed.). 1988. *Les langues chamito-sémitiques.* In Jean Perrot (general ed.), *Les langues dans le monde ancien et moderne,* part 3. Paris: CNRS Editions.

Cohen, M. 1947. *Essai comparatif sur le vocabularie et la phonétique du chamito-sémitique.* Bibliothèque de l'Ecole des Hautes Etudes 248. Paris: Champion.

Diakonoff, I. 1988. *Afrasian Languages.* Moscow: Nauka.

______. 1998. "The earliest Semitic society: linguistic data." *Journal of Semitic Studies* 43:209–219.

Diem, W. 1975. "Gedanken zur Frage der Mimation und Nunation in den semitischen Sprachen." *Zeitschrift der Deutschen Morgenländischen Gesellschaft* 125:239–258.

Faber, A. 1984. "Semitic sibilants in an Afro-Asiatic context." *Journal of Semitic Studies* 29:189–224.

______. 1985. "Akkadian evidence for Proto-Semitic affricates." *Journal of Cuneiform Studies* 37:101–107.

______. 1989. "On the nature of Proto-Semitic **l.*" *Journal of the American Oriental Society* 109:33–36.

Fleming, H. 1999. "Afroasiatic internal taxonomy: new methods and better results." Paper presented at the 26th annual meeting of the North American Conference on Afroasiatic Linguistics, Baltimore, April 1999.

Fleming, H., A. Yilma, A. Mitiku, *et al.* 1992. "Ongota (or) Birale: a moribund language of Gemu-Gofa (Ethiopia)." *Journal of Afroasiatic Languages* 3:181–225.

Fox, J. 1998. "Isolated nouns in the Semitic languages." *Zeitschrift für Althebraistik* 11:1–31.

______. 2003. *Semitic Noun Patterns.* Harvard Semitic Studies. Winona Lake, IN: Eisenbrauns.

Fronzaroli, P. 1964–1971. "Studie sul lessico commune semitico." *RANL* 19 (1964):155–172 (I), 243–280 (II); 20 (1965):135–150 (III), 246–269 (IV); 23 (1968):267–303 (V); 24 (1969): 285–320 (VI); 26 (1971):603–642 (VII).

Garbini, G. and O. Durand. 1994. *Introduzione alle lingue semitiche.* Brescia: Paedeia.

Gensler, O. 1997. "Reconstructing quadriliteral verb inflection: Ethiopic, Akkadian, Proto-Semitic." *Journal of Semitic Studies* 42:229–257.

______. 1998. "Verbs with two object suffixes: a Semitic archaism in its Afroasiatic context." *Diachronica* 15:231–284.

Goldenberg, G. 1994. "Principles of Semitic word-structure." In G. Goldenberg and S. Raz (eds.), *Semitic and Cushitic Studies,* pp. 29–64. Wiesbaden: Harrassowitz.

Gray, L. 1934. *Introduction to Semitic Comparative Linguistics.* New York: Columbia University.

Greenberg, J. 1950. "The patterning of root morphemes in Semitic." *Word* 6:162–181.

______. 1952. "The Afro-Asiatic (Hamito-Semitic) present." *Journal of the American Oriental Society* 72:1–9.

______. 1955a. "Internal *a*-plurals in Afroasiatic (Hamito-Semitic)." In J. Lukas (ed.), *Afrikanistische Studien,* pp. 198–204. Berlin: Academie-Verlag.

______. 1955b. *Studies in African Linguistic Classification.* New Haven.

______. 1970. *The Languages of Africa* (3rd edition). Indiana University Research Center for Language Sciences, Publication 25. Bloomington: Indiana University Press.

Hayward, R. 2000. "Afroasiatic." In B. Heine and D. Nurse (eds.), *African Languages: An Introduction,* pp. 74–98. Cambridge University Press.

Hetzron, R. 1974. "La division des langues sémitiques." In A. Caquot and D. Cohen (eds.), *Actes du premier congrès international de linguistique sémitique et chamito-sémitique, Paris 16–19 juillet 1969,* pp. 181–194. The Hague/Paris: Mouton.

______. 1976. "Two principles of genetic reconstruction." *Lingua* 38:89–108.

______. 1980. "The limits of Cushitic." *Sprache und Geschichte in Afrika* 2:7–126.

______. 1987. "Afroasiatic languages." In B. Comrie (ed.), *The World's Major Languages*, pp. 645–53. New York: Oxford University Press.

Hetzron, R. (ed.). 1997. *The Semitic Languages.* London/New York: Routledge.

Hodge, C. (ed.). 1971. *Afroasiatic: A Survey.* The Hague/Paris: Mouton. Reprinted from T. A. Sebeok (ed.), *Current Trends in Linguistics.* Vol. VI: *Linguistics in South West Asia and North Africa*, pp. 237–661. The Hague/Paris: Mouton, 1970.

Huehnergard, J. 1991. "Remarks on the classification of the Northwest Semitic languages." In J. Hoftijzer and G. van der Kooij (eds.), *The Balaam Text from Deir ʿAlla Re-evaluated. Proceedings of the International Symposium held at Leiden 21–24 August 1989*, pp. 282–293. Leiden: Brill.

______. 2002. "Comparative Semitic linguistics." *Israel Oriental Studies* 20 (S. Izre'el, ed., *Semitic Linguistics: The State of the Art at the Turn of the Twenty-First Century*):213–245.

Khan, G. 1988. *Studies in Semitic Syntax.* London Oriental Studies 38. Oxford: Oxford University Press.

Kienast, B. 2001. *Historische semitische Sprachwissenschaft.* Wiesbaden: Harrassowitz.

Kouwenberg, N. 1997. *Gemination in the Akkadian Verb.* Studia Semitica Neerlandica. Assen: Van Gorcum.

Kuryłowicz, J. 1973. *Studies in Semitic Grammar and Metrics.* London: Curzon Press. (Translation and revision of *L'apophonie en sémitique* 1961.)

Lieberman, S. 1986. "The Afro-Asiatic background of the Semitic N-stem: toward the origins of the Semitic and Afro-Asiatic verb." *Bibliotheca Orientalis* 43:577–628.

Lipiński, E. 1997. *Semitic Languages: Outline of a Comparative Grammar.* Orientalia Lovaniensia Analecta 80. Louvain-la-Neuve: Peeters/Departement Oosterse Studies.

McCarthy, J. 1979. *Formal Problems in Semitic Phonology and Morphology.* Ph.D. dissertation, MIT. (= New York: Garland, 1985.)

Militarev, A. 1994. "Home for Afrasian: African or Asian? Areal linguistic arguments." In C. Griefenow-Menis and R. Voigt (eds.), *Cushitic and Omotic Languages: Proceedings of the Third International Symposium, Berlin, March 17–19, 1994*, pp. 13–32. Cologne: Rüdiger Köppe.

Moscati, S. (ed.). 1964. *An Introduction to the Comparative Grammar of the Semitic Languages: Phonology and Morphology.* Wiesbaden: Harrassowitz.

Nebes, N. 1994. "Zur Form der Imperfektbasis des unvermehrten Grundstammes im Altsüdarabischen." In W. Heinrichs and G. Schoeler (eds.), *Festschrift Ewald Wagner zum 65. Geburtstag.* Vol. I, *Semitische Studien unter besonderer Berücksichtigung der Südsemitistik*, pp. 59–81. Beirut/Stuttgart: Steiner.

Nöldeke, T. 1904. *Beiträge zur semitischen Sprachwissenschaft.* Strasburg: Trübner.

______. 1910. *Neue Beiträge zur semitischen Sprachwissenschaft.* Strasburg: Trübner.

O'Connor, M. 1996. "The Berber Scripts." In P. Daniels and W. Bright (eds.), *The World's Writing Systems*, pp. 112–116. New York/Oxford: Oxford University Press.

Orel, V. and O. Stolbova. 1995. *Hamito-Semitic Etymological Dictionary: Materials for a Reconstruction.* Leiden: Brill.

Pennacchietti, F. 1968. *Studi sui pronomi determinativi semitici.* Publicazioni del seminario de semitistica, ricerche 4. Naples: Istituto Orientale.

Petráček, K. 1988. *Altägyptisch, Hamitosemitisch und ihre Beziehungen zu einigen Sprachfamilien in Afrika und Asien.* Praha: Univerzita Karlova.

Porkhomovsky, V. 1997. "Modern South Arabian languages from a Semitic and Hamito-Semitic perspective." *Proceedings of the Seminar for Arabian Studies* 27:219–223.

Ratcliffe, R. 1998. *The Broken Plural Problem in Arabic and Comparative Semitic: Allomorphy and Analogy in Non-Concatenative Morphology.* CILT 168. Amsterdam: John Benjamins.

Retsö, J. 1989. *Diathesis in the Semitic Languages: A Comparative Morphological Study.* Studies in Semitic Languages and Linguistics 14. Leiden: Brill.

Rössler, O. 1950. "Verbalbau und Verbalflexion in den semitohamitischen Sprachen. Vorstudien zu einer vergleichenden semitohamitischen Grammatik." *Zeitschrift der Deutschen Morgenländischen Gesellschaft* 100:461–514. Translated as "The structure and inflection of the verb in the Semito-Hamitic Languages: preliminary studies for a comparative Semito-Hamitic grammar," in Y. Arbeitman and A. Bomhard (eds.), *Bono Homini Donum: Essays in Historical Linguistics in Memory of J. Alexander Kerns*, pp. 679–748. Amsterdam: John Benjamins, 1981.

Rundgren, F. 1955. *Über Bildungen mit* s/š- *und* n-t-*Demonstrativen im Semitischen.* Uppsala: Almqvist and Wiksell.

———. 1959. *Intensiv und Aspektkorrelation.* Uppsala: Lundequistska; Wiesbaden: Otto Harrassowitz.

Sasse, H.-J. 1984. "Case in Cushitic, Semitic and Berber." In J. Bynon (ed.), *Current Progress in Afro-Asiatic Linguistics: Papers of the Third International Hamito-Semitic Congress*, pp. 111–126. Amsterdam/Philadelphia: John Benjamins.

Sasse, H.-J., L. Störk, and E. Wolff. 1981. "Afroasiatisch." In B. Heine, T. Schadeberg, and E. Wolff (eds.), *Die Sprachen Afrikas*, pp. 129–262. Hamburg: Helmut Buske.

Speiser, E. 1952. "The 'Elative' in West-Semitic and Akkadian." *Journal of Cuneiform Studies* 6:81–92.

Steiner, R. 1977. *The Case for Fricative-Laterals in Proto-Semitic.* American Oriental Series, 59. New Haven: American Oriental Society.

———. 1982. *Affricated Ṣade in the Semitic Languages.* The American Academy for Jewish Research Monograph Series 3. New York.

Stempel, R. 1999. *Abriß einer historischen Grammatik der semitischen Sprachen.* Nordostafrikanisch/Westasiatische Studien 3. Frankfurt am Main: Peter Lang.

Testen, D. 1998. *Parallels in Semitic Linguistics: The Development of Arabic la- and Related Semitic Particles.* Studies in Semitic Languages and Linguistics 26. Leiden: Brill.

Tropper, J. 1990. *Der ugaritische Kausativstamm und die Kausativbildungen des Semitischen: Eine morphologisch-semantische Untersuchung zum Š-Stamm und zu den umstrittenen nichtsibilantischen Kausativstämmen des Ugaritischen.* Abhandlungen zur Literatur Alt-Syrien-Palästinas 2. Münster: Ugarit Verlag.

Voigt, R. 1987a. "Derivatives und flektives *t* im Semitohamitischen." In H. Jungraithmayr and W. Müller (eds.), *Proceedings of the Fourth International Hamito-Semitic Congress, Marburg, 20–22 September, 1983*, pp. 85–107. CILT, 44. Amsterdam/Philadelphia: John Benjamins.

———. 1987b. "Die Personalpronomina der 3. Personen im Semitischen." *Welt des Orients* 18:49–63.

Zaborski, A. 1995. "Problems of Hamitosemitic pronouns." *Sprawozdania z Posiedzeń Komisji Naukowych* 38:59–62.

APPENDIX 2

Full tables of contents from *The Cambridge Encyclopedia of the World's Ancient Languages*, and from the other volumes in the paperback series

Table of contents of *WAL*

	List of figures		page vii
	List of tables		xi
	List of maps		xiv
	List of contributors		xv
	Preface		xvii
	List of abbreviations		xviii
1	Introduction	ROGER D. WOODARD	1
2	Sumerian	PIOTR MICHALOWSKI	19
3	Elamite	MATTHEW W. STOLPER	60
4	Hurrian	GERNOT WILHELM	95
5	Urartian	GERNOT WILHELM	119
6	Afro-Asiatic	JOHN HUEHNERGARD	138
7	Ancient Egyptian and Coptic	ANTONIO LOPRIENO	160
8	Akkadian and Eblaite	JOHN HUEHNERGARD and CHRISTOPHER WOODS	218
9	Ugaritic	DENNIS PARDEE	288
10	Hebrew	P. KYLE MCCARTER, JR.	319
11	Phoenician and Punic	JO ANN HACKETT	365
12	Canaanite dialects	DENNIS PARDEE	386
13	Aramaic	STUART CREASON	391
14	Ge'ez (Aksum)	GENE GRAGG	427
15	Ancient South Arabian	NORBERT NEBES and PETER STEIN	454
16	Ancient North Arabian	M. C. A. MACDONALD	488

17	Indo-European	HENRY M. HOENIGSWALD, ROGER D. WOODARD, and JAMES P. T. CLACKSON	534
18	Hittite	CALVERT WATKINS	551
19	Luvian	H. CRAIG MELCHERT	576
20	Palaic	H. CRAIG MELCHERT	585
21	Lycian	H. CRAIG MELCHERT	591
22	Lydian	H. CRAIG MELCHERT	601
23	Carian	H. CRAIG MELCHERT	609
24	Attic Greek	ROGER D. WOODARD	614
25	Greek dialects	ROGER D. WOODARD	650
26	Sanskrit	STEPHANIE W. JAMISON	673
27	Middle Indic	STEPHANIE W. JAMISON	700
28	Old Persian	RÜDIGER SCHMITT	717
29	Avestan	MARK HALE	742
30	Pahlavi	MARK HALE	764
31	Phrygian	CLAUDE BRIXHE	777
32	Latin	JAMES P. T. CLACKSON	789
33	Sabellian languages	REX E. WALLACE	812
34	Venetic	REX E. WALLACE	840
35	Continental Celtic	JOSEPH F. ESKA	857
36	Gothic	JAY H. JASANOFF	881
37	Ancient Nordic	JAN TERJE FAARLUND	907
38	Classical Armenian	JAMES P. T. CLACKSON	922
39	Etruscan	HELMUT RIX	943
40	Early Georgian	KEVIN TUITE	967
41	Ancient Chinese	ALAIN PEYRAUBE	988
42	Old Tamil	SANFORD B. STEEVER	1015
43	Mayan	VICTORIA R. BRICKER	1041
44	Epi-Olmec	TERRENCE KAUFMAN and JOHN JUSTESON	1071
45	Reconstructed ancient languages	DON RINGE	1112
	Index		1129

Table of contents of *The Ancient Languages of Asia and the Americas*

	List of figures		vi
	List of tables		vii
	List of maps		viii
	List of contributors		ix
	Notes on numbering and cross-referencing		x
	List of abbreviations		xi
	Preface	ROGER D. WOODARD	xv
	Preface to the first edition	ROGER D. WOODARD	xix
1	Language in ancient Asia and the Americas: an introduction	ROGER D. WOODARD	1
2	Sanskrit	STEPHANIE W. JAMISON	6
3	Middle Indic	STEPHANIE W. JAMISON	33
4	Old Tamil	SANFORD B. STEEVER	50
5	Old Persian	RÜDIGER SCHMITT	76
6	Avestan	MARK HALE	101
7	Pahlavi	MARK HALE	123
8	Ancient Chinese	ALAIN PEYRAUBE	136
9	Mayan	VICTORIA R. BRICKER	163
10	Epi-Olmec (Zapotec appendix)	TERRENCE KAUFMAN and JOHN JUSTESON	193
	Appendix 1. Reconstructed ancient languages	DON RINGE	234
	Appendix 2. Full tables of contents from The Cambridge Encyclopedia of the World's Ancient Languages, *and from the other volumes in the paperback series*		251
	Indexes		256

Table of contents of *The Ancient Languages of Asia Minor*

List of figures		vi
List of tables		vii
List of maps		viii
List of contributors		ix
Notes on numbering and cross-referencing		x
List of abbreviations		xi
Preface	ROGER D. WOODARD	xv
Preface to the first edition	ROGER D. WOODARD	xix

1	Language in ancient Asia Minor: an introduction	ROGER D. WOODARD	1
2	Hittite	CALVERT WATKINS	6
3	Luvain	H. CRAIG MELCHERT	31
4	Palaic	H. CRAIG MELCHERT	40
5	Lycian	H. CRAIG MELCHERT	46
6	Lydian	H. CRAIG MELCHERT	56
7	Carian	H. CRAIG MELCHERT	64
8	Phrygian	CLAUDE BRIXHE	69
9	Hurrian	GERNOT WILHELM	81
10	Urartian	GERNOT WILHELM	105
11	Classical Armenian	JAMES P. T. CLACKSON	124
12	Early Georgian	KEVIN TUITE	145

Appendix 1. The cuneiform script 166
Appendix 2. Full tables of contents from The Cambridge Encyclopedia of the World's Ancient Languages, *and from the other volumes in the paperback series* 173
Indexes 178

Table of contents for *The Ancient Languages of Europe*

List of figures		vi
List of tables		vii
List of maps		ix
List of contributors		x
Notes on numbering and cross-referencing		xi
List of abbreviations		xii
Preface	ROGER D. WOODARD	xv
Preface to the first edition	ROGER D. WOODARD	xix

1	Language in ancient Europe: an introduction	ROGER D. WOODARD	1
2	Attic Greek	ROGER D. WOODARD	14
3	Greek dialects	ROGER D. WOODARD	50
4	Latin	JAMES P. T. CLACKSON	73
5	Sabellian languages	REX E. WALLACE	96
6	Venetic	REX E. WALLACE	124
7	Etruscan	HELMUT RIX	141
8	Continental Celtic	JOSEPH F. ESKA	165

9 Gothic — JAY H. JASANOFF — 189

10 Ancient Nordic — JAN TERJE FAARLUND — 215

Appendix 1. Indo-European — HENRY M. HOENIGSWALD, ROGER D. WOODARD, and JAMES P. T. CLACKSON — 230

Appendix 2. Full tables of contents from The Cambridge Encyclopedia of the World's Ancient Languages, *and from the other volumes in the paperback series* — 247

Indexes — 252

Table of contents of *The Ancient Languages of Mesopotamia, Egypt, and Aksum*

List of figures — *page* vi

List of tables — vii

List of map — viii

List of contributors — ix

Notes on numbering and cross-referencing — x

List of abbreviations — xi

Preface — ROGER D. WOODARD — xv

Preface to the first edition — ROGER D. WOODARD — xix

1 Language in ancient Mesopotamia, Egypt, and Aksum: an introduction — ROGER D. WOODARD — 1

2 Sumerian — PIOTR MICHALOWSKI — 6

3 Elamite — MATTHEW W. STOLPER — 47

4 Akkadian and Eblaite — JOHN HUEHNERGARD and CHRISTOPHER WOODS — 83

5 Egyptian and Coptic — ANTONIO LOPRIENO — 153

6 Ge'ez (Aksum) — GENE GRAGG — 211

Appendix. Full tables of contents from The Cambridge Encyclopedia of the World's Ancient Languages, *and from the other volumes in the paperback series* — 238

Indexes — 243

Index of general subjects

Abecedaria 185, 191, 208
Acco 82
Acrophonic principle 84
Africa 83, 100, 225, 226, 228
Aḥiram 84
Aleppo 108, 109, 113
Alexander the Great 79
Al-Ǧawf 181
Algeria 83, 225, 226
Alphabet 84
Al-ʿulā 146, 181
Amorites 5
Anatolia 100, 103, 104
Antioch 106
Arabia (Arabian) 145, 146, 176, 179, 180, 181, 183, 185, 189, 191, 205, 211, 213, 220
Arabs (Arab) 109, 181, 184, 191
Arameans 84, 108, 109, 112
Asia (Asian) 103, 225, 228
Asia Minor 82, 95, 98
Assyria (Assyrian) 37, 108, 145
Assyrian Empire 79
Atlas Mountains 225
Awām-temple 145

Bab-al-Mandab 146
Babylon 104
Babylonia (Babylonian) 37, 38, 39, 190
Babylonian Empire 109, 183
Babylonian Exile 36, 38
Balearic Islands 82, 83
Balikh River 108
Barth, Jacob 52
Beeston, A. F. L. 145
Beja 226
Beqaʿ Valley 83
Beth-Shemesh 7
Bible 6, 36, 37, 39, 40, 50
Boustrophedon 83, 84, 86, 146, 186
  Late Bronze Age 5, 36
Byblos 82, 83, 93, 95, 97, 105

Cairo 189
Cameroon 226
Canaan (Canaanite) 82, 103, 104, 105
Canary Islands 226
Carthage 83, 84
Central African Republic 226
Chad 226
Christianity (Christian) 111
Consonantal scripts 6–8, 38, 84, 85, 105, 110, 151, 185
Cuneiform 6–7, 104, 105, 228
Cypro-Minoan 6
Cyprus (Cypriot) 82, 84, 93

Dadan 181, 208
Damascus 108, 109, 189
Dead Sea Scrolls 37, 109
Decipherment 7, 105
Deir ʿAlla 109
Delos 146
Demotic 228
Diacritics 39, 40, 43, 111–112
Dūmā 181

Egypt (Egyptian) 82, 88, 100, 103, 104, 106, 109, 146, 181, 190, 191, 208, 225, 226, 227
Eritrea 226, 228
Estrangelo 110
Ethiopia (Ethiopian) 226, 227, 228
Eusebius 88

France 83

Galilee (Galilean) 37, 38, 47
Gebleh Plain 6
Ginsberg, H. L. 52
Glossenkeil 104
  Arab 179, 184, 188, 190, 216
  Medieval Hebrew 63
Graphemes 7, 8
Greece (Greek) 82, 84, 85

Hadramawt 146
Haram 210, 212
Hattuša 104
Ḫawr Rūrī 146
Hebrews 84, 108
Hegrā 183
Hellenism (Hellenistic) 36, 88
Hermopolis 109
Herodotus 191, 208
Hexapla 37, 59, 67
Himyar 145, 146
Ḥismā 183
Hittites (Hittite) 6, 104, 108
Hurria (Hurrian) 108

Indian Ocean 146
Iraq 108, 189
Iron Age 36, 47, 37 38, 78, 79, 82
Islam (Islamic) 179, 185, 200, 220, 225
Israel 36, 37, 38, 82, 228
ʿIzbet Ṣarṭah 105

Jabal al-ʿAwd 146
Jebel al-Aqraʿ 5

Jebel Ansariyeh 5
Jerusalem 37, 38, 51, 189
Jewish script 38
Jordan 108, 181, 183
Josephus 88
Judaea 37, 79
Judah 36, 37, 38, 79
Judaism (Jewish) 36, 111

Karatepe 95, 98, 99, 100
Kenya 226
Khabur River 108

Lachish Ewer 105
Lebanon 82, 83, 103, 108
Libya 83, 226
Logograms (Logographic) 104
Luxor 84

Madā'in Ṣāliḥ 183
Mali 226
Malta 82, 83
Mari 5, 103
Marib 145, 146, 150
Masoretes (*See also* Masoretic text) 48, 49, 62
Masoretic text 40, 43, 44, 46, 50, 51, 60, 67, 48 49
Matres lectionis 9, 18, 38, 40, 63, 85, 98, 105, 111, 112, 114, 149, 186
Mauritania 226
Mediterranean 82, 83, 99, 103, 108, 181
Mesopotamia (Mesopotamian) 103, 104, 181
Minaeans 183
Mishnah 37
Morocco 225, 226
Mount Amanus 108
Mukish 6

Nabataeans (Nabataean) 183, 189
Nahal Hever 37
Near East 108, 109, 141, 220
Neo-Babylonian Empire 38
Neolithic period 5
Niger 226
Nigeria 226
Nora 83

Oasis of Dedān 146
Old Testament 37
Oman 228, 146
Omo River 226
Origen of Caesarea 37

Palestine 7, 37, 38, 39, 83, 84
Pentateuch (*See also* Samaritan Pentateuch) 62
Persia (Persian) 36, 103
Persian Empire 38, 79, 109
Petra 183
Philistines 82
Phoenicia (Phoenician) 82, 85, 99, 100, 105, 108, 110
Pictograms 84
Plautus 83
Plene spelling 44, 72, 151
Punctuation 146

Qumran 37, 39, 41, 42, 47, 59, 60, 67, 109

Ramlat as-Sabʿatayn 145
Ras Ibn Hani 5
Ras Shamra 5
Red Sea 146, 227
Rhodes 82
Rif Mountains 225
Rome (Roman) 38, 79, 94, 179, 186, 191
Rubʿ al-ḫālī 145

Sabaʿ 146
Sabeans 145
Šabwa 146
Sahara 225
St. Augustine 83
St. Jerome 47
Sakākā 181
Salāla 146
Sam'al 109
Samaria 37
Samaritan Pentateuch 36, 38, 40, 47, 59, 66
Samārum 146
Sardinia 82, 83
Saudi Arabia 146, 181, 183, 205
Ṣayhad 145
Sea Peoples 82
Semitic 108
Septuagint 42
Serabit al-Khadem 84
Sicily 82, 83
Sidon 95
Sinai peninsula 84, 104, 189
Ṣirwāḥ 145
Siyannu 6
Somalia 226
Spain (Spanish) 82, 83
Sudan 225, 227
Syllabary (Syllabic script) 185
Syllabic spelling 52
Syllabic symbols 8
Syria (Syrian) 108, 110, 179, 181, 183, 189, 210

Talmud 47
  Babylonian 37
  Jerusalem 37
Tanzania 226
Targums 133
Taymā' 181
Tel Fekheriye 109, 113
Tell al-Maskhūṭah 208
Tell el-Amarna 5, 51, 88, 104, 105
Tell Sukas 82
Tiberias 40
Tifinagh 226
Tifinigh 226
Timnaʿ 146
Tofseta 37
Transcription 42, 86, 88, 90, 98, 112, 191
Transjordan 36, 37, 78, 103
Transliteration 40–41, 113, 116, 120, 186, 188, 191, 192
Tuareg 226
Tunisia 83, 226
Turkey 108, 109

Ugarit 5, 6–7, 32, 36
Ur 93
Urartian 108
  Babylonian vocalization 39, 46, 48, 49, 57, 111, 116
  Hexaplaric vocalization 45, 46, 47, 48, 49, 57, 60
  Jacobite vocalization 111–112, 117

Urartian (*cont*)
  Nestorian vocalization 111–112
  Palestinian vocalization 39
  Tiberian vocalization 40–41, 43, 46, 48, 49, 57, 60, 63, 111–112, 116

Vowel points 39

Wadi Bayḥān 146
Wadi Hadramawt 146
Wadi Ḥarīb 146
Wadi Maḏāb 146
Wadi Murabba'at 37
Wadi Ramm 183
Woito River 227
Word division (dividers) 186, 199
Writing systems 5, 9, 6–8, 38–41, 84–86, 104–105, 108, 110–112, 113, 114, 116, 146–147, 181, 185–188

Yemen (Yemeni) 145, 146, 176, 179, 210, 212, 228,
Ẓafār 145, 146

Index of grammar and linguistics

Ablaut 18, 21, 24, 28, 52, 119, 126
Absolute chronology 115
Accent 89
  Stress accent 49–50, 117, 232
Adjectives (*See also* Comparative adjectives; Superlative adjectives) 13–14, 31, 90, 135, 196–197
Adverbs 25–26, 132
Agreement 12, 14, 17, 31, 62, 73, 77–78, 135, 136, 137, 138, 174–175, 196, 212, 214, 217
Allophonic variation 114
Analogy 16, 65, 70, 72, 97, 129
Anaptyxis 45, 46, 47, 48, 57, 118
Annexation 216
Antecedents 17, 30, 31, 32, 60, 171, 172, 175, 219
Apodosis 27, 29, 30, 139, 168, 170
Articles 63
  Definite articles 18, 25, 78, 94–95, 98, 152, 179, 196, 198, 208–209, 216
  Indefinite articles 63, 120
Aspect 20–21, 64–65, 128, 238
  Durative 64
  Imperfective 21, 63, 64, 95, 128, 238
  Nonimperfective 20
  Perfective 20, 21, 63, 64, 95, 128, 238
  Punctual (Punctiliar) 64
Assimilation 17, 18, 42, 68, 71, 87, 98, 117–118, 121, 126, 150, 189, 192, 193, 204, 230
Asyndeton 29, 171, 172, 175

Basic verb stems (*See also* Derived verb stems) 202, 203
  G stem 19, 66, 95, 96, 97, 240
  Qal stem 66
Bghadhkphath 188
Binyānîm (*See also* Derived verb stems) 63, 69, 72
Broken plurals 151, 235

Case 12, 31–32, 54, 90, 91, 152, 193, 196, 233, 235
Chiastic concord (*See also* Gender polarity) 15, 136
Clitics 16–17, 153, 241
  Enclitics 16, 17, 18, 25, 27, 59, 91–93, 121, 123, 159, 163, 193, 197–198, 217, 234
  Proclitics 16, 55, 56, 62, 63, 74, 84, 98, 132, 133
Cognates 94
Cohortative 65–66
Comparative adjectives 14, 119, 140, 234
Compensatory lengthening 47, 68
Compounds 28
Conditional clauses 30, 76, 139, 168–170
Consonants 8–9, 41–42, 50–51, 86–87, 105, 112–114, 148–149, 188–193
Construct chains 28, 55, 56, 77, 78, 90, 136, 154, 174
Converted imperfect 64, 65, 75
Converted perfect 64, 65–66, 75
Coordinate clauses 29, 139
Coordination (*See also* Coordinate clauses) 74–76, 165, 242

Declension 236
Deixis 25
Derived verb stems (*See also* Basic verb stems) 19–20, 69–72, 97, 126–128, 157, 202–204, 240
  C stem 95, 97, 240
  D stem 19, 95, 97, 240
  Ethpa“al / ’Ithpa“al 126, 127
  Ethpəʿel / ’Ithpəʿel 126, 127
  ’Ettaphʿal / ’Ittaphʿal 126–127
  Haphʿel / ’Aphʿel 126, 127
  Hipʿil 71
  Hitpaʿel 71
  Hitpolel 72
  Hopʿal 72
  L stem 19
  Minor stems 127–128
  N stem 19, 95, 97, 240
  Nipʿal 70
  Pa“el 126, 127
  Pəʿal 126, 127
  Piʿel 70
  Polal 72
  Polel 72
  Puʿal 70
  R stem 19, 240
  Š stem 19
  t stems 19, 95, 97

Dissimilation 46, 106, 118, 208
  Qatqat-qitqat dissimilation 51, 58

Emphatic consonants 41, 113, 189, 191, 227, 230
Ergativity 235

Fusional morphology 10, 52, 118, 232

Gender 12, 20, 31–32, 53, 63, 89, 91, 95, 118, 119, 125, 128, 134, 135, 136, 137, 138, 151, 153, 193–194, 196, 200, 207, 212, 214, 217, 233, 234–235, 238
Gender polarity 160
Glottalic consonants (*See also* Emphatic consonants) 41
Glottalization 227

Hendiadys 99, 139
Hypotaxis 74

Imperatives 22, 65, 95, 97, 131, 157, 206–207
Infinitives 24, 97, 131–132, 139–140, 158, 163, 173–174, 175, 239, 242
  Infinitive absolute 24, 66, 70, 95, 96, 97, 99, 140
  Infinitive construct 66, 70, 95, 96, 97
Innovations 62
Isogloss 5, 32

Jussive 65–66, 99, 130, 157, 206, 218

Lexicalization 127
Lingua franca 6, 103, 108, 109, 141
Loanwords 32, 53, 111, 128, 141–142, 190, 191

Mergers 7, 9, 38, 41, 50, 62, 87
Metathesis 71, 117, 128, 150, 203
Mimation 152, 175
Monophthongization 10, 24, 46, 48, 192, 193–198
Mood (*See also* Imperatives; Jussive; Precative; Vetitive) 21–22, 206–207
  Indicative mood 206, 238
  Optative mood 207, 218
  Subjunctive mood 206, 218
Morphophonemics 40, 44, 114

Nominal morphology 11–14, 53–59, 89–90, 119–121, 151–152, 161, 193–209, 233–237
Noun endings 90
Noun formation 11, 56–58
Number 12, 20, 31–32, 53–54, 63, 89, 91, 93, 95, 118, 120, 128, 135, 137, 138, 151, 193, 194–196, 200, 207, 214, 217, 233, 235–236, 238
Numerals 14–15, 72–73, 134–135, 159–161, 163, 212–214, 240–241
  Cardinal numerals 14, 15, 72, 73, 134–135, 136, 159–160, 212–214, 240, 241
  Fractions 160
  Multiplicatives 161
  Ordinal numerals 14, 15, 73, 135, 136, 160, 214, 241
Nûn energicum 65

Palatalization 97
Parataxis 74
Participles 21, 25, 64, 66, 95, 96, 97, 128, 132, 141, 158, 194, 195, 207–208, 218–219, 239
Particles 18, 25–27, 28, 29, 30, 56, 62, 66, 74, 94, 98, 117, 126, 133, 136, 138, 139, 140, 158, 163, 199, 208–212, 242
  Negative particles 133, 139, 159, 163, 218
Perfective adjective 239
Person 20, 31, 63, 91, 93, 95, 128, 200, 238
Pharyngealization 41, 113, 118, 227
Phonotactic constraints 48–49, 118
Precative 157
Prefix conjugation 96, 97, 155, 156–157, 163, 205, 206, 218, 219, 227
Prepositions 26–27, 98, 132, 158–159, 209, 210–211, 242
  Demonstrative adjectives 209, 216, 217
  Demonstrative pronouns 18, 22, 25, 32, 62, 63, 74, 84, 93, 125, 135, 153, 154, 162, 196, 199–209, 227, 238
    Far demonstratives 93, 125
    Near demonstratives 93, 125
  Determinative-relative pronouns 62, 94, 238
  Indefinite pronouns 18, 32, 63, 94, 154, 162
  Interrogative pronouns 18, 32, 62–63, 93, 199, 238
  Personal pronouns 16–17, 31, 59–62, 74, 91–93, 121–125, 131, 132, 135, 137, 153, 161, 172, 197–198, 217, 227, 237–238
  Possessive pronouns 126
  Reflexive pronouns 125, 237
  Relative pronouns 17, 18, 25, 27, 30, 31, 32, 62, 63, 84, 94, 99, 154, 162, 171, 172, 198–199, 219
  Resumptive pronouns 77, 164
Protasis 27, 139, 168
Prothetic vowels 84, 118, 213
Purpose clauses 97, 98

Reconstruction 188
Relative chronology 115
Relative clauses 30, 31, 77, 99, 154, 164, 170–172, 175, 219

Segholates (Segholation) 48, 57
State 12, 55–56, 90, 120, 135, 151–152, 196, 233–234

Absolute state 12, 13, 55, 90, 120, 135, 136, 137, 138
Construct state (*See also* Construct chains) 12, 13, 28, 55, 56, 61, 90, 120, 136, 152, 171, 172, 175, 193, 233
Determinate state 152, 196
Emphatic state 120, 136, 137
Pronominal state 12, 13
Strong verbs 23
Subordinate clauses (*See also* Subordination) 29–31, 76–77, 139
Subordination (*See also* Subordinate clauses) 74, 165–170, 242
Suffix conjugation 96, 97, 155, 156, 162, 204, 205–206, 207, 217–218, 219, 228
Superlative adjectives 14, 119, 234
Syllable structure 48–49, 117, 231–232
Syncope 231

Temporal clauses 76–77
Tense 20, 128–130
Topicalization 29
Triphthongization 45, 46, 48, 51

Verb inflection 66–69
Verbal conjugations 204–206, 217–218
Verbal morphology 19–25, 63–72, 95–97, 126–132, 154–158, 162–163, 200–208, 238–240
Vetitive 157
Voice 21, 127, 206, 207
Vowel shift 88
Vowels 9–10, 43–47, 51–52, 87–89, 114–117, 149, 193

Weak verbs 24, 67–69, 151, 157
Word classes 10–11
Word formation 10, 119, 126–128
Word order 28–29, 73–74, 98, 139, 164–165, 215–217, 241
Word structure 52–53, 89, 151, 232–233

Index of languages

Afar-Saho 226
Afro-Asiatic (*See also* Common Afro-Asiatic; Proto-Afro-Asiatic) 36, 52, 89, 225–228, 239, 240, 243
  North Afro-Asiatic 227
Akkadian 5, 6, 8, 10, 13, 14, 15, 20, 21, 27, 51, 66, 79, 83, 88, 94, 103, 104, 105, 106, 108, 112, 118, 120, 128, 139, 141, 171, 188, 191, 192, 228, 230, 231, 232, 234, 235, 236, 238, 239, 241, 242
  Assyrian 86, 88, 231
    Neo-Assyrian 79
  Babylonian 230
    Neo-Babylonian 79
  Old Akkadian 94, 235, 242
Alagwa 226
Amharic 228
Amorite 5, 79
Arabic (*See also* Proto-Arabic) 5, 9, 12, 13, 17, 22, 25, 27, 31, 32, 36, 41, 54, 60, 89, 90, 94, 98, 99, 104, 108, 109, 148, 155, 156, 167, 175, 176, 179–181, 184, 188, 189, 190, 191, 192, 193, 194, 195, 196, 197, 198, 200, 201–206, 207, 208, 209–212, 214, 216, 217, 220, 225, 227, 228, 230, 231, 232, 234, 235, 240, 241, 242
  Classical Arabic 179, 184, 188, 189, 191, 192, 194, 196, 197, 198, 199, 200, 201, 204, 205, 206, 207, 208, 212–214, 215, 217, 218, 219, 220, 221
  Dialects 179, 189, 191, 192, 193, 194, 198, 199, 200, 209, 217, 220
  Middle Arabic 179
  Modern Standard Arabic 191
  Old Arabic 179, 180, 181, 189, 193, 208, 209
Aramaic (*See also* Proto-Aramaic) 5, 10, 16, 25, 32, 36, 37, 38, 39, 46, 47, 49, 54, 55, 59, 78, 79, 85, 87, 94, 98, 100, 103, 104, 106, 108–143, 176, 179, 180, 188, 189, 190, 191, 192, 208, 228, 230, 231, 234, 235
  Biblical Aramaic 133
  Christian Palestinian Aramaic 109, 110
  Dialects 109
  East Arabian Aramaic 181
  Galilean Aramaic 109
  Hatran 109
  Imperial Aramaic 109, 113–114, 118, 119, 123–124, 125, 128, 129, 130, 131, 132, 134, 138, 139, 140, 141, 142, 191
  Jewish Babylonian Aramaic 109, 122, 123–125, 129, 130, 131, 133, 138
  Jewish Palestinian Aramaic 109, 122, 123, 124, 125, 129, 131, 132, 134
Late Aramaic 109, 110, 111, 112, 114, 116–117, 119, 120, 122, 123, 124, 125, 126, 127, 128, 129, 131, 132, 134, 135, 136, 137, 138, 140, 141
  Eastern Late Aramaic 130
  Western Late Aramaic 130, 142
Ma'lulan 109
Mandaic 109
Middle Aramaic 109, 111, 114, 115, 116, 119, 120, 125, 126, 128, 129, 130, 131, 132, 134, 135, 138, 140, 141
Modern Aramaic 109, 114, 116
Nabatean 109, 180, 189, 191, 200, 206
Old Aramaic 109, 113, 114, 118, 119, 120, 121, 122, 123–124, 125, 127, 128, 129, 130, 131, 132, 138, 140
  Sam'al dialect 113, 120, 121, 123, 125, 130
Official Aramaic 109
Palmyrene 109
Samaritan Aramaic 109, 122, 123, 124, 125, 129, 130, 131, 134
Standard Literary Aramaic 109
Syriac 109, 110, 120, 122, 123–125, 129, 130, 131, 132, 133, 134, 138, 139, 209
Ṭuroyo 109

Avestan 79
Awgni 226

Bauchi 226
Beja 227
Berber 225–226, 227, 228, 239
Bilin 226
Birale 227
Birelle 227
Bura 226
Burunge 226

Canaanite (*See also* Canaanite Dialects; Proto-Canaanite) 5, 22, 36, 51, 78, 82, 84, 86, 88, 89, 94, 100, 108, 121, 180, 228, 238
  North Canaanite 78, 103
  Old Canaanite 63
  South Canaanite 78, 103
Canaanite Dialects (*See also* Canaanite) 51, 103–107, 113, 120, 125
  Ammonite 36, 55, 62, 63, 78, 82, 94, 103
  Edomite 36, 78, 82, 94, 103
  Moabite 36, 55, 62, 78, 82, 94, 103, 108
Chadic 226, 227
  Central Chadic 226
  Eastern Chadic 226
  West Chadic 226
Common Afro-Asiatic (*See also* Proto-Afro-Asiatic) 233, 236, 238
Common Semitic (*See also* Proto-Semitic) 62, 230, 231, 243
Cushitic 226, 228, 239
  Central Cushitic 226
  East Cushitic 226
    Highland East Cushtic 226
    Lowland East Cushtic 226
  North Cushitic 226, 227
  South Cushitic 226

Eblaite 228, 242
Egyptian 6, 8, 17, 79, 84, 100, 141, 142, 225, 227, 228, 233, 239
  Demotic 112
Ethiopic (*See also* Ge'ez; Semitic) 41, 176, 179, 185, 229, 230, 231, 234, 238, 241, 242

Galla 226
Gaunche 226
Ge'ez 229
Greek 37, 38, 42, 47, 79, 83, 84, 86, 88, 100, 110, 112, 119, 133, 134, 139, 141, 142, 176, 179, 180, 186, 188, 191, 243
  Koine Greek 186

Hamitic 204
Hamito-Semitic 225
Hausa 226
Hebrew (*See also* Proto-Hebrew) 9, 10, 11, 12, 13, 15, 16, 17, 18, 25, 26, 32, 36–81, 82, 83, 85, 86, 87, 89, 94, 98, 103, 104, 105, 106, 108, 110, 114, 125, 133, 139, 140, 141, 142, 148, 150, 186, 188, 189, 190, 191, 192, 208, 210, 228, 230, 231, 232, 234, 235, 238
  Archaic Biblical Hebrew 36
  Archaic Hebrew 36, 62
  Biblical Hebrew 5, 8, 10, 18, 20–21, 24, 26, 29, 30, 31, 36, 37, 42, 43, 53, 54, 55, 58, 59, 60, 62, 64, 65, 66, 78, 79, 89, 92, 93, 94, 95, 97, 98, 99
  Classical Hebrew 36
  Israeli Hebrew 37
  Israelite Hebrew 51, 62, 79
  Judahite Hebrew 51, 62, 94
  Late Biblical Hebrew 36, 37, 41, 54, 56, 59, 62, 65, 67, 69, 79
  Late Classical Hebrew 36
  Medieval Hebrew 37
  Middle Hebrew 37
  Modern Hebrew 37
  Northern Hebrew 51, 56
  Pre-Hebrew 58
  Rabbinic Hebrew 37, 41, 42, 47, 53, 54, 55, 56, 58, 59, 60, 62, 63, 64, 65, 66, 67, 69, 70, 71, 72, 79
  Southern Hebrew 51
Hittite 6, 32, 243
Hurrian 6, 8, 32

Indo-European 60, 94, 119, 141, 227, 235, 243
Iraqw 226

Jibbāli 228, 194, 230

Kabyle 225
Kemant 226
Kera 226
Kotoko-Logone 226
Kurdish 108

Latin 52, 63, 79, 83, 84, 86, 88, 90, 94, 98, 100, 141, 142, 191
Libyan 226
Libyco-Berber 226
Luvian (Luwian) 98, 100

Margi 226
Masa 226
Mehri 228, 194
Migama 226
Mubi 226

North Arabian 145, 146, 176, 179, 186, 208
  Ancient North Arabian 179–224
    Chaldaean 181
    Dadanitic 180, 181, 184, 185, 186–188, 189, 190, 191, 192, 193, 194, 195, 196, 197, 198, 199, 200–210, 211–213, 214–215, 216–217, 218, 220, 221
    Dedanite 181
    Dialects 181
    Dispersed Oasis North Arabian 181
    Dumaitic 181, 186, 191, 192, 210

North Arabian (*cont.*)
Hasaitic 181, 183, 185, 186, 191, 192, 197, 198, 199, 208, 210, 212, 214, 220
Hismaic 181, 183, 184, 185–186, 188, 189, 191, 192, 195, 196, 197, 198, 199, 200, 208, 209–210, 211, 214, 218, 219, 220, 221
Jawfian 181
Lihyanite 181, 220, 221
Oasis North Arabian 181–183
Safaitic 181, 183, 184, 185–186, 188, 189, 190, 191–192, 193, 194, 195–196, 197, 198, 199, 200, 201–202, 204–205, 207, 208, 209–211, 212, 213–214, 215–216, 218, 219, 220–221
South Safaitic 183
Southern Thamudic 181, 183
Tabuki Thamudic 183
Taymanitic 181, 183, 184, 185, 186, 190, 191, 192, 193, 197, 198, 199, 208, 209–210, 211, 220, 221
Thamudic 183, 184, 199, 221
Thamudic A 183
Thamudic B 181, 183, 185, 186, 191, 192, 194, 197, 198, 199, 201, 207, 208, 209–210, 211, 218
Thamudic C 181, 185, 186, 191, 197, 198, 199, 208, 209–210
Thamudic D 181, 183, 185, 186, 191, 197, 198, 199, 208, 209–210
Thamudic E 183
Nostratic 227
Numidian 84, 100, 226

Omotic languages 226
Ongota 227
Oromo 226

Persian 141
Old Persian 79
Phoenician (*See also* Punic) 7, 10, 17, 25, 32, 36, 38, 49, 55, 62, 63, 78, 82–102, 103, 104, 105, 106, 108, 228
Common Phoenician 83
Cypriot Phoenician 93
Old Byblian 83, 84, 91, 94, 99
Standard Phoenician 83, 84, 87, 91, 93
Proto-Afro-Asiatic (*See also* Common Afro-Asiatic) 225, 227, 228, 230, 231
Proto-Arabic 179
Proto-Aramaic 109, 112, 114–115, 117, 118, 119, 127, 128, 134
Proto-Canaanite 43, 96, 103, 104–105
Proto-Central Semitic 86, 89
Proto-Hebrew 18, 49, 51
Proto-Northwest Semitic 50–52, 54, 55, 62, 63, 64, 65, 69, 86, 90
Proto-Semitic (*See also* Common Semitic) 5, 10, 38, 41, 43, 44, 46, 48, 50–52, 54, 55, 56, 57, 59, 60, 62, 63, 67, 86, 87, 88, 90, 93, 103, 115, 148, 190, 227, 229–243
Proto-Sinaitic 104–105
Proto-Ugaritic 11
Punic 226, 10, 62, 83, 84, 85, 87, 88, 90, 92, 93, 94, 98, 103
Early Punic 92
Late Punic 83, 85, 90, 92, 97
Latino-Punic 83, 90
Neopunic 10, 83

Ron languages 226
Ṣayhadic 228, 145, 230, 231, 235

Semitic (*See also* Common Semitic; Proto-Semitic) 5, 6, 7, 10, 12, 13, 14, 16, 17, 19, 21, 22, 27, 28, 32, 36, 54, 55, 63, 66, 67, 70, 73, 74, 78, 82, 85, 86, 87, 89, 90, 93, 94, 95, 98, 99, 100, 105, 108, 109, 119, 147, 148, 151, 153, 155, 160, 176, 185, 186, 191, 193, 194, 197, 204, 216, 220, 225, 226, 227, 228–229, 242, 243
Central Semitic (*See also* Proto-Central Semitic) 36, 82, 180, 228, 231, 233, 238, 239, 242
East Semitic 5, 20, 228, 241
Ethiopian Semitic 229, 231, 235, 241
Mahrian Semitic 229, 231, 235
Northwest Semitic (*See also* Proto-Northwest Semitic) 5, 7–8, 9, 11, 12, 32, 36, 49, 55, 64, 78, 82, 89, 95, 96, 97, 103, 105, 106, 108, 113, 128, 185, 186, 228, 230, 231, 235, 241
South Semitic 7, 145, 185, 186, 208
South West Semitic 180
West Semitic 5, 7, 8, 10, 14, 15, 19, 20, 21, 25, 26, 28, 32, 36, 94, 104–105, 228, 230, 238, 239, 241, 242
Semito-Hamitic 225
Sidamo 226
Somali 226
Soqoṭri 228
South Arabian 7, 183, 186, 190, 199, 228
Ancient South Arabian 145–178, 179, 180, 184, 185, 189, 190, 196
Hadramitic 145, 146, 150, 161–163, 229
Haramic 145, 167, 168, 169, 176
Ma<u>dh</u>ābic 183
Minaic 145, 146, 150, 175, 161–163
Qatabanian 145, 146, 175, 161–163

Sabaic 145, 146, 147, 150, 158, 162, 163, 171–172, 175, 176, 180, 184, 185, 200, 210, 212, 220
Early Sabaic 145, 146, 152, 156, 160, 161, 165
Late Sabaic 145, 146, 150, 153, 160, 165, 167
Middle Sabaic 145, 150, 156, 160, 165, 167, 174
Modern South Arabian 229, 176, 179, 190
Old South Arabian 41
Sumerian 6, 104, 228, 239, 241, 242

Tamazight 225
Tarafit 225
Taselhit 225
Tigrinya 228
Tuareg 226

Ugaritic (*See also* Proto-Ugaritic) 5–35, 46, 52, 54, 55, 60, 63, 66, 78, 99, 103, 105, 106, 113, 188, 228, 235, 238

Welsh 190
Wolaytta 226

Xamir 226

Index of named linguistic laws and principles

Barth-Ginsberg Law 21, 24, 46, 52, 106

Canaanite Shift 10, 51, 88, 103, 106

Philippi's Law 45, 56
Phoenician Shift 88